Histories of City

MW01128459

In this path-breaking and multi-layered account of one of the least explored societies in the Middle East, Nelida Fuccaro examines the political and social life of the Gulf port city and of its hinterland, as exemplified by Manama in Bahrain. Written as an ethnography of space, politics and community, it addresses the changing relationship between urban development, politics and society before and after the discovery of oil. By using a variety of local sources and oral histories, Fuccaro questions the role played by the British Empire and oil in state-making. Instead, she draws attention to urban residents, elites and institutions as active participants in state- and-nation building. She also examines how the city has continued to provide a source of political, social and sectarian identity since the early nineteenth century, challenging the view that the advent of oil and modernity represented a radical break in the urban past of the region.

NELIDA FUCCARO lectures on modern Middle Eastern history at the School of Oriental and African Studies, University of London.

CAMBRIDGE MIDDLE EAST STUDIES 30

Cambridge Middle East Studies has been established to publish books on the nineteenth- to twenty-first-century Middle East and North Africa. The aim of the series is to provide new and original interpretations of aspects of Middle Eastern societies and their histories. To achieve disciplinary diversity, books will be solicited from authors writing in a wide range of fields including history, sociology, anthropology, political science and political economy. The emphasis will be on producing books offering an original approach along theoretical and empirical lines. The series is intended for students and academics, but the more accessible and wide-ranging studies will also appeal to the interested general reader.

A list of books in the series can be found after the index.

Histories of City and State in the Persian Gulf

Manama since 1800

Nelida Fuccaro

University of London

CAMBRIDGE
UNIVERSITY PRESS

CAMBRIDGE UNIVERSITY PRESS
Cambridge, New York, Melbourne, Madrid, Cape Town,
Singapore, São Paulo, Delhi, Tokyo, Mexico City

Cambridge University Press
The Edinburgh Building, Cambridge CB2 8RU, UK

Published in the United States of America by Cambridge University Press, New York

www.cambridge.org
Information on this title: www.cambridge.org/9781107404441

First published 2009
First paperback edition 2011

A catalogue record for this publication is available from the British Library

ISBN 978-0-521-51435-4 Hardback
ISBN 978-1-107-40444-1 Paperback

In memory of Clinio

The past is not dead. In fact, it's not even past.
William Faulkner

Contents

Illustrations

Maps

Acknowledgements

This book has been a long time coming. I owe it to my father, who is no longer with us, and to Ali Akbar Bushehri of Manama, a formidable Bahraini who epitomises the generosity, historical memory and exceptional qualities of Bahrain, a complex and fascinating frontier society. Without them, this book could have never been written. My deepest gratitude goes to Ali Akbar Bushehri for having been so generous with his time, knowledge, documents and contacts, as well as with his friendship, wit and hospitality during the various stages of this research. Together we have retrieved the history of Manama from obscurity, overcoming the academic uncertainties facing historians working in this part of the world.

Many other people in Bahrain have made this book possible. Their help has compensated for the limited availability of historical materials. A number of them deserve a special mention for their generous assistance offered over the years and for their inquisitive attitude towards Bahraini history: Mirza al-Sharif (particularly for photographs), Ahmad Abdulrahman al-Jowder (for his insights into urban space and architecture and for having drawn some of the maps), Ali Qasim Rabia (for his passionate understanding of Bahraini politics), Hamid al-Awadhi (for his memory of al-ʿAwadiyyah) and Manaf Yousuf Hamza (for his knowledge of land surveying). I also wish to thank (with apologies for inevitable omissions): Abdulrahman Hussain Abdulrahman, Adel Yousif Ajoor, Jasim H. Ali, Ismail Alshafei, Muhammad Jabir al-Ansari, Majid Asghrar, Muhammad Jafar Muhsin al-Arab, Abd al-Razzak Yusuf al-Awadhi, Ibrahim Muhammad Bashmi, Khalid al-Bassam, Saif al-Binali, Abed Yousif al-Bousta, Ibrahim Buhassan, Angela Clarke and her husband, Ali Dawaygher, Habib Hassan, Tayyeba Hoodi, Ali Aba Husayn, Yousif Husain, Mansur al-Jamri, Sawsan Karimi, Salman Abdullah Hamad Al Khalifah, Muhammad Ishaq Abdulrahman al-Khan, Seema Ahmed al-Lengawi, Faieq Juma Mandeel, Abd al-Rahim Muhammad, Jassim Muhammad Murad, Baqer Salman al-Najjar, Abdulrahman Saud Musameh, Abdallah Sayf, the late Yousuf Shirawi, Khalifa Ahmed Sulaibeekh, Ibrahim Uthman and Abdallah Yateem.

In Bahrain, I am also indebted to a number of institutions and government departments. Abdallah al-Rifai, the former President of the Arabian Gulf University, and his personal assistant Layla offered accommodation and much needed logistical support during my first trip to Bahrain in 1998. Shaykh 'Abdallah ibn Khalid Al Khalifah has shared with me some insights into the history of Manama. The Directorate of Legal Affairs, the Department of Land Registration, the Ministry of Housing and Municipalities and the Historical Documentation Centre of Rifa' have kindly provided invaluable documentation on the old town.

This project started several years ago under the aegis of the former Centre of Arab Gulf Studies at Exeter University where I first developed an interest in the Gulf region. My former colleagues deserve much praise for their moral encouragement and concrete support, particularly the former director of the Centre, Kamil Mahdi, and Ruth Butler and Roberta Cole, the two extraordinary fun-loving ladies in charge of the Documentation Unit of the Centre (now Arab World Documentation Unit). In London, the staff of the India Office Library and of the Public Record Office have been equally kind and efficient. I have also benefitted from the help of other individuals and institutions in the United Kingdom. Robert Jarman, Saed Shehabi, the late Fuad Khuri, the late Rosemarie Said Zahlan and Madawi Al Rasheed have shared with me their insights into Gulf politics and society. The Leverhulme Trust has generously funded a year's research leave for the writing up of the project and the British Academy and the Arts and Humanities Research Board (now both Arts and Humanities Research Council) funded different stages of the fieldwork. The research for Chapter 5 on violence and public disorder was partly funded by the Social Science Research Council of New York as part of an international project on the urban public sphere in the Arab Middle East. I wish to thank the members of this research group, particularly Franck Mermier and Sharon Nagy with whom I discussed some of the general themes developed in this chapter. A special thanks also to Aurora Sottimano who helped me with the archival research for this chapter.

I owe a considerable intellectual debt to colleagues and friends whose work on the Middle East, Persian Gulf and on cities has been a source of inspiration for this study. Some of them have kindly read and commented on drafts and on the final manuscript: Salwa Ismail, James Onley, Roger Owen, Dina Khoury, John Parker, Lawrence Potter, Peter Sluglett, Gabriele Vom Bruck and Sami Zubaida. A very special thanks goes to Salwa Ismail whose work on Cairo and urban politics in the Middle East has been very influential on my thinking about this book. Of course any shortcomings are only mine.

Lastly, and on a personal note, my family has been a constant source of support; my mother Paola, with her cooking and concern for myself and Ida; Shaalan with his impeccable thoughtfulness, measured understanding and relentless love of jazz; my brother Villiam and his family with their discreet presence; and Peter with his generosity and ebullient personality.

Note on transliteration and terminology

The transliteration for Arabic and Persian terms follows that of the *International Journal of Middle East Studies*. While diacritical marks have been omitted, the letters *hamza* and *'ayn* are shown as ' and ' in the text. The words suq, shariah, mulla and qadi appear in their common English spelling.

The geographical denomination 'Persian Gulf' or 'Gulf' (as opposed to 'Arab Gulf' or 'Arabian Gulf') is used throughout the book. The choice of terminology follows an established convention in the historiography of the region in the English language and carries no political connotation.

As some local informants interviewed for this study requested to maintain their anonymity, their names have been omitted from the references.

Glossary

'amarah (pl. *'amarat*)	warehouse
'arish	see *barasti*
'asabiyyah	tribal solidarity
'ashura'	anniversary of the death of Imam Husayn
a'yan	notables
Baharna	Shi'i Arab population
Baladiyyah	municipality
Banyan	Hindu merchants
barasti	thatched hut
al-barriyyah	uncultivated land
Bayt	house/merchant mansion
Bayt al-Dawlah	British Political Agency
dallal (pl. *dallalun*)	broker
Dar al-Hukumah	tribal government
farij (pl. *firjan*)	urban quarter
al-fidawiyyah	armed retinue of tribal leaders and of members of the ruling family
al-fitnah	dissent/strife of religious nature
hala'il	villagers
Hasawi	inhabitant of al-Ahsa'
Hawala	mercantile group of tribal descent from southern Iran
'imarah	tribal principality
khums	Shi'i religious tax
majlis	council/tribal council/reception room
ma'tam	Shi'i congregation/house of mourning
Muharram	the first month of the Islamic calendar
mujtahid	Shi'i cleric

al-mazra'ah (also collective noun)	agricultural allotment/cultivated land
nakhudah	captain of a pearling boat
na'tur	municipal guard
qasr (pl. *qusur*)	tribal mansion/palace of a member of the ruling family
qassab (pl. *qassabun)*	butcher
shaykh	member of the ruling family/ tribal leader/member of the religious establishment
shaykh al-ra'is (pl. *shuyukh al-ra'is*)	chief Shi'i cleric of Bahrain
al-Shuyukh	the ruler of Bahrain
al-sukhrah	collection of tribal tax following customary rights
al-tabu	land registration
tamthiliyyah	play enacting the killing of Imam Husayn
tawwash (pl. *tawawish*)	pearl merchant
waqf ja'fariyyah/al-sunnah (pl. *awqaf*)	Shi'i/Sunni pious foundation

Abbreviations

AWDU	Arab World Documentation Unit (Exeter, UK)
BA	Bushehri Archive (Manama)
DSQ	*Da'irah al-Shu'un al-Qanuniyyah* (Directorate of Legal Affairs, Manama)
HA	Hamza Archive (Manama)
IOR	India Office Records (London)
IT	*Idarah al-Tabu* (Department of Land Registration, Ministry of Justice and Islamic Affairs, Manama)
MMBM	*Mahadir li Majlis al-Baladiyyah (al-Manamah)* Minutes of Manama Municipal Council
MWT	*Markaz al-Watha'iq al-Tarikhiyyah* (Historical Documentation Centre, Rifa', Bahrain)
PRO	Public Record Office (London)
WIB	*Wizarah al-Iskan wa al-Baladiyyat* (Ministry of Housing and Municipalities, Manama)

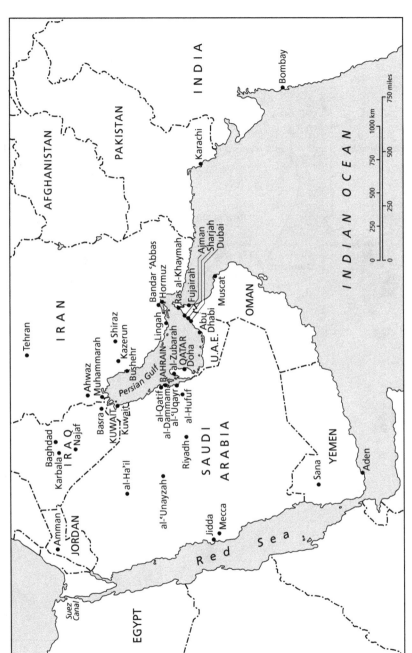

1 The Persian Gulf and Bahrain in the regional context

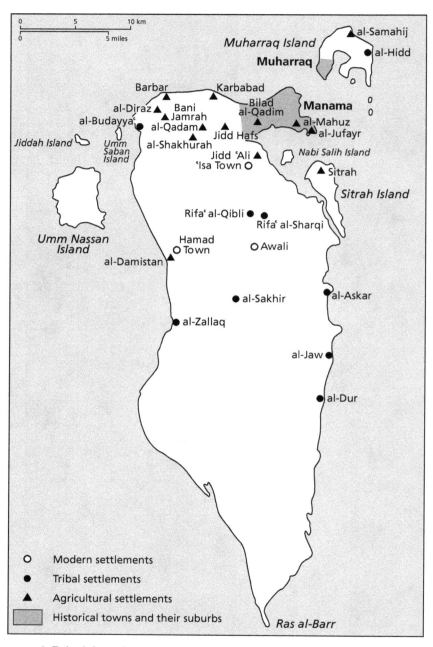

2 Bahrain's settlements

Introduction

Why cities and urban history?

It is peculiar that urban history has been conspicuously absent from the study of the Arab coast of the Persian Gulf in the nineteenth and twentieth centuries, peppered as that region is by a chain of city-states – or quasi city-states – stretching from Kuwait to Oman. The history of cities and urban societies in this region has featured only as a corollary to that of tribes, British Empire and oil. Of course the pivotal role of tribesmen, British officials and oil wealth as agents of historical change can be hardly overstated. Tribal communities constituted the backbone of the political infrastructure of the Gulf coast in the nineteenth century and developed a symbiotic, albeit often conflicting, relationship with the British authorities who controlled the region between 1820 and 1971. British protection ensured the political stability of the local tribal principalities within the new regional order of nation-states which took shape after World War I. After the 1930s, the discovery of oil gradually transformed the lives of Gulf peoples beyond recognition, altering their social and political identities and their relationship with their living environments.

The study of the politics of empire and tribalism, which has been the staple of regional historiography, has imposed a number of constraints on our understanding of indigenous societies and political cultures. External factors have been paramount in explaining historical change through the lens of British influence. The focus on imperial encroachment has also tended to restrict the scope of investigation to those elite groups which came into closer contact with British 'gunboat diplomats' (the officials of the Government of India supported by the Royal Navy in their diplomatic pursuits) and imperial administrators, particularly the ruling families and those segments of the merchant classes involved in pearling or European shipping. In parallel, the rich literature on tribes has often contributed to the typecasting of the region as a fragmented political universe. Traditional ethnographic studies, particularly on the Arabian Peninsula, have often reproduced the Orientalist clichés first publicised by travellers and colonial officials who visited and described the region in the early twentieth century. Discussing tribal and religious authority in the Yemen, R. B. Serjeant famously wrote: 'As each tribe ... is an independent unit, tribal Arabia is to be conceived of as normally in a state of anarchy.'[1] More recently, ethnographers, anthropologists and historians have discussed tribes either as state makers, forces opposed to state centralisation, or as the building blocks of social and political cohesion at the local level. Historical anthropologists, in particular, have presented a nuanced picture of tribal societies by engaging with the multiform manifestations of kinship solidarities across time and space: from the states which emerged in Central Arabia after the eighteenth century to the pearling communities of Trucial Oman (since 1971 the United Arab Emirates) in the 1950s.[2]

Without losing sight of tribal folk and imperial politics, this study shifts the context of investigation to urban milieus and to port towns and oil cities in particular. In drawing a composite picture of political and social life in Manama and in the islands of Bahrain, it explores the city as an organic entity and as the point of intersection of the political, social and cultural universe of the Gulf coast. Before oil, mercantile port towns such as Manama, Dubai and Kuwait provided the interface between their tribal and agricultural hinterlands, and the cosmopolitan world of trade which gravitated around the Gulf waters. In the oil era, regional ports were transformed into capital cities and showcases of modernisation. Their development epitomised the making of a new oil frontier populated by modern entrepreneurs, consumer goods and oil companies.

Revisiting the history of port towns and oil cities also responds to contemporary concerns. In the last decades or so, the manipulation of the region's urban past has acquired an increasing relevance in the practices of legitimacy promoted by Gulf governments. Efforts on the part of the ruling families to enforce political consensus among national populations gathered momentum in the various countries of the region after they

---

[1] R. B. Serjeant, 'The Interplay between Tribal Affinities and Religious (Zaydī) Authority in the Yemen', *al-Abhath*, 30(1982), 11–50 (12). For a critique of the literature on Gulf tribes written both by local historians and Western 'Orientalists' see K. al-Naqeeb, *Society and State in the Arabian Peninsula: A Different Perspective* (London: Routledge, 1990), pp. 1–4.

[2] See N. N. Ayubi, *Over-Stating the Arab State* (London: I. B. Tauris, 1995), pp. 123–6, for an excellent discussion of Gulf tribalism and state formation in a historical setting. As representative of this type of literature see M. al-Rasheed, *Politics in an Arabian Oasis: The Rashidis of Saudi Arabia* (London: I. B. Tauris, 1991); P. Lienhardt, *Shaikhdoms of Eastern Arabia*, ed. by Ahmad al-Shahi (Basingstoke: Palgrave MacMillan, 2001); P. Khoury and J. Kostiner (eds.), *Tribes and State Formation in the Middle East* (Berkeley: University of California Press, 1990), particularly contributions by Joseph Kostiner and Paul Dresch; P. Dresch, *Tribes, Government and History in Yemen* (Oxford: Clarendon Press, 1989); J. Kostiner, *The Making of Saudi Arabia: From Chieftaincy to Monarchical State* (Oxford University Press, 1993).

achieved independence from British control between 1961 and 1971. Accordingly, Gulf metropolises have become instruments of statecraft, tools to promote state formation.[3] Since the 1990s, the historical centres of Dubai, Kuwait and, to a lesser extent, Manama have been gradually transformed into spaces which embody a new idea of 'homogenous' national culture and political community. The recuperation of pre-oil urban traditions and settings and the establishment of national museums have set in motion a movement of heritage revival (*ihya' al-turath*) which constitutes the most tangible manifestation of state-sponsored nationalism in the region. Historical sites and natural harbours have become recreational, educational and tourist spaces emphasising the tribal and Arab character of pre-oil Gulf societies, often to the detriment of their cosmopolitan traditions. The Dubai Heritage Village established in 1996 in the old harbour of the city includes replicas of its old quarters, spaces for folklore performances and the reconstruction of a diving village with miniatures of pearling boats. Since 1998, when the village was officially transformed into a living museum (*mathaf hayy*), it has become a venue where 'cultural representations and displays are organized, thematized and presented to viewers as discourses of Emirati national culture'.[4]

As an integral part of the teleological narrative of legitimacy promoted by ruling families, historic towns have also become the symbols of loyalty or opposition to contemporary Gulf regimes. Old Muharraq – the capital of the Al Khalifah administration of Bahrain in the nineteenth century – still evokes and reinforces allegiance to the ruling family among Bahrain's Sunni population. The celebrated historical novel *Mudun al-Milah* ('Cities of Salt') by 'Abd al-Rahman al-Munif expresses the author's dissent by presenting a powerful and imaginative political geography of the early modern oil city, a neocolonial city shaped since the 1940s by the

---

[3] E. Davis, 'Theorizing Statecraft and Social Change in Arab Oil-Producing Countries' in E. Davis and N. Gavrielides (eds.), *Statecraft in the Middle East: Oil, Historical Memory and Popular Culture* (Miami: Florida International University Press, 1991), pp. 1–35 (p. 12).

[4] S. Khalaf, 'Globalization and Heritage Revival in the Gulf: An Anthropological Look at Dubai Heritage Village', *Journal of Social Affairs* 19.75 (2002), 13–41 (19). A similar project is being undertaken in Kuwait City with the development of the Village of the Seaman (Qaryah Yawm al-Bahhar) which started in 2003. 'al-Baladiyyah du'yat mukhat-tatat al-mawqi' wa talabat khamsin alf dinar', *al-Abraj*, 24 Dhu al-Hijjah 1427 (13 January 2007). For a recent discussion of historical identity and globalisation in Sharjah and in Saudi Arabia see J. W. Fox, N. Mourtada-Sabbah and M. al-Mutawa, 'Heritage Revivalism in Sharjah' in J. W. Fox, N. Mourtada-Sabbah and M. al-Mutawa (eds.), *Globalization and the Gulf* (London: Routledge, 2006), pp. 266–87 and G. Okruhlik, 'Struggle over History and Identity: "Opening the Gates" of the Kingdom to Tourism' in M. al-Rasheed and R. Vitalis (eds.), *Counter-Narratives: History, Contemporary Society and Politics in Saudi Arabia and Yemen* (New York: Palgrave Macmillan, 2004), pp. 201–28. On statecraft and history in the oil states of the Middle East see Davis, 'Theorizing Statecraft'.

international oil economy. Munif's literary representation of the fragility and ephemeral nature of Harran, a fictional oil town in Saudi Arabia, is a critique of the coercive power of the neo-tribal governments which emerged in the early oil era in collusion with American imperialism and the nascent oil industry.[5] By focussing on the displacement of an urbanised Bedouin community, the author also gives a voice to the social malaise and political insubstantiality of large segments of Gulf societies.

In an equally subversive message, some Gulf intellectuals have used the demise of the pluralistic civic tradition and cosmopolitan culture of port towns as a symbol of the violation of cities and urban lives by oil and modernity. The tolerant milieus of pre-oil Kuwait Town and Manama have been often contrasted with the forced policies of 'Arabisation' (and in the case of Kuwait City also 'Bedouinisation') enforced by the Al Sabah and Al Khalifah families. In the United Arab Emirates, these processes have also become apparent in recent decades but have so far not aroused dissident voices.[6] In a similar vein, the Kuwaiti sociologist Khaldun al-Naqeeb sees the metropolitan oil city as the personification of the authoritarian state, the ghetto of a 'decrepit *lumpenproletariat*'.[7] Such caustic criticism echoes the bitter contestation over thorny issues of citizenship and of political and economic entitlements on the part of disenfranchised groups such as the *bidun* (indigenous communities without passport), second-class citizens and immigrant labourers. Without accepting at face value this idealised portrayal of the pre-oil era, it is beyond doubt that the intervention of the oil state profoundly transformed the fluid trans-national character of Gulf ports. In the case of Manama this transformation is striking. As will be discussed in Chapters 3 and 6, since the 1950s the emergence of political and legal divisions between citizens (*al-muwatinun*), expatriate communities and migrant workers contrasts starkly with the open milieus which characterised the mercantile settlement of the nineteenth century.

The question of how historic port towns and their populations were bequeathed to modern oil states features prominently in this study of Manama. As shown by the literature on the post-Ottoman world, the notion of 'imperial legacy' offers a key to understanding the historical

---

[5] A. Munif, *Cities of Salt*, trans. by Peter Theroux (New York: Random House, 1987).

[6] See for instance 'Ali al-Tharrah, 'Family in the Kinship State', paper presented at the conference 'The Gulf Family: Modernity and Kinship Policies', School of Oriental and African Studies, University of London, April 2005.

[7] al-Naqeeb, *Society and State*, p. 91. On Gulf indigenous historiography with a reformist agenda and the reinterpretation of the broad categories of tribe, state, class and British imperialism see A. Dessouki, 'Social and Political Dimension of the Historiography of the Arab Gulf' in E. Davis and Gavrielides (eds.), *Statecraft in the Middle East*, pp. 96–115.

Introduction 5

roots of the states and urban societies which emerged in the Middle East after World War I. Philip Khoury and James Gelvin, for instance, have demonstrated how the politics of urban notables and popular nationalism provided a crucial element of continuity in the political infrastructure of Damascus between Ottoman and French rule and shaped the outlook of the city as the new capital of the Syrian state in the interwar period. In a similar vein, Jens Hanssen's study of urbanism in *fin de siècle* Beirut sets out to challenge the dichotomy between the Ottoman and French imperial histories of the city.[8] It is true that European imperialism and state building in the Gulf followed a different trajectory. Yet, particularly in Bahrain, the remarkable longevity of British informal empire (which lasted some 150 years) was instrumental in maintaining the urban and tribal elites of the pre-oil era in power as the 'natural' leaders of their populations. With oil revenue and British support, the Al Khalifah of Bahrain – in much the same way as the Al Sabah of Kuwait and the Al Maktum of Dubai – were able to refashion their profile as the political elites of the oil state, providing a term of comparison with the post-Ottoman Arab world, at least in the period between the two World Wars. This study develops this comparison by focussing on the politics of notables in Manama and on the role played by the municipality in upholding their position in the oil era.

In the first place, the absence of a comparative agenda in the study of Gulf towns and cities stems from the very limited interest in the region on the part of urban specialists. Historians have often been discouraged by the apparent 'exceptionalism' of the historical experience of the Gulf coast. The scarcity of local records and the seemingly 'obfuscated' historical memory of Arab Gulf societies have undoubtedly played a major role, as if oil modernisation had swept away urban history along with the traditional urban landscapes. Among specialists of the Muslim world in particular, this attitude is also reinforced by a general bias towards the study of 'lesser cities', urban centres which do not conform to normative ideas of Islamic urbanism in the same way as the capitals and provincial centres of Muslim Empires: Cairo, Delhi, Istanbul, Damascus and

[8] L. C. Brown (ed.), *Imperial Legacy: The Ottoman Imprint on the Balkans and the Middle East* (New York: Columbia University Press, 1996); J. L. Gelvin, *Divided Loyalties: Nationalism and Mass Politics in Syria at the Close of Empire* (Berkeley: University of California Press, 1998); P. Khoury, *Syria and the French Mandate. The Politics of Arab Nationalism, 1920–1946* (London: I. B. Tauris, 1987); P. Khoury, *Urban Notables and Arab Nationalism: The Politics of Damascus, 1860–1920* (Cambridge University Press, 1983); J. Hanssen, *Fin de siècle Beirut: The Making of an Ottoman Provincial Capital* (Oxford: Clarendon Press, 2005), pp. 266–9.

Aleppo, to name a few.[9] Moreover, the little attention devoted to the urban history of the Arab Gulf States (including Saudi Arabia) is partly a symptom of the effects of the 'modernist' and 'state-centric' paradigm which has permeated the study of the region, the brainchild of the modernisation literature produced in the 1950s and 1960s. In focussing on the evolution of the state in oil-producing countries, this literature not only portrayed state formation as following a Western model of development but also construed it as an irreconcilable break with the past.[10] As social anthropologists would put it, the oil era was typecast as a process exemplifying the sudden withdrawal of 'tradition' in the face of 'modernity', contributing to dissociate processes of city formation from the cumulative experience of change over the long *durée* of regional history.

The dependency approach that has dominated the study of the political economy of oil countries since the 1970s has reframed the developmental process under the rubric of 'rentierism', with an emphasis on oil income as an externally generated source of state revenue.[11] Yet, with the exception of the studies by Jill Crystal on Kuwait and Qatar and by Fuad Khuri on Bahrain, what we often miss from these accounts is the historical perspective which should underpin the study of oil development.[12] One of the additional pitfalls of the 'rentierist' approach is the emphasis placed upon the preponderant role played by the world economy over the Gulf 'periphery'. This emphasis has led scholars to view politics and economics through the lens of global processes and thus often to underplay historical and regional specificities.[13] In examining further the limitations of the 'rentierist'/dependency approach, it must be simply noted that it has not been concerned with urban issues. Even studies on the Oil City, which to some extent draw on this approach, promote an 'essentialist' view of

---

[9] The Islamic City has a long pedigree in Middle Eastern historiography. For the earliest poignant critique to this concept see J. Abu Lughod, 'The Islamic City – Historic Myth, Islamic Essence and Contemporary Relevance', *International Journal of Middle East Studies*, 19(1987), 155–86.

[10] J. Crystal, *Oil and Politics in the Gulf: Rulers and Merchants in Kuwait and Qatar* (Cambridge University Press, 1990), pp. 3–5.

[11] Literature on the rentier state is vast. See Ayubi, *Over-Stating the Arab State*, pp. 224–30; H. Beblawi and G. Luciani (eds.), *The Rentier State* (London: Croom Helm, 1987); J. S. Ismael, *Kuwait: Dependency and Class in a Rentier State* (Gainesville: University of Florida Press, 1993).

[12] Crystal, *Oil and Politics in the Gulf*; F. I. Khuri, *Tribe and State in Bahrain: The Transformation of Social and Political Authority in an Arab State* (University of Chicago Press, 1980).

[13] I here draw on Sami Zubaida's discussion of historical continuity, dependence and the peripheral state in the Middle East. S. Zubaida, *Islam, the People and the State: Political Ideas and Movements in the Middle East* (London: I. B.Tauris, 1993), pp. 140–5.

urban development with poor conceptual elaboration and limited empirical substance.[14]

A line of enquiry which seems to have much resonance for the study of urbanisation in the Arab Gulf is that pioneered by Anthony King who has opened new ways of investigating continuities in the evolution of 'colonial' and 'world' cities in the nineteenth and twentieth centuries.[15] First, this approach links the development of non-Western cities to the long *durée* of the world global economy, broadening considerably the scope for research on Gulf urbanism encompassing the period before and after the discovery of oil. Secondly, it focusses on the 'language' of urbanisation, that is, on how processes such as colonialism, imperialism, modernisation and development became 'concretized in the built environment'.[16] Although the port towns and oil cities of the Persian Gulf were not colonial creations and do not conform to the definition of 'world' city (with the notable exception of Dubai),[17] they deserve attention as the physical embodiment of historical processes, more so in the light of the dramatic transformations of their cityscapes over the last two centuries.

In spite of the heuristic potential of the macro-economic approach pioneered by King, this study of Manama between 1783 and 1971 is not underpinned by an analysis of the changes in the world economy. Primarily conceived as a history of urban space, politics and community, it uses regional and international trends as a backdrop: the resurgence of tribal power across Asia and the Arabian Peninsula in the eighteenth century, British political and commercial expansion in the long nineteenth century, internationalism and state building after World War I, the consolidation of the international oil economy, particularly after 1945

---

[14] For a critique of the literature on Gulf cities see N. Fuccaro, 'Visions of the City: Urban Studies on the Gulf', *Middle East Studies Association Bulletin* 35.2 (2001), 175–87.
[15] See in particular A. D. King, *Colonial Urban Development. Culture, Social Power and Environment* (London: Routledge and Kegan Paul, 1976); A. D. King, *Urbanism, Colonialism and the World Economy: Cultural and Spatial Foundations of the World Urban System* (London: Routledge, 1990); J. Hosagrahar, *Indigenous Modernities. Negotiating Architecture and Urbanism* (London and New York: Routledge, 2005). On colonial and world cities see A. D. King, *Global Cities: Post-Imperialism and the Internationalization of London* (London and New York: Routledge, 1990), pp. 33–68.
[16] King, *Global Cities*, p. 35.
[17] Studies of global Dubai have increased in the last few years, starting to challenge the static paradigm of the Oil City. See A. Kanna, 'Not Their Fathers' Days: Idioms of Space and Time in the Arabian Gulf', unpublished PhD dissertation, Harvard (2006); B. Ghoul, 'Les Transformations d'une cité-marchande: Doubaï, 1971–2001: impact global et dynamique interne', *Monde Arabe Maghreb-Machrek*, 174 (2001), 70–4; R. Marchal, 'Dubai: Global City and Transnational Hub' in M. al-Rasheed (ed.), *Transnational Connections in the Arab Gulf* (London: Routledge, 2005), pp. 93–110.

and, last but not least, the demise of the British Empire in India and in the Middle East. Yet, to some extent King's 'language' of urbanism has provided inspiration for this urban history which is partly concerned with the transformation of urban spaces and how key players such as state, tribe, empire, oil and modernisation intersected with them.

Histories of city and state in Manama

Before the development of modern states and national cultures, urban centres often symbolised the identity of entire regions. The nature of the relationship between city and state in the pre-modern period has long engaged historians and urban specialists. In the context of the Islamic world, Ira Lapidus has referred to cities as plural societies and as the microcosms of wider political processes. Taking a broader cross-cultural approach, Kirti Chaudhuri has discussed the city in the Indian Ocean as the architectural sign and symbol of 'the abstract concept of the state, government, society, and economic activities'.[18] The common matrix of urban development and state building is particularly apparent in the ports of the Arab coast of the Persian Gulf and in the Arabian Peninsula. Here towns constituted veritable 'central places' with important political and economic functions. In an area which offered scarce resources and was located on the fringes of large territorial empires, the control of key commercial and religious centres allowed tribal groups to raise revenue and to establish centralised administrations. Along the Arab coast, maritime trade emporia dominated physically and politically the tribal principalities, which in some cases did not extend much further beyond the precincts of port settlements. With the discovery of oil these trade emporia made a relatively smooth transition to capitals of modern states: Manama in the 1920s, followed by Kuwait, Abu Dhabi and Doha some decades later. The situation was not dissimilar in Central Arabia. In Najd, the Sau'di and Rashidi Emirates developed along the axis which connected the towns of al-Ha'il and Riyadh, centres of caravan trade which were intersected by pilgrimage routes. It was from Riyadh that Ibn Sa'ud started the unification of what is today Saudi Arabia at the turn of the twentieth century.

In the heterogeneous society of the islands of Bahrain the interface between city and state resulted in a complex 'politics of urbanisation'

---

[18] I. M. Lapidus, 'The Muslim Cities as Plural Societies: The Politics of Intermediary Bodies' in *The Proceedings of the International Conference on Urbanism and Islam (ICUIT)*, 4 vols (Tokyo: The Middle East Culture Centre, 1989), vol. I, pp. 134–63 (p. 136); K. N. Chaudhuri, *Asia before Europe: Economy and Civilisation of the Indian Ocean from the Rise of Islam to 1750* (Cambridge University Press, 1990), p. 338.

whose repercussions were still felt in the twentieth century. This politics antagonised tribes, agriculturalists and mercantile communities, and triggered economic and political competition between Manama, the cosmopolitan trade centre of the islands, and Muharraq, the seat of the administration of the Al Khalifah family. While Muharraq resembled many of the tribal settlements scattered along the coast, Manama represented the microcosm of Bahrain as *the* frontier society of the Persian Gulf.[19] The mixed ethnic and sectarian composition of the urban population reflected a long history of immigration associated with trade, pearling, pilgrimage and military conquest. Moreover, the town was situated at the intersection of the Arab and Iranian and the Sunni and Shi'i worlds. It lay at the southern end of an imaginary axis running along southern Iraq through the Shi'i holy cities of Najaf and Karbala and was the terminus of the overland route which connected Wahhabi Najd to the shores of the Gulf, continuing further west to Mecca and Medina in the Hijaz.

In the study of the 'unruly' multicultural society of Bahrain, the familiar theme of Gulf tribes as almost 'natural' state-makers has had considerable academic currency. As stated by Fuad Khuri in the late 1970s: 'In the absence of state structures with standardized and centralized systems of authority, tribal groupings and alliances … emerged [before oil] as the *logical* forms of social organisation. The Shi'a [cultivators] and urban Sunni [of Manama], lacking tribal organization, prevailed in those occupations and careers that were not related to government and the control of resources' [my emphasis].[20] In focussing on cosmopolitan Manama, this study challenges the restrictive definition of state – both pre-modern and modern – as a structure built into the tribal (or neo-tribal) system supported by the Al Khalifah since their arrival in Bahrain in 1783. In contrast, it draws attention to the resources offered by this port town and oil city, which developed as the centre of the booming pearling economy of the Gulf and of the region's nascent oil industry, after the 1880s and 1932

[19] As a frontier society, the islands of Bahrain differed considerably from their American and African counterparts. They functioned as areas of contact and cultural exchange, rather than as empty zones inhabited by 'uncivilised' natives, or border regions exposed to the absorbing power of centralised states and their dominant cultures. Gulf frontiers have been discussed only in the context of regional trade. H. Fattah, *The Politics of Regional Trade in Iraq, Arabia and the Gulf, 1745–1900* (Albany: State University of New York Press, 1997), pp. 19–23. For a review of the conceptualisation of the Asian, European and North American frontier in history see P. R. Gaubatz, *Beyond the Great Wall. Urban Form and Transformation on the Chinese Frontiers* (Stanford University Press, 1996), pp. 15–19. The classic studies on the Eurasian and world frontiers are by W. H. McNeill, *Europe's Steppe Frontier, 1500–1800* (Chicago University Press, 1964) and *The Great Frontier: Freedom and Hierarchy in Modern Times* (Princeton University Press, 1983).
[20] Khuri, *Tribe and State in Bahrain*, p. 67.

respectively. These resources were not only economic but also political and ideological. Until 1971, Manama continued to be a locus of a strong civic identity and of British imperial influence, both of which restrained the authority of Bahrain's rulers. Throughout the two centuries covered in this book, changes in the sociopolitical organisation of urban society and in Manama's built environment and urban layout clearly signposted the emergence and consolidation of Bahrain's state administration under the aegis of the British Empire and oil. Treating Manama as an integral part of the pedigree of the oil state broadens the reductive understanding of Gulf modernisation as a more or less simple transition between 'pastoral nomadism to petroleum tribalism'.[21]

In fact, the entry of Manama into the modern world was not shadowed exclusively by the oil boom and by the integration of the northern Gulf into the industrial world economy in the 1940s and 1950s. In this respect, the town's imperial history is instrumental in fine-tuning the penetration of modernity in the region. To this effect, this study takes the 1880s as a point of departure, a period which marked the first era of 'global' capitalism and the boom of Bahrain and Gulf pearls in the world markets. Renewed British expansion in Bahrain and the Persian Gulf paralleled the accelerated economic and political penetration of the British Empire in India, Egypt and in the Ottoman world. As shown by studies on the ports of the Mediterranean and Indian Ocean in this period, the development of urban milieus in the age of European expansion embodied a new 'set of relationships between Europe, Middle East and South-East Asia'.[22] Although Manama remained essentially a 'native' town, it became increasingly connected to the world of empires which stretched from the Ottoman Mediterranean to British-controlled India. This is also suggested by the consolidation of an eclectic trans-regional culture among the town's merchants, which fused elements from different areas of the Indian Ocean rim.[23] This imperial connection was furthered after World

---

[21] M. Dahir, *al-Mashriq al-'Arabi al-mu'asir min al-badawah ila al-dawlah al-hadithah*, quoted in Ayubi, *Over-Stating the Arab State*, pp. 125–6.

[22] Quote from C. A. Bayly and L. T. Fawaz, 'Introduction: The Connected World of Empires' in Fawaz and Bayly (eds.), *Modernity and Culture: From the Mediterranean to the Indian Ocean* (New York: Columbia University Press, 2002), p. 1. For an overview of the development of port cities in the Indian Ocean in this period see K. McPherson 'Port Cities as Nodal Points of Change: The Indian Ocean, 1890s–1920s' in Fawaz and Bayly (eds.), *Modernity and Culture*, pp. 75–95.

[23] J. Onley, *The Arabian Frontier of the British Raj: Merchants, Rulers, and the British in the Nineteenth-Century Gulf* (Oxford University Press, 2007); J. Onley, 'Transnational Merchants in the Nineteenth-Century Gulf: The Case of the Safar Family' in M. al-Rasheed (ed.), *Transnational Connections in the Arab Gulf*, pp. 59–89. On merchants as the modernist elites of the Indian Ocean see U. Freitag and W. Clarence-Smith (eds.),

War I with the establishment of a British-sponsored municipal government which became the first nucleus of the modern administration of
Bahrain.

In dealing with the question of how oil transformed the town until
independence, this study does not treat modernisation as a linear process
of urban change. This is not a tale of transformation from 'rags to riches',
the story of an economic miracle which created a more uniform landscape, and a 'rational', disciplined and affluent society. On the contrary,
the transformative powers of oil enforced new political, social and spatial
divisions, from the creation of new lines of separation between Manama
and its former agricultural hinterland, and between immigrants and the
indigenous population, to the formation of new social classes and political
movements which antagonised the government. To expose further the
fallacies of the 'exceptionalism' of oil development, it must be noted that
manifestations of modernity in Manama did not differ substantially from
those across the colonial world. Essentially, as will be highlighted in the
concluding sections of this book, they fostered the creation of new ideas
about race and class, and new spaces of political contestation.

The themes of city, state and modernisation which provide the framework for this study are developed through three specific lines of enquiry.
The first links processes of urbanisation to state formation, with particular
reference to the relationship between the development of Manama and
that of its historic agricultural and tribal hinterlands. The notion that pre-
modern cities cannot be understood without their hinterlands is particularly true of Manama, bounded as it was by once prosperous agricultural
districts which in the nineteenth century were under the control of the
ruling family. Moreover, the town of Muharraq itself was part of the wider
tribal hinterland surrounding Manama whose political importance
increased dramatically after the arrival of the Al Khalifah in Bahrain. A
focus on urban–rural relations in the oil era seems equally appropriate in
order to understand the nature and directives of state building given the
fast pace of oil modernisation.

The second line of enquiry focuses on transformations in urban spaces
and institutions as indicators of changing relations of power between
urban residents, and between them and the state. Besides recognising
the importance of King's global 'language' of urbanisation, this approach
draws on some of the literature which discusses space both as the recipient

Hadrami Traders, Scholars and Statesmen in the Indian Ocean, 1750s–1960s (Leiden: Brill,
1997); D. Lombard and Jean Aubin (eds.), *Asian Merchants and Businessmen in the Indian
Ocean and in the China Sea* (Delhi: Oxford University Press, 2000); C. Markovits, *The
Global World of Indian Merchants, 1750–1947: Traders of Sind from Bukhara to Panama*
(Cambridge University Press, 2000).

of historical change and as the expression of localised social and political relations. Michel de Certeau, for instance, famously asserted that 'places are fragmentary and inward-turning histories ... accumulated times that can be unfolded.'[24] Moreover, studies of colonial urbanism inspired by Michel Foucault have emphasised the political nature of space; that is, how changing urban forms and institutions provide an insight into relations of power.[25] In exploring these relations in the non-colonial context of Manama, this study considers the agency of both urban residents and the state. While merchants, immigrants and labourers developed and organised the town of the pearl boom given the absence of a centralised urban administration (Chapter 3), after the 1920s the government took an increasingly active role in urban development, which by the 1950s had become one of the primary tools for modernisation (Chapter 6).

The third approach is concerned with the evolution of the urban body politic and public sphere under the aegis of patronage politics, grassroots organisations cum religious institutions, particularly the Shi'i houses of mourning (ma'tams), professional and political associations, and the municipality. 'Informal' networks of political mobilisation continued to be prevalent in Manama in the oil era. As argued by Diane Singerman for Egypt, these associations allowed individuals and groups to carve out vital political space.[26] In order to understand the foundations of a 'modern' domain of public contestation (and how this domain shaped state and nation building) Chapter 5 analyses different episodes of unrest and the performance of Muharram rituals. As in British India before partition, the violence and ritual performances staged in Manama were the key activities which underscored the consolidation of Bahrain's nationalist politics in the 1950s. In the same way as many Indian cities Manama was in fact a society starkly divided along communal and sectarian lines.[27] Its transformation into a forum of Arab nationalist politics and anti-British

---

[24] M. de Certeau, *The Practice of Everyday Life*, trans. by Steven Rendall (Berkeley: University of California Press, 1984), p. 108.

[25] See for instance Z. Celik, *Urban Forms and Colonial Confrontations: Algiers under French Rule* (Berkeley: University of California Press, 1997); W. Cunningham Bissel, 'Conservation and the Colonial Past: Urban Space, Planning and Power in Zanzibar' in D. Anderson and R. Rathbone (eds.), *Africa's Urban Past* (Oxford: Currey, 2000), pp. 246–61; M. Dossal, *Imperial Designs and Indian Realities: The Planning of Bombay City, 1845 –1875* (Bombay: Oxford University Press, 1991); G. A. Myers, *Verandahs of Power: Colonialism and Space in Urban Africa* (New York: Syracuse University Press, 2003).

[26] D. Singerman, 'Informal Networks: The Construction of Politics in Urban Egypt' in T. Sato (ed.), *Islamic Urbanism in Human History: Political Power and Social Networks* (London and New York: Kegan Paul International, 1997), pp. 77–106.

[27] The literature on communalism and violence in British India is abundant. See for instance S. Freitag, *Collective Action and Community: Public Arenas and the Emergence of*

sentiment, a development which triggered the progressive Arabisation of the state in the 1960s, reflected the exclusive nature of modern nationalism. The emergence of Manama as an 'Arab' city, this study argues, was one of the most visible signs of the demise of the cosmopolitan town of the pearling era.

Besides reflecting the thematic agenda of this study, the organisation of the chapters emphasises the plurality of contexts which framed the history of Manama, hence the plural *Histories* in the title. The periodisation follows the rhythm of both urban change and state building and takes the 1880s, 1919 and 1932 as the beginnings of three different stages of urban development characterised by the pearl boom, municipal government and oil. The next important dates are 1937, 1957 and 1971. In 1937, the enforcement of provisions of nationality had a profound impact on Manama's historic communities; 1957 marked the collapse of the urban order championed by the municipality and of Bahrain's nationalist movement; with independence in 1971 Manama became the official capital of the Arab State of Bahrain.

Chapter 1 discusses urbanisation and state formation in Bahrain during the rule of the Safavid Empire (1602–1717) and in the Al Khalifah era (1783–1923). The principal focus of this chapter is to explore the making of new rural and urban landscapes after the Al Khalifah occupation of the islands in 1783, particularly the establishment of Muharraq and of new tribal towns. This chapter discusses the close relationship between tribes, urbanisation, Sunni Islam and state building in the nineteenth century, and explains how the political and socio-economic inequalities between Sunni tribesmen and Shi'i cultivators were reflected in the organisation of towns and villages, and in the enforcement of separate domains of public and communal life for the Sunni and Shi'i population living outside Manama.

Chapter 2 shifts to the regional and international contexts in order to situate the development of Manama as a port town in the wider setting of coastal urbanisation. The aim is to draw a picture of urban development across the Gulf in the eighteenth and nineteenth centuries against the backdrop of tribal migrations and British expansion, and to analyse the socio-economic and political structure of port towns in the age of pearl urbanisation. While making a distinction between tribal centres and

Communalism in North India (Berkeley: California University Press, 1989); G. Pandey, *The Construction of Communalism in North India* (Delhi: Oxford University Press, 1990); A. Jalal, *Self and Sovereignty: Individual and Community in South Asian Islam since 1850* (London and New York: Routledge, 2000); P. A. Grossman, *Riots and Victims: Violence and the Construction of Communal Identity among Bengali Muslims, 1905–1947* (Boulder: Westview Press, 1999); R. Kaur, *Performative Politics and the Cultures of Hinduism: Public Uses of Religion in Western India* (New Delhi: Permanent Black, 2003).

cosmopolitan settlements, these ports are characterised as 'city-societies' – rather than city-states – on the basis of a number of key features of their body politic.

Chapter 3 refocusses on Bahrain and deals with Manama during the pearl boom and before the establishment of municipal government in 1919. The distinctive character of Manama's urban system is explained through an analysis of its dual connection with rural Bahrain and with the maritime economy of the Persian Gulf. The making of the town as a major trade emporium and as the world centre of pearling is explained through a number of symbiotic relationships. On the one hand, the evolution of the harbour, markets and residential areas is linked to the presence of immigrants, the accumulation of merchant capital, and the consolidation of a class of foreign merchants who acted as the brokers between the population, the Al Khalifah family and Bahrain's overseas economy. On the other, the organisation of urban space is considered from the perspective of changing patterns of land control, a key factor in defining the political profile of merchants as urban elites.

Chapter 4 discusses the development of Manama between 1919 and 1957 through the lens of its municipality, the first modern institution of government established along the Arab coast. While urban reform is treated as an integral part of the process of state building initiated by the Government of India in Bahrain in the 1920s, this chapter is particularly concerned with the influence of the new municipal order on urban politics and society. The socially conservative outlook of the municipal council (*majlis al-baladiyyah*) and changes which affected the markets are analysed in order to illustrate the ambiguous role played by the municipality in processes of political and social modernisation leading to the explosion of sectarian and labour conflict in the early 1950s.

Under the rubric of urban 'disorder', Chapter 5 investigates how episodes of violence, Muharram rituals and mass events defined domains of political mobilisation for residents and urban elites, and spaces of contestation against the government. The aim is to show how unrest marked crucial junctures in the process of state and nation building before and after oil, while signposting changes in the political organisation of urban society. Episodes of unrest are also examined as symbols of political communication in order to trace the cumulative experience of popular politics leading to the nationalist agitations of the 1950s.

Chapter 6 explores and contrasts the impact of state intervention on Manama and on its agricultural hinterland in the oil era. Drawing on the discussion of pre-oil urbanisation and state formation in Chapters 1 and 3, it identifies a new phase in Bahrain's 'dialectic of urbanisation' brought about by oil revenue and political centralisation, both of which pitted the development of Manama as a modern capital city against its rural districts. The land policies enforced by the administration after 1925 are singled out as a crucial instrument through which the state exerted control over urban and rural development favouring the continuation of old social and political divisions between city and countryside, and the survival of Shi'ism as an ideology of resistance against state power.

The concluding sections develop further some of the general themes discussed in the introduction in the light of the evidence from Manama, outlining some social and political developments which consolidated the position of the city as the 'progressive' and turbulent frontier of modern Gulf politics in the 1960s and early 1970s. It also underlines some key features of urban and rural development in the 1970s and 1980s which underscored the transformation of Bahrain into a metropolitan state, pointing at the crucial political legacy of Bahrain's urban and rural histories.

1   Indigenous state traditions and the dialectics of urbanisation in Bahrain, 1602–1923

Before the discovery of oil, the presence of water and the rich pearl fisheries of Bahrain supported the growth of towns and agricultural hamlets. The continuity of settlement can also be readily explained by a long history of trade and by the political realities of a frontier society in flux. The strategic position of the islands favoured the consolidation of local administrations under the aegis of the regional powers and of the maritime and land empires which dominated the Gulf coast. Yet until the establishment of the Pax Britannica in the first half of the nineteenth century, the absence of fixed military and political frontiers fostered continuous instability throughout the region. Bahrain was a busy 'buffer' zone between the Arab and Iranian worlds and the point of intersection between the tribal and agricultural frontiers of the Persian Gulf. The coastline did not constitute a barrier but a permeable border in a region which had a long history of indigenous seafaring supported by an advanced maritime technology. Over the centuries, migrations from the mainland were the engine of political change as suggested by the sequence of dynasties of tribesmen, merchant seafarers and imperial administrators which ruled the islands. Newcomers had a profound influence on the economic and demographic make-up of Bahrain; the mainland was a reservoir of manpower but migrations could easily carry the seeds of societal and political collapse.

Bahrain also featured prominently in the 'battle for Eastern Arabia' which witnessed the confrontation between Sunni and Shi'i Islam as political and religious movements. As noted by Juan Cole, since the consolidation of the Carmathian movement in the area in the ninth century, Shi'ism expressed a quest for local autonomy from surrounding imperial powers, an ideology of resistance against 'foreign' intrusion.[1] Moreover, for the Shi'i peasants who formed the majority of the settled population of Bahrain, and of the oasis of al-Qatif and al-Ahsa' on the mainland, it served as an instrument of 'resistance' against Sunni tribes, which constituted the most dynamic and eclectic

---

[1] J. R. Cole, 'Rival Empires of Trade and Imami Shi'ism in Eastern Arabia, 1300–1800', *International Journal of Middle East Studies*, 19.3 (1987), 177–204 (178).

political force of the region. With the Safavid occupation of Bahrain in 1602, the 'battle for Eastern Arabia' entered a new phase. As Twelver Shi'ism was elevated to state religion in Iran, the Safavid Empire established a ground-breaking tradition of imperial government in the islands. The collapse of the dynasty in 1722 re-ignited tribal conflict across Iran and the Gulf. Persian influence in Bahrain continued under Nadir Shah Afshar (1688–1747), the new tribal leader of Iran who sought to restore the Sunni orthodoxy, and continued until the arrival of the Sunni Al Khalifah family in 1783, a branch of the al-'Utub confederation from mainland Arabia.

The consolidation of tribal government and the inflow of Sunni tribes from the mainland radically transformed the social, political and urban fabric of the islands. In the nineteenth century the imposition of tribal authority over Bahrain's Shi'i agricultural communities created strict divisions along sectarian lines reinforced by the opposition, as well as by the symbiotic relationship, between tribesmen and agriculturalists. These divisions became enshrined in the different sociopolitical organisations and built environments of towns and villages, and in the strictly compart-mentalised religious and political life of their Sunni and Shi'i residents.

Safavid Bahrain

The Safavids occupied Bahrain in 1602 as part of their expansionist drive to counterbalance Portuguese and Ottoman influence along the southern Iranian coast and in Iraq.[2] Soon after the conquest, the majority of the population of Bahrain embraced Imami Shi'ism. As a political movement, Shi'i Islam had a long tradition in the region. Eastern Arabia had been the centre of the state established by Carmathian dissidents in the tenth and eleventh centuries, and Ismaili chieftains like the Banu Jarwan continued to rule Bahrain from al-Ahsa' and al-Qatif until the middle of the fifteenth century. It is not clear to what extent Imamism was widespread in Bahrain before the Persian occupation established the less intransigent doctrine of Twelver Shi'ism. In the thirteenth century Shaykh Maytham ibn 'Ali al-Bahrani (d. 1280), a renowed Shi'i theologian, accepted the theory of the occultation of the Twelfth Imam. A century later Muhammad Öljaytü (1309–16), the Ilkhanid ruler of Iran, requested the religious services of *'ulama'* from Bahrain after his conversion to Imamism.[3]

---

[2] W. Floor, *The Persian Gulf: A Political and Economic History of Five Port Cities, 1500–1730* (Washington: Mage, 2006), p. 202.

[3] Cole, 'Rival Empires', 177–83. Archaeologists have discovered coins minted on the occasion of the death of Öljaytü under the title of Zayn al-'Abidin. Interview with 'Ali Akbar Bushehri, Manama, 24 March 2004.

The town of Bilad al-Qadim became the provincial capital of Safavid Bahrain and the seat of the chief *mujtahid* of the islands, the second most important political figure after the Persian governor. The religious credentials of Bahrain's *shaykh al-islam*, locally known as *shaykh al-ra'is*, were carefully vetted by Isfahan, as his office was under the direct control of the central government. The legacy of Bilad al-Qadim as a centre of Twelver Shi'ism continued after the collapse of the Safavid administration. Several *shuyukh al-ra'is* were buried on the holy grounds of the site at least until 1792, and the mosque of Suq al-Khamis, the oldest religious complex of the area, has continued to attract widespread popular devotion ever since.[4] In Safavid Bilad al-Qadim, piety and learning thrived alongside a flourishing market-place supported by the lush date farms, orchards and vegetable gardens of the rich agricultural region of northern Awal, the main island of the archipelago. In the early Safavid period the Portuguese traveller Pedro Teixeira also noted extensive cultivation of wheat and barley. It can be surmised that the opening of southern Iranian markets to Bahrain's produce, particularly dates and pearls, boosted the islands' export economy.[5] Migration also contributed to Bahrain's agricultural prosperity. In fear of religious discrimination, Shi'i cultivators from al-Qatif and al-Ahsa' flocked to the islands after the temporary Ottoman occupation of Eastern Arabia in 1537.[6]

The *shaykh al-ra'is* and a network of local Arab clerics became the pillars of the Safavid provincial administration of Bahrain, which was supported by taxation on agriculture and pearling earmarked in accordance with the Islamic principle of *khums*. The spiritual authority and political influence of the clergy derived from the control of religious institutions: mosques and schools (*hawzat*), endowments which provided essential services to the population, the celebration of the Friday prayer in the name of the Safavid Shah, and the *hisbah* which allowed clerics to regulate prices and transactions in the local markets in accordance with Islamic principles. One of the titles of the *shaykh al-ra'is* was that of

---

[4] J. Belgrave, *Welcome to Bahrain*, 8th edn (Manama: The Augustan Press, 1973), pp. 87–9; 'Ali A. Bushehri, 'Archaeological evidence on the graves of the *shuyukh al-ra'is* of Bahrein', typescript, 12 pages, 1996. On the early history of al-Khamis mosque see 'Abd al-Rahman Musameh, *Muqaddimah fi tarikh al-Bahrayn al-qadim* (Manama: [n.pub.], 1998), p. 3.

[5] P. Teixeira, *The Travels of Pedro Teixeira*, trans. by William F. Sinclair (London: Hakluyt Society, 1902), pp. 174–5.

[6] C. E. Larsen, *Life and Land Use on the Bahraini Islands: The Geoarchaeology of an Ancient Society* (University of Chicago Press, 1983), pp. 67, 99, 205; *The Gazetteer of the Persian Gulf, Oman and Central Arabia*, by John George Lorimer, 2 vols. (Calcutta: Office of the Superintendent Government Printing, 1908; repub. by Gregg International, Farnborough, 1970), vol. II, pp. 298–9.

mutawalli al-'umur al-hisbiyyah, an indication of his political importance as the executive of the provisions of the religious law.[7]

Evidence on the activities of Shi'i *'ulama'* is anecdotal and coated in the celebratory and rhetorical images of the Imami tradition. It seems that the higher echelons of the clergy combined religious office with the control of agricultural estates and direct involvement in the pearling industry. Crucially, some *'ulama'* families owned date plantations, financed pearling expeditions, owned boats and recruited labour.[8] One famous example was Shaykh Muhammad ibn Sulayman al-Maqabi (d. 1674), the imam of the village of al-Qadam who became the chief religious dignitary of Bahrain. He bought the entire catch of the village at the end of the season from pearl divers in exchange for advances on profit, and acted as a wholesaler of pearls, attracting buyers from all corners of the islands.[9]

Villages became organised around a hierarchy of place dictated by the influence of local clerics with connections to the Shi'i religious establishment in and outside Bahrain. In the absence of detailed evidence, the importance of the settlements of Safavid Bahrain can be inferred from the recurrence of their names in the *nisbah*s of religious elites: al-Mahuzi, al-Qadami, al-Jidd Hafsi and al-Dirazi. Regional networks of politics and learning contributed further to the integration of Bahrain into the world of Shi'i Islam. Influential clerics attended the religious schools of the holy cities of Najaf and Karbala and those of the Safavid provincial capitals.[10] While pilgrims crowded the shrines of Iran and Iraq, Bahrain's *mujtahid*s held a prominent position in the cadres of the Safavid Empire and by the second half of the seventeenth century they had replaced their colleagues of Jabal 'Amil in Lebanon who had provided the early foundations of the state.

Piety, popular Shi'ism and the collapse of the 'Islands of Paradise'

The family history and biography of Yusuf ibn Ahmad al-Bahrani (1695–1772) sheds light on the combined tradition of learning and mundane

---

[7] Cole, 'Rival Empires', 187–90.
[8] These developments are analysed in Cole, 'Rival Empires', pp. 190–2.
[9] On Shaykh Muhammad ibn Sulayman al-Maqabi see Yusuf ibn Ahmad al-Bahrani, *Lu'luat al-Bahrayn fi al-ijazat wa tarajim rijal al-hadith* (Najaf: Matba'ah al-Nu'man, 1966), pp. 86–90; 'Ali ibn Hasan al-Bahrani, *Anwar al-badrayn fi tarajim 'ulama' al-Qatif wa al-Ahsa' wa al-Bahrayn* (Najaf: Matba'ah al-Nu'man, 1960), pp. 125–7.
[10] M. Salati, 'La Lu'lua al-Bahrayn fi l-ijāza li qurratay al-'ayn di Šayh Yûsuf b. Ahmad al-Bahrânî (1107-1186/1695-1772): per lo Studio della Ši'a di Bahrayn', *Annali di Ca' Foscari*, 28.3 (1989), 111–45 (124–36).

pursuits which dominated the Shi'i circles of Bahrain. It is also a poignant testimony of the collapse of the Imami tradition in the early eighteenth century as a result of the fierce contest between the Safavid Empire and Oman, the new maritime power which emerged after the relinquishment of Portuguese rule over Muscat in the mid seventeenth century.[11]

Born into a religious family from the village of al-Diraz with connections to the pearling industry, Yusuf's father Ahmad ibn Ibrahim (d. 1719) moved to al-Mahuz to join the circle of Shaykh Sulayman ibn 'Abdallah al-Mahuzi (d. 1709), a renowned cleric. After a long and debilitating illness Sulayman ibn Salih (d. 1675), the paternal uncle of Yusuf's grandfather, abandoned his business as the owner of pearling boats and became the *imam al-jum'ah wa al-jama'ah* (the prayer leader) in the village of al-Diraz. In 1700, when Yusuf was five, Bahrain became the battleground between the al-'Utub and the al-Haram Sunni tribes, the latter called in by the *shaykh al-ra'is* of Bahrain to defend the islands from tribal incursions. Prolonged hostilities and the fear of a military occupation by the Imam of Muscat forced many clerics, including Yusuf's father, to leave Bahrain. On his way to al-Qatif, Ahmad left his young son in charge of the family properties in the village of al-Shakurah. As the Safavid administration collapsed in 1717, Yusuf joined his father on the mainland but returned to Bahrain two years later to tend the family's date plantations. Shortly after, he ran into financial difficulties and left the islands for good. His peregrinations continued in Iran and Iraq, where he died after a distinguished career in 1772.[12]

The departure of Yusuf al-Bahrani from Bahrain in 1717 anticipated the religious diaspora which plagued the islands throughout the eighteenth century and continued after the takeover by the Al Khalifah in 1783. Agriculturalists and merchants left for Iraq and Iran after the Omani invasion of 1800–1. The influx of refugees into the port town of Bushehr led to the creation of a new quarter there which was named after the Bahraini village of al-Damistan. In recollecting his personal experience of the first Omani attack in 1700, Yusuf al-Bahrani illustrates the extent to which the survival of Imami learning had become by then closely associated with the political vicissitudes of the islands. Yusuf recounts that when he sought sanctuary in the Portuguese fort, he brought with him only the family collection of religious texts, his most cherished possessions. Once the invaders entered the fort Yusuf's books were burnt, the majority of the

---

[11] On the Omani-Persian war see B. J. Slot, *The Arabs of the Gulf, 1602–1784*, 2nd edn (Leidschendam: the author, 1995), pp. 217–47.

[12] Y. al-Bahrani, *Lu'luat*, pp. 87, 442–3; Salati, 'La Lu'lua al-Bahrayn', pp. 115–17, 124, 129.

population that had taken refuge there was killed or captured and the date farms owned by his family in the village of al-Shakurah were taken over by new settlers. Only the successful despatch of some books to his father in al-Qatif soon before the beginning of the hostilities secured the idealised transfer of religious knowledge outside Bahrain.[13]

Yusuf al-Bahrani's story might well suggest that spiritual wealth survived in the face of the confiscation and destruction of material possessions. Yet by the time the Al Khalifah consolidated their rule over Bahrain, the departure of religious leaders and the loss of agricultural land had irreversibly transformed the position of Bahraini Shi'ism. In his introduction to *Anwar al-Badrayn*, 'Ali ibn Hasan al-Bahrani, a local cleric writing at the beginning of the twentieth century, summed up these changes with fervour and nostalgia:

Speaking about their forefathers some people of good reputation told me that … in the old days every corner of the islands was renowned for the piety of its inhabitants … but the forces of ignorance and sin prevailed after the departure of the *'ulama'* … Foreigners replaced them. They appropriated properties unlawfully and plundered the resources of the country.[14]

After the demise of the Safavid administration, rural Bahrain suffered severe destruction. Carsten Niebuhr, who visited the islands in 1765, remarked that some villages had virtually disappeared as a result of depopulation and warfare. During the rule of the Sunni Al Khalifah, agricultural production suffered from the depletion of water resources under a new system of land tenure. Although the majority of cultivators retained rights of usufruct (*tasarruf*) over their village plots and some were able to buy land, they became accountable to new tribal lords who regarded villages and their population as their personal properties. The shaykhs fixed rents, imposed a poll tax (*raqbiyyah*), agricultural corvees (*al-sukhrah*) and a water tax (*dawb*).[15]

It is easy to understand how in the Al Khalifah era the intellectual and political engagement of Yusuf al-Bahrani and of his predecessors became the flagship of lost 'just' governance and the symbol of bygone economic prosperity. Large numbers of cultivators resented arbitrary exploitation and violence. Starving and defenceless, they were left with a bare

---

[13] Y. al-Bahrani, *Lu'luat*, pp. 442–3.   [14] 'Ali al-Bahrani, *Anwar al-badrayn*, pp. 52–3.
[15] C. Niebuhr, *Travels through Arabia, and other Countries in the East*, trans. by Robert Heron, 2 vols. (Edinburgh: R. Morison & Son, 1792), vol. II, p. 152; R. B. Serjeant, 'Customary Irrigation Law among the Baharnah of Bahrain' in A. Ibn K. al-Khalifah and M. Rice (eds.), *Bahrain through the Ages: The History* (London: Kegan Paul International, 1993), pp. 471–96 (pp. 474–5); Khuri, *Tribe and State in Bahrain*, p. 41; Lorimer, *Gazetteer*, vol. II, pp. 241–3, 248–9.

minimum to survive. In the words of a Persian traveller who visited Bahrain in 1836: 'They get the inedible dates and the rotten fish.'[16] A song still remembers the dire economic conditions of the peasantry in the period of the joint rulership of the two sons of Ahmad al-Fatih, the first Al Khalifah ruler of Bahrain: 'An ankle ring for 400 rupees, I wish it was a sour lemon / grown in the garden / 'Abdallah peels it and Salman eats it.' Similarly, the decadence of Bilad al-Qadim as a centre of religious devotion is still lamented in a nursery rhyme: 'Pray for Muhammad, pray for the Prophet / the springs of Bilad al-Qadim are dry / and no longer bring male children.'[17]

In response to such dire circumstances, villagers drew on a rich repertoire of oral tradition which celebrated the pillars of rural life, particularly water and agriculture. In offering an idealised and idyllic representation of Bahrain before the arrival of the Al Khalifah, Shi'i folklore echoed the Sumerian and Akkadian myths which celebrated Bahrain as the 'Islands of Paradise' featuring the hero Gilgamish and the prosperous Dilmun civilisation.[18] Water entered Shi'i popular imagery as a supernatural force which symbolised prosperity, political stability and urban regeneration. Springs and wells, in particular, featured in epic tales set in the early Islamic period which recounted stories of emancipation from 'foreign' yoke. In 1860 Lieutenant Whish, a British naval officer, collected a folk tale about an invading army which blocked a large spring near Suq al-Khamis, a place of Shi'i worship, in order to weaken the resistance of the local population. The water suddenly resurfaced in a myriad of sea springs which allowed villagers to drive the invaders away thus rescuing the population from the humiliations of foreign rule. Theodore Bent and his wife, two amateur archaeologists who visited the region in 1899, recorded a similar story set during the reign of the Umayyad Caliph 'Abd al-Malik ibn Marwan (685–705).[19] Local tradition also attributed to 'Abd al-Malik the covering of 'Ayn Sujur, a large spring in the village of al-Diraz, in order to punish the population for having sheltered religious dissidents from

[16] Muhammad Ibrahim Kazeruni, *Athar shahr-ha-ye-bastani savahil va jaza'ir-i Khalij-i Fars va darya-ye 'Umani*, annotated by Ahmad Iqtidari (Teheran: [n.pub.], 1996), p. 881.
[17] Salah 'Ali al-Madani and Karim 'Ali al-'Urayyad, *Min turath al-Bahrayn al-sha'abi* (Beirut: Matba'ah Samia, n.d.), pp. 202, 208.
[18] R. Alster, 'Dilmun, Bahrain and the Alleged Paradise in Sumerian Myth and Literature' in D. T. Potts (ed.), *Dilmun: New Studies in the Archaeology and Early History of Bahrain* (Berlin: Reimer, 1983), pp. 39–74; G. Bibby, *Looking for Dilmun*, 2nd edn (London: Stacey International, 1996), pp. 23–35.
[19] Lieutenant R. W. Whish, 'Memoir on Bahreyn' in *Records of Bahrain: Primary Documents, 1820–1960*, 8 vols. (Slough: Archive Editions, 1993), vol. I, p. 174; T. Bent, *Southern Arabia* (London: Smith and Elder, 1900), p. 15.

Iraq. Once the stones blocking the flow of water were removed, villages used them to build new houses.[20]

Springs also regenerated and consoled the oppressed. Their healing powers were often associated with miraculous events which involved the most sacred figures of Imami Shi'ism. The Persian community of Manama attributed the appearance of the famous spring of 'Ayn al-Adhari near Bilad al-Qadim to Imam 'Ali ibn Abu Talib (d. 661). The story recounts that water started to gush out of the ground after the sword of the Imam hit the soil during a fictitious contest staged in Bahrain against the Caliph 'Umar ibn al-Khattab (634–44). In the 1950s, this spring was used as a symbol of social and political alienation which marked the early oil era. The saying *"Ayn al-'adhari tasqi al-ba'id wa tukhalli al-qarib"* (literally: ''Ayn al-'Adhari waters far-away lands but neglects what is at hand') lamented the appropriation of Bahrain's resources by foreigners, particularly by the oil company. *'Adhari* also referred to individuals who neglected their families for strangers.[21]

The vitality and vigour of Shi'i folklore can be explained by the importance assumed by the lower clergy in the life of agricultural communities after the departure of leading *mujtahids* and clerics from Bahrain. The Omani army dealt a final blow to the higher echelons of the indigenous religious establishment in 1801 when Husayn Muhammad al-'Asfur al-Shakhuri, the last *Shaykh al-Ra'is*, was killed in battle. As the learned tradition of Imamism languished, Shi'i piety survived mainly in the ritualistic and textual context of *'ashura'*, the anniversary of the death of Imam Husayn. Mullas and *khatibs* (preachers) became the interpreters and custodians of the stories of the *Ahl al-Bayt* (the family of Imam Husayn) and of local tradition which came to life during the celebration of religious festivities.[22] The clergy continued to control *khums* donations and the extensive network of *waqf* properties dating from the Safavid period. In the 1830s approximately one third of the date plantations of Bahrain were *awqaf ja'fariyyah* (Shi'i pious foundations). Their income supported the upkeep of mosques, shrines and canals, and provided funds to accommodate guests and pilgrims. Endowments were a crucial and

[20] Muhammad 'Ali Tajir, *'Aqd al-lal fi tarikh al-Awal* (Manama: al-Maktabah al-'Ammah, 1994), pp. 39–40.
[21] R. P. Serjeant, 'Customary Irrigation Law among the Shi'ah Baharinah of al-Bahrayn', typescript, 33 pages, 1960, p. 7; interview with 'Ali Akbar Bushehri, Manama, 19 March 2004.
[22] In the eighteenth century we have information on a number of *shuyukh al-ra'is*: Muhammad Ahmad Ibrahim al-'Asfur (d. 1768), Muhammad 'Ali 'Abd al-Nabi al-Maqabi (d. 1786), 'Ali Hasan 'Abdallah al-Biladi (in office at least until 1789). Salim al-Nuwaydri, *'Alam al-thaqafah al-Islamiyyah fi al-Bahrayn khilal arba'at 'asharah qarnan*, 3 vols. (Beirut: al-'Arif, 1992), vol. II, pp. 221, 298, 338.

long-lasting legacy of more than a century of Shiʻi government under the Safavids. When the modern administration started to register land and properties after 1925, Shiʻi endowments by far outnumbered their Sunni counterparts.[23]

Upheaval from the sands: the tribal 'revolution'

The collapse of Safavid rule in 1717 revolutionised the political and urban landscape of the islands. Between 1735 and 1783, the year of the arrival of the first tribal contingents of the Al Khalifah, some thirteen different governors seized power including the al-Madhkur family from Bushehr which acted as the representatives of Iran.[24] In an important respect the Al Khalifah family, a section of the al-ʻUtub confederation from Najd, differed from their predecessors: they transformed Bahrain into a colony of tribal settlement and imposed the organisation of the nomadic polities of Central Arabia upon its agricultural and mercantile society. A three-tier system of settlement emerged in the nineteenth century. The newcomers established new tribal towns which became their strongholds: Muharraq, al-Budayyaʻ, al-Hidd, Rifaʻ al-Qibli and Rifaʻ al-Sharqi. These towns developed separately from the Shiʻi agricultural hamlets and from Manama, the most important port and entrepôt centre of the islands. The reorganisation of the territory reflected a competition between 'the desert and the sown' in a variety of ideological contexts. *al-ʻAsabiyyah* (tribal solidarity) and kinship which united the tribal elites and their allies became the organising principles of politics, superseding the strong religious ideals which had sustained the Safavid polity. Further, as the new tribal settlers were Sunni (mostly adhering to the Maliki school of law) their relations with large sections of the indigenous population were tinged with strong sectarian overtones.

The making of the islands of Bahrain into a tribal principality (*ʻimarah*) was part of the fractured power politics which antagonised the successors of Ahmad ibn Muhammad Al Khalifah, also known as Ahmad al-Fatih (the Conqueror), who first captured the islands in 1783. Although the Al Khalifah were no longer nomadic when they arrived in Bahrain from Qatar, they still followed the tradition of the desert. Family members fought among themselves over the distribution of the spoils of war, vying for the control of the new fiefdom. After the civil war which opposed the descendants of Ahmad al-Fatih in 1842–3, the branch of his son Salman took permanent control of government. The first Al Khalifah

[23] Kazeruni, *Athar*, pp. 880–1; Khuri, *Tribe and State in Bahrain*, p. 83.
[24] Tajir, *ʻAqd al-lal*, pp. 97–100.

rulers established their strongholds in the arid regions of the main island of the archipelago at some distance from the agricultural areas of the north. Salman (r. 1796–1825) founded Rifaʿ al-Sharqi which became the residence of his son Khalifah after 1830. The second Rifaʿ, known as al-Qibli, became the headquarters of ʿAli ibn Khalifah (r. 1868–9), while ʿAbdallah (r. 1796–1843), the second son of Ahmad al-Fatih, established the town of Muharraq on an island to the north east of Manama in 1809–10.[25]

During the long reign of ʿIsa ibn ʿAli (r. 1869–1932), Muharraq became the seat of the Dar al-Hukumah, a central administration under British protection. The intervention of the Government of India in Bahrain was regulated under a convention stipulated in 1861 with the Shaykh of Bahrain which affirmed his autonomous status under the auspices of Great Britain.[26] As Shaykh ʿIsa became the sole administrator of the islands under 'treaty relations', he allocated the agricultural regions of the islands to his relatives following tribal customs. His sons received a considerable share: ʿAbdallah ruled the village of Jidd Hafs, Hamad controlled Bilad al-Qadim, and Muhammad the agricultural hamlets of Karbabad, Jidd ʿAli and al-Jufayr. Isa's brother Khalid ruled the islands of Sitrah and Nabi Salih and was given control of Rifaʿ al-Sharqi and Rifaʿ al-Qibli.[27] The distribution of permanent rights over land, villages and labour force underpinned the establishment of a quasi feudal administration thus altering the fractured political organisation of al-ʿimarah before 1869.

Yet the tribal allies of the Al Khalifah who now controlled the pearling industry consolidated their independent position. Their leaders maintained councils (majlises) where they deliberated on diving matters and on internal disputes. Only in the case of conflict with other tribes did they resort to the arbitration of the ruler who presided over umbrella institutions based in Muharraq: his personal majlis and the al-salifah court in charge of the pearling industry, which included prominent merchants

[25] Muhammad al-Nabhani, al-Tuhfah al-Nabhaniyyah fi tarikh al-Jazirah al-ʿArabiyyah (Beirut: Dar Ihyaʾ al-ʿUlum, 1976), pp. 47–9, 87–9, 108–9; Tajir, ʿAqd al-lal, pp. 41–2; G. B. Brucks, 'Memoir Descriptive of the Navigation of the Gulf of Persia with Brief Notices of the Manners, Customs, Religion, Commerce and Resources of the People Inhabiting Its Shores and Islands' in Arabian Gulf Intelligence: Selections from the Records of the Bombay Government, new series, no. XXIV, 1856, ed. by R. Hughes Thomas (Cambridge: Oleander Press, 1985), p. 566; A. B. Kemball, 'Memoranda on the Resources, Localities, and Relations of the Tribes Inhabiting the Arabian Shores of the Persian Gulf' (1845), fiche 1090–1, 106, V 23/217 India Office Records (hereafter IOR); Kemball, 'Historical Sketch of the Utoobee Tribe of Arabs (Bahrein) ... from the Year 1832 to August 1844' (1844), fiche 1094, 392 ff, V 23/217 IOR.
[26] H. M. Albaharna, The Arabian Gulf States: Their Legal and Political Status and International Problems (Beirut: Librairie du Liban, 1978), pp. 31–2.
[27] Khuri, Tribe and State in Bahrain, p. 43; Lorimer, Gazetteer, vol. II, p. 248.

cum tribal notables. Tribal autonomy fostered political factionalism and continued to expose the islands to the turbulent politics of the mainland. The al-Dawasir, for instance, a tribal group from Najd under the protection of the Al Sa'ud family, were treated by Shaykh 'Isa as very special 'guests' in Bahrain. They kept the authority of the ruler at arm's length and acquired landed estates and properties in Manama.[28]

Bahrain's prosperous pearl industry constituted the main resource base for the tribal newcomers. Pearl production was tightly organised around tribal affiliations and alliances. The powerful pearling tribes of Muharraq, such as the Al Jalahimah and Al Ibn 'Ali, owned a large number of ships and financed expeditions. Their leaders became the wealthiest pearl merchants of Bahrain. The Al Musallam, a branch of the Banu Khalid confederation of Eastern Arabia, specialised in the marketing of pearls. The clients of the al-'Utub groups provided pullers and divers while other minor tribes supplied the rank and file of the military force which protected tribal leaders, locally known as al-fidawiyyah. The concentration of Africans and Baluchis in the main pearling centres suggests that tribes also held the monopoly over slave labour, as elsewhere along the Gulf coast. At the turn of the twentieth century many slaves had become gradually integrated into the tribal system. Lorimer reported nearly 5,000 emancipated slaves in Bahrain who maintained close involvement with the sea, particularly with pearling. He also mentioned an equal number still in captivity, listing them among the tribal population.[29]

Tribal mercantilism was the single most important agent of urbanisation along the coast. By the early twentieth century, approximately 60 per cent of the population had become concentrated in a handful of maritime outposts which, with the exception of Manama, grew as a result of successive migrations of Arab tribes. After 1869 Muharraq consolidated its position as the stronghold of the Al Khalifah and of groups which belonged to the al-'Utub confederation, including the Al Fadhil and Al Jalahimah. As the largest tribal settlement of Bahrain, the town developed as the powerhouse of the pearl economy of the islands and continued to occupy a special place in the epic of tribal colonisation. The pious Muhammad al-Nabhani, the official historian of the Al Khalifah family, described retrospectively the foundation of their capital in 1809–10 as *nuzul al-Muharraq ba'da al-Zubarah* (lit. the descent upon Muharraq after al-Zubarah). This Koranic image evoking the first revelation of the

---

[28] Khuri, *Tribe and State in Bahrain*, pp. 35–67.
[29] Lorimer, *Gazetteer*, vol. II, pp. 62–4, 238–41, 1160–1, 1282–3; 'List of Some of the Families into which the Tribes Residing in Bahrain are Divided' in 'Memo on the Islands of Bahrain', 11 July 1875, R/15/2/192 IOR.

Archangel Gabriel to the Prophet Muhammad was of course intended to endow the ruling family with a sense of divine mission. The event marked the establishment of the Al Khalifah in Bahrain on a permanent basis and the relinquishment of their possessions in mainland Qatar after the fall of the town of al-Zubarah in 1796, the previous stronghold of the family.[30] al-Hidd, the second largest and richest pearling centre of Bahrain, remained a satellite of Muharraq under the powerful Al Ibn 'Ali tribe while al-Budayya' and al-Zallaq remained the personal fiefdom of the al-Dawasir tribe which arrived from al-Dammam on the mainland after 1845.[31]

The transfer of productive activity from the agricultural hinterland to the coast lay at the heart of the political economy of tribal government. The concentration of revenue from pearling in the hands of tribal entrepreneurs allowed the Al Khalifah to construct a tight network of political allegiances. At the same time, the family derived most of its income from customs dues and agricultural taxation. The islands began a period of rapid commercial expansion before the outbreak of the civil war in the early 1840s as a result of increased activities in the pearl banks. In the mid eighteenth century Carsten Niebuhr reported an annual income of approximately 100,000 rupees from Bahrain's pearl fisheries and dates, while in 1833 David Blane, the British Resident in the Persian Gulf, estimated annual production from pearling at about £200,000–240,000 (between two and three million rupees) with approximately 30,000 men and 2,500 vessels employed around Bahrain.[32]

As rural communities became an integral part of Bahrain's new 'colonial' economy, the population and size of agricultural hamlets decreased steadily. Although there are no population statistics or evidence for rural production for much of the nineteenth century, as early as 1836 villages such as al-Diraz and al-Shakurah were reported in a state of ruin with large tracts of land lying waste. It is also significant that Shaykh 'Isa's agricultural revenue halved between 1873 and 1904. In 1906 Bahrain was

---

[30] al-Nabhani, *al-Tuhfah al-Nabhaniyyah*, pp. 82–98; Tariq Wali, *al-Muharraq: 'umran madinah khalijiyyah 1783–1971* (Manama: Matbu 'at Banurama al-Khalij, 1990), pp. 67–8. For the history of Zubara see A. M. Abu-Hakima, *History of Eastern Arabia, 1750–1800: The Rise and Development of Bahrain, Kuwait and Wahhabi Saudi Arabia* (Beirut: Khayats, 1965), pp. 63–77.

[31] Lorimer estimated the total population of Bahrain at 99,275 of which 60,800 were concentrated in Manama, Muharraq, al-Hidd and al-Budayya'. He reported only 16,000 Shi'i urban residents (mainly in Manama) as opposed to approximately 45,000 Sunnis. Lorimer, *Gazetteer*, vol. II, pp. 62–4, 237–8, 324–35, 596–7, 1270, 1364, 1917–19.

[32] Niebuhr, *Travels through Arabia*, vol. II, p. 152; J. B. Kelly, *Britain and the Persian Gulf, 1795–1880* (Oxford: Clarendon Press, 1968), pp. 29–30.

already importing fairly large quantities of dates from al-'Ahsa' to provision the population.[33] In search of new opportunities many agriculturalists abandoned their plots and moved to Manama, which in the last quarter of the nineteenth century replaced Muscat in Oman as the leading commercial emporium of the Arab coast. Desperate to find new sources of income and a modus vivendi with the regime, a segment of the rural notability also abandoned their ancestral homes.[34] Families of religious standing (such as the Ibn Rajabs, al-Jishis and al-'Alawis) recreated economic and religious networks in Manama in symbiosis with the town's growing mercantile communities.

Developments in the legal sphere also explain the deterioration of the social and economic conditions of rural Bahrain at the turn of the twentieth century in contrast with the growing prosperity of urban settlements. The customary law (al-'urf) in force among the tribes continued to be applied consistently only in the villages while shariah and British Indian law became important instruments of government in the towns. On the one hand, the consolidation of a system of Islamic courts, both Sunni and Shi'i, was an integral part of the progressive centralisation and administrative specialisation of the Dar al-Hukumah.[35] On the other, it can be explained by the threat to the authority of the Al Khalifah posed by the gradual imposition of British extraterritorial jurisdiction in Manama. Most notably, the application of shariah law had important implication for the property regime inside Manama and Muharraq. Here the presence of religious courts favoured the commercialisation of real estate, and the acquisition of properties by merchants as qadis certified sale transactions between notables, and between them and the Al Khalifah. In the villages, customary rights continued to protect tribal landlords and discouraged the penetration of merchant capital which could have injected a new lease of life to the ailing agriculture of the islands. Additional factors prevented urban-based merchants and entrepreneurs from investing in agriculture. They looked to the sea as their main source of income, social prestige and political legitimacy. Even those Shi'i notables of rural extraction living in

---

[33] 'Report on the Administration of the Bushehr Residency and Muscat Political Agency for 1873–1874' in *The Persian Gulf Administration Reports 1873–1949*, 10 vols. (Gerrards Cross: Archive Editions, 1986), vol. I, p. 66; Lorimer, *Gazetteer*, vol. II, p. 251; Sulayman Da'wud 'Abdallah, *Samahij fi al-tarikh* (Manama, 1996), 100; Kazeruni, *Athar*, pp. 91, 94.

[34] Lorimer, *Gazetteer*, vol. II, pp. 222, 238, 298; J. Onley, 'The Politics of Protection in the Gulf: The Arabian Rulers and the British Resident in the Nineteenth Century', *New Arabian Studies* 6 (2004), 30–82 (34); C. H. Allen, 'The State of Masqat in the Gulf and East Africa, 1785–1829', *International Journal of Middle East Studies*, 14 (1982), 117–27.

[35] Lorimer, *Gazetteer*, vol. II, pp. 249–50.

Manama maintained social distance from their former constituents, attracting the continuous resentment of rural folks.[36]

Urban and rural spheres in the Al Khalifah era

Approaching the coast from the mainland in the late nineteenth century, northern Bahrain still appeared as a large oasis surrounded by the sea, a place of shelter and recovery from the harshness of the desert. The 'Islands of Paradise' were certainly alive in the imagination of foreign observers who were captivated by Bahrain's lush landscape. In 1879 Captain Durand, the Assistant British Political Resident in Bushehr, noted: 'On looking out to sea on the morning of a clear sky and a fresh nor'wester, it would seem as if nature, at all times lavish of effect, had here, however, exhausted every tint of living green in her paint box.'[37] The economic profile of the towns and villages which merged into this idyllic scenery differed from the oasis settlements of Central Arabia. Muharraq, al-Hidd and al-Budayya' did not serve as nodes of exchange between the sedentary and nomadic populations but developed as the passageways into the pearl banks which surrounded Bahrain.[38] In contrast with al-Ha'il and 'Unayzah in Najd, market towns which lived off caravan trade and revenue from the pilgrimage to Mecca in the Hijaz, their economy was heavily dependent upon Manama, the centre of pearl exports to Bombay and the hub of Bahrain's import trade. The socio-economic and demographic divisions between these pearling towns and their immediate agricultural hinterland also reflected deep sectarian cleavages. While in Central Arabia, Kuwait and Qatar the terms *badu* and *hadar* distinguished the tribal from sedentary populations, the corresponding status groups in Bahrain were *'Arab* (Sunnis of tribal origin) and *Baharna* (Arab Shi'i agriculturalists).[39]

Yet it was tribal solidarity (*al-'asabiyyah*) as opposed to sectarian sentiment which articulated ideal urban hierarchies, often irrespective of the size and the importance of settlements. In the early twentieth century Muhammad al-Nabhani, the official historian of the Al Khalifah, expressed this taxonomy of place by celebrating the primacy of Muharraq and al-Hidd over Manama, by then arguably the largest and

---

[36] Interview with Mansur al-Jamri, London, 13 March 1999.

[37] E. L. Durand, 'Notes on the Islands of Bahrain and Antiquities' in Political Resident Bushehr to Secretary to the Government of India, 1 May 1879, R/15/2/192 IOR.

[38] al-Rasheed, *Politics in an Arabian Oasis*, pp. 9–28, 95–132; S. Altorki and D. P. Cole, *Arabian Oasis City: The Transformation of 'Unayzah* (Austin: University of Texas Press, 1989), pp. 15–82.

[39] For a cogent discussion of the distinction between *badu* and *hadar* in al-Ha'il see al-Rasheed, *Politics in an Arabian Oasis*, pp. 117–32.

most important economic centre of the islands. He referred to them as *al-qasbat*, the architectural strongholds which constituted the inner core of the tribal polity. With no citadel or fortifications protecting Muharraq or al-Hidd when al-Nabhani was writing, *al-qasbat* were the figurative bastions which guarded *al-'asabiyyah*.[40] These towns held a strong emotional appeal for Bahrain's population. They awoke the sense of prowess and superiority of groups with a tribal pedigree, and demarcated the physical and ideal separation between them and the Shi'i agriculturalists, between Bahrain's 'urban' and 'rural' spheres. In the minds of the villagers, towns became the image of oppression, places of coercion dominated by *al-fidawiyyah*, the armed retainers of tribal leaders and members of the ruling family who were in charge of public security. During the reign of Khalifah ibn Salman (1825–34) public order in the then capital Rifa' was exclusively in the hands of slaves of African origin. In Muharraq, the governorship of the town was entrusted to a high-ranking retainer of Shaykh 'Isa while in Manama *al-fidawiyyah* of the Al Khalifah governor controlled the markets. The *lawhah al-aqfal*, the notorious 'board of chains' where offenders were exposed to public scrutiny became the hallmark of the injustice dispensed by the government.[41]

The close identification of tribes with urban milieus is also evident from the use of the term for tribal section and Bedouin encampment (*farij*, pl. *firjan*) to denote urban quarters. This was evident even in Manama, whose population included small numbers of tribesmen and a majority of Shi'is. The pre-eminent position occupied by *al-'asabiyyah* in the organisation of new spaces of settlement is also reflected in the observations of outsiders who took a keen interest in the complex population mosaic of the islands. At the turn of the twentieth century Lorimer classed Shi'i villagers as a 'race' as opposed to a 'tribe', attributing their poverty and oppression to the lack of tribal bonds between them. He described the Hawala in similar terms since they also lacked the political cohesion which characterised the Al Khalifah and their allies. In contrast, in 1875 an anonymous British official included the Shi'i artisans and sail makers of Muharraq (*al-hayyakin*) among the tribal population. He clearly viewed their economic specialisation and tight spatial organisation in exclusive neighbourhoods as a form of communal solidarity comparable to *al-'asabiyyah*, but devoid of any political connotation.[42]

---

[40] al-Nabhani, *al-Tuhfah al-Nabhaniyyah*, pp. 42–4.
[41] W. H. Wyburd, 'Journals of an Excursion into Arabia' (1832) in *Records of Bahrain*, vol. I, p. 148; Khuri, *Tribe and State in Bahrain*, pp. 51–2; Wali, *al-Muharraq*, p. 37.
[42] Lorimer, *Gazetteer*, vol. II, pp. 237–41, 622; 'List of Some of the Families into which the Tribes Residing in Bahrain are Divided' in 'Memo on the Islands of Bahrain', 11 July

Distinctions between the urban and rural spheres were also enshrined in the spatial and socio-economic organisation of settlements. The neighbourhoods of al-Hidd and al-Budayya' constituted close networks of solidarity which reflected the organisation of pearl production. Clients, slaves and divers concentrated around tribal leaders cum pearling entrepreneurs. In contrast, Shi'i villages were organised around agricultural allotments (*mazra'ah*) which included huts, canals and water wells. Customary water rights played a crucial role in the organisation of neighbourhoods. Described from a distance by foreign travellers as clusters of poor dwellings hidden by greenery and date clumps, the history of the development of these villages is mainly preserved in local tradition.[43] The oldest nucleus of al-Samahij on the Muharraq Island, for instance, maintained a predominantly agricultural landscape until the mid-1950s with agricultural allotments, gardens and springs.[44]

The contrasting spatial order of Muharraq and Manama was testimony to the different patterns of social organisation which underlined the evolution of the two largest settlements of Bahrain. In Muharraq, economic specialisation and sectarian affiliation played a part in the organisation of residential districts at the turn of the twentieth century. While the oldest and largest quarters of the town housed the tribal aristocracy of the town, subordinate tribes, Shi'i artisans and Hawala merchant communities (the only non-tribal commercial elites of the town) formed their own enclaves.[45] Muharraq's traditional urban layout was still apparent in the oil era. Although by the 1960s the government had reorganised urban districts following a numbering system (allegedly in order to avoid disputes over the names of localities), inner-city neighbourhoods were still known by the names of members of the Al Khalifah family and of leading tribes (see Map 3). In contrast, the residential areas of Manama had a fairly mixed population and developed primarily as immigration units, as will be explained in Chapter 4. It is in these neighbourhoods that

1875, R/15/2/192 IOR. According to oral tradition the Shi'i population of Muharraq did not belong to the indigenous population of Bahrain but arrived from the mainland with the Al Khalifah.
[43] General information on Shi'i villages are included in Lorimer, *Gazetteer*, vol. II, pp. 217–29; Tajir, *'Aqd al-lal*, pp. 27–48; Muhammad Ibrahim Kazeruni, *Tarikh banadir va jaza'ir Khalij-i Fars* (Teheran: Mu'assasah-i Farhangi-i Jahangiri, 1367 [1988–9]), pp. 86–101. The few accounts of rural Bahrain by the missionaries of the American Dutch Reformed Church based in Manama focussed primarily on pearling settlements. H. G. Van Vlack, 'A Tour of the Bahrein Villages' in *The Arabian Mission: Field Reports, Quarterly Letters, Neglected Arabia, Arabia Calling*, 8 vols. (Gerrards Cross: Archive Editions, 1993), vol. III, 94 (July–September 1915), pp. 8–11; G. J. Pennings 'A Trip to Zellag' in *The Arabian Mission*, vol. III, 82 (July–September 1912), pp. 11–13.
[44] 'Abdallah, *Samahij fi al-tarikh*, pp. 60, 101–4, 150.
[45] The pre-oil town and its neighbourhoods are described by Lorimer in *Gazetteer*, vol. II, pp. 1269–71.

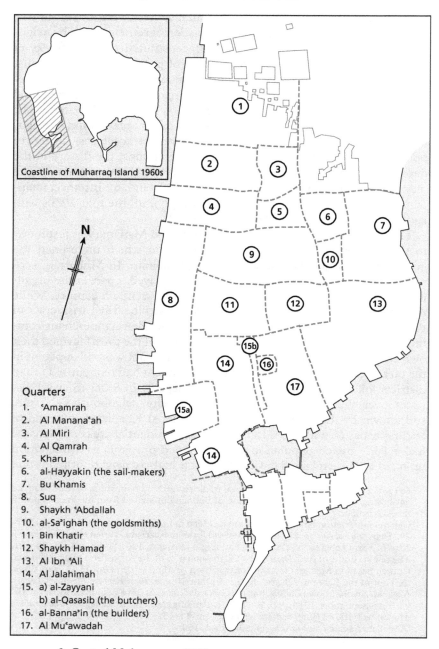

Coastline of Muharraq Island 1960s

N

Quarters

1. 'Amamrah
2. Al Manana'ah
3. Al Miri
4. Al Qamrah
5. Kharu
6. al-Hayyakin (the sail-makers)
7. Bu Khamis
8. Suq
9. Shaykh 'Abdallah
10. al-Sa'ighah (the goldsmiths)
11. Bin Khatir
12. Shaykh Hamad
13. Al Ibn 'Ali
14. Al Jalahimah
15. a) al-Zayyani
    b) al-Qasasib (the butchers)
16. al-Banna'in (the builders)
17. Al Mu'awadah

3 Central Muharraq: *c.* 1960

the multi-layered organisation of Bahrain's settled life became manifest. Unlike in Muharraq, merchants were of mixed background. *al-Tawawish*, the most prestigious pearl merchants, were Sunni, Shi'i and Hawala (Arabs with a tribal pedigree but originally from southern Iran). Persians and Indians monopolised food imports from Iran and British India. Moreover, the majority of the urban population was located socially and politically outside the tribal system, and capitalised on the utilitarian ethos and outward-looking orientation of the port's economy. The presence of different ethnic and religious groups created a distinctively Manami Shi'i and Sunni culture whose heterogeneous character contrasted with that of tribal towns and rural communities.

The layout of the inner city of Muharraq also reflected political orders which were in contrast with those of Manama. Under Shaykh 'Isa ibn 'Ali, central Muharraq evolved as the centre of the Dar al-Hukumah and embodied the tribal hierarchies and allegiances which supported the administration. The tribal quarters were located around a central area inhabited by prominent members of the Al Khalifah family which was organised around the palace of the ruler and which after the 1930s was named after Shaykh Hamad, 'Isa's successor. In the celebratory words of Muhammad al-Nabhani, Bayt Shaykh 'Isa stood among the residences of his relatives as 'the moon among shining stars'.[46] In contrast, the landscape of Manama encapsulated the acephalous political organisation of a cosmopolitan port town with the seafront constituting its political and administrative centre. At the turn of the twentieth century the creation of a new warehouse district and the building of the British political agency marked the consolidation of a class of powerful merchants who controlled overseas trade in partnership with Shaykh 'Isa and with the Government of India, whose representatives came to dominate Manama's political life.[47]

Built environments and spaces of socialisation

The evolution of new architectural styles, and the creation of new venues of political and religious socialisation were part and parcel of the dialectics of urbanisation which characterised the Al Khalifah era. As the majority of the population continued to live in huts, stone buildings made a vivid impression on locals and visitors alike. In both urban and rural districts, masonry buildings mirrored the increasing socio-economic, ethnic and cultural stratification of the population. Their architectural language

---

[46] al-Nabhani, *al-Tuhfah al-Nabhaniyyah*, p. 141.   [47] See p. 81.

communicated the wealth and political influence of the elites: the ruling family, the tribal leaders cum pearling entrepreneurs and the foreign merchants. Tribal architecture also became a permanent feature of both the urban and rural landscapes affirming the Bedouin heritage of the Al Khalifah family and their allies as a counterpoint to the more cosmopolitan, and ostensibly more sophisticated, culture of Bahrain's commercial classes. The 'introvert' and inward-looking character of the built environment mirrored the religious and political life of the population. Both vernacular and public architecture protected and prioritised security: masonry houses were organised around internal courtyards and hut compounds were surrounded by walls and fences which guarded extended families, Shi'i villages and overseas immigrants. Similarly, spaces of private and public utility tended to safeguard kinship networks, mercantile interests and sectarian ideals.[48]

For the majority of the urban population housing continued to represent a moveable asset as thatched huts made of palm branches with stone or mud walls (known as *barasti* and *'arish*) dominated towns and villages. In the villages they were passed from father to son and considered an integral part of the property of tribal landowners. In Manama and Muharraq the life span of *barasti* compounds was dependent on the precarious nature of land occupancy, which was not protected by private property rights. As it took from three to five days to erect a *barasti*, their building materials (*al-athat*, lit. furniture) were considered an integral part of the possessions of a household. With the commercialisation of land at the turn of the twentieth century the economic meaning of 'informal' housing started to change. Their *al-athat* were often mentioned in contracts of sale, if they affected the price or the rent value of the property. Moreover, evidence suggests that *barasti* compounds started to became a source of investment for the notables of Manama who acquired land and built cheap accommodation for rent (see Figure 1).[49]

[48] For a discussion of the architecture and Islamic tradition of the Arabian Peninsula see J. King, *Traditional Architecture of Saudi Arabia* (London: I. B. Tauris, 1998). On Bahraini housing and architecture see: *Al-Malamih al-'umraniyyah li al-mudun al-taqlidiyyah fi al-Bahrayn* (Ministry of Housing, Physical Planning Directorate, State of Bahrain, [n.d]); Tariq Wali, *al-Bayan wa al-tibyan fi al-'imarah wa al-'umran* (Manama: [n.pub.], 1993); Rashid al-'Urayfi, *al-'Imarah al-Bahrayniyyah* (Manama: al-Matba'ah al-Sharqiyyah, 1978); *al-Khifaz 'ala khasa'is al-madinah al-'Arabiyyah wa ala turathiha al-'Arabi al-Islami*, by Ibrahim 'Uthman (Central Municipal Committee, State of Bahrain, [n.d]).
[49] Wali, *al-Muharraq*, pp. 116–18; *Mahadir li Majlis al-Baladiyyah (al-Manamah)* (Minutes of Manama Municipal Council, hereafter MMBM), 15 Rajab 1355 (1 October 1936) R/15/2/1923 IOR; E. I. Majed, *The Traditional Construction of Early Twentieth Century Houses in Bahrain* (Doha: Arab States Folklore Centre, 1987), pp. 37–8; *Ayyam zaman / Old Days* (Manama: Matbu'at Banurama al-Khalij, 1986), p. 42; files n. 36, 56, 57, Idarah al-Tabu (Department of Land Registration, hereafter IT).

1 Children with *barasti* in the background surrounded by a stone wall, Manama mid 1930s

The proliferation of *barasti* settlements in the outskirts of Manama and Muharraq during the pearl and trade boom of the last quarter of the nineteenth century constituted the most conspicuous phenomenon of pre-oil urbanisation. Inhabited by overseas and rural immigrants, these veritable shanty towns epitomised the deepening class divisions which separated the urban workforce from mercantile and tribal communities. The boom of 'informal' housing and the overall better living conditions of the urban population also led to development of different building styles. *al-'Arish al-bahrani* which predominated in the villages was simpler in structure and built with cheaper materials, while the *al-manami* which was predominant in Manama stood on a platform which insulated it from the ground.[50]

Wealth from the pearl banks rapidly transformed the dwellings of the members of pearling tribes from tents to masonry structures built in timber, coral aggregate, gypsum and limestone. In the 1820s, only a decade after its establishment, Muharraq displayed a fine architecture in coral stone as pearl merchants built their mansions around internal courtyards with elegant decorations in plaster work. Outside the more densely

---

[50] al-'Urayfi, *al-'Imarah al-Bahrayniyyah*, pp. 10–13.

populated areas, newly built houses distinguished tribal from agricultural communities. Even small pearling centres had permanent housing in contrast with the majority of villages whose landscape was dominated by *barastis*.[51] Manama's housing boom coincided with the expansion of its port economy after the 1880s which brought to the town large numbers of immigrants and considerable wealth to the import–export merchants. al-'Awadiyyah, the most affluent residential district of the town, was built with the capital of immigrants from Iran who left the port of Lingah after the establishment of a customs administration in 1900. In the same way as the al-Bastakiyyah quarter of Dubai, its wind towers (*al-kashtil*) became the most architecturally distinctive feature of Manama. The history of Bayt Khadim, one of the large mansions of the district, illustrates the ways in which family and commercial connections from overseas contributed to transform the built environment. The house was first built by Muhammad Latif Khadim (b. 1899), a young trader from Lingah, as a simple structure in palm branches and coral stone. It was rebuilt as a large merchant house after his nephew Muhammad Sa'id joined him from Iran sometime in the early 1920s, married his daughter and helped him to expand his business in the carpet trade.[52]

The architectural style of upper-class mansions displayed the cultural influences and the ethnic divisions between tribal and cosmopolitan entrepreneurs, and between them and the ruling family. In Muharraq the palaces of the Al Khalifah (*al-qusur*, sing. *al-qasr*) resembled the tribal forts of the desert. They were organised around internal courtyards and protected by high walls; their inward-looking and defensive architecture made them an integral part of the ideal *al-qasbah* celebrated by Muhammad al-Nabhani. The residences of merchants in Muharraq, Manama and al-Hidd shared the cosmopolitan influences of the Indian Ocean trade. Expensive varieties of wood used for doors and windows, such as mangrove, teak and sandal, were imported from India, as well as building techniques and large items of wooden household furniture. The facades and exterior decorations of the merchant houses of Manama showed more openness to the outside world and a strong Persian influence. Many followed the style of the ports of the Gulf coast, and of Bushehr in particular, with two floors and reception rooms at roof level.[53] In the words of the British Indian lawyer Manockjee Cursetjee who visited Manama in 1917:

[51] C. Belgrave, *The Pirate Coast* (Beirut: Librairie du Liban, 1972), p. 76; Lorimer, *Gazetteer*, vol. II, pp. 217–29.
[52] Interview with Hamid al-Awadhi, Manama, 19 April 2004.
[53] Belgrave, *The Pirate Coast*, p. 76; al-Nabhani, *al-Tuhfah al-Nabhaniyyah*, pp. 141–4; R. Lewcock, *Traditional Architecture in Kuwait and Northern Gulf* (London: Archaeology Research Papers, 1978), pp. 15–23, 46.

2 Bayt Faruq in al-'Awadiyyah, *c.* 1955. After World War II it became the Taj Mahal Hotel, demolished soon after independence.

Many of the houses imitate the Persian style, with terraced roofs, ornamented with open work stucco balustrades or parapets, hanging balconies, porticoes with some pretence to elegance and windows with fretted wooden shutters or sliding panels which gave them a pretty look.[54]

The house of Yusuf Ridha' built after 1921 in al-'Awadiyyah was renowned for its balustrades, whose style imitated the European taste widespread in late Qajar Iran. In Manama, architecture not only spoke the language of an urbanite trans-regional culture but also of ambivalent political allegiances to the Al Khalifah. The two carved lions at the entrance of Bayt Faruq, the residence of the wealthy 'Arshi family, paid homage to the Iranian imperial tradition which rallied the loyalties of many of Manama's Persian residents (see Figure 2).[55]

In the nineteenth century new architectural styles also expressed the changing nature of tribal government. In the first decades of their rule, the Al Khalifah built military outposts, forts and watchtowers to control

---

[54] Quote from M. Cursetjee, *The Land of the Date* (Reading: Garnet, 1994), p. 75.
[55] Majed, *The Traditional Construction*, pp. 88–128; interviews with 'Ali Akbar Bushehri and Hamid al-Awadhi, Manama, 15 and 19 April 2004.

the territory and to bind the agricultural population to submission.[56] After Shaykh 'Isa's accession in 1869, the *al-qusur* of Muharraq, which housed the Al Khalifah and the leaders of the pearling tribes, became the centres of the new Dar al-Hukumah which emerged under British protection. Modelled on the Bayt Shaykh 'Isa (the residence of the ruler built in the late 1820s) they became the powerful symbols of tribal authority.[57] In this period, the consolidation of dynastic rule led to the emergence of a new type of public architecture which affirmed the tribal pedigree of the ruling family and celebrated the Bedouin arts of generosity, hospitality and physical prowess. The palatial complex built in 1900–1 by Shaykh Hamad (the son of Shaykh 'Isa and heir apparent) in al-Sakhir followed the tradition of the early Al Khalifah rulers who had established their strongholds far from populated areas. Yet it embodied the more elaborate protocol of the twentieth-century court with separate quarters for guests, breeding areas for animals, and grounds for camel and horse races. Younger members of the family followed suit and sponsored their own public residences in the vicinity of al-Sakhir: relatively small buildings to entertain guests with central chambers surrounded by arched galleries.[58]

The residences of merchants, tribal leaders and members of the ruling family were the venues where the majority of the urban and rural population constructed their views of self and community. Shi'i merchants sponsored *'ashura'* and hosted in their houses the congregations, known as *ma'tam*s, which celebrated the martyrdom of Imam Husayn. They also subsidised communal gatherings in open spaces (*barahih*, sing. *barahah*) which were established social institutions across pre-oil Eastern Arabia, usually named after their benefactors.[59] Among the Sunnis community life evolved around the houses of merchants, *'ulama'* and tribal leaders who organised assemblies in their *majlis*es, reception rooms located in their mansions.

*Ma'tam*s and *majlis*es constituted the setting for the political socialisation of large segments of the urban population in the pre-oil era. As social institutions, they illustrate the different political organisation and religious worldviews of Shi'is and Sunnis. *Ma'tam*s nurtured the link

---

[56] Brucks, 'Memoir Descriptive of the Navigation of the Gulf' in *Arabian Gulf Intelligence*, p. 566, 568; Lorimer, *Gazetteer*, vol. II, p. 1589. For the sketches of Bahrain's forts see Onley, 'The Politics of Protection', 62.

[57] C. Hardy-Guilbert and C. Lalande, *La Maison de Shaikh 'Isa à Bahrayn* (Paris: ADPF, 1981).

[58] al-Nabhani, *al-Tuhfah al-Nabhaniyyah*, pp. 48–9; Tajir, *'Aqd al-lal*, p. 42; Lorimer, *Gazetteer*, vol. II, p. 227; C. Hardy-Guilbert, 'A Bahraini Architect in Qatar at the Beginning of our Century: Houses and Palaces in the Arabian Gulf Countries', conference abstract, [n.d], Typescripts, 1990–2006 Bushehri Archive, hereafter BA.

[59] 'Abdallah, *Samahij fi al-tarikh*, p. 211.

between religion and politics which has been a constant feature of the history of Shi'ism. Through rituals and religious performance *ma'tam* congregations reinforced sectarian bonds among the population irrespective of status and socio-economic divisions. They also provided a platform for the expression of ill-feeling against the Sunni government. The *majlis*es were Sunni institutions which centred on family and kinship. Although each household had a *majlis* as a separate room to entertain visitors, the *majlis*es presided over by members of the ruling family, the heads of pearling tribes and by the merchant notables of Muharraq and al-Hidd were the lifeline of the Dar al-Hukumah. Here the powerful and influential negotiated alliances with the Al Khalifah and with their peers and, most crucially, attended to the administration of the tribal towns and of the agricultural regions they controlled. Moreover, as the institutions which regulated tribal affairs, *majlis*es had a strong hierarchical ethos. Leaders and merchant patrons of tribal stock received their protégées and interacted with them as subordinates, settled internal disputes and in some cases dispensed justice.[60]

The strong political profile of the *majlis*es of wealthy Muharraqis with connections to the ruling family created a demarcation between public and private spaces in their residences. This is suggested by the presence of a *majlis khususi* and *majlis 'umumi*: the former used for private audiences and for family business, the latter open to visitors.[61] In the houses of the sponsors of *ma'tam* congregations the boundaries between religious, domestic and public space were often blurred. The history of the *ma'tam* sponsored by the al-Sabt family in the village of al-Samahij is a case in point. Around 1910 the family, whose economic background is unclear, built a mosque and started to sponsor *'ashura'*. Typically, the congregation which mourned the death of Imam Husayn was first organised inside the family residence. Subsequently, villagers collected funds for the acquisition of a piece of land adjacent to the house. In the austere but allusive words of 'Abdallah Sayf who collected the oral account in the 1990s: 'Hajj 'Abbas [the builder] from al-Jufayr [a village to the south-east of Manama] … built a courtyard in order to transform the land into a *ma'tam*.'[62] This account rehearses a theme which is familiar in the

[60] Wali, *al-Muharraq*, pp. 71, 118–19: Khuri, *Tribe and State in Bahrain*, pp. 35–6. As venues for socialisation and informal politics the *majlis*es of Bahrain were similar to the *al-diwaniyyat* of pre-oil Kuwait.
[61] Wali, *al-Muharraq*, pp. 118–19, 142–3. The term *al-khususi* also defined spaces in the house which could not be accessed by visitors.
[62] 'Abdallah Sayf, *al-Ma'tam fi al-Bahrayn*, 2 vols. (Manama: al-Matba'ah al-Sharqiyyah, 1995; Maktabah Fakrawi, 2004), vol. I, pp. 348–52 (p. 349, my translation); 'Abdallah, *Samahij fi al-tarikh*, pp. 76–7.

tradition of early Islam and continued to be predominant in the architecture of mosques in the Gulf and Arabian Peninsula: the creation of places of worship as a courtyard for public assembly through the donations of the community of faithful.[63] Moreover, the description of the creation of a new religious space by Hajj 'Abbas (probably by erecting a fence or a wall around the property, in the literal translation of Sayf's account by 'adding' the land to the *ma'tam*) suggests the physical and symbolic inclusion of barren land into the house, whose private quarters became a space of public use as a result of the presence of the Shi'i congregation. Similar histories of *ma'tam*s and sponsors feature prominently in the oral tradition of Manama and of the villages. Although they often offer an idealised portrayal of Shi'i society, they are indicative of the importance of *ma'tam*s as centres of popular devotion throughout Bahrain.

For urban and rural Shi'is alike, religion was of course no longer built in the structure of government. The ancient mosque of Suq al-Khamis of Bilad al-Qadim, a major symbol of the Islamic past of Bahrain, was last rebuilt in the fourteenth century and was not used for worship under the Al Khalifahs. Towns lost their role of places of encounter between the administration and the rural population as centres of religious and spiritual life. In Muharraq, Manama and al-Hidd the rulers sponsored Sunni Friday mosques and had prayers officiated in their names.[64] Formal religious education was also confined to the Sunni population and sponsored by pearl merchants who established the leading religious schools of Muharraq.[65] Public life was dominated by a class of Sunni *'ulama'* who had either emerged from tribal ranks or through connections with the ruling family. Such was the profile of Muhammad al-Nabhani, the official historian of the Al Khalifah, and of Qasim al-Mahzah, the most famous Sunni cleric of his generation who served as the leading qadi of Bahrain during the reign of Shaykh 'Isa. Religious office was also linked to the entrepreneurial world of Bahrain's tribal aristocracy which had the necessary means to provide for the religious education of their scions in Mecca, al-Qatif and al-Ahsa'.[66]

---

[63] See S. Bianca, *Urban Form in the Arab World: Past and Present* (London: Thames and Hudson, 2000), 101–5; Wali, *al-Bayan wa al-tibyan*, pp. 135–59.

[64] al-Nabhani, *al-Tuhfah al-Nabhaniyyah*, p. 42.

[65] Salih ibn Yusif al-Jawdar, *Ibn Jawdar qadhi al-Muharraq* (Manama: al-Khalij al-'Arabi, 1999), pp. 35–41.

[66] al-Nuwaydri, *'Alam al-thaqafah*, vol. II, pp. 629–30, 751–2; vol. III, p. 430. Mubarak al-Khatir, *al-Qadhi al-Ra'is Qasim ibn Mahza*, 2nd edn (Manama: Matba 'ah Wizarat al-'Ilam, 1986), pp. 16–18, 23 ff., 35–6; al-Jawdar, *Ibn Jawdar qadhi al-Muharraq*, pp. 12–16.

Conclusion

Since 1602, the history of the towns and agricultural hamlets of Bahrain was part of a 'dialectics of urbanisation' which embodied the key sources of state building in Eastern Arabia and in the Persian Gulf: religious ideals (*al-din*) and kinship solidarity (*al-'asabiyyah*). The demise of Safavid Bilad al-Qadim and the emergence of Muharraq as the new seat of government in the early nineteenth century conform to the patterns of city making described by Ibn Khaldun, the medieval Muslim intellectual who famously wrote that the life of a dynasty in the Islamic world coincided with that of the town.[67] In Bilad al-Qadim, state-sponsored religiosity became manifest in the prominent political and social position occupied by Shi'i clerics in the agricultural villages surrounding the settlement. In contrast, a combination of tribal ideals and mercantile interests guided the development of Muharraq as the centre of the Dar al-Hukumah which emerged after 1869 under the rulership of Shaykh 'Isa ibn 'Ali Al Khalifah. Here Sunni Islam made its presence felt as a corollary of tribal ethics and organisation, rather than acting as a source of political legitimacy per se.

The Al Khalifah era witnessed accelerated sectarian tensions and deepening divisions between tribesmen and agriculturalists. These divisions were political, administrative and institutional, as well as socio-economic and spatial. Inequalities encompassed several aspects of individual, community and public life, and mirrored the transformation of urban and rural landscapes. Urban and architectural forms gradually enshrined the ethos of Sunni towns and tribal polities in the making with their quarters (*al-firjan*), residences of the members of the ruling family (*al-qusur*) and *majlis*es. As Shi'i agricultural areas remained politically and socially at the very periphery of the tribal system, they became synonymous with decadence and oppression. Most notably, however, the vibrant popular religious culture which coalesced around *ma'tam* congregations permeated rural life and framed the quest for political and social emancipation of the Shi'i population.

In parallel, the networks of politics, trade and migrants which in the course of the nineteenth century increasingly connected Bahrain to the Gulf coast and to British India triggered a new type of urbanisation in Manama. Unlike the other urban centres which flourished under the Al Khalifah, Bahrain's leading port developed as a cosmopolitan settlement where mercantile groups, immigrant communities, tribesmen, former agriculturalists, Sunnis and Shi'is rubbed shoulders with each other. If

---

[67] Ibn Khaldun. *al-Muqaddimah: An Introduction to History*, trans. by Franz Rosenthal, 3 vols. (London: Routledge and Kegan Paul, 1958), vol. II, pp. 233–7.

urban history – as remarked by Kirti Chaudhuri – is not only a history of objects but also of meaning,[68] then the cosmopolitan character of Manama was antithetical to the exclusive religious and tribal ideals which had shaped the civic and political cultures of Bilad al-Qadim and Muharraq. As a hybrid 'frontier' society under tribal government, Manama played an increasingly critical role in redefining trajectories of state building in the second half of the nineteenth century. These developments were rooted in the history of the penetration of the British Empire in the Persian Gulf and can be related to, and contrasted with, the development of other regional ports.

[68] Chaudhuri, *Asia before Europe*, p. 338.

2   The making of Gulf port towns before oil

In the Al Khalifah era, Manama developed as part of a network of port settlements which connected the Persian Gulf to the world of trade, merchants and trans-continental routes extending from the Mediterranean and the Red Sea to South East Asia. Viewed from the perspective of this maritime world, these commercial emporia were essentially 'brides of the sea'. Yet, as clearly suggested by the case of Manama, they also constituted the microcosm of the complex political and economic dynamics which bound coastal societies to their agricultural and tribal hinterlands. That this dual relationship with hinterlands and forelands underpinned the urbanisation of the Gulf coast is evident from the vicissitudes of the tribal and imperial histories of the region before the discovery of oil.

Developments in Bahrain reflected wider processes of political and urban change which were triggered by the resurgence of tribal power throughout the Persian Gulf in the eighteenth century. Alongside the Al Khalifah, a powerful cohort of tribal rulers came to control the Arab coast, favouring the consolidation of a new constellation of maritime outposts. From Kuwait in the west to Ras al-Khaymah in the east, these port settlements under tribal regimes started to compete for the control of regional and long-distance trade with the leading commercial emporia of Basra, Bushehr and Muscat in Oman. As was the case of Manama and Muharraq in Bahrain, fully fledged port towns with complex socio-political organisations only began to take shape in the second half of the nineteenth century under the combined forces of the pearl boom and of British informal empire. If on the one hand the increasing demand of Gulf pearls in the world market accelerated urban development, on the other the establishment of a new port regime under the aegis of the Government of India provided the necessary political conditions for urban economies to prosper. The Pax Britannica championed by the British Crown after 1820 sheltered the main commercial emporia of the Gulf in a variety of ways. The Government of India provided military protection to the coast against novel tribal threats and consolidated the precarious position of local ruling dynasties. At the same time, it granted privileges of extraterritorial jurisdiction to segments of the urban populations.

In spite of the importance of the new 'Indian connection', the making of Gulf coastal towns as part of tribal fiefdoms continued to reflect the fragmentary nature of patterns of state building across the region and to depend on the close relationship between merchants, rulers and urban residents. In this respect, the demography and socio-political organisation of these towns offers excellent vistas on the evolution of pre-oil coastal societies and political cultures from an indigenous perspective. They also illustrate the different character of Gulf ports as towns in the making in order to situate the development of Manama in the larger narrative of pre-oil urbanisation.

Gulf ports as 'native' towns

Until the eighteenth century there is not much information on the port settlements of the Arab coast, as the area did not rise to commercial and political prominence. Even the history of Basra, one of the most important ports of the Gulf under Ottoman control since 1546, is largely unexplored. Few studies focussing on the eighteenth century have convincingly shown that the town grew in importance as a regional emporium after the establishment of a factory of the English East India Company in 1723 and the transfer of the Company's headquarters from Bandar 'Abbas on the Persian coast in 1763.[1] Literature on the Arab coast outside Ottoman control is particularly instructive on regional and tribal politics but does not focus on port settlements. Besides portraying the region as a theatre of relentless tribal confrontation, these studies emphasise the influence of the English, Dutch and French East India Companies, of the Ottoman administration of Iraq and, in the nineteenth century, of the Government of India.[2]

---

[1] R. Matthee, 'Boom and Bust: the Port of Basra in the Sixteenth and Seventeenth Centuries', paper presented at the Conference 'The Persian Gulf in History', 7–10 October 2004. For a reassessment of the fortunes of Basra's trade in the eighteenth century, see T. A. J. Abdullah, *Merchants, Mamluks and Murder: The Political Economy of Trade in Eighteenth-century Basra* (Albany: State University of New York Press, 2001), pp. 49–56, 117–19. For the nineteenth century see H. Fattah, *The Politics of Regional Trade*, particularly 102 ff.

[2] See for instance Slot, *The Arabs of the Gulf*; W. Floor, 'Dutch Trade with Mascat during the Eighteenth Century', *Journal of Asian and African Studies*, 16 (1982), 197–213; Sultan ibn Muhammad al-Qasimi, *Power Struggles and Trade in the Gulf, 1620–1820* (University of Exeter Press, 1999); F. Anscombe, *The Ottoman Gulf: The Creation of Kuwait, Saudi Arabia and Qatar* (New York: Columbia University Press, 1997); Onley, *The Arabian Frontier of the British Raj*.

A useful starting point to discussing the history of Gulf coastal settlements is to consider the relative influence of indigenous and foreign actors in their development. Economically, the port towns of the Gulf were part of that regional trading world so evocatively portrayed by Hala Fattah, which included southern Iraq and Iran, and the Arabian Peninsula.[3] As nodes of commercial exchange they became the natural focus of tribal and imperial competition. While the fortunes of port economies relied on the delicate balance between tribal rulers and merchants, the presence of the East India Companies since the seventeenth century affected the ability of ruling families to use revenue from maritime trade for the purpose of political centralisation. Yet regional ports were prone to develop autonomously from the land empires which controlled Iran, Iraq and the Arabian Peninsula. In the eighteenth and early nineteenth centuries the settlements of the Arab coast, with the notable exception of Basra under Ottoman control, became the seats of independent tribal governments: the Al Sabah and Al Khalifah principalities based in Kuwait Town, Muharraq and Manama; the confederation of city-states controlled by the al-Qawasim (sing. al-Qasimi), including Sharjah and Ras al-Khaymah; and the Al Bu Falasah and the Banu Yas principalities based in Dubai and Abu Dhabi. Until the mid nineteenth century, the ports of southern Iran also prospered under Arab families of tribal descent which succeeded in keeping the Qajar government at arm's length.

Reflecting a long history of empire by proxy, the commercial and political encroachment of Europe in the Persian Gulf did not affect substantially the spatial and socio-political organisation of its port towns. Coastal settlements remained essentially 'native' towns untouched by the transformative powers of foreign military outposts and colonies of settlement. In Indonesian ports, in contrast, the Dutch East India Company enforced an elaborate system of administration and the segregation of native populations from Company employees.[4] Since European trading stations made their appearance in the Persian Gulf in the seventeenth century, the bulk of foreign trade continued to be conducted by local intermediaries and by transient foreign merchants, soldiers and administrators. Ottoman Basra, for instance, had large numbers of Greek, Italian, Dutch and English traders. In the same way as Manama, patterns of residential settlement suggest that it developed as an open port

---

[3] Fattah, *The Politics of Regional Trade.*
[4] See for instance the case of colonial Makassar. H. Sutherland, 'Eastern Emporium and Company Town: Trade and Society in Eighteenth-Century Makassar' in F. Broeze (ed.), *Brides of the Sea: Port Cities of Asia from the 16th–20th Centuries* (Kensington: New South Wales University Press, 1989), pp. 97–128.

town organised around professional activities, religious sites and local notables.[5] In the other ports of the Arab coast there were only a handful of European and American residents until the discovery of oil, although by the end of the nineteenth century they had become important stations of British shipping to and from India.

The movement of tribal peoples and merchant capital, rather than European intervention, constituted the dynamic matrix of regional urbanisation. Ruling families themselves had started their careers as urban leaders by embracing merchant seafaring. The Al Khalifah and Al Sabah, for instance, had abandoned pastoral nomadism during their overland migration from Najd to the Gulf coast. Once settled there they acquired vessels and sailed across the Gulf waters, attracted by its rich pearl fisheries and by the opportunities offered by the pearl trade.[6] The history of the Hawala, a group of nomadic maritime traders originally from the Iranian coast, is equally instructive on the importance of this itinerant maritime tradition. At the end of the seventeenth century, some Hawala tribes started to compete for the control of the pearl banks around Basra and Bushehr. A few decades later, they ruled Bahrain and Qatar, opposing the consolidation of the Al Khalifah and the Al Sabah on the coast.[7] Moreover, after the collapse of the Safavid Empire, the rise of the al-Qawasim in the eastern Gulf was closely associated with their profile as tribal warriors cum merchant seafarers.

With the gradual imposition of the Pax Britannica after 1820, British naval technology and commercial culture had a considerable impact on trade, communications and on the portfolios of some indigenous entrepreneurs. Gulf ports, however, did not become the powerhouses of colonial global economies in the same way as Bombay, Colombo or Shanghai. As British interests in the Gulf remained confined to its maritime security, coastal settlements did not serve as the lynchpins of economic and political penetration into the hinterland. Since the 1880s, for instance, Colombo boomed as a reflection of the expansion of Sri Lanka's plantation agriculture and the export of commercial crops such as coffee, tea and rubber. Colonial Bombay gained prominence as a gateway to western India as a result of the extensive railway network which was developed

---

[5] D. R. Khoury, 'Merchants and Trade in Early Modern Iraq', *New Perspectives on Turkey*, 5–6 (1991), 53–86 (55); Abdullah, *Merchants, Mamluks and Murder*, p. 23.

[6] al-Nabhani, *al-Tuhfah al-Nabhaniyyah*, pp. 82–3, 85.

[7] In Arab milieu the name Hawala is said to have derived from the Arabic verb *tahawwala* ('to move around') while Niebuhr in the 1750s suggested that their tribal name meant immigrants. Slot, *The Arabs of the Gulf*, pp. 18–19, 195–6, 230; Muhammad Gharib Khatam, *Tarikh 'Arab al-Huwilah* (Beirut, 2003), pp. 79–85.

around the city after 1853.[8] The Gulf did not offer resources for expanding European economies and industries. Moreover, after the establishment of Aden as a British colony in 1839 and the opening of the Suez Canal in 1869, the region remained largely peripheral to trans-continental European commercial routes as the Red Sea replaced the old overland passage from the Indian Ocean to the Mediterranean through Iraq and Syria.[9] Useful comparisons can be also drawn with contemporary developments in the Eastern Mediterranean, where British and French economic penetration had momentous implications for ports nominally under Ottoman control. Beirut, Haifa and Alexandria boomed with the influx of foreign capital, and were profoundly transformed by the integration of Lebanon, Palestine and Egypt into the world economy.[10]

The regional context: the long eighteenth century and the Pax Britannica

The 'tribal breakout', as Christopher Bayly puts it, which undermined the authority of the Ottoman, Mughal and Safavid Empires in the eighteenth century reverberated across the Persian Gulf generating a surge in tribal power throughout the region.[11] In the east, the al-Qawasim and Hawala tribes strengthened their position as the result of the power vacuum left by the collapse of the Safavids in 1722 followed by the death of Nadir Shah in 1747, and by the decadence of the Omani Empire which had been involved in a long war with Iran.[12] In the west, al-'Utub groups, and particularly the Al Khalifah and the Al Sabah, took advantage of the multiple threats faced by the Ottoman Empire in southern Iraq and in the Arabian Peninsula: the establishment of local rule by Georgian Mamluks in Basra and Baghdad and the emergence of the first Sa'udi state in Central Arabia between 1744 and 1818.

---

[8] For a discussion of colonial port cities in relation to their hinterlands see D. K. Basu, *The Rise and Growth of the Colonial Port Cities in Asia* (Berkeley: University of California Press, 1985), pp. 1–22; K. Dharmasena, 'Colombo: Gateway and Oceanic Hub of Shipping' in Broeze (ed.), *Brides of the Sea*, pp. 156–69; R. Murphy, 'Colombo and the Re-Making of Ceylon' in F. Broeze (ed.), *Gateways of Asia: Port Cities of Asia in the 13th–20th Centuries* (London and New York: Kegan Paul, 1997), pp. 195–209.

[9] K. McPherson, 'Port Cities as Nodal Points of Change: The Indian Ocean, 1890s–1920s', pp. 84–7.

[10] R. Ilbert, 'De Beyrouth à Alger: la fin d'un ordre urbain', *Vingtième Siècle*, 32 (1991), 15–24; M. Seikaly, 'Haifa at the Crossroads: An Outpost of the New World Order' in Fawaz and Bayly (eds.), *Modernity and Culture*, pp. 96–111; C. Issawi, 'British Trade and the Rise of Beirut, 1830–1860', *International Journal of Middle East Studies*, 7 (1977), 91–101.

[11] C. A. Bayly, *Imperial Meridian: The British Empire and the World, 1780–1830* (Harlow: Pearson Education, 1989), pp. 35–52.

[12] Slot, *The Arabs of the Gulf*, pp. 346–53.

The new Sa'udi threat was ideological as well as military. The religious doctrine of Wahhabism undermined the precarious Pax Islamica which the Ottoman and Iranian Empires had established in the Gulf region since the sixteenth century. As a revivalist movement, Wahhabism disputed the claims of the Ottoman Sultan to the universal caliphate. Moreover, its fanatic monotheism rebutted the beliefs of Imami Shi'ism and the 'heretical' manifestation of Sufi cults and of popular religion which permeated the life of tribal, urban and rural populations.[13] At the close of the eighteenth century, the new Sau'di administration of al-Ahsa' in Eastern Arabia implemented a ruthless policy of eradication of Shi'i religious beliefs and institutions as a manifestation of *shirk* (idolatry). Moreover, in 1801 Wahhabi forces sacked the Shi'i shrine city of Karbala and two years later they occupied Mecca, sending shockwaves through the Islamic world.

Political instability in the age of Wahhabi expansion reconfigured the fractured political complex of the Gulf. The Wahhabi *da'wah* (religious propaganda) offered the al-Qawasim an ideological instrument to fight the Omani Empire and a novel military alliance with the Sa'udi leaders. In contrast, the al-'Utub did not espouse the Wahhabi creed but gained power through political expediency. Both the Al Khalifah and Al Sabah took advantage of the precarious position of the Banu Khalid, the tribal confederation which controlled the region between Basra and al-Qatif. In the second half of the eighteenth century, as the Banu Khalid succumbed to the military power of the Wahhabis, the Al Sabah consolidated their position in Kuwait while the Al Khalifah occupied Qatar and Bahrain.[14]

A brief description of Kuwait around 1756 by the Dutch resident on Kharg Island offers a fairly exceptional glimpse of the fierce competition faced by coastal rulers which severely tested their ability to remain in control of expanding trading settlements:

At the exit of the Euphrates near the Arabian coast is the island of Feltscha [Faylaka] and of Grien [Kuwait]. Both are inhabited by an Arab tribe ... called Eutobis [al-'Utub]. They possess about 300 vessels, but all of these are very small, because they only use them for pearl-diving ... They are about 4,000 men strong, who almost all have swords, shields and spears, but almost no firearms, they even do not know how to handle these. This nation is always in conflict with the Houlas [Hawala of Bushehr who controlled Bahrain], whose mortal enemies they are.[15]

---

[13] For a cogent reading of the political and doctrinal challenges faced by the Sunni orthodoxy in an Asian context, see Bayly, *Imperial Meridian*, pp. 179–84.

[14] The early history of Kuwait and of migrations of al-'Utub is unclear. See as the main contribution Abu-Hakima, *History of Eastern Arabia*, pp. 45–90 and Slot, *The Arabs of the Gulf*, p. 351. On the Banu Khalid and Wahhabi power in Eastern Arabia see Abu-Hakima, *History of Eastern Arabia*, pp. 125–64.

[15] 'Kniphausen Report', fol. 10, quoted by Slot, *The Arabs of the Gulf*, p. 350.

As the need for security from external threats increased, the network of tribute relations which moulded security pacts and cemented alliances between Gulf tribes became increasingly complex. At the turn of the nineteenth century, the al-Qawasim of Sharjah still played off the Imam of Muscat and the Wahhabis one against the other. At the same time both the Imam and the rulers of Najd received tribute from the Al Khalifah who had just occupied Bahrain and provided for their own security with the subsidies collected from their possessions in Qatar. After Bahrain was occupied by Omani forces in 1800, the Al Khalifah regained the islands by becoming tributaries of 'Abd al-'Aziz ibn Muhammad al-Sa'ud. Yet, by 1805 they started to appeal to the Imam of Muscat and to the British resident in Bushehr to shake off the Wahhabi yoke.[16]

The long and troubled eighteenth century came to a close only after 1820 with the restoration of 'peace and security' at sea by British gunboat diplomacy. As after the 1780s the Royal Navy became in control of African and Asian routes, British naval power started to be deployed in the Gulf. Armed by the desire to protect trade and by the moral imperative to defeat piracy, British vessels intervened as early as 1775 at the request of the East India Company factory based in Bushehr. Between 1809 and 1820 British naval expeditions against Ras al-Khaymah crushed the power of the al-Qawasim, setting in motion a system of maritime truces which culminated with the establishment of the Perpetual Maritime Peace of 1853. Along with piracy, these maritime truces supported the abolition of the slave trade with the African coast which supplied large numbers of labourers to the pearl industry.[17] By placing the Gulf waters under Royal Navy patrols, the new treaty system isolated further the coastal principalities from the political influence of their hinterlands. The new apparatus of imperial control was minimal. It relied on a network of British native agents, usually local merchants, posted in regional ports under the authority of the British resident in Bushehr who answered to the Government of India. The residency had started its activities in 1763 as a commercial subsidiary of the factory of the East India Company in Basra. In 1822 it acquired political status after the headquarters of the Company was moved to Baghdad and Bushehr following the Persian occupation of Basra in 1788.[18]

[16] Onley, 'The Politics of Protection', 44–5; Fattah, *The Politics of Regional Trade*, pp. 56–8.
[17] A. B. Khalifa, 'Slaves and Musical Performances in Dubai: Socio-Cultural Relevance of African Traditions', unpublished PhD dissertation, University of Exeter, (2003), pp. 89–92.
[18] M. Yapp, 'British Policy in the Persian Gulf' and R. M. Savory, 'A.D. 600–1800' in A. Cottrell et al., *The Persian Gulf States: A General Survey* (Baltimore: Johns Hopkins University Press, 1980), pp. 70–100 (pp. 72–7), 14–40 (p. 37). On the British naval expeditions against the al-Qawasim see C. Belgrave, *The Pirate Coast*, pp. 28–37, 133–49.

The Gulf coast was integrated further into the sphere of British informal empire in the second half of the nineteenth century. The Anglo-Persian war of 1856–7 and the Indian Mutiny of 1857 consolidated the British military presence in southern Iran. The fear of an Ottoman occupation of Bahrain, which by then had become the basis of British commercial operations in the Gulf, prompted the Government of India to stipulate exclusive agreements with Gulf rulers. The first was signed with Bahrain in 1880, followed by what became known as the Trucial States in 1892, including Dubai, Abu Dhabi and the al-Qasimi strongholds. Kuwait and Qatar entered treaty negotiations in 1899 and 1916 respectively. The newly acquired control over the external relations of the Gulf principalities coincided with a new phase of British imperial expansion in the Ottoman Middle East, culminating in the military occupation of Egypt in 1882.[19]

The new global era of 'steam and steel', as Rhoads Murphey has aptly called the age of European imperialism, transformed the Gulf into a maritime station for British shipping to and from India.[20] The introduction of steam navigation along the rivers of Iraq, and its extension to the Gulf, led to the concentration of commercial activities in leading entrepôt centres served by British steamers, which ensured fast communications with the Indian subcontinent. After 1862, ports like Basra, Manama and Bushehr developed as intermediary stations between Iraq and Bombay as the agricultural areas around Basra were gradually integrated into the world economy and European goods started to make their appearance in local and regional markets. As was to happen in the 1930s with the introduction of Imperial Airways, the arrival of British steamships fostered increasing interconnections between regional centres and their historical emporia overseas.[21]

British inroads in the Gulf recomposed the 'tribal breakout' of the eighteenth century in a variety of ways. Politically, the Government of India protected the position of local dynasties and restrained tribal conflict. It also sheltered coastal rulers from the renewed expansionist drive of the second Sa'udi 'imarah after the capture of Riyadh by 'Abd al-'Aziz Al Sa'ud (Ibn Sa'ud) in 1902. After 1820 the residency adopted Bedouin

---

[19] Yapp, 'British Policy in the Persian Gulf' pp. 77–84; Albaharna, *The Arabian Gulf States*, pp. 25–57; Lienhardt, *Shaikhdoms of Eastern Arabia*, pp. 1–16.

[20] R. Murphey, 'On the Evolution of the Port City' in Broeze (ed.), *Brides of the Sea*, pp. 223–46 (pp. 241–2).

[21] R. Kubicek, 'The Proliferation and Diffusion of Steamship Technology and the Beginnings of "New Imperialism"' in D. Killingray, M. Lincoln and N. Rigby (eds.), *Maritime Empires: British Maritime Trade in the Nineteenth Century* (Woodbridge: Boydell Press, 2004), pp. 100–10.

customs to deal with episodes of tribal warfare at sea. Coastal rulers were
forced to pay compensation for lives and properties and often collaborated
to punish culprits. Economically, the Pax Britannica restored a degree of
security to regional trade. A new political and commercial era for Gulf
ports opened up soon after the collapse of Ras al-Khaymah in 1820. This
era was symbolically marked by the despatch under British escort of al-
Qasimi warships to the port of Lingah to be newly equipped for commercial ventures.[22] The volume of goods entering local ports grew steadily as
a result of the prosperity generated by the demand for Gulf pearls and
mother-of-pearl in the world markets. As pearl jewellery, buttons and
luxury household articles became fashionable among the European
and North American upper classes, regional ports refashioned themselves
as *mudun al-ghaws*, pearling towns.[23]

Of tribes, pearls and empire: directives of urbanisation

In the long eighteenth century, the migration of Bedouin and Hawala
merchant seafarers towards the coast and across the Gulf brought the
segmentary opposition of tribal life to the forefront of processes of urbanisation.[24] In the early years of the Pax Britannica, tribal secession and the
competition between tribes over the control of pearl banks continued to
be an integral part of the process of sedentarisation and town making. As
noted in the 1840s by A. B. Kemball, the Assistant Political Resident at
Bushehr:

it is by no means uncommon for one of the branches of a tribe [of the Gulf
shores] … with a view to secure to themselves greater immunities and advantages,
to secede from the authority and territory of their lawful and acknowledged chief
into that of another, or to establish themselves and build a fort on some other
spot.[25]

Kemball's observations accurately reflect the early history of some of the
most important pearling centres and port settlements of the pre-oil

---

[22] G. B. Brucks, 'Memoir Descriptive of the Navigation of the Gulf of Persia with Brief
  Notices of the Manners, Customs, Religion, Commerce, and Resources of the People
  Inhabiting its Shores and Islands' (1829–35), fiche 1096, p. 543, V 23/217 IOR.
[23] The value of pearl exports from the region grew from £483,767 in 1893–4 to £1,076,310
  in 1904–5. al-Naqeeb, *Society and State*, p. 56.
[24] We have no detailed information on the history of the port settlements on the Arab coast
  before the Government of India started to survey the Persian Gulf in the early nineteenth
  century. These surveys are included in V 23 IOR, 'Selections from the Records of the
  Government of India, 1849–1937'.
[25] Kemball, 'Memoranda on the Resources, Localities, and Relations' (1845), fiche 1090–1,
  p. 94, V 23/217 IOR.

era. al-Zubarah in mainland Qatar was established by the Al Khalifah after
they had relocated from Kuwait to Qatar around 1766, possibly as a result
of dissent with the Al Sabah but most likely in search for new commercial
and pearling ventures.[26] Approximately forty years later the Al Khalifah
continued their journey to Bahrain and founded Muharraq. The transition of Dubai from a small village to a port town started with the occupation of the Al Bu Falasah tribe in 1833 after a quarrel with the Banu Yas of
Abu Dhabi.[27] Forts, bastions and towers built in mud, stone or lime were
the landmarks of new tribal settlements and functioned as the poles of
urban expansion. Built to guard natural harbours, water supplies and
pearl banks, over time they distinguished urban rulers (hukkam, sing.
hakim) from the leaders of the nomadic and semi-nomadic tribes of the
hinterland (shuyukh, sing. shaykh) whose authority was still identified with
the tent.[28] Forts in particular attracted the settlement of client tribes and
non-tribal protégés. Their small size, however, did not allow the development of intra-mural residential and commercial areas. Kemball reported
in the 1840s that the largest tribal fort along the Arab coast could shelter a
maximum of 400 to 600 people in case of enemy attack. Towns like
Dubai, Abu Dhabi, 'Ajman and Sharjah developed outside the perimeter
of the fortified residences of their shaykhs which towered over surrounding neighbourhoods and harbours.[29]

Although forts had been the predominant (and the least transient)
feature of the built landscape of the Gulf coast for centuries, those built
by ruling families of tribal descent differed substantially from the larger
Portuguese forts of Hormuz, al-Qatif and Manama. In the age of tribal
expansion the proliferation of small forts mirrored the chronic insecurity
which marred sea and land routes and the fragmented political economy

---

[26] 'Historical Sketch of the Utoobee Tribe of Arabs (Bahrein) from the Year 1716 to the
Year 1817 prepared by Mr. Francis Warden' (1817), fiche 1094, p. 362, V 23/217 IOR.
The date and circumstances of the establishment of Zubara are controversial. al-Nabhani
reports that Shaykh Muhammad ibn Khalifa Al Khalifah (the grandfather of Ahmad, the
conqueror of Bahrain) built the Mirir fort in Zubara in 1768/9. al-Nabhani, al-Tuhfah al-
Nabhaniyyah, p. 73.

[27] Kemball, 'Memoranda on the Resources, Localities, and Relations'(1845), fiche 1090–1,
pp. 103–4, V 23/217 IOR.

[28] For a discussion of forts and rulership in Bahrain see Onley, 'The Politics of Protection',
60–4. Lienhardt suggests that the title hakim is a translation of the English word 'ruler'
which started to be used by British officials after the 1910s. Yet the local use of the term
Dar al-Hukumah for Shaykh 'Isa's administration in pre-oil Bahrain suggests the contrary. Urban rulers were also referred to by British observers as chiefs or shaykhs.
Lienhardt, Shaikhdoms of Eastern Arabia, p. 185.

[29] Kemball, 'Memoranda on the Resources, Localities, and Relations' (1845), fiche 1090–1,
p. 99, V 23/217 IOR; Brucks, 'Memoir Descriptive of the Navigation of the Gulf' (1829–
35), fiche 1096, pp. 541, 544, 547, V 23/217 IOR; Lorimer, Gazetteer, vol. II, pp. 410,
1761–2.

of the region. In the sixteenth century forts had served the expansion of Portuguese mercantilism in the Persian Gulf. As the seats of local governors who were tributary to the King of Portugal, they linked together key regional ports and provided shelter for merchants and cargo along trans-regional and trans-oceanic routes. For the leading shaykhs of emerging tribal principalities, the ability to build permanent defences was commensurate to their control of pearl banks and sea trade, which in turn depended on the support of tribal contingents and mercenary armies (al-'askariyyah). The town of Ras al-Khaymah developed into the model fortress town of the era under its al-Qasimi rulers, whose fleets patrolled commercial routes, imposed the payment of safe passages and seized cargo. Before it was destroyed by the Royal Navy in 1820, the settlement was protected by a shallow lagoon from the sea and surrounded on three sides by walls which were defended by cannons and by 7,000 armed men.[30] While the al-Qasimi ports of the eastern Gulf became the showcase of the defensive architecture which boomed under tribal mercantilism, in the west the strongholds of the Al Sabah and Al Khalifah had more precarious defences. Until the early nineteenth century, the rulers of Kuwait and al-Zubarah had neither artillery to protect their outposts nor large ships to carry out sea raids, although they commandeered the loyalty of large numbers of tribal fighters.[31] Their military capabilities had somewhat increased by the 1820s and 1830s as suggested by the use of guns and artillery for the defence of Muharraq.

The imposition of the Pax Britannica imparted a new direction to Gulf urbanisation. While fortifications lost much of their military and political importance, British policies favoured the growth of port settlements by stabilising the boundaries of tribal influence across the region and by lending political support to rulers in exchange for their military quiescence. Leading shaykhs could no longer pursue territorial expansion outside their domains, particularly as a result of the treaties negotiated after the 1880s which entrusted the Government of India with the conduct of the foreign affairs of Gulf ports. These agreements prevented 'the cessation or the disposal of their territories by means of sale, lease, mortgage, or by other means, without the agreement of the United Kingdom'.[32] British influence was also instrumental in reshaping the hierarchy of regional ports. As the Bushehr residency came to control the external relations of the Gulf principalities, Bushehr and Manama consolidated their

---

[30] Brucks, 'Memoir Descriptive of the Navigation of the Gulf' (1829–35), fiche 1096, p. 541, V 23/217 IOR.
[31] Slot, *The Arabs of the Gulf*, pp. 250–1.
[32] Albaharna, *The Arabian Gulf States*, pp. 70–5 (p. 73).

position as the political and commercial strongholds of British informal empire in the Gulf. They replaced Ras al-Khaymah, which had dominated the eastern Gulf in the eighteenth century, and Muscat, which by the end of the nineteenth century suffered from the partition of the Omani Empire following the establishment of an independent ruler in Zanzibar in 1856.

The growth of port settlements mirrored the expanding horizons of their fast-growing economies. Bombay – now closer to the Persian Gulf as a result of the establishment of steamship services – increasingly supplied brokers, merchants and capital to finance pearl exports, besides providing political and military protection. Overseas migrations to the coast intensified as the booming pearl industry and evolving entrepôt economies demanded an increasing supply of labour. Manama and Dubai blossomed as the cosmopolitan centres of the pearl era. Manama's population increased threefold in the last quarter of the nineteenth century, due mainly to an influx of labourers and mercantile groups from Bahrain's agricultural hinterland, Iran, East Africa and from al-Ahsa' and al-Qatif.[33] The rise of Dubai was even more spectacular. Inhabited by around 800 Al Bu Falasah tribesmen in 1833, the town had approximately 10,000 inhabitants by 1905. Dubai's port economy boomed with the establishment of a customs administration in Lingah in 1900, which followed the reimposition of direct Qajar rule over southern Iranian ports. Fixed tariffs on imports and exports precipitated a large scale migration of Arab and Persian merchants towards the southern Gulf, who came to control much of the trade with India and East Africa. Like Manama, Dubai became a port of call for British steamships with influential Persian and Indian mercantile communities.[34]

Kuwait doubled in size in the last quarter of the nineteenth century. The town outgrew the wall which separated it from the desert, becoming an open settlement until a new wall was built in 1922. Commercially and politically, Kuwait looked towards southern Iraq and Najd as until World War I it was the most important market centre outside direct Ottoman control which served central and northern Arabia. The bulk of the town's sea trade, which was confined to the northern Gulf and to the estuary of the Shatt al-'Arab, remained in the hands of the descendants of the first

[33] For details see pp. 90–5.
[34] Brucks, 'Memoir Descriptive of the Navigation of the Gulf' (1829–35), fiche 1096, pp. 545–6, V 23/217 IOR; Lorimer, *Gazetteer*, vol. II, pp. 454–6; F. Heard-Bey, *From Trucial States to United Arab Emirates* (London and New York: Longman, 1999), pp. 243–5; Kemball, 'Memoranda on the Resources, Localities, and Relations' (1845), fiche 1090–1, p. 100, V 23/217 IOR.

tribal settlers.[35] As late as 1930, the tribal character of Kuwait contrasted with the cosmopolitan outlook of Manama as noted by H. V. Briscoe, the British Political Resident in the Gulf:

It may be asked why we should not allow Bahrain [Manama] to be run as, for instance, Kuwait is, as an Arab city on Arab lines. The answer is that the population of the two cities is wholly dissimilar. The population of Kuwait is largely Bedouin: their outlook is towards the desert ... The population of Bahrain is heterogeneous and divided by racial and religious difference – Nejdis, Wahhabis, Persians, Sunnis, Shias and large colonies of Muhammedan and Hindu Indians. Bahrain is a purely commercial centre, its outlook is towards Bombay and the stock markets of the world on which it depends to sell its pearls.[36]

Merchants, tribal rulers and urban economies

In the age of informal empire Gulf ports maintained the distinctive features of 'indigenous' trading towns which had characterised their early development. The close relationship between merchants and tribal rulers, and the control of the pearling industry and of intercoastal trade, continued to define their political and social hierarchies as urban settlements. The merchant capital produced and invested inside these settlements was the most important resource base which underpinned the consolidation of tribal dynasties. Arab and Hawala merchants financed regional and long-distance trade and the pearling industry, the pillars of the indigenous maritime economy. Those pearling entrepreneurs of tribal descent who had played a crucial role in the establishment of port facilities provided direct financial and political support to ruling families until the discovery of oil, often in the form of loans and tribal fighters. The most influential mercantile groups of Kuwait either claimed descent from the first al-'Utub settlers or had intermarried with the Al Sabah in the course of the nineteenth century.[37] As already noted, in Bahrain the majority of the Sunni pearl merchants belonged to the tribal entourage of the Al Khalifah, often to groups which had arrived in the islands with them from al-Zubarah and Kuwait.

The fiscal regime enforced inside port settlements tended to favour indigenous capitalists and merchants of tribal descent involved in pearling, reinforcing their symbiotic relationship with ruling families. Rulers

[35] Kuwait's population increased from approximately 6,000 in the 1840s to 35,000 in 1905. Lorimer, *Gazetteer*, vol. II, p. 1051; Brucks, 'Memoir Descriptive of the Navigation of the Gulf' (1829–35), fiche 1096, pp. 575–6, V 23/217 IOR.
[36] H. V. Briscoe in Political Resident Bushehr to Foreign Secretary to the Government of India, 13 February 1930, n. 43, R/15/1/332 IOR.
[37] Crystal, *Oil and Politics in the Gulf*, pp. 19, 24–6.

56   Histories of City and State in the Persian Gulf

conceived the imposition of customs duties as the extension of the customary rights acquired through the military control of harbours at the time
of the establishment of new commercial outposts. Yet pearl exports were
generally not subject to taxation, while entrepôt and long-distance traders
often paid duty on imports and on goods in transit as a form of ground rent
which allowed them to maintain their businesses in Gulf ports. The
structure of the pearl industry also accentuated the privileged position of
tribal entrepreneurs. As was the case in Bahrain, pearl production was
managed independently by tribal groups which had the usufruct of pearl
banks and exercised jurisdiction over the labour force through their
own councils. With the expansion of the pearling industry and the concomitant growth of the urban labour force, however, the influence of non-
tribal entrepreneurs, particularly of Persian and Indian merchants who
imported textiles and foodstuffs, increased. The mercantile communities
of Manama, including Persians, Banyan (a Hindu subcaste specialising in
commerce), Hawala and Jews, produced a class which competed with
Bahrain's pearling entrepreneurs in wealth and lifestyle. Exceptionally,
some foreign traders were also able to gain a share in the pearling industry
by capitalising on British protection and on closer commercial links with
India. In Dubai, a syndicate of Indian entrepreneurs started to control the
production and marketing of pearls as part of their import–export trade.
After 1865, they were able to finance expeditions to the pearl banks and
used revenue from the sale of pearls in Bombay to pay for the transport of
Indian imports back to the Gulf.[38]

Despite the enhanced position of merchants with no tribal credentials,
their ability to diversify their portfolios was limited, particularly with
regard to income from agricultural rent or to the establishment of trade
monopolies. In other words, unlike their counterparts in Ottoman or
Qajar provincial centres, they could not make inroads into the hinterland
of Gulf ports as landlords, tax-farmers or collectors of tribute. Tribal
considerations and military alliances guided the distribution of tax-
farms, pearl-fishing rights and rural estate on the part of rulers, as exemplified by the case of Bahrain. Import–export merchants were integrated
into the tribal administration of port towns such as Manama and Abu
Dhabi only as customs collectors and tax-farmers in the urban markets.[39]
The scarcity of economic choices at their disposal contrasts with the more
fluid picture of southern Iraq. Here, Baghdadi and Basrawi merchants

---

[38] F. al-Sayegh, 'Merchants' Role in a Changing Society: The Case of Dubai, 1900–90',
    Middle Eastern Studies 34 (1998), 87–102 (87–8, 189–90).
[39] Heard-Bey, *From Trucial States to United Arab Emirates*, p. 249. For Manama see
    Chapter 3, pp. 88–9.

benefited from the competition between Ottoman governors, tribes and British traders for the control of agricultural regions, particularly after the application of the 1838 Anglo-Ottoman commercial convention. By the 1860s, for instance, the al-Danyal family from Baghdad controlled the production and marketing of grain and rice outside the town.[40] An additional factor which disadvantaged Gulf merchants with no tribal connections was their inability to control militias in order to defend their cargo and shipments. Weapons and armed retainers were the preserve of tribes which accrued part of their revenue through the imposition of protection fees.

The mobility of merchant capital, however, worked to the advantage of Gulf traders, regardless of their background and specialisation. With tribal secession, the relocation of merchants across the region is a constant theme in the history of Gulf coastal towns. Entrepreneurs moved their business if they could not secure for themselves advantageous terms or conduct their trade in a safe environment. During the Bahrain civil war of 1842–3, for instance, Manama's merchants fled en masse to Kuwait and Lingah, reducing the commercial fleet of the islands to a quarter of its size.[41] The fear of merchant secession had crucial implications: it restrained the authority of rulers and forced them to impose relaxed customs duties in order to assuage the sensibility of merchants and entrepreneurs who in turn acquired considerable political leverage. In 1831 the import tariff on goods entering the harbour of Kuwait was only 2 per cent of value, and by 1845 taxes were collected only on commodities purchased by Bedouin visitors to the town. In Bahrain, a customs administration slowly emerged after 1869 under 'Isa ibn 'Ali Al Khalifah, while Dubai had no custom facilities for much of the nineteenth century.[42]

This 'free' port regime, as Hala Fattah has called it,[43] not only constituted one of the pillars of the urban political economy but was also a necessary condition for the development of trading emporia at the periphery of centralised administrations, which tended to enforce protectionist polices in order to raise state revenue. Between 1792 and 1818 al-'Uqayr, the main seaport under Sa'udi control in Eastern Arabia, charged up to 20 per cent ad valorem on dates and agricultural produce imported from

---

[40] Fattah, *The Politics of Regional Trade*, pp. 141–4.
[41] Kemball, 'Memoranda on the Resources, Localities, and Relations' (1845), fiche 1090–1, p. 106, V 23/217 IOR.
[42] Brucks, 'Memoir Descriptive of the Navigation of the Gulf' (1829–35), fiche 1096–7, p. 576, V 23/217 IOR; Lorimer, *Gazetteer*, vol. II, p. 1760; Kemball, 'Memoranda on the Resources, Localities, and Relations' (1845), fiche 1090–1, p. 109, V 23/217 IOR. Heard-Bey, *Trucial States to United Arab Emirates*, p. 191.
[43] Fattah, *The Politics of Regional Trade*, pp. 25–8.

other Gulf ports.[44] After 1838, the enforcement of the Anglo-Ottoman commercial convention and Ottoman centralisation damaged the position of local merchants with bases of operation in Basra. Horse dealers trading with Bombay moved to Kuwait and Muhammarah, one of the ports on the Iranian coast, and started to do business with British shippers, thus circumventing Ottoman port duties. Similarly, increasing trade restrictions and onerous taxation by the Qajar authorities in the southern Iranian ports after 1900 favoured the relocation of merchant capital to the Arab coast. By 1905 the ruler of Dubai had abolished the 5 per cent customs duty and declared the town a free port.[45]

The structure of the pearl industry had profound socio-economic implications for urban life. Besides favouring the concentration of wealth and political influence in the hands of tribal entrepreneurs, it also allowed them to control large segments of the urban population employed in the business. Although in Kuwait and Abu Dhabi pearl divers of Bedouin origin were able to establish free cooperatives and finance their own boats, the majority of the labour force worked on a system of seasonal advances. These advances, whose repayment depended on the catch and the sale of pearls, forced divers and their families to rely on ship captains, financiers, tribal leaders and pearl merchants for their living. In bad seasons crew members were not able to pay back the monies received before they boarded pearling boats, leading to the accumulation of debt year after year and from one generation to another. Further, a chain of dependency also bound boat captains, pearl dealers and the workforce employed in the industry of native crafts to tribal entrepreneurs. The fluctuation of the pearl market influenced patterns of consumption: any reduction in the quantity of food imports caused prices in urban markets to soar and in extreme cases brought famine to the population. As divers and pullers became indebted to boat captains and financiers, they were inevitably drawn into forced labour to make up for their losses.[46]

Accounts of the industry by Europeans often stressed its exploitative nature, in some cases denouncing it as a form of slavery. In 1924 Paul Harrison noted that in Bahrain 'the diver is known as a slave for the rest of his life'.[47] While the association between debt and slavery featured

[44] R. Taylor, 'Extracts from Brief Notes Containing Historical and Other Information Connected with the Province of Oman; Muskat and the Adjoining Countries; the Islands of Bahrain, Ormus, Kishm, and Karrak; and Other Ports in the Persian Gulf' (1818), fiche 1089–90, pp. 17–18, V 23/217 IOR; Fattah, *The Politics of Regional Trade*, p. 67.

[45] Fattah, *The Politics of Regional Trade*, pp. 171–8; al-Sayegh, 'Merchants' Role in a Changing Society', 90; Lorimer, *Gazetteer*, vol. I, p. 322.

[46] Lorimer, *Gazetteer*, vol. I, pp. 2220–93; Lienhardt, *Shaikhdoms of Eastern Arabia*, pp. 150–64.

[47] P. W. Harrison, *The Arab at Home* (London: Hutchinson, 1925), p. 80.

prominently in the pre-capitalist economies of mercantile systems, particularly across South East Asia, in the Gulf ports capitalist and labourer
were partners in an 'unequal' relationship as both shared an interest in
increasing the margin of profit.[48] Moreover, indebtedness carried little or
no social stigma as suggested by the British anthropologist Peter
Lienhardt who in the 1950s gathered oral testimonies on the conditions
of the pearling communities of Trucial Oman: '[In the past] debt
restricted people's freedom of action, tied them to their work, and laid
them open to exploitation. But, being endemic, it involved no disgrace.
Nor could a creditor practice the level of extortion and emotional perse-
cution possible to English moneylenders in the last century.'[49] One significant implication of the advance system was that the cycle of debt
prevented the accumulation of capital, thus severely restricting the social
mobility of pearl labourers as the largest productive sector of Gulf ports.

The survival of the pearling industry as a local enterprise explains the
continuity of the socio-political organisation of port settlements in the
nineteenth century. It also suggests that the indigenous economy of
the Gulf did not collapse under the pressure of European trade, contrary
to what is generally assumed for many areas of the Middle East.[50]
Although some local merchants started to work as agents and employees
of European shipping companies, local shipping maintained a solid profile
sustained by the pearl trade with India and by the exchange of goods for
local consumption with Iran, Iraq and the Arabian Peninsula. The continuation of intercoastal trade was also assisted by the size of British ships,
which could approach only large harbours. Native shipping was also able
to support the bulk of regional trade in the late 1920s and early 1930s,
when the collapse of pearling and the depression in the world markets
restrained the circulation of international commodities.[51] The resilience
of the Gulf's traditional maritime economy is also further testimony to the
protectionist policies adopted by the Government of India in order to
ensure the political stability of the Gulf ports. In keeping the pearling
industry firmly under tribal control, imperial policies buttressed the position of urban rulers, cementing their alliance with tribal entrepreneurs.

---

[48] A. Reid, 'The Organisation of Production in the Pre-Colonial South Eastern Asian Port
City' in Broeze (ed.), *Brides of the Sea*, pp. 54–74 (pp. 61–4).
[49] Lienhardt, *Shaikhdoms of Eastern Arabia*, p. 152.
[50] This is in contrast for instance with developments in Iraq where Fattah concludes that by
1900 'the autonomy of regional merchants had been shattered'. Fattah, *The Politics of
Regional Trade*, p. 207.
[51] For an analysis of the political implications on indigenous trade following the establishment of British monopolies see al-Naqeeb, *Society and State*, pp. 51–78; Crystal, *Oil and
Politics in the Gulf*, p. 26.

Not only did the British residency provide effective arbitration for the delimitation of the rights of exploitation of pearl banks but in some cases also initiated the process of delimitation of territorial waters by declaring pearl banks the inalienable property of local tribes.

Manama, Bahrain: the town of foreigners

The history of Manama pre-dated the tribal scramble of the long eighteenth century. Manama developed as true 'bride of the sea' as it was a port before becoming a town. Before the nineteenth century, its development can be linked to the presence of Qal'ah al-Bahrayn, the Portuguese fort which overlooked the town's natural harbour. Long before the arrival of the Portuguese in the sixteenth century, the harbour was an important trade centre, as suggested by the ruins of an old city located near the fort which served a large agricultural region in the third millennium BC. In the early thirteenth century, when Bahrain became a dependency of Iran, the extension of trade networks furthered regional integration, and consolidated the position of Manama in a grid of maritime connections linking Gulf port settlements to the Indian Ocean, East Africa and the Far East.[52]

Before the nineteenth century, the history of the town survives merely as a locality whose name was recorded in few documents. The first mention dates back to 1347 when Turan Shah, the King of Hormuz, occupied the islands after his nephew Shambeh, who acted as local governor, was killed by an army mutiny. We can assume that the harbour was of some importance, as in the same period Persian records name the future capital of Safavid Bahrain as 'Bilad al-Qadim' (the Old Town), implying the existence of a new settlement. Two centuries later, another military campaign against Bahrain suggests the strategic importance of the area. In 1559 the Ottoman commander Mustafa Pasha, the governor of al-Ahsa', launched an attack against Qal'ah al-Bahrayn in an attempt to wrest the control of the islands. After a long siege he was defeated by Portuguese forces and died in Bahrain. Sixteen years later the military command in Baghdad resumed plans for the occupation of the fort in order to establish an Ottoman outpost in Manama harbour which was to be provisioned from al-Qatif, then under Ottoman control.[53]

---

[52] Larsen, *Life and Land Use on the Bahraini Islands*, pp. 20–1, 95–8, 205; Bibby, *Looking for Dilmun*, pp. 60–85.

[53] 'Ali Akbar Bushehri, 'Bilad al-jadid – mawlid madinah al-Manamah' and 'Mashad 'asimah al-Bahrayn' in *al-Wasat*, July 2003; Teixeira, *The Travels of Pedro Teixeira*, p. 175; 'Taqarir hawla al-hamlah al-'uthmaniyyah 'ala al-Bahrayn' ('Documents concerning the Ottoman Attack against Bahrain'), 996h./1559 and 983h./1575, Markaz

The vicissitudes of the fort established the historic credentials of Manama among the local population, who named it Qal'ah al-Faranji, the fort of the Europeans, at least since the mid nineteenth century.[54] Despite its powerful impression upon popular imagery, Qal'ah al-Bahrayn guarded Manama's harbour from a distance and it seems that no permanent fortifications integrated the fort into the town's defensive and administrative system. A temporary line of defence which protected the harbour was erected by the local governor Muqrin in 1521 during the first Portuguese siege of Bahrain. The wall had disappeared by 1605 when the Portuguese fleet attempted to reconquer the islands after the occupation by the forces of Shah 'Abbas.[55] According to Carsten Niebuhr, Manama (which he referred to as Bahrain or Awal) was a fortified town in 1765. His description is confirmed by the Persian traveller Muhammad Ibrahim Kazeruni, who in the early nineteenth century described Manama as a gated port which was protected by fortifications and guarded by twenty-eight towers. Although the presence of the remains of town walls is confirmed by twentieth-century observers, the surveys and accounts produced by British naval officers after the 1820s do not confirm Kazeruni's observations. His representation of Manama is somewhat striking and unique, a stylised vision of a fabled port town which emerged from the desert and from the squalor of rural deprivation surrounding it. The condition of the agricultural population held a particularly emotional and political appeal to the writer, a devout Shi'i Muslim whose visit to the Gulf region was sponsored directly by the Qajar shah.[56]

In the absence of detailed historical records, cartography offers some clues on the position of the settlement in Bahrain's changing politics of urbanism in the sixteenth and seventeenth centuries. A detailed Portuguese picture map dating from 1538 provides an impressionistic illustration of the northern coast of Bahrain from the point of view of a sailor approaching the main island from the northwest. While Qal'ah al-Bahrayn takes the centre stage with flags indicating the headquarters of the Portuguese administration, Manama is sketched as a dense conglomeration of white buildings overlooking the seafront. In this period a

al-Watha'iq al-Tarikhiyyah (Historical Documentation Centre, Rifa', hereafter MWT); M. Kervran, *Bahrain in the 16th Century: An Impregnable Island* (Manama: Ministry of Information, 1988), pp. 24–30, 40.

[54] The name Manama is also connected with the presence of the fort as indicated by the toponymic *qasr al-manam* often used to explain the origins of the town as the sleeping quarter of the ruler, from the Arabic root *nama* (to sleep). *Ihya' madinah al-Manamah al-qadimah/Manama Urban Renewal Project* (Ministry of Housing, Physical Planning Directorate, State of Bahrain, 1987), p. 7; Lorimer, *Gazetteer*, vol. II, p. 52.

[55] Kervran, *Bahrain in the 16th century*, pp. 16–20, 31–4, 41–2.

[56] Kazeruni, *Athar*, pp. 880 ff.; Niebuhr, *Travels through Arabia*, vol. II, p. 152; Belgrave, *The Pirate Coast*, p. 76.

Portuguese observer provided the first brief description of the town's built environment as an assembly of tall mansions with wind towers.[57] Another Portuguese naval survey produced around 1635 when Bahrain was a province of the Safavid Empire presents Manama as a cluster of small dark houses, most likely huts. The Portuguese fort, now with an additional wide moat, is connected by a bridge to a large inland settlement with stone buildings and a tall minaret, clearly Bilad al-Qadim. Taking into account a margin of inaccuracy in the stylised representation of the two Portuguese cartographers, Manama appears prosperous under Portuguese rule but was sidelined in favour of Bilad al-Qadim in the Safavid period. The deterioration of Manama's urban environment resonates in the accounts of the period by local *'ulama'*, who rather puzzlingly do not make any reference to the settlement.[58]

The separation of the harbour from the fort and Bilad al-Qadim underlines what seems to have been a continuum in the town's more recent pre-modern history; that is, the struggle between its independent civic tradition and constituted authority. While providing continuity in the entrepôt economy of Bahrain, Manama defied the crystallisation of a state-sponsored urban tradition. As part of a 'littoral society' resulting from the interface between land and sea over the centuries, Manama constructed its image of dissidence as a stopover of seafarers, privateers, pearl divers, adventures and fishermen who sought provisions, shelter and rest during or after their long journeys at sea. As suggested by the etymology of its name (from the Arabic verb *nama*, to sleep), the harbour was a 'resting place' which allowed almost unrestricted access to a heterogeneous crowd of occasional visitors and permanent settlers. In the nineteenth century Manama was a commercial emporium in flux, as the harbour was not a geographical, political and economic barrier but a highly permeable border. Cosmopolitanism was the building block of urban society and mercantilism the ideology of its audacious free entrepreneurs. The wide array of opportunities offered to newcomers by the harbour economy worked as a double-edged sword, guaranteeing a cycle of prosperity but also fostering political instability.

In the 1860s the British traveller W. G. Palgrave celebrated the exhilarating atmosphere of Manama as a counterpoint to the strikingly different geographical and political horizons of Najd under Sa'udi influence. Unfavourably impressed by the restrictions imposed in Central Arabia

---

[57] For a reproduction of this map see Kervran, *Bahrain in the 16th Century*, p. 41; Jean Aubin, 'Le royaume d'Ormuz au début du XVIe siècle' *Mare Luso-Indicum* (Geneva: Droz, 1973), vol. II, pp. 77–179 (p. 99).

[58] A reproduction of the 1635 map is included in Kervran, *Bahrain in the 16th Century*, p. 51.

by the Wahhabis, he captured a snapshot of life in the town's harbour by recalling his encounters in a tavern called the 'Sailor's Home':

the profound ignorance of Nejed regarding Europeans and their various classifications is here exchanged for a partial acquaintance with those topics; thus 'English' and 'French', disfigured into the local 'Ingleez' and 'Fransees', are familiar words in Menamah, though Germans and Italians, whose vessels seldom or never visit these seas, have as yet no place in the Bahreyn vocabulary; ... But Russians, or 'Moscôp' (that is, Muscovites), are alike well known and well feared, thanks to Persian intercourse. Besides, the policy of Contantinople [sic] and Teheran are freely and at times sensibly discussed in these coffee-houses, no less than the stormy diplomacy of Nejed and her dangerous encroachments; ship news, commerce, business, tales of foreign lands, and occasionally literature, supply the rest of the conversation. Of religious controversy I never heard one word. In short, instead of Zelators and fanatics, camel-drivers and Bedouins, we have at Bahreyn [Manama] something like 'men of the world, who know the world like men', a great relief to the mind; certainly it was so to mine.[59]

The making of public opinion reflected the contingencies of local politics in so far as these affected business and overseas connections. The khans and coffee houses around the harbour are seldom portrayed as spaces of subversion and disorder but as the centres of the commercial life of the town. Here entrepreneurs met partners, assessed the feasibility of new commercial ventures in the light of current political events, negotiated deals and recruited crews for their vessels. By the beginning of the twentieth century Manama's largest merchant houses were part of international trade networks which operated in the proto-globalised trans-regional world championed by the British Empire. The Kanu, al-Safar and Sharif families had branches across the Gulf region and connections to Indian Ocean ports and Europe, capitalising on the new technologies in communication and shipping introduced by British firms in India and southern Iran. In 1913 the office of Yusuf ibn Ahmad Kanu, one of the largest import–export merchants of Manama and the local agent of the Anglo-Persian Oil Company, displayed: 'office desks and chairs used by the clerks, presses for duplicating correspondence, a type-writer, a wall-calendar in English, and an American clock or time-piece, an iron safe of the newest pattern and with a Portuguese or Eurasian clerk imported from Bombay, to look after the English letters'.[60]

A familiarity with Arabic, English, Farsi and Hindi were prerequisites for the commercial and political success of the upper echelons of Manama's notability. Hindu and Persian merchants acted as the British

---

[59] al-Nabhani, *al-Tuhfah al-Nabhaniyyah*, pp. 141–4; W. G. Palgrave, *Narrative of a Year's Journey through Central and Eastern Arabia (1862–63)*, 2 vols. (London and Cambridge: Macmillan, 1865), vol. II, pp. 218–19.
[60] Cursetjee, *The Land of the Date*, p. 83.

native agents throughout the nineteenth century, reflecting the triangular relationship which linked the Al Khalifah administration to the Bombay Government, and to the British residency in Bushehr. Between 1872 and 1900 the agency under 'Abd al-Nabi al-Safar and his son Muhammad Rahim was staffed by Persians and Hawala clerks who were fluent in English, Arabic and Farsi.[61] With no indigenous bureaucratic tradition surviving from the Safavid period, literacy and record-keeping among Arabs was almost exclusively the preserve of merchants and clergy. The absence of suitably trained locals was a crucial factor in the employment of many foreigners in areas which demanded specialised clerical skills, particularly in shipping. Foreigners also monopolised the few contracts offered by the ruler: Indians occupied key positions in the customs and Persians were employed as landing contractors in the harbour. Even powerful Hawala entrepreneurs were relative latecomers to the business, and their public profile, as was the case with Yusuf ibn Ahmad Kanu, was established only when they became attached to European firms (see Figure 3).[62]

The Arab pearl merchants of the town were a heterogeneous lot. Both Sunni and Shi'is looked at Bombay as the commercial, cultural and religious capital of the region with its import–export offices, Arabic printing presses, and thriving religious and intellectual life. They invested in urban properties and maintained family residences in the Indian port. The primary and secondary schools of Bombay, which offered both scientific and commercial education, further fashioned the Arab urban elites of the turn of the century. The offspring of pearl merchants also joined the Islamic University of Aligarh founded by the reformist Sayyed Ahmad Khan (1817–98), which promoted Islamic values, followed a western curriculum and constituted the training ground for Indian Muslim activists who opposed British rule.[63]

After 1900, the newly built British political agency (locally known as Bayt al-Dawlah) further promoted Manama's mercantile and multi-ethnic tradition. It introduced a new public ceremonial which emphasised the position of the agency as the protector of the town's commercial classes. The representatives of the Bombay Government skilfully orchestrated official events following British Indian protocol as the counterpoint to the tribal pomp of the court of Shaykh 'Isa in Muharraq. In June 1926 Charles

[61] Onley, 'Transnational Merchants in the Nineteenth-Century Gulf', pp. 63–77; Onley, *The Arabian Frontier of the British Raj*, p. 107.
[62] Political Agent Bahrain to Political Resident Bushehr, 17 May 1914, n. 546, R/15/1/331 IOR.
[63] 'Abd al-Karim al-'Urayyad, *Nafidhah 'ala al-tarikh: Bayt al-'Urayyad* (Manama al-Mu'assah al 'Arabiyyah li al-Tiba'ah wa al-Nashr, [n.d.]), pp. 40–3; *Ayyam al-zaman*, p. 84.

3 Muhammad Rahim al-Safar, the British Native Agent between 1893
and 1900

Belgrave, the British advisor to Shaykh Hamad (who became regent after
the deposition of Shaykh 'Isa ibn 'Ali in 1923) noted in his diary his first
encounter with the town's merchants organised by Major Daly, the British
Political Agent. Wearing his official uniform, Daly introduced Belgrave to
the notables as the representatives of the urban population with short
speeches in Arabic, Urdu and Persian. The visitors politely reciprocated
in their own mother tongues, and the conversation continued briskly in
various languages during the reception (see Figure 4).[64]

[64] Belgrave Diaries, 5 June 1926, Arab World Documentation Unit (AWDU hereafter).

4 The staff of the British political agency in front of the agency building.
Sitting in the centre of the front row is Charles Geoffrey Prior, British
Political Agent between 1929 and 1932

Urban elites were the mirror image of the communities they led, organised along lines of ethnicity, religion and sect. Until the oil era, the heterogeneous make-up of the urban population did not generate a process of cultural osmosis between different urban groups. Dress, taste and material culture continued to distinguish members of individual communities regardless of their social status. Blue was always worn by Baharna women, while their Persian and Sunni Arab counterparts were wrapped in Islamic dress and black shawls. The distinctive features of male settlers of tribal origin were their white robes and different headgear, often tied with headbands made of camel hair in Bedouin style.[65] European visitors generally disdained the manners of the Arab notables, preferring the more sophisticated and worldly etiquette of the Persians. British observers took for granted the superior taste of Manama's Persians. A British report on Bahrain trade compiled in 1902 noted that:

[65] Palgrave, *Narrative of a Year's Journey*, vol. II, pp. 211–12; G. N. Curzon, *Persia and the Persian Question* (London: Longmans, 1892), pp. 467–8.

'the influx of Persian settlers during the past two years is creating demand for a better class of prints, woollen cloths, cheap velvets and silks.' The consumption of dates and coffee was central to the lore of the Arab population of the town, irrespective of their wealth. The Indian lawyer Manockjee Cursetjee was dutifully instructed in the 'correct Arab style of eating dates' while dining in one of Manama's rich households. The ceremony of serving coffee in long beaked pots was an indication of high social status among Arab notables in the same way as tea, rose water and shoes dictated trends among the Persians following the fashion of Bushehr.[66]

The diversity of idioms used for trade and administration is suggestive of the fragmentation of Manama's commercial and public life. Sindi and Gujarati were the languages of bookkeeping in the customs house, replaced by English only after the appointment of a British director in 1923. Arabic was *lughah al-ghaws*, the language of pearling, and that of the Al Khalifah court in Muharraq. In the same way as Hindu merchants, Bohrah shopkeepers from Bombay who controlled the retail of cheap Japanese and British household goods on the eve of World War I spoke very poor Arabic, conducting their business in English. Persian continued to be the language of trade and education among the community, although second generation settlers adopted a variant heavily infused with Arabic and English. Moreover, the variant of Arabic spoken by the indigenous Shi'i population, which was mostly of rural extraction, differed substantially from that of their Sunni counterparts.[67]

The acceptance of religious diversity and social separation constituted the foundations of a tacit social contract which permeated Manama's civic spirit. It was commonplace to encounter a Hindu performing his ritual ablutions in tight white cotton pants and silk-fringed cloth wrapped around his waist alongside a well-to-do Persian wearing a waistcoat, pantaloons, woollen socks and shoes. Travellers and foreigner residents tended to portray diversity as an exotic trope, and underlined the peaceful coexistence of the town's communities. Their impressionistic sketches of urban society seldom depict episodes of conflict. Instead, they are instructive on the visual and cultural texture of the urban landscape. This blend of settlers and outsiders, and kaleidoscope of languages, colours and dress

---

[66] 'Administration Report on the Persian Gulf Political Residency and Maskat Political Agency for 1902–1903' in *The Persian Gulf Administration Reports 1873–1949*, vol. V, p. 35; Lorimer, *Gazetteer*, vol. II, p. 345; Cursetjee, *The Land of the Date*, pp. 80–2 (p. 85).
[67] Political Agent Bahrain to Political Resident Bushehr, 21 September 1920 and 2 September 1923, R/15/1/331 IOR; Cursetjee, *The Land of the Date*, p. 87; C. Holes, *Language Variation and Change in a Modernising Arab State: The Case of Bahrain* (London and New York: Kegan Paul, 1987), pp. 16–17.

prompted George Curzon, the future Viceroy of India, to note that: 'a more curious study in polyglot and polychrome could not well be conceived'.[68]

At the grassroots the meaning of community was translated into a sectarian and ethnic division of labour. The Arab Shi'is or Baharna, who formed approximately three-fifths of the town's population in 1905 and the most compact urban group, monopolised urban crafts and traded in local produce.[69] They also provided manpower for the markets and the harbour as labourers, porters and pearl divers. Their 'natural' leaders were those rural notables who had moved to Manama and capitalised on the pearling industry. The Persians were divided both by sect and by deep socio-economic cleavages, which reflected their long history of immigration from southern Iran. The Shi'i majority, approximately 1,500 individuals in 1904, were mostly from the district of Dashti. Like their Arab counterparts they were of humble background and of very limited means, and depended upon a few families who became rich as import merchants dealing with major Iranian ports, particularly Bushehr. By the 1920s the Persian Sunnis included a minority of extremely wealthy individuals from the district of Bastak with business interests in India, Lingah and Bandar 'Abbas, and a mass of destitute rural immigrants who had arrived via the port of Lingah.[70]

The Arab Sunnis were the most socially and politically compartmentalised of Manama's residents. Najdis with tribal associations gravitated around the Al Khalifah and monopolised pearling as boat captains, middle men or al-tawawish, the most prestigious pearl dealers. Those who had no tribal connections, particularly from al-'Unayzah in Najd, followed the patterns of other upcoming immigrant communities: they maintained social and political distance from the tribal mercantile aristocracy of the town, and worked as hammal (porters), mughawis (coffee boys) and petty traders. Although al-'Unayzah was an important centre for the long distance trade in camels, horses and sheep, the Najdi community of Manama did not engage in the export of animals to India. The trade was monopolised by transport agents (al-'uqaylat) operating from Kuwait and Basrah, ports which had strong links with the tribal hinterlands where these animals were bred.[71]

---

[68] Curzon, *Persia and the Persian Question*, p. 468.

[69] Lorimer, *Gazetteer*, vol. II, p. 1160.

[70] 'Note on the Persian Communities at Bahrein', 4 November 1929, in Political Agent Bahrain to British Resident Bushehr, L/P&S/10/1045 IOR; Lorimer, *Gazetteer*, vol. II, p. 1160; interviews with Tayyebah Hoodi and Hamid al-'Awadhi, Manama, 21 March and 10 April 2004.

[71] At the beginning of the twentieth century the numerical distribution of Arab Sunnis was as follows: 250 individuals from Basra, 850 from Kuwait, Najd and al-Ahsa', 500 'Utub,

Hawala residents, whom Lorimer includes among the Arab population of the town, were looked upon with diffidence by both tribal Arabs and Baharna. Although some families had been in Bahrain for several generations and spoke Arabic, they continued to be considered Persians. At the turn of the century the community included an important segment of the town's commercial elite who had acquired wealth and political connections by tapping into European shipping and trade.[72] Indians, mainly Hindus from Gujarat, were a small community of traders and clerks who 'live among the motley crowd [of Manama], "among them, but not of them" ', as noted by Palgrave in the mid nineteenth century.[73] Often employed as accountants and English translators for local merchants, they started to play an important role in the modern administration after 1920. Jewish families such as the Khadduri, Nunu and Rubin, originally from Iraq and Iran, worked in the markets as bankers and money lenders.[74] Very few Christians and Europeans lived in Manama before the discovery of oil, mostly working with the British agency and in the mission established by the Dutch Reformed Church of America in 1892.

In a social landscape dominated by newcomers and settlers, perceptions of outsiders and insiders were blurred. Family bonds, local identities and sectarian feelings were rarely subject to negotiation, and individuals and groups maintained strong trans-local referents long after their settlement in the town. Non-tribal residents born in Manama from foreign parents continued to be identified with their places of origin through their family names, providing an important subdivision to Manama's ethnic groups. Although members of the extended household settled in the town were the preferred choice as marriage partners, overseas relatives and former neighbours supplied business associates and matrimonial ties to the Bushehris, Shirazis, Bastakis, al-Ahsa'is and al-Qatifis of Manama.[75] The Arab Shi'i population maintained strong connections to the villages, where marrying into one of the families living in Manama was highly prized. A song still celebrates the aspirations of the young males of Bahrain's agricultural communities: 'I wish I could get 2,000 rupees,

1,000 residents of uncertain origin and 2,300 Africans of which 800 were slaves. Lorimer, *Gazetteer*, vol. II, p. 1160. Interview with Khalid al-Bassam, Manama, 20 March 2004. On pre-oil al-'Unayzah see Altorki and Cole, *Arabian Oasis City*, pp. 15–82.
[72] 5,000 Hawala were reported in Manama in 1905. Lorimer, *Gazetteer*, vol. II, p. 1160. Belgrave to Political Agent Bahrain, 17 February 1948, R/15/2/485 IOR.
[73] Palgrave, *Narrative of a Year's Journey*, vol. II, p. 212. In the early 1830s Brucks reported the presence of one hundred Banyan merchants in the town. Brucks, 'Memoir Descriptive of the Navigation of the Gulf' (1829–35), fiche 1096–7, p. 566, V 23/217 IOR.
[74] Only fifty Jews lived in Manama in 1905. Lorimer, *Gazetteer*, vol. II, p. 1160.
[75] N. Fuccaro, 'Mapping the Transnational Community: Persians and the Space of the City in Bahrain, c.1869–1937' in al-Rasheed (ed.), *Transnational Connections in the Arab Gulf*, pp. 39–58 (pp. 45–8).

and a high *ghurayfah* [a rudimentary mechanical lifter of underground water used for irrigation] with a woman from Manama.' No collective name denoted 'immigrant' throughout the town as individual communities continued to define them in their own terms: the Baharna referred to Arab Shi'i newcomers as *al-hala'il* (villagers), and the Persians called their immigrants *farsi* denoting their rural origin.[76]

Conclusion: unity and diversity in the evolution of port polities

Compared with the other *mudun al-ghaws* (pearling towns) of the Persian Gulf, Manama had a distinctive character. Its demography encapsulated the ancient agricultural tradition of Bahrain and the geographic position of the islands. Uniquely among the ports of the Arab coast controlled by dynasties of Bedouin descent, Manama had very few tribal settlers and a large Shi'i population with strong economic and social ties to rural areas. In contrast, Kuwait and Dubai were 'new' ports which had emerged out of the tribal scramble of the long eighteenth century. Like Muharraq, they combined political and commercial functions as the centres of tribal administrations and of pearl production. Moreover, large segments of their populations maintained a clannish tradition and strong loyalties to the ruling families, features which were not so prominent in the socio-political landscape of Manama.

By the beginning of the twentieth century Bahrain's 'special relationship' with the British Empire and Bombay, the imperial metropolis of the Gulf region, had accentuated the cosmopolitan character of the islands' leading port. In the years of the pearl boom the British connection empowered further the mercantile groups of Manama and contributed to defining the town's semi-autonomous position in relation to the Dar al-Hukumah based in Muharraq. At the turn of the twentieth century Kuwait followed a divergent path. Taking advantage of the rivalry between the Government of India and the Ottoman Empire, Mubarak al-Sabah (r. 1896–1915) was able to pursue a vigorous programme of urban centralisation, mainly by instituting a regular system of taxation, which transformed the town into the prototype of the tribal city-state of the pre-oil era.[77]

---

[76] Interviews with 'Abdallah Sayf, Tayyebah Hoodi, Khalid al-Bassam and 'Ali Akbar Bushehri, Manama, March and April 2004; al-Madani and al-'Urayyad, *Min turath al-Bahrayn*, p. 211; Serjeant, 'Customary Irrigation Law', pp. 8–9.

[77] Lorimer, *Gazetteer*, vol. II, pp. 2286–9; S. Alghanim, *The Reign of Mubarak al-Sabah: Shaikh of Kuwait, 1896–1915* (London: I. B. Tauris, 1998), pp. 135–41.

Despite their diversity, the pearling and trading towns of the Arab coast shared a similar social organisation and political institutions which were tied to both the desert and the sea. The political supremacy of tribes and the absence of centralised administrations set them apart from the ports under Ottoman and Qajar control, contributing to the instability of local government and to the precariousness of urban public security. The tension between mercantile communities, immigrants and tribesmen, often the only militarised segments of urban society, compounded by infighting among ruling families, accentuated their political disunity. For much of the nineteenth century, ruling dynasties exercised control over residents through their militias and by forging crucial political alliances with merchants and community leaders. These constraints facilitated the autonomous organisation of large segments of urban society, particularly in towns with a more heterogeneous population. Ports such as Manama and Dubai, in particular, evolved almost as 'voluntary' associations with their immigrant populations of non-tribal stock and mobile workforce. Immigrants were often able to maintain links to their countries of origin and their religious and linguistic specificity. In this respect, rather than city-states, these port polities evolved as relatively open 'city-societies' in the sense suggested by the historical anthropologist Richard O'Connor with reference to the city states of pre-modern South East Asia.[78]

From this perspective, urban polities emerged out of consensus and a balance of power, rather than conflict. As clearly suggested by the mobility of merchants across the region, the port towns of the Arab coast constituted a sort of commonwealth whose success depended on their ability to attract settlers with benefits of residence. Urban rulers faced further challenges in the wake of the economic and demographic expansion of the late nineteenth century. Towns-in-the-making had increasingly complex societies and stood in stark contrast with the mobile and relatively egalitarian environment which had produced their tribal rulers. While in Bedouin life, public order and the position of leaders was based on the supremacy of the tribe, in the towns, as noted by Lienhardt for the Trucial States, 'the primacy of the sheikhs is not so much primacy in an ethnic group [i.e. the tribe] as primacy in a fixed place: the town itself'.[79] In other words, bonds other than tribal solidarities started to provide a source of

---

[78] S. Chutintaranond and C. Baker (eds.), *Recalling Local Pasts: Autonomous History in Southeast Asia* (Chiang Mai: Silkworm Books, 2002), pp. 171–4; R. A. O'Connor, 'A Regional Explanation of the Tai *Müang* as a City-State' in Moregns Herman Hansen (ed.), *A Comparative Study of Thirty City-State Cultures* (Copenhagen, Kongelige Danske Videnskabernes Selskab, 2000), pp. 431–44, (433–8).
[79] Lienhardt, *Shaikhdoms of Eastern Arabia*, p. 210.

social and political cohesion. For instance, the increasing reliance of the pearling industry on immigrant labour of non-tribal extraction created a rudimentary class system which started to antagonise merchants and capitalists on the one hand, and divers on the other. Similarly, the enforcement of British extraterritorial jurisdiction over British Indian subjects and foreign merchants after the issue of the Foreign Jurisdiction Acts of 1890 and 1913 (followed by the enforcement of Orders-in-Councils) created new political divisions among the urban population and empowered British agents at the expense of ruling families.[80]

Transformations which affected merchants are the most illuminating examples of how in the first two decades of the twentieth century Gulf towns became the focus of new political identities and class solidarities. As the benefits of residence increased, urban environments started to provide Gulf merchants with a source of wealth in the form of property ownership. It was the consolidation of a new class of urban landowners among the merchant classes of Manama and Kuwait which inaugurated a new type of urban politics. Merchants were no longer prone to express political dissent by relocating their business elsewhere. In Kuwait they performed their very last 'act of secession', as Jill Crystal puts it, in 1909 when they fled to Bahrain as a result of the strict fiscal policies of Mubarak al-Sabah. By 1911 they had returned to the town and started to organise themselves politically, affirming their sense of belonging to Kuwait.[81] As will be illustrated in the following chapter, the landed aristocracy of Manama also coalesced into a fairly united political force. Operating in symbiosis with the ruling family and with British political agents, they took control of the urban administration and effectively guided the development of the town on the eve of the discovery of oil.

---

[80] H. M. Al Baharna, *British Extra-Territorial Jurisdiction in the Gulf, 1913–1971* (Slough: Archive Editions, 1998), pp. 10–12, 19–20. For a general discussion of the issue of extraterritoriality and port cities before the twentieth century see R. Murphey, 'On the Evolution of the Port City' pp. 236–7.

[81] Crystal, *Oil and Politics in the Gulf*, pp. 24–5 (p. 25); Lorimer, *Gazetteer*, vol. II, p. 1058.

3 Ordering space, politics and community in Manama, 1880s–1919

Between the accession to power of Shaykh 'Isa ibn 'Ali Al Khalifah in 1869 and the establishment of municipal government in 1919, the growth of Manama reflected the evolution of Bahrain's pearling and entrepôt economies and the increasing importance of the Government of India in fostering its semi-autonomous position within the Al Khalifah domains. At the turn of the twentieth century, the urban layout revealed the relative weakness of the tribal administration and the critical role played by trade and immigration in the expansion of the previous decades. Unlike Muharraq, which developed around the residences of the Al Khalifah family, Manama did not have a clearly defined administrative and political centre. Its configuration was to a great extent the result of the spatial and demographic requirements of the maritime economy which dominated urban life. The successive waves of rural and overseas immigrants and the increasing volume of trade were matched by the development of the harbour and the markets, fostering the growth of residential districts along the seafront.[1]

While the town developed gradually throughout the nineteenth century, its political and social orders crystallised in the years of the pearl boom, particularly after the 1880s. In this period the accelerated development of the harbour, markets, neighbourhoods and religious institutions unveils the 'dynamics of power' which characterised the rise of a powerful merchant class and the contest, as well as the symbiotic relationship, between merchants and rulers on the one hand and the Al Khalifah and British agents on the other. Moreover, in the absence of a strong government, immigrants, entrepreneurs and labourers had the upper hand in the creation of new urban space and in the making of the town's socio-political orders. In this respect, three elements were crucial to the evolution of Manama as a 'city-society' in the sense suggested in the previous chapter: the accumulation of merchant capital, communal solidarities and

---

[1] I am indebted to Ahmad al-Jowder for suggestions on the socio-economic and political implications of the different spatial organisation of Manama and Muharraq.

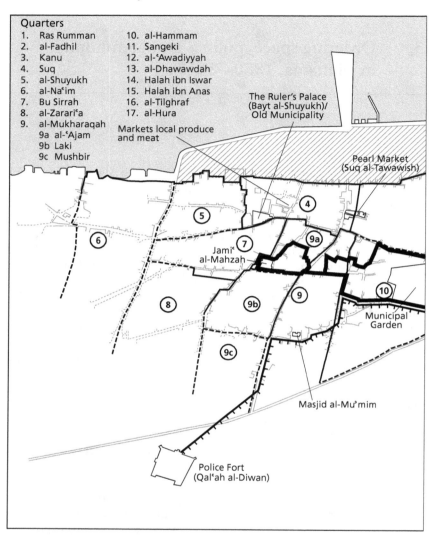

4 The town of the pearl boom: Manama, 1926

the consolidation of clientele networks which bound the population to
merchants cum community leaders. Merchant patrons financed the
development of residential areas and the provision of services for the
population, including the establishment of mosques and of buildings for
ma'tam congregations. Immigrant communities were able to develop an

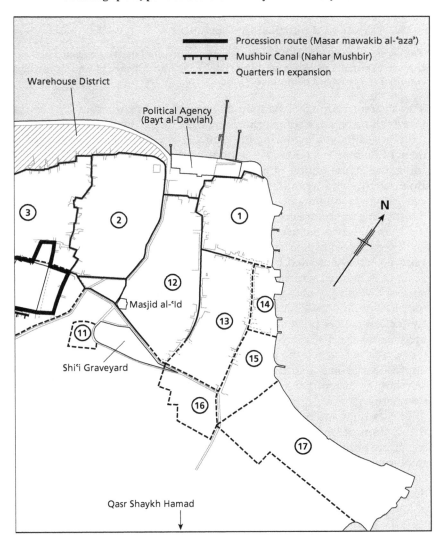

Procession route (Masar mawakib al-ʿazaʾ)

Mushbir Canal (Nahar Mushbir)

Quarters in expansion

Warehouse District

Political Agency
(Bayt al-Dawlah)

N

Masjid al-ʿId

Shiʿi Graveyard

Qasr Shaykh Hamad

ethos of cooperation and association which promoted civic values and
shared codes of morality. While this ethos dictated a modus vivendi based
upon patterns of consensus which often eluded tribal diktat, merchant
patrons as urban leaders accommodated the presence of the tribal government by acting as the intermediaries between the Al Khalifah family and
the population.

Trade and politics: the harbour

The protection of the British Government has converted the island from a scene of chronic external aggression and intestinal feud into a peaceful and flourishing centre of industry and commerce. (*Lord Curzon, 1904*)[2]

This characterisation of Bahrain as tranquil and prosperous by George Curzon is reminiscent of the charming vignette of Manama he drew some ten years earlier while touring the Gulf.[3] His typically flamboyant assessment of Bahrain's economic conditions as the newly appointed Viceroy of India evokes the notion of a 'renaissance' under the aegis of the British Empire. By the time Curzon celebrated the island's wealth, Manama's economy was dominated by pearl exports and transit trade, the latter constituting approximately one-third of the total volume of imports into the islands.[4] The picturesque sight evoked by Curzon was certainly in stark contrast with the desolate view of the shore in the mid nineteenth century, often lamented by visitors approaching the town from the sea. Huts of fishermen and sailors formed 'a coastline of filthy beaches and *barastis*' which lay alongside the customs house, a small shed with a thatched roof in 1864. The journey to the heart of the town was tortuous. As shallow waters prevented large ships from approaching the coast, all merchandise and passengers had to be transferred to small sailing boats. Once visitors reached the beach, they entered Manama through its warehouse district and markets, while cargo was either distributed to the warehouses of the merchants on the seafront, or reloaded for overseas destinations.[5]

The harbour and trade were the focal points of urban life. They shaped the division of labour of Manama's residents and structured the town's social and political hierarchies. Merchants involved in pearling, European shipping and intercoastal trade formed the commercial and political elites of early twentieth-century Manama. As part of a living chain which distributed vital overseas supplies to the urban population, the traders operating from the town's markets had far more socio-economic mobility than the artisans and farmers who tended the gardens and palm groves in the hinterland. Moreover, the immigrant and casual labourers which sustained the harbour economy were less exposed to exploitation than pearl divers, as work was organised around wages which were dependent

---

[2] Lord Curzon to Secretary of State for India, 21 April 1904, n. 85, R/15/1/330 IOR.
[3] See Chapter 2, pp. 67–8.   [4] Lorimer, *Gazetteer*, vol. II, pp. 245–6.
[5] Lorimer, *Gazetteer*, vol. I, p. 246; Belgrave, *The Pirate Coast*, p. 76; Palgrave, *Narrative of a Year's Journey*, vol. II, pp. 205, 207–8. For the earliest photographic evidence of Manama harbour see *Ayyam zaman*, pp. 16 ff.

on supply and demand. Particular professional groups were able to organise themselves in informal syndicates which protected employment. For instance, the Faramansis, a group of immigrants from the hinterland of Lingah renowned for their physical prowess and stout build, monopolised the unloading and distribution of cargo to Manama's warehouses.[6]

Besides illustrating trends which were specific to the Gulf region, the harbour economy of Manama encapsulated the tension between merchants and pre-modern states which characterised the development of many trading ports across the Indian Ocean. The absence of a class of state-affiliated merchants was testimony to the inability on the part of the Al Khalifah family to impose monopolies on the marketing of pearls. Shaykh 'Isa did not draw direct income from the industry as pearl exports were not subject to customs duties or taxation. The limited control he exercised over the customs revenue was a measure of his restricted capacity to take advantage of Manama's entrepôt trade and to negotiate alliances with local merchants. Indeed, it was largely receipts from trade that determined his ability to consolidate tribal government inside the town. In fact, the customs house (*al-gumruk*) was the lynchpin of tribal government in Manama, a position which was tellingly summed up by its popular name *Dar al-Hukumah*, the term used for the tribal administration of Muharraq.

Evidence of customs collection in the first half of the nineteenth century is sporadic. Although Khalifah ibn Salman (r. 1825–34) imposed a 5 per cent duty on imports from India, the Persian coast, Basra and Muscat, we can assume that customs fees were collected at very irregular intervals as his attempts at levying regular customs failed in 1832. By 1845 the ruling family did not derive any income from imports or exports.[7] Under Shaykh 'Isa a regular system of collections started to emerge after 1869, but he controlled the flow of commodities into Bahrain by proxy by farming out essential services to local contractors. The system relied on the payment of cash advances to the ruler, a practice which explains his close dependence on the foreign merchants and their growing influence towards the end of the century. The building of a warehouse around 1860 by Ahmad ibn 'Ali, 'Isa's brother, anticipated the organisation of the customs administration in the second half of the nineteenth century. When Ahmad died in 1888, Shaykh 'Isa started to farm out the collection of customs to Indian

---

[6] 'Note on the Persian Communities at Bahrain', 4 November 1929, in Political Agent Bahrain to Political Resident Bushehr, L/P&S/10/1045 IOR; interview with Tayyebah Hoodi, Manama, 21 March 2004.

[7] Brucks, 'Memoir Descriptive of the Navigation of the Gulf' (1829–35), fiche 1096, p. 566, V 23/217 IOR; Kemball, 'Memoranda on the Resources, Localities, and Relations' (1845), fiche 1090–1, p. 105, V 23/217 IOR.

merchants, while the Al Khalifah *'amarah* (warehouse) came under the separate management of a tax-farmer who was directly responsible to the ruler.[8]

As the harbour was the only fiscal barrier separating Manama from its maritime foreland, the consolidation of the customs administration reflected the trade boom of the late nineteenth century. Between 1888 and 1898 alone the volume of trade increased by more than 40 per cent and the value of pearl exports grew more than twofold. Foreign trade engaged increasing numbers of merchants, labourers and native vessels as a result of growing European economic penetration in the Gulf. In 1903 the British agency asked Grey Mackenzie, the firm which represented the British India Steam Navigation Company in Bahrain, to grant a large interest-free loan to the harbour's contractors for the purchase of additional craft. The contractors complained that most lighters neglected their duties, preferring to trade directly with the mainland, a practice which had become increasingly lucrative as a result of the circulation of European goods. Boat building had expanded accordingly, and the extent of the importance of this industry in the local market can be gauged by the wages of skilled labourers, which had doubled in comparison with previous years.[9]

Increased wealth coupled with the growing influence of the British agency fuelled economic and political competition. Shaykh 'Isa refused any interference in the management of Manama's rudimentary port facilities on the part of European firms, as he considered it a violation of his personal monopoly over the harbour. At the same time, the ruler of Bahrain could not make use of growing receipts from trade to consolidate his authority. As the Government of India had successfully imposed his son Hamad as heir apparent in 1900 in order to ensure a smooth succession, Shaykh 'Isa was forced to distribute large amounts of cash, lavish gifts and land grants to assuage the sensitivities of Shaykh 'Ali, the Al Khalifah governor of Manama, and of his tribal allies. Unable to extract revenue from the town's markets which were under 'Ali's control, Shaykh 'Isa raised the duty on the export of oysters, mussels and of mother-of-pearl shells in an attempt to pocket the surplus directly, bypassing the authority of the syndicate of Indian merchants. The Banyan responded swiftly, and the ruler was eventually forced to farm out the additional

[8] Assistant Political Agent Bahrain to Political Resident Bushehr, 19 December 1903, n. 277, 26 March 1904, n. 76, R/15/2/49 IOR. Lorimer, *Gazetteer*, vol. I, p. 928.
[9] Lorimer, *Gazetteer*, vol. I, pp. 298–312, 938, 2552; Political Agent Bahrain to Grey Mackenzie, 6 May 1903, n. 77 of 1903, R/15/2/49 IOR; 'Administration Report on the Persian Gulf Political Residency and Maskat Political Agency for 1903–1904' in *The Persian Gulf Administration Reports 1873–1949*, vol. V, pp. 60–1.

1 per cent to their leader Gungaram ibn Tika.[10] By 1904 the prestige of Shaykh 'Isa in Manama was 'at a very low ebb' according to Lorimer, and rumours were even circulating of impending hostilities as a result of the renewed factionalism within the Al Khalifah family.[11]

In the general climate of distrust and uncertainty which characterised the period before and after the appointment of Shaykh Hamad as heir apparent, foreign merchants were able to profit extensively from contracts. Sometime before 1908, a group of entrepreneurs from the Ahwaz district in Iran took over the harbour, replacing 'Abd al-Nabi Kazeruni, the former Persian landing contractor (*hammal bashi*) and keeper of Shaykh 'Isa's warehouse in Manama. Despite the considerable sums paid to the ruler in advance by the syndicate of Indian merchants which controlled the customs, only two-fifths of the revenue collected by them was pocketed by Shaykh 'Isa between 1895 and 1899. Although contracts were stipulated to run over a three-year period, the syndicate started to buy new leases two years in advance by the early 1890s, partly out of fear of losing the business and partly prompted by Shaykh 'Isa's demands for ready cash.[12]

The mid 1890s also marked a palpable shift in British policy as imperial concerns for the protection of trade started to be directed towards the management of the customs house. In 1899, the Political Resident M. J. Meade visited Bahrain to discuss the employment of a customs official from the Indian civil service. As Shaykh 'Isa had already signed a new contract with the Indian syndicate for a further two years starting in March 1902, the residency swiftly withdrew its support from the Indian tax-farmers as 'the continued possession of the customs contract by the Banias is not to the advance [*sic*] of British interests in Bahrain'.[13] Besides paralleling the recognition of Shaykh Hamad as heir apparent, plans for customs reform resulted in the posting of an assistant political agent to Manama in 1900 who replaced the native agent. Moreover, the upgrading of the British representative to political agent in 1904 coincided with yet another refusal by Shaykh 'Isa to bow to British pressure for

---

[10] R/15/1/315 IOR: Declaration by Shaykh 'Isa ibn 'Ali Al Khalifah, Jumada al-Ula 1314/ October 1897; Native Agent Bahrain to Political Resident Bushehr, 19 Muharram 1318/ 29 May 1899; Native Agent Bahrain to Political Resident Bushehr, 2 and 27 August 1898.

[11] Lorimer, *Gazetteer*, vol. I, pp. 928 ff. and 2552.

[12] R/15/1/315 IOR: Note by Assistant Political Resident Bushehr, 27 May 1899; Customs Agreement, 5 Jumada al-Thaniyyah 1315; memo by Assistant Political Agent Bahrain, 23 December 1899; correspondence Political Resident Bushehr to Government of India, 8 January 1800, n. 3 of 1900. Assistant Political Agent Bahrain to Tax-Farmers, 31 October 1904, n. 251, R/15/1/330 IOR.

[13] Confidential correspondence from Political Resident Bushehr to Calcutta, 8 January 1900, n. 3 of 1900, R/15/1/315 IOR.

customs reform.[14] It was only when military operations began in Iraq in 1914 that the residency of Bushehr was forced to adopt a more lenient stance in customs matters, and sought to gain influence by appointing locally based clerks who could monitor receipts on behalf of the Bahrain's agency.[15]

New patterns of commercial arbitration contributed to undermine further the position of Shaykh 'Isa in Manama where the settlement of trade disputes had enormous political implications. With the de facto imposition of British extraterritorial jurisdiction in 1861, following the treaty negotiated by the Indian authorities with the then ruler Shaykh Muhammad ibn Khalifah, an informal court was established in the native agency which catered for foreigners as protected subjects. Moreover, the native agent started to attend the sessions of the *Majlis al-'Urf*, the indigenous commercial council presided over by the ruler of Bahrain, in order to protect the interests of Manama's foreign merchants. British influence in the *Majlis al-'Urf* became more consistent as foreign trade grew exponentially by the end of the century, and peaked after 1919, when half of its members started to be nominated directly by the agency.[16]

Yet the granting of British protection in nineteenth-century Manama was neither straightforward nor necessarily directly beneficial to imperial interests. The boundaries of jurisdiction of the *Majlis al-'Urf*, Manama's indigenous commercial council, and of the court convened in the native agency were blurred. Until 1900 the official duties of native agents were often overshadowed by their personal interests as merchants, as well as by their relations with the rulers. Moreover, as Bahrain was in a far corner of the British Empire, procedures took a while to become established, even in the case of the Indians, who in theory were the privileged recipients of British protection. A group of Hindu traders claimed this entitlement as early as 1843, but it was not until the 1870s that the majority of Manama's Banyan could produce certificates of British nationality. After 1853, for instance, the Indian authorities even discontinued the issue of these certificates in Bahrain, fearing to fuel dissent among the members of the

---

[14] R/15/1/315 IOR: Notes by Assistant Political Resident Bushehr, 27 May 1899; customs agreement, 5 Jumada al-Thaniyyah 1315/31 October 1897; memo by Assistant Political Agent Bahrain, 23 December 1899; Political Resident Bushehr to Government of India, 8 January 1800, n. 3 of 1900. Assistant Political Agent to Tax-Farmers, 31 October 1904, n. 251, R/15/1/330 IOR. Political Resident Bushehr to Secretary to the Government of India, 4 June 1914, n. 1693, R/15/1/331 IOR.

[15] Political Resident Bushehr to Secretary to the Government of India, 4 June 1914, n. 1693, R/15/1/331 IOR.

[16] Onley, *The Arabian Frontier of the British Raj*, pp. 119–27; M. A. al-Tajir, *Bahrain 1920–1945: Britain, The Shaikh and the Administration* (London: Croom Helm, 1987), pp. 22–6. The dissolution of the *Majlis al-'Urf* in 1917–18 is discussed extensively in R/15/2/12 IOR.

Al Khalifah family who competed with the native agent for the protection of the town's Indian mercantile community.[17]

Uncertainty as to who was entitled to British protection persisted after the appointment of a British assistant political agent in 1900, as the concept of 'foreigner' continued to spark fierce controversy. Even cases involving European merchants, whose interests were championed by the agency as an extension of its concern for British trade, produced no clear-cut guidelines. In 1908 Messrs Wonckhaus & Co., a German firm based in Bahrain which represented the Hamburg–America Steamship Line, lodged a complaint with the Bushehr residency against the landing contractors of Manama's harbour. The company maintained that the contractors had not sent sufficient lighters to one of their steamers and that only a fraction of the goods destined for Manama reached the shore, thus causing considerable financial loss. When the case was referred to India the company was eventually informed that the Government was in no position to uphold the claim.[18]

Besides integrating merchants and rulers into the 'inner' circle of British informal empire, British protection and the trade boom of the late nineteenth century transformed the landscape of Manama's water-front in ways which suggest the progressive empowerment of the town's merchant classes. By 1904 local merchants had built a new district with separate landing facilities whose warehouses and offices towered over the seafront. Lorimer noted that the new district offered the best accommodation in town, although the Native Agent Muhammad Rahim complained in 1898 that the new quays were built precariously and boats were often crushed before they could land their cargo.[19] The outbreak of World War I, which caused great economic hardship throughout the region, forced Shaykh 'Isa to resort to merchant capital in order to rescue the town from famine. In 1917, as no commercial steamers had called at the harbour for several months and the prices of basic commodities were soaring in the central markets, he solicited a subscription for the construction of a pier to facilitate the arrival and entry of goods into Bahrain.[20]

---

[17] R/15/1/138 IOR: Political Resident Bushehr to Government of India, 10 February 1853, n. 56, 5 and 6 September 1853, n. 247; Native Agent Bahrain to Political Resident Bushehr, 16 May 1853.

[18] Registers n. 1354 and 1153 with enclosures, L/P&S/10/83 IOR.

[19] BA: Taqrir al-bai' (sale registration), 4 Rajab 1316/18 November 1898, 26 Jumada al-Thaniyyah 1315/21 November 1897 and 16 Ramadan 1341/3 May 1923; waraqah al-hibah (certificate of royal donation), Jumada al-Ula 1315/September–October 1897. Lorimer, *Gazetteer*, vol. II, p. 1159; Cursetjee, *The Land of the Date*, p. 93.

[20] Subscribers also included the leaders of the most influential pearling tribes of Muharraq such as Shahin ibn Saqar Al Jalahimah, 'Ali ibn Ibrahim al-Zayyani, Ahmad ibn Jasim ibn Jawdar and Salman ibn Husayn al-Matar. R/15/2/49 IOR: Agreement dated 5 Safar 1335/

This project, which sealed a new partnership between the merchants and Shaykh 'Isa, laid the foundation for the development of modern port facilities in the following decades. The increasing visibility of Bahrain on the map of the Government of India was only temporarily obfuscated by the outbreak of the war. The end of the hostilities marked a new phase of British imperial expansion which consolidated the political and commercial role of Manama as the lynchpin of British imperial influence in the Persian Gulf.

The markets

The organisation of trade in the inner city reflected the function of the harbour as a gateway to faraway regions which gathered supplies for the urban population beyond the town's immediate agricultural hinterland. Only a very few items apart from agricultural produce reached the shops of Manama from the villages: palm mats and baskets, sails and some types of earthenware, particularly from the village of al-'Ali which had a long tradition of pottery making.[21] Regardless of status, occupation and wealth, the average urban dweller relied heavily on overseas imports, as suggested by a list compiled by the British agency in 1903: rice, wheat, meat, coffee, tea, sugar, soap, candles, matches, pottery, glassware, charcoal, firewood, spices, cotton, wool and silk. If compared with the first available trade statistics on Bahrain collected by Captain Brucks of the Royal Navy in 1826, the 1903 list suggests that new patterns of consumption had emerged as a result of increased wealth among the upper classes.[22] Yet the majority of commodities still came from overseas. In the late nineteenth century, for instance, some villages started to produce garments as a result of the availability of cotton cloth from India, but most clothing continued to be imported in accordance with the requirements and dressing styles of the town's communities. Foodstuffs continued to be the largest item of imports, particularly rice, which was the most important item in the local diet. Moreover, the large numbers of shops reported by the Persian traveller Muhammad Ibrahim Kazeruni in 1836 and by Lorimer in 1904 (400 and 450, respectively) cannot be explained by the demands of the urban population alone but also by the requirements of

1 December 1916 in Shaykh 'Isa to Political Agent, 7 Safar 1335/3 December 1916. R/15/2/958 IOR: Shaykh 'Isa to Political Agent, 12 Ramadan 1334/13 July 1916 and 18 Rajab 1335/ 10 May 1917; petition, 13 Rajab 1335/5 May 1917.

[21] For village production in Bahrain see Lorimer, *Gazetteer*, vol. II, p. 245. Tajir, *'Aqd al-lal*, pp. 28–42; Brucks, 'Memoir Descriptive of the Navigation of the Gulf' (1829–35), fiche 1096, pp. 568–9, V 23/217 IOR.

[22] 'Schedule of the Proposed Wharfage Dues to Be Levied on All Goods' in Assistant Political Agent Bahrain to Political Resident Bushehr, 3 May 1903, n. 74, R/15/2/49 IOR.

the surrounding hamlets and tribal settlements which were provisioned from Manama.[23]

As large sections of the markets sold overseas merchandise, wholesale merchants with foreign connections enjoyed paramount social and political influence. Rice, cotton and coffee reached Manama's warehouses mainly from India, wheat from Iran, India and southern Iraq, and meat and cattle from Muscat, al-Qatif, southern Iraq and Iran. The dependence of Manama's economy on imports was a double-edged sword for the majority of the town's trading communities. Under Shaykh 'Isa fiscal arrangements favoured entrepreneurs with overseas connections and shopkeepers dealing with foreign commodities. Goods were taxed only at the point of entry in Bahrain and were not subject to systematic taxation once they reached the markets of the inner city. Yet merchants could be badly affected by the fluctuation of the regional and international markets as retail prices followed basic rules of supply and demand. By the early twentieth century, for instance, the prices of some goods imported from India such as cotton cloth increased considerably as a result of the stiff competition of British monopolies which forced some local entrepreneurs to abandon the trade or to become attached to British firms.

Moreover, the fortunes of the pearling season, which determined the spending power of groups partaking in the diving chain (divers, boat captains, middlemen and financiers), were also crucial to securing the business turnover of Manama's wholesalers and retailers. The livelihood of the pearl divers was always on the line as they depended almost exclusively on advances, although some of them supplemented their income with fishing and trade in oyster shells.[24] The period 1902–4 aptly illustrates the economic cycle which bound the prosperity of traders to the circulation and availability of commodities on the one hand, and to the pearling industry on the other. In 1902 and 1903 divers were able to make up most of the advances they had received at the beginning of the season, but pearl dealers faced considerable losses on exports as a result of low prices in Bombay and Europe. Good returns for the lower echelons of the industry stimulated consumption and consequently rice imports, and by the end of 1903 the town's supplies were fairly low. The following year the large stock of unsold pearls started to affect the divers' margin of

---

[23] The large number of shops reported by Kazeruni in 1836 in comparison with the figure proposed by Lorimer confirms that the former's description of Manama is generally hyperbolic. Kazeruni, *Athar*, pp. 881 ff.; Lorimer, *Gazetteer*, vol. II, p. 1162.

[24] See for instance documents of purchase of oyster shells by 'Abd al-Nabi Bushehri and 'Ali Kazim Bushehri between 1908 and 1910. In this period the two Persian merchants carried out some twenty-five transactions for a total of 1,915 sacks of shells purchased from divers residing in al-Diraz, Karranah, Ras Rumman, Bani Jamrah, al-Budayya' and Sitrah, BA.

profit, and consequently their ability to purchase food in the market. Large quantities of rice remained unsold, partly also as a result of an outbreak of cholera which killed 5,000 people across the islands between May and September 1904.[25]

Mapping the marketplace

The scarcity of both written documentation and systematic statistics makes it extremely difficult to trace the development of Manama's economy throughout the nineteenth century in any detail. The morphology and social texture of the marketplace can be reconstructed in broad outline on the basis of some archaeological and documentary evidence, surveys undertaken by the government of Bahrain after the 1920s, oral histories and land records dating from the 1880s.[26] The layout of the markets and local tradition tell a complex story of the development of multiple spaces of commercial exchange which articulated the symbiosis between the rural and maritime economies of Bahrain on the one hand, and local industries and long-distance trade on the other. Although the precise phases of this development are open to speculation, it seems that the growth of specialised suqs around the harbour marked the transition from the warehouse/entrepôt camp which had characterised the waterfront in earlier periods to the town of the pearl boom.

The oldest commercial complex developed under the aegis of the pearl industry. In the years of the pearl boom Suq al-Tawawish (the Pearl Market), the most prestigious commercial area of the town, was connected to the harbour by a covered market (Suq al-Musaqqaf), a long and narrow lane of shops built on reclaimed land. al-Tawawish was the base of the rich pearl dealers of Bahrain who conducted their complex financial operations from large shops including a reception room for clients (*majlis*), and small workshops for the cleaning and piercing of pearls. The job of *tawwash* (pl. *tawawish*, pearl dealer) was not only that of retailer but was often closely linked to pearl production. A *tawwash* could own boats, finance pearling expeditions, or simply buy the catch

---

[25] 'Administration Report on the Persian Gulf Political Residency and Maskat Political Agency for 1902–1903, 1903–1904, 1904–1905' in *The Persian Gulf Administration Reports 1873–1949*, vol. V, pp. 35, 60–1, 150–1.

[26] I am indebted to 'Ali Akbar Bushehri for his invaluable help in supplying documentation and archaeological evidence, and for the mapping of Manama's old market area. Maps 'Manamah City', April 1926, and 'Manamah – Plan of Port and Town', January 1933 in *Historic Maps of Bahrain, 1817–1970*, ed. by R. L. Jarman, 3 vols. (Gerrards Cross: Archive Editions, 1996), maps n. 29 and 30; 'Map of Manamah', Bombay Survey Department, 1946, BA.

directly from the pearl banks. Unlike in Muharraq, where the trade was exclusively in the hands of Sunnis of tribal origin, Manama's *al-tawawish* included members of Baharna families such as the al-Mudayfa', al-'Urayyad and Ibn Rajab which specialised exclusively in this trade, and the Hawala al-Wazzans and the al-Qusaybis from Najd, who were also import–export general merchants. The Baharna *tawawish* embodied the indigenous seafaring tradition of Manama, and were able to establish highly successful family businesses.[27]

Patterns of exchange and distribution of commodities to the population supported the formation of the two market blocs which dominated the town in the late nineteenth century. The first and the largest commercial complex gravitated around the import economy and local crafts. The second, which grew alongside it, specialised in agricultural produce and developed as an appendix of the rural estates controlled by the Al Khalifah.

Suqs trading in imported goods were sustained by immigrants, and their development is an indication of the consolidation of commercial links between the wealthy import merchants who owned the large *al-'amarat* on the seafront and regional and international ports. The mention of Suq al-'Ajam and Suq al-Garashi (the Persian and Garashi markets, the latter a village in the hinterland of Lingah) in local records dating between 1860 and 1872 suggests the consolidation of a group of influential Persian food dealers who displaced their Indian counterparts, the community which had monopolised much of the trade in foodstuffs in previous decades.[28] The small Jewish suq (Suq al-Yahud), mentioned for the first time around 1890, emerged as an integral part of Manama's expanding financial sector, facilitating money transfers for export merchants to India or Europe and supporting a lucrative pilgrimage business in the form of loans granted to Muslim pilgrims en route to Mecca, Karbala and Najaf.[29]

As was the case in many pre-modern port settlements, the marketplace fostered the social unity of immigrants from particular villages, towns and regions. Traditional skills, crafts and family connections were activated to suit the needs of the population and harmonised with the requirements of the harbour economy. Social advancement and professional mobility among the rank-and-file of the labour force employed in the markets

---

[27] Interview with Ibrahim Uthman, Manama, 14 June 1998; Rashid al-Zayyani, *al-Ghaws wa al-tawwashah* (Manama: Nashr al-Ayyam, 1998), p. 121; Sayf, *al-Ma'tam*, vol. I, pp. 103 ff.

[28] 'Ali Akbar Bushehri, 'al-Manamah al-qadimah: dhakaraha al-Burtughaliyyun wa al-'Uthmaniyyun', *Banurama al-Khalij*, July 1991.

[29] 'al-Yahud bayna al-Bahrayn', *al-Mar'at al-Yawm*, 9 July 2002; 'Ali A. Bushehri, 'The Jews of Bahrain', typescript, 5 pages, December 2003.

were generally confined within an individual's community. A specific profession or trade continued to identify the popular classes over time, as suggested by the names of old suqs which indicated specialisation or ethnic origin. Manama's richer households were supplied with cushions and mattresses from Suq al-Naddafah, which gathered together wool carders from Bastak in southern Iran. Sellers of dry nuts and fruit, sweets, rice and cooking oil from the village of Garash were based in Suq al-Garashi. Textile dealers, mostly Indians linked to wholesalers or Baharna, were based in Suq al-Aqmisha. By 1891 sweet makers, mostly Baharna and Persian Shi'is, had their own market in Suq al-Halwa. Baharna of rural extraction formed the artisan class which was identified with the various specialised suqs, although their workshops could move from one warehouse to another.[30]

The outlook of the markets selling local produce contrasted with those of their counterparts across the town. As shopkeepers were exclusively Baharna who had retained strong village connections, they were the least affected by overseas immigration and by the fluctuations in international trade. Located at the western extremity of the import markets, these commercial areas represented the terminus of the axis of transport which linked Manama to the agricultural belt lying to the west and north-west of the town. Their stalls were stocked with produce from the estates controlled by the Al Khalifah, particularly fruit, vegetables, fish and water. There are no statistics on the supplies which reached Manama from the villages but the open landscape of some of these market areas suggests that peasants could sell their produce in makeshift stalls, often independently of their tribal overlords. Ibrahim Kazeruni reported in 1836 that villagers flocked to this end of the bazaar every Friday and that many of them aspired to establish a business in the town.[31]

Attitudes towards professional specialisation and trade reinforced the social and cultural cleavages between tribal and non-tribal residents. Individuals of tribal descent expressed their feeling of superiority vis-à-vis the shopkeeper and artisan population by displaying their attachment to strong moral codes stemming from religious and social diktats. Arabs who maintained connections with the Arabian Peninsula did not deal in tobacco as a result of the ban on smoking imposed by Wahhabism. Tribesmen looked down on any occupation outside the traditional remit of pearling, particularly the sale of foodstuffs, which was in the hands of Persians and Indians. For their part, Persians and Indians tended to look

---

[30] Transcripts of interview with 'Abbas Qannati (b. 1913), 8 December 1990, by 'Ali Akbar Bushehri; Sayf, al-Ma'tam, vol. I, pp. 136–7.
[31] Kazeruni, Athar, pp. 880 ff.; Lorimer, Gazetteer, vol. II, p. 246.

down upon the Bahrana artisans and retailers employed in the markets selling local produce given their position of subordination to the Al Khalifah.

Merchants and rulers: coercion, taxation and the politics of real estate

Affected far less conspicuously than the harbour by the growing influence of the Government of India, the markets continued to be the showcase of the 'indigenous' political economy of Manama. The growing prosperity of the town after the 1880s created a closer association between the Al Khalifah and its merchants, and contributed to the consolidation of the latter as tax-farmers and landowners.

Anecdotal evidence confirms that the position of the Al Khalifah in the inner city was defined by the exercise of customary rights in the markets. For Manama's shopkeeper population the practice of imposing sporadic collections in specie and in kind (*al-sukhrah*) constituted the reality of tribal government, and informed their perception of the rulers. Like *al-khuwwah*, the brotherhood tax collected by tribesmen in the hinterlands of the Arabian Peninsula, *al-sukhrah* bound residents to their masters in a relationship of protector and protégé which epitomised the exercise of tribal power. Narratives of *al-sukhrah* in Manama are closely intertwined with the violence, coercion and abuse of authority perpetrated by *al-fidawwiyyah*, the armed retainers of the Al Khalifah. The following account was related to Charles Belgrave, the British advisor to the ruler of Bahrain, in 1932, long after the practice was abolished:

In those days if any of the Shaikhs' hangers on [*al-fidawiyyah*] saw anything in the bazaar that they liked the looks of they just took it and paid a modicum of the price saying it was for the Shaikhs. A woman had nothing but a few chickens and the fidawis came to her and demanded some payment to the Shaikhs. She said she had nothing so he [*sic*] took half of her chickens. If a man had any money he never built a good house as if he did the Shaikhs would say he was rich and would demand money from him. The rich men always dressed in old clothes as well in order to hide the fact that they possessed anything.[32]

Although *al-sukhrah* was a curse for rich and poor, it affected the most vulnerable segments of the population, primarily Baharna shopkeepers and artisans based in the local markets. The political, economic and symbolic importance of the imposition of *al-sukhrah* in these markets can hardly be overestimated. Before 1900, they became the theatre of

---

[32] Belgrave Diaries, 29 March 1932, AWDU.

the contest between Shaykh 'Isa and Shaykh 'Ali, the Al Khalifah governor
of Manama, as each routinely sent their retainers to enforce collections.
Further evidence of the crucial position of these suqs in the political
economy of tribal government is the transfer of the fruit and vegetable
markets from Shaykh 'Ali to Shaykh Hamad (Isa's son and designated
successor), after British intervention established the principle of succession by primogeniture in 1900. In 1912, Shaykh 'Isa also donated the
meat market to Shaykh Salman, Hamad's own designated successor who
was still an infant, in order to ensure for him a future power base in
Manama.[33]

After the 1880s, however, a new system of tax collection started to be
enforced in the local markets in parallel with the reorganisation of the
customs administration in the harbour. While the imposition of *al-sukhrah*
continued to plague retailers, Shaykh 'Isa became increasingly reliant
on the cooperation of appointed tax-farmers and brokers (*al-dallalun*)
who pocketed fees on sales. In the eyes of traders, there continued to be
a fine line between the collection of brokerage fees and the imposition of
al-sukhrah, as many brokers continued to be recruited from the rank-and-
file of *al-fidawiyyah*. Yet the most influential tax-farmers were Shi'i entrepreneurs who were able to capitalise on the social connections and strong
sectarian loyalties which bound the shopkeeper population together.[34]
In their new capacity as tax-farmers these entrepreneurs were also able
to diversify their portfolios by organising tenancies and providing for the
upkeep and repair of shops. The activities of 'Abd al-Nabi Bushehri,
a Persian merchant, provide an insight into the scale of the business.
From 1904 he controlled part of the fruit and vegetable markets on behalf
of Shaykh Hamad, the heir apparent, and managed a large number of
rented properties which included warehouses, coffee shops and open
areas used by itinerant traders.[35] Shi'i merchants also came to control
the markets selling meat and wood for domestic consumption, the only
two items of import monopolised by Shaykh 'Isa. At least until 1920
Ahmad ibn Sallum, a Baharna landowner, and Abu Qasim Shirazi, a
Persian wholesaler specialising in foodstuffs, acted as tax-farmers and brokers
on the sale of meat and sheep skins. From 1910 Ahmad ibn Sallum controlled Manama's meat market almost single-handedly. Besides being

[33] File n. 53, IT; waraqah al-iltizam (tax-farming contract), Rabi' al-Awwali 1347/August–
September 1928, BA; waraqah al-hibah (certificate of royal donation) from Shaykh 'Isa,
Jumada al-Thaniyyah 1330/May–June 1912, R/15/2/806 IOR.
[34] Secretary Municipality of Manama to Political Agent Bahrain, 19 Rabi' al-Thani 1351/22
August 1932, 15/2/1921 IOR.
[35] Waraqah al-iltizam (tax-farming contract), Rabi' al-Awwali 1347/August–September
1928 and Muharram 1323/March–April 1905, BA.

economically rewarding, association with the meat trade brought him social prestige and a large following among the population, particularly during Ramadan when the ruler ordered the distribution of meat to the poor.[36]

Access to market properties became a sign of the growing political importance of the merchant class in general, and of those tax-farmers who served the tribal administration in particular. The acquisition of shops and warehouses gathered momentum in the early twentieth century when tax-farmers were able to capitalise on Shaykh 'Isa's incessant shortages of cash. Although there is evidence of sales conducted through the shariah court, market properties continued to be exchanged according to customary practice. Shaykh 'Isa could not alienate land through sale, as it was part of his estate which he distributed routinely to family members. Instead, he granted personal donations (*al-hibah*) to merchants and circumvented tribal custom by receiving cash. Merchants generally favoured this agreement as a guarantee of repayment against their fear of future confiscation. Tax-farmers, in particular, used their position to develop their own properties. After 1899 Ahmad ibn Sallum entered into a partnership with the contractor of the Shaykh's *'amarah*, 'Abd al-Nabi Kazeruni, to develop an exclusive cluster of shops near the harbour. Abu Qasim Shirazi, Shaykh 'Isa's meat contractor, acquired large sections of the wood market, as suggested by the sale of these properties between 1925 and 1928.[37]

The rise of a new class of Shi'i landholders, however, did not radically transform patterns of ownership of real estate in both import and local markets. The majority of properties continued to be under the control of Al Khalifah and of key Sunni allies as family endowments (*awqaf dhurriyah*). By the 1890s at least two-thirds of the properties in Suq al-'Ajam were in the hands of Hawala merchants; the Baharna retailers who sold herbs, opium and spices in Suq al-'Attarah were also paying rent to Hawala landlords. The control of market properties partly explains the paramount economic position enjoyed by the Hawala in the early Al Khalifah period. The mosaic of partners in inheritance displayed by some of these properties suggests that the community was able to maintain its position over time through a tight web of marriage alliances, which allowed many households to have a share in the control of endowments.

---

[36] Waraqah al-hibah (certificate of royal donation) from Shaykh 'Isa, Jumada al-Thaniyyah 1330/May–June 1912, R/15/2/806 IOR.

[37] File n. 53, IT; taqrir al-bai' (sale registration), 26 Jumada al-Thaniyyah 1315/21 November 1897, 29 Rajab 1326/27 August 1908 and 9 Jumada al-Thaniyyah 1326/8 July 1908, BA.

Even a trader of modest means such as Ahmad ibn 'Abd al-Rahman al-Sahhaf, who died around 1915, owned his own shop and was related to the most powerful Hawala families of Manama (including Kanu, al-Mutawwa' and al-Mahmid) through numerous marriages.[38]

The Sunni court presided over by the qadi Qasim al-Mahzah was also a key player in the politics of real estate of early twentieth-century Manama. During his long tenure of office the judge, who supervised *awqaf* properties and acted as the official *muhtasib* (market regulator according to Islamic law), was instrumental in protecting the land regime and the interests of the Al Khalifah. As the milk brother of the ruler, he also came to enjoy the rights and privileges of the royal household and became the largest owner of property in central Manama after Shaykh 'Isa. Examples of real estate turned to public use also suggest that Sunnis continued to have privileged access to the markets. Unlike in the residential districts of Manama, Shi'i merchants were unable to establish religious or community institutions. The mosques, for instance, were strictly supported by endowments under *awqaf al-sunnah* the largest was built by 'Abd al-'Aziz Lutf 'Ali Khunji, a rich Persian merchant from Lingah, between 1910 and 1912.[39]

Urban quarters

Multiple traditions of settlement supported the unregulated and often random growth of Manama, whose harbour economy sustained the expansion of its population from an estimated 8,000 inhabitants in the early 1860s to approximately 25,000 in 1904. Earlier accounts concentrate on the harbour and the central markets, and make only occasional references to the residential districts. In 1862, Palgrave reported an impoverished town whose landscape was dominated by *barasti*s with only a few dilapidated stone buildings.[40] At the turn of the century Lorimer described Manama as 'damp, squalid and depressing ... the habitations in the outskirts are for the most part huts with sloping roofs standing in courtyards surrounded by hurdles of upright date fronds.' The

---

[38] File n. 49, IT; Bushehri, 'al-Manamah al-qadimah'.

[39] Tasjil Idarah al-Tabu (land registration document) n. 288/367 of 1345 (1926–7), BA. *I'lanat Tabu al-Bahrayn*, I'lan n. 303 of 1360, April 1941, Da'irah al-Shu'un al-Qanuniyyah (Directorate of Legal Affairs, hereafter DSQ). al-Nabhani, *al-Tuhfah al-Nabhaniyyah*, p. 46. After 1883 the oldest mosque on record, Muhammad ibn Jum'an, was partly supported by the properties of the Bashmi family, the largest rice importers of Manama. Wasiyyah waqf ahli (family waqf will), Safar 1293/February–March 1876; waqfiyyah (certificate of endowment), Rabi' al-Awwali 1300/January–February 1883, BA; interview with Ibrahim Bashmi, Manama, 18 March 2004.

[40] Palgrave, *Narrative of a Year's Journey*, vol. II, pp. 208–9.

ephemeral nature of Manama's built environment, in stark contrast with the majesty of some of the provincial capitals of the Ottoman Middle East and of British India, prompted visitors to assume a state of decadence. Yet what seemed a chaotic and unregulated layout concealed a deep-seated urban order: Lorimer reported the existence of fourteen neighbourhoods, from the oldest residential areas of eastern Manama on the seafront, to the popular quarters south and west of the harbour whose expansion accounted for much of the town's growth in the second half of the nineteenth century.[41]

The landscape and social organisation of Manama's neighbourhoods reflected the multiple modes of community implantation in the town by agriculturalists, tribesmen and overseas immigrants. Important elements of the village tradition of Safavid Bahrain resurfaced in the popular neighbourhoods of Manama. Rural migration cannot be quantified in the absence of census statistics, but the family histories of Baharna émigrés suggest that, throughout the nineteenth century, settlement in the town offered an opportunity to escape the exploitative system of the tribal estates. Urban residents had an ambivalent relationship with villagers. People with no rural pedigree were disdained in the predominantly Shi'i neighbourhoods of Manama where association with the old families of al-Diraz, Jidd Hafs and Bilad al-Qadim brought social and political influence. At the same time villagers were looked down upon as *al-hala'il*, a term which mocked their condition of servitude.[42]

Archaeological evidence suggests that changing patterns of land use around the Mushbir canal, the most important water supply around the harbour, account for the formation of the Shi'i popular neighbourhoods of Manama. The Mushbir canal featured prominently in the folk tales which surrounded the creation of the al-Hammam district, originally a large agricultural hamlet, and of the establishment of two of the oldest religious institutions of the town: the Jami' al-Mu'min, mentioned for the first time in 1738, and Ma'tam Bin Aman, a building for the celebration of *'ashura'* established at the turn of the nineteenth century.[43] Mushbir was also part of the epic which surrounded the Al Khalifah occupation of Bahrain as the

---

[41] Lorimer, *Gazetteer*, vol. II, pp. 1159–61 (p. 1159); *The Gulf Pilot* by C. G. Constable and A. W. Stiff (London: Hydrographic Office, 1864), p. 112.

[42] See Sayf, *al-Ma'tam*, vol. I, for family histories; Kazeruni, *Athar*, pp. 880 ff.; interview with 'Abdallah Sayf, Manama, 20 March 2004. Although the etymology of *hala'il* is contested, it seems that the term is the plural of *halali* (my property) used by the Al Khalifah to lay claims of ownership over the villages. Interview with Muhammad Jabar al-Ansari, Manama, 8 June 1998.

[43] Interview with Shaykh 'Abdallah ibn Khalid Al Khalifah, Manama, 15 June 1998; al-'Urayyad, *Nafidha 'ala al-tarikh*, p. 33; Sayf, *al-Ma'tam*, vol. I, p. 179.

al-ʿUtub had used the canal to capture Qalʿah al-Diwan, the inland fort which was the headquarters of the Persian administration. In the Al Khalifah era Mushbir fell into disrepair following the general decline of Bahrain's old canal system, although in 1904 Lorimer noted the remnants of a lush date grove in the heart of the al-Hammam district.[44]

Given the absence of cartographic and documentary evidence the transition from agricultural hamlets to urban quarters is not easy to detect. The boundaries between the town and its cultivated hinterland (*al-mazraʿah*) were blurred as agricultural allotments (*al-daliyyah*) and empty land surrounded by fences (*al-hawtat*) still dotted the urban landscape in the early twentieth century. The gradual expansion of the harbour economy, overcrowding and declining water supplies inexorably undermined agricultural pursuits over the years with a proliferation of huts, shelters, masonry houses, walled structures and family warehouses used for the storage of food and goods. The constitution of popular neighbourhoods replicated the compound organisation of the villages. Their growth by accretion through immigration and the diversification of the economic activities of their residents paralleled and complemented the expansion of the harbour and commercial districts, rather than developing *ex novo* as their direct appendix.

Descriptions of Farij Bu Sirrah transmitted by generations of former residents illustrate the ways in which village activities combined with the maritime economy of the town. As part of the old agricultural belt surrounding the harbour, this district was often associated with the coastal village of al-Naʿim and often referred to as Bu Sirrah al-Naʿim (Bu Sirrah of Naʿim). In the early twentieth century its population included a majority of Shiʿis of mixed background, status and wealth. Influential Baharna families of rural origin like the Ibn Sallums and al-Habishis owned agricultural land outside Manama and employed villagers or immigrants from al-Ahsaʾ to cultivate their properties. The al-Shabibs, al-Marhums and Sayfs were involved in pearling and in ship building. Persian immigrants like the Bushehris capitalised on their overseas connections and traded in general foodstuffs. Baharna, Persian, Omani and Hasawi residents worked as carpenters, builders, porters and pearl cleaners. While the wealthy owned the few houses built of mud, gypsum and stone constructed around a central courtyard, the majority of the population lived in *barasti*s which clustered in garden plots intersected by a rudimentary road system. Less is known about the early history of the large district of al-Mukharaqah which, with al-Hammam, was the stronghold of

---

[44] Tajir, *ʿAqd al-lal*, pp. 103–5; Lorimer, *Gazetteer*, vol. II, p. 1159.

Manama's Baharna population. Its name (from the Arabic verb *kharaqa*, piercing) suggests a close connection with the pearling industry but also with local crafts, possibly referring to the presence of tailors in the neighbourhood.[45]

Immigration from overseas added a crucial dimension to processes of urbanisation as it fostered the creation of clusters of 'informal' communities which started to colonise *al-barriyyah*, insalubrious land impoverished by the infiltration of sea water located to the east and southeast of the harbour. With the exception of al-'Awadiyyah, which became the most elegant district of Manama in the first decades of the twentieth century, localities such as Sangeki and Zulmabad, inhabited by a mixture of Persians, Baluchis and former slaves, remained peripheral to the premodern town. These impoverished peasants and unskilled workmen constituted the rank-and-file of the dispossessed, a crucial reservoir of casual labour for the harbour and pearling industry.[46] The numbers of emancipated slaves in Manama, mostly employed in the pearl industry, had increased after 1897 when the British government set up an official manumission programme in the Persian Gulf.[47] Slaves, who were granted freedom after they presented a petition to local British agents, arrived in Manama from other Gulf ports, particularly Lingah and Muscat.

The role played by tribal immigrants in the development of the residential districts of the inner city is unclear, although Farij al-Fadhil located east of the harbour was named after a Najdi tribe which had settled in the area before the Al Khalifah conquest. Alongside with Kanu, this neighbourhood grew along the axis of transport which connected Muharraq Island to the harbour of Manama. The majority of the population of tribal origin was concentrated in this district in the second half of the nineteenth century, including several families of al-'Utub and al-Dawasir under the guardianship of the Najdi pearl merchant Muqbil al-Dhakir, the closest personal advisor of Shaykh 'Isa. As the centre of British influence and European shipping, Kanu housed those who had acquired political influence through outside connections: Yusuf ibn Ahmad Kanu, after whom the quarter was named in the early 1920s, 'Abd al-'Aziz al-Qusaybi,

---

[45] Sayf, *al-Ma'tam*, vol. I, pp. 86–7; 119–20; interview with 'Ali Akbar Bushehri, 17 March 2000.

[46] Interviews with Tayyebah Hoodi and Muhammad Ishaq 'Abd al-Rahman al-Khan, Manama 21 March and 8 April 2004. There are no historical records on the development of these neighbourhoods. For a general impression and location see the sketch attached to the letter of S. M. Zwemer to the American Board of Foreign Missions, 28 November 1899, MWT; Political Resident Bushehr to Government of India, 10 November 1923, n. 626-S of 1923, R/15/2/127 IOR.

[47] Khalifa, 'Slaves and Musical Performances in Dubai', pp. 103–4.

the representative of Ibn Sa'ud in Bahrain, and the Sharif and al-Safar families, the British native agents who acted as the representatives of the shippers Grey Mackenzie. The area attracted immigrants who had business ambitions and could afford a more expensive lifestyle. By the early 1900s inflated property prices and the lack of opportunity for investment in real estate forced many foreign entrepreneurs to move to the 'new' neighbourhoods of western Manama.

In the inner city few individuals were able to organise their lives and activities around tribal connections, since sectarian and economic considerations prevailed. The *halat* settlements along the eastern coast, which accommodated some Sunni tribal groups, lived off pearling and fishing and had strong social and economic ties with Muharraq. The history of the al-Dawawdah, a tribe of pearl divers, is fairly typical of the ways in which integration into Manama was characterised by a loosening of tribal bonds. In 1875 some thirty families, most likely from al-Hidd, lived around Manama's Portuguese Fort. At the turn of the century, they relocated closer to the town, moving between Halah Ibn Iswar and Halah Ibn Anas, the largest settlements along the eastern coast of the town. By the 1930s the formation of a new neighbourhood named Farij al-Dawawdah suggests that this group had lost its tribal exclusivity through sedentarisation and intermarriage.[48] In the case of the al-Lahmada tribe, it was their conversion en masse to Shi'ism sometime in the second half of the nineteenth century which favoured their integration into Manama's satellite village of Ras Rumman.[49]

In pre-modern Manama, neighbourhoods had no administrative, fiscal or corporate personality. The Jewish community, for instance, neither formed a distinctive urban cluster nor was subject to a separate fiscal regime as suggested by attempts on the part of Shaykh 'Isa to impose a head tax on the community in April 1906.[50] With no spatial, administrative or cultural markers separating the various districts, locals conceptualised the identity of urban quarters as the domain of influential merchants and as a continuous process of colonisation of *al-mazra'ah* and *al-barriyyah*. As will be explained in the following sections, at the turn of

---

[48] Lorimer, *Gazetteer*, vol. II, p. 1011; 'List of Some of the Families into which the Arab Tribes Residing in Bahrain are Divided' in 'Memo on the Islands of Bahrain', 11 July 1875, R/15/1/192 IOR; interview with 'Abd al-Rahim Muhammad, Manama, 17 April 2004.

[49] Lorimer, *Gazetteer*, vol. II, p. 1161; interviews with 'Ali Akbar Bushehri and Muhammad Ishaq 'Abd al-Rahman al-Khan, Manama, 18 March and 8 April 2004.

[50] 'Administration Report on the Persian Gulf Political Residency and Maskat Political Agency for 1906–1907' in *The Persian Gulf Administration Reports 1873–1949*, vol. VI, p. 67.

the twentieth century this process was expressed through a new language of patronage and public architecture. The hierarchical organisation of the quarters of Muharraq, determined by the status and economic special-isation of its resident tribes and non-tribal groups, contrasted with the multiplicity of localities intersecting the urban map of Manama whose political, social and geographical boundaries were continuously in the making.

While *al-qarabah* (closeness) was perceived by immigrant groups as their guarantee of security and protection, patronage politics defined the spatial hierarchy of power and privilege. Civic identity coalesced around the powerful figures of local men of reputation, usually merchants, and became manifest in the central place occupied by their residences and by the religious buildings they sponsored in the new districts. In the 1890s the eastern part of al-Fadhil developed around the residence and mosque of Muqbil al-Dhakir, while southern al-Hammam expanded after Ahmad Salman Khalaf, the doyen of Manama's pearl merchants, built his large family residence there in 1914.[51] Toponymic names employed by the Sunni and Shi'i religious courts confirm that urban localities emerged from the grass roots, shaped by the daily practices of patronage bonds. While al-Hammam, al-Mukharaqah and al-Fadhil were used sporadically (although their locations do not necessarily coincide with their modern counterparts), popular usage informed the taxonomy of place. In Bu Sirrah, Farij Ahmad ibn Sallum was named after Shaykh 'Isa's meat contractor, and in al-Fadhil the area around the residence of Muqbil al-Dhakir was known by his name. Upmarket Kanu included districts named after the Hawala and Banyan communities.[52]

Merchants as urban leaders

The circle of men of influence who constituted Manama's political elite at the turn of the twentieth century represented a loose coalition of mer-chants cum entrepreneurs, whose alliance of interests with the rulers varied a great deal. Some of the features of the body politic of the town, however, contributed to mould them into an 'alliance of equals'. Although positions as tax-farmers in the markets brought considerable financial

[51] Sayf, *al-Ma'tam*, vol. I, pp. 19, 171–3; Lorimer, *Gazetteer*, vol. II, p. 1161; Majed, *The Traditional Construction*, pp. 131–3; Political Resident Bushehr to Government of India, n. 626-S of 1923, 10 November 1923, R/15/2/197 IOR; waraqah al-hibah (certificate of royal donation), 10 Shawwal 1350/17 February 1932 and 18 Ramadan 1353/25 December 1934, BA; files n. 25, 61, 67, IT.

[52] Evidence on names of localities between 1880 and 1920 is included in files n. 40 to n. 106, IT; Lorimer, *Gazetteer*, vol. II, p. 1161; Sayf, *al-Ma'tam*, vol. I, p. 86.

reward to some, advancement in the public arena under the aegis of the tribal government was an unlikely option. Unlike their counterparts who populated Ottoman provincial centres during the Tanzimat period, the notables of Manama lacked the means to gain influence through government appointments.[53] The administrative apparatus supported by Shaykh 'Isa was truly minimal. Apart from the Al Khalifah governor and the Sunni qadi, the rank-and-file of the administration was provided by *al-fidawiyyah* recruited among loyal tribes, mercenary units and former slaves, and thus imported into the town. Beside the Customs House, the palace of the governor (Bayt al-Shuyukh) was the centre of Manama's tribal administration. Built as a self-sufficient compound on the coast east of the harbour around 1840 by 'Ali ibn Khalifah Al Khalifah (the ruler of Bahrain before Shaykh 'Isa), Bayt al-Shuyukh was guarded by high walls and resembled the tribal *al-qusur* of Muharraq.[54] Its architecture was a powerful reminder of the social distance between rulers, merchants and the urban population. The rigid spatial boundaries which demarcated the residence of the governor from Manama's markets and residential districts mirrored the inability on the part of merchant notables to gain influence through intermarriage with the ruling family.

As already mentioned, connections to the tribal establishment of Muharraq guaranteed a few influential Sunni and Shi'i merchants economic privileges and access to real estate in the markets. Yet, strictly speaking, they did not form a state-sponsored elite as this role was confined to the tribal clients of Al Khalifah who gravitated around the council of Shaykh 'Isa in Muharraq. The majority of these pearling entrepreneurs opted for the exclusivity and security offered by the new tribal towns of the Al Khalifah era, and treated Manama with a mixture of contempt and distrust. For merchants with no tribal pedigree based in Manama, the kind of state patronage promoted by membership in the *Majlis al-'Urf*, the town's commercial council which brought together influential members of its communities, did not automatically grant prestige, connections and wealth, although it certainly helped to maintain it. Rather, it offered recognition of the notables' position in the urban economy, their political connections outside Bahrain and their influence among the population.

In Manama status and pedigree were not a guarantee of economic and political success. The group of merchants who took the centre stage of

[53] See for instance the rise to power of the landowning families of Ottoman Damascus after 1860 as a result of their monopoly of positions in the civil bureaucracy of the Tanzimat, Khoury, *Urban Notables and Arab Nationalism*, pp. 35–46.

[54] Lorimer, *Gazetteer*, vol. I, pp. 927–8 and vol. II, p. 1161; J. Dieulafoy, *A Suse: Journal des Fouilles, 1884–1886* (Paris: Hachette, 1888), p. 47 (drawing of Bayt al-Shuyukh).

urban politics during the reign of Shaykh 'Isa were upstarts as the majority of them had settled in the town in the second half of the nineteenth century. This generation of self-made newcomers had amassed fortunes with the entrepôt trade and with the pearl boom and run large family business: the al-Qusaybis and Muqbil al-Dhakir from Najd, the Khunjis, Bushehris, and Kazerunis from Iran, and the Ibn Rajab, al-Mudayfa', and al-'Urayyad from Bahrain's agricultural districts. The political instability of the eighteenth and early nineteenth centuries and the fast turnover of Bahrain's rulers suggest the concomitant rise and fall of the urban notability. In other words, Manama did not have an established leadership in 1869 when Shaykh 'Isa became the ruler of Bahrain. It is significant that family traditions portray the second half of the nineteenth century as a major rupture in the history of Manama, the beginning of a radically new era.

The position of religious households is another important indication of the relative unimportance of status in influencing urban political life. Families renowned for their piety were in short supply in early twentieth century Manama, as hierarchies of influence were moulded by utilitarian ideas of social order. The Sunni religious establishment drew extensively on the tribal ethos of the Al Khalifa, while the Shi'i clerical and scriptural tradition languished. The reputation of Shi'i individuals with a religious pedigree such as Ahmad ibn Sayyid al-'Alawi and 'Abd al-'Ali ibn Rajab (a descendent of Muhammad Hasan ibn Rajab al-Maqabi who became *Shaykh al-Ra'is* of Bahrain in 1602) was due primarily to their association with the earthly and ritualistic universe of *'ashura'* and with *ma'tam* congregations. They were able to establish and maintain as men of trade the houses of mourning where *ma'tam* congregations gathered, and it was the popularity of their *ma'tam*s which formed the basis of their political standing (see Figure 5).[55]

Two sets of relationships distinguished the notables of Manama as political actors. The first was their association with the Al Khalifa administration and with foreign powers, not only the Government of India but also the Qajar administration of Iran and the Sa'udi amirs of Central Arabia. The second was their degree of access to the urban population.

With the expansion of Manama's entrepôt economy, the wealth of merchants involved in long-distance and transit trade became increasingly dependent on connections to powerful foreign protectors. Yusuf ibn

[55] For the family histories of the al-'Alawis and Ibn Rajabs see Sayf, *al-Ma'tam*, vol. I, pp. 104–5, 127–9.

5 'Abd al-'Ali ibn Rajab, the Shi'i merchant and patron of
the homonymous house of mourning, early 1930s

Ahmad Kanu, for instance, started his career as a young man in 1893 (or
1898–9: the date is not clear) as an employee for the British native agency.
Acting as a middleman, he became enormously rich and influential and
built up a fortune in shipping. His identification with British interests in
Manama antagonised Shaykh 'Isa to such an extent that in 1920 Major
Dickinson, the British Political Agent, remarked that '[Yusuf Kanu]
undoubtedly would get into serious trouble if [the] British ever withdrew

from Bahrain'.[56] Wahhabi politics also played a role in the rise of powerful merchant houses in Manama. As the political and commercial representative of Ibn Sa'ud in Bahrain, 'Abd al-Aziz al-Qusaybi built up a mercantile empire as a pearl merchant, and supplier of wheat and foodstuffs to Eastern Arabia after al-Ahsa' came under Wahhabi control in 1913. After he arrived in Bahrain from al-Dammam in 1898 with his two brothers, the family enlisted in the entourage of Shaykh 'Isa. 'Abd al-'Aziz , a flamboyant character notorious for his arrogance, entered into competition with the royal household in terms of wealth and lifestyle, surrounded by his own *al-fidawiyyah*. He built one of his residences in al-Rifa', the fiefdom of the Al Khalifah family.[57] Another example is that of the al-Safar family, which throughout the nineteenth century used their position as British native agents in Bahrain to consolidate the family's international network of merchant houses which branched as far as Yemen and India.[58]

Unlike the majority of the town's merchants, the power base of these entrepreneurs who capitalised on foreign connections was generally dissociated from the popular quarters of Manama. It was above all the influence these merchants were able to exercise at the grass roots which transformed them into a fairly cohesive group of *a'yan*, a class of notables who represented the interests of the population vis-à-vis the tribal administration. Not only did this kind of authority underscore the consolidation of a powerful cohort of Shi'i tax-farmers cum landowners in the markets, it also allowed merchants to exercise state-like functions in the residential districts almost single-handedly. Taking advantage of developing community networks, they provided protection, representation and welfare to the town's immigrant population. Mostly of humble background, these leaders started off their careers as petty traders, or labourers in the port and in the markets. At the turn of the twentieth century, *a'yan* with popular constituencies were predominant in Manama, particularly among the Baharna and the Persian Shi'is which constituted the poorest as well as the largest section of the urban population. These two groups were able to produce community leaders (the Bushehris, Ibn Rajabs, al-'Urayyads) with a strong power base in al-Mukharaqah, al-Hammam and

[56] Dickinson, 'Note on the Political Situation in Bahrain' in Political Agent Bahrain to Civil Commissioner Baghdad and Political Resident Bushehr, 5 January 1920, n. 6-C, R/15/2/785 IOR. K. M. Kanoo, *The House of Kanoo: A Century of an Arabian Family Business* (London: Centre of Arab Studies, 1997), pp. 1–15; M. Field, *The Merchants: The Big Business Families of Saudi Arabia and the Gulf States* (New York: Overlook Press, 1985), pp. 266–7.

[57] 'Confidential Memo on the Qusaybi Family' in Political Agent Bahrain to Political Resident Bushehr, 2 June 1931, R/15/2/101 IOR; interview with Khalid al-Bassam, Manama, 20 March 2004; Field, *The Merchants*, p. 219.

[58] Onley, 'Transnational Merchants in the Nineteenth-Century Gulf', pp. 63–77.

Bu Sirrah, while the Najdis and Persian Sunnis coalesced around the al-Bassams, al-Tamims, Khunjis and al-Khadims of al-'Awadiyyah and al-Fadhil.[59]

In comparison with their Ottoman counterparts, these popular notables seemed to have enjoyed a greater degree of political leverage with the state administration.[60] Besides possessing popular followings and benefitting from the 'informal' nature of tribal government, the assistance of powerful foreign protectors characterised their career paths. The leaders of the Persian community, for instance, had a long history of involvement with the Qajar administration which continued apace into the Pahlavi era.[61] The Ibn Rajab family was linked both to the Al Khalifah and to the British. 'Abdallah ibn Rajab served as the agent of the British India Steam Navigation Company between 1873 and 1889, and his cousin Ibrahim was British Native Agent in the 1850s. Only the Ibn Sallums seem to have relied almost exclusively on the support of the ruling family as also suggested by the name *Shi'ah al-Shuyukh* (the partisans of the ruler) with which they were known among their detractors. Originally from al-Hufuf on the east coast, they converted to Shi'ism when they settled in Bahrain in the 1820s and started to manage the stables of the Al Khalifah before Ahmad ibn Sallum became Shaykh 'Isa's meat tax-farmer.[62]

Immigrants and the politics of patronage

Bonds of patronage represented the single most important chain of authority shaping the settlement of Manama's immigrant population. At the most basic level, many of the newcomers needed food and housing to start a new life. They also necessitated the creation of an environment which reproduced their ideals of community life and spiritual fulfilment. Protection was neither granted at random, nor dominated by sheer economic interests. On the patron's side, it was dictated by the necessity to create constituencies in tune with personal and family connections and to conform to the prevailing moral and religious norms which sanctioned the

[59] Interviews with Khalid al-Bassam, Muhammad Ishaq 'Abd al-Rahman al-Khan and Hamid al-'Awadhi, Manama, March and April 2004.

[60] Literature on the *a'yan* in the Arab provinces of the Ottoman Empire is vast. Classic studies are: A. Hourani, 'Ottoman Reform and the Politics of Notables' in A. Hourani, P. Khoury and M. Wilson (eds.), *The Modern Middle East: A Reader* (London: I. B. Tauris, 1993), pp. 83–109 and Khoury, *Urban Notables and Arab Nationalism*.

[61] Fuccaro, 'Mapping the Transnational Community'; interview with 'Ali Akbar Bushehri, 21 March 2004.

[62] Mayy Muhammad Al Khalifah, *Muhammad ibn Khalifah 1813–1890: al-usturah wa al-tarikh al-muwazi* (Beirut: al-Mu'assasah al-'Arabiyyah li al-Dirasat wa al-Nashr, 1999), p. 582; Ibn Sallum family tree, BA; Sayf, *al-Ma'tam*, vol. I, p. 8.

social separation between Sunnis and Shiʻis. The rich present-day popular traditions concerning Manama during the age of pearling concentrate almost exclusively on the feats and misfortunes of residents, immigrants and local merchants. These oral narratives reflect the strong corporate identities of urban communities in the making. Personal accounts of immigration and patronage, which are still handed down from one generation to the other, reflect the process by which individuals carved out new social, economic and political spaces in the urban arena.

The history of Jaʻfar Muhammad Qannati can be taken as representative of that of thousands of immigrants who arrived in the last quarter of the nineteenth century. He was born in Brazajan in the district of Fars in 1875 and reached the harbour of Muharraq in 1902 from the Persian port of Kangun. He had no trade or skill, unlike his travelling companion who was a sweet maker from the same village. Both had lost all their immediate families and possessions as a result of a severe drought which had decimated the population of Brazajan a few months earlier. With no money or contacts in Bahrain they were offered accommodation in a makeshift hut near the harbour. As Jaʻfar and his friend could not pay rent, the same individual who provided them with sleeping quarters also bought the ingredients to make sweets. They then rented a stall in the suq of Muharraq, paid back their creditor and eventually established their own business. Realising that most Shiʻis lived in Manama, and that no *'ashura'* was celebrated in Muharraq, they joined *jamaʻah al-ʻAjam*, the congregation of the homonymous house of mourning, by then the largest in the town. Eventually they moved to Manama with the help of the *maʻtam* and, eager to contribute to its upkeep, rented one of its properties.[63]

Jaʻfar Muhammad Qannati ended his journey from Iran as a member of the vast network of clients who gravitated around Maʻtam al-ʻAjam al-Kabir, a house of mourning which was established in the al-Mukharaqah district following the inflow of immigrants from Iran after the 1860s. A large majority of the congregation came from the district of Dashti, whose capital Bushehr had suffered from chronic political instability and cyclical food shortages after the consolidation of direct Qajar rule. After 1880 the Bushehri and Kazeruni families, both closely associated with the *maʻtam*, brought approximately 30 per cent of the Persian population of Dashti under their protection to Manama. The heads of these two families were themselves immigrants and representative of rising community leaders who came to control Manama's neighbourhoods. ʻAbd al-Nabi Kazeruni, the contractor of Shaykh ʻIsa's warehouse in the harbour and one of the

---

[63] Transcript of interview with ʻAbbas Qannati (b. 1913), 8 December 1990, kindly provided by ʻAli Akbar Bushehri.

first leaders of al-'Ajam al-Kabir, arrived in Manama in the 1890s. He quickly rose to prominence by establishing matrimonial alliances with prominent Baharna families associated with houses of mourning, becoming the representative of the Persian community in the *Majlis al-'Urf* and styling himself 'Persian Consul' in Bahrain.[64] More is known about the life of 'Ali Kazim Bushehri, the head of the Kazimi branch of the family. Truly a self-made man, he worked as porter in the harbour after reaching Manama around 1860 and then accumulated a fortune as an import dealer in household commodities, particularly foodstuffs. Like the anonymous benefactor who helped Ja'far Muhammad Qannati, 'Ali Kazim established credit lines with many of the Persian immigrants who flocked to the town, as recounted by the oral history of the Bushehri family. Ahmad Bushehri, the head of the Muniri branch of the family, arrived in Bahrain in 1890 under the protection of 'Ali Kazim, who employed Ahmad's son 'Abd al-Nabi in his shop in the suq. In 1906 'Abd al-Nabi Bushehri became the business partner of 'Ali Kazim, started a spectacular career as a building contractor and took over the management of the *ma'tam* around 1927.[65]

The careers of 'Abd al-Nabi Bushehri and 'Abd al-Nabi Kazeruni provide examples of the inner workings of Manama's patronage system and of the close relations between the accumulation of merchant capital and the development of the town at the turn of the twentieth century. 'Abd al-Nabi Kazeruni used his connections to issue travel permits to Iran, allegedly with the connivance of the Qajar authorities. As building contractors, the two 'Abd al-Nabis capitalised on their overseas connections and obtained a large pool of skilled labour from Iran. Many of Manama's master builders, builders and carpenters started their careers under their protection. 'Abd al-Nabi Bushehri built the British political agency in 1900 and renovated the al-Khamis mosque in 1927, while Kazeruni contributed to the construction of the Victoria Memorial Hospital in 1902–3, the first modern medical facilities established in Bahrain.[66] The portfolio of investments by the two 'Abd al-Nabis in the residential neighbourhood of Manama provides a further insight into the consolidation of merchants as the landed aristocracy of the town. In fact, Persian notables became the largest owners of urban properties before the

[64] Fuccaro, 'Mapping the Transnational Community', pp. 45–6; Kazeruni family tree, BA.
[65] 'Ali A. Bushehri, 'The Struggle of a Family', typescript, 225 pages, n.d., pp. 115–19, 121, 124–5.
[66] Dickinson, 'Note on the Political Situation in Bahrain' in Political Agent Bahrain to Civil Commissioner in Baghdad and Political Resident Bushehr, 5 January 1920, n. 6-C, R/15/2/785 IOR. Oral history of the Bushehri family, Manama, 15 June 1998; 'Ali A. Bushehri, 'The Master Builder of Bahrain', *The Gulf Mirror*, February 1987, issue n. 8.

discovery of oil as suggested by large numbers of holdings registered in the name of both Sunni and Shi'i merchants after the issue of the Bahrain Nationality and Property Law in 1937.[67]

For a'yan with popular constituencies, the acquisition of real estate in the residential districts not only generated considerable income but also represented crucial political and social capital. Houses, plots and barastis were distributed or rented out to family members, distant relatives, clients and skilled labourers, ensuring the continuation and enlargement of patronage networks. The consolidation of a class of property owners benefited the merchant class as a whole. As with the markets, residential properties became a crucial item of exchange for loans and political support with Shaykh 'Isa, members of his entourage and tribal allies.[68] Unlike in Ottoman Damascus during the Tanzimat period, Manama's new landed elite did not emerge as a result of processes of state centralisation and of the institution of private property. Particularly after the Government of India appointed Shaykh Hamad as heir apparent in 1900, it was the financial crisis that hit the treasury of Shaykh 'Isa which turned many of the town's prominent merchants into landowners.[69]

By the 1920s the role of entrepreneur and patron had become synonymous with that of landowner. Yusuf Luft 'Ali Khunji and Mustafa 'Abd al-Latif, two of the wealthiest Persian Sunnis of al-'Awadiyyah quarter, for instance, employed attorneys to manage their estates in Manama as part of the network of agents who supervised their import–export offices overseas.[70] Sunni Persian notables also acquired properties in Muharraq, al-Hidd and the two al-Rifa's, the tribal towns with an overwhelming majority of Sunni residents. A handful of Baharna merchants turned their attention to the villages. As explained in Chapter 1, investment in rural estate was not particularly profitable given the lack of commercialisation of Bahrain's agriculture, but it cemented social ties and political

---

[67] Minutes by Political Agent Bahrain, 21 January 1938, and letters by 'Abd al-Wahid Faramasi, Muhammad Khoeji, Muhammad Hadi ibn Mahmud Bastaki and Nasrallah ibn Zainal al-'Abidin to Political Agent Bahrain, February 1928, R/15/2/151 IOR.

[68] Evidence of the sale of land by members of Shaykh 'Isa's household is included in the documentation from the Idarah al-Tabu. See also Political Agent Bahrain to Political Resident Bushehr n. 204 of 1904, 31 December 1904, R/15/2/10 IOR, and memo from Belgrave to Political Agent Bahrain, 19 November 1931, R/15/2/1807 IOR.

[69] In Ottoman Damascus the rise of the landowning bureaucratic elites of the Tanzimat period was closely associated with provincial reform, state centralisation and the application of the 1858 Land Code. Khoury, *Urban Notables and Arab Nationalism*, pp. 27–30. Evidence of ownership rights acquired by the merchant notability of Manama before the enforcement of land registration in 1925 is included in the documentation of the Land Department. Files n. 29 to 54, IT.

[70] Interviews with Muhammad Ishaq 'Abd al-Rahman al-Khan and Hamid al-'Awadhi, Manama, 8 and 10 April 2004.

connections between Manama's Shi'i leaders and the rural population. The Ibn Rajabs, for instance, acquired land in their ancestral village,
Bilad al-Qadim.[71] Merchants also invested in the outskirts of the town as
the ownership of garden properties became a sign of political prestige and
social visibility. On particular days of the week they were used as the
extensions of the *ma'tam*s and *majlis*es of the inner city as the heads of
prominent families received and entertained their guests or celebrated
religious holidays.

Religious sentiment, patronage and public architecture

The story of Ja'far Muhammad Qannati illustrates the ways in which piety
constituted an important resource base at the disposal of the mercantile
elites of the pearl boom. Regardless of confessional orientation, the mosques and *ma'tam* buildings which mushroomed in the town shared important features: sponsorship by local *a'yan* as a crucial dimension of their
politics of patronage with their membership organised by ethnicity, locality and occupation.

The architectural idiom and decor of religious buildings did not leave a
powerful impression upon foreign visitors. Driven by prejudice and
Christian zeal, Theodore Bent and his wife in 1899 dismissed
Manama's mosques as 'little better than barns'. A few years later
Cursetjee remarked that even the Friday mosque of Manama was far
from 'picturesque and graceful'.[72] Yet religious buildings were an important projection of the town's collectivities upon urban space. On the one
hand, their lack of visual prominence reflected the relatively low profile of
Sunni *'ulama'*, Shi'i clergy and mosque imams in urban society. On the
other, their modest appearance signposted the utilitarian outlook of
Manama's civic ethos and the intimacy and exclusivity of its community
networks. Religious sentiment found expression in the discreet combination of mercantile wealth and individual devotion, rather than reflecting
the flamboyancy of power and legitimacy emanating from a state-
sponsored religiosity. Although the imams of Sunni mosques gravitated
around the entourages of the ruler and of leading pearling tribes,
Manama's religious institutions rarely enjoyed the direct patronage of
the tribal government as suggested by the tight network of endowments
by merchants and residents which permeated the property structure of the
town. Even Jami' al-Mahzah, the Friday mosque, one of the strongholds
of the tribal administration, was partly supported by merchant capital. In

[71] Minutes by Political Agent Bahrain, 21 January 1938, R/15/2/151 IOR.
[72] Bent, *Southern Arabia*, p. 12; Cursetjee, *The Land of the Date*, pp. 88–9.

1909 Shaykh 'Isa resorted to 'Abd al-Nabi Kazeruni to provide for its upkeep as part of the conditions imposed on the sale of a piece of land to the Persian entrepreneur. The price demanded by the ruler was exceptionally low but Kazeruni had to endow part of the property as a *waqf* after his death for the benefit both of the mosque and of the Persian *ma'tam* located in the vicinity.[73]

The political controversies which surrounded the family of the Sunni qadi Qasim al-Mahzah epitomised the relations of power between Sunnis and Shi'is and underlined the importance of sectarian worldviews in Manama's political life. Their monopoly of religious office dated back to 1853 when Qasim's father was appointed imam of the personal mosque of Shaykh 'Ali ibn Khalifah (r. 1868–9). At least since 1904 his youngest son Ahmad served as the imam of Manama's Friday mosque, while Qasim presided over the court. The family had a reputation for being partisan; the piety and moral probity of Qasim al-Mahzah continued to be celebrated by Sunnis of his generation, but his cruelty, greed and vanity became notorious among the Shi'i population. Stories still circulate about the severity of his punishment of offenders and his occasional beatings of women brought to his court accused of practising prostitution.[74] The influence of the al-Mahzah brothers decreased alongside that of the ruling family, especially after 1904 when Ahmad was blacklisted by the British agency for having instigated violence between Persians and Arabs.[75]

Religious buildings in Manama were largely an attribute of mercantile power, a symbol of wealth and an integral part of the welfare services offered by notables. 'Abd al-'Aziz Lutf 'Ali Khunji, the merchant from Lingah who sponsored the large mosque in the suq, was one of the most prominent religious philanthropists in town. He became famous for the several mosques he founded for the benefit of destitute Persian and Baluchi immigrants in the shanty towns of eastern Manama, the most popular being an open air mosque on empty land known as Masjid al-'Id. Around 1900 he surrounded the property with a low wall and paid for the construction of a *minbar* (pulpit) to conduct the prayers.[76] Styles of

---

[73] Khalifah Sulaybikh, *Hikayat min al-Hurah* (Manama: [n.pub.], 2004), pp. 17–18; taqrir al-bai' (sale registration), 16 Jumada al-Thaniyyah 1327/4 July 1909, BA.

[74] Belgrave to Political Agent Bahrain, 25 Rabi' al-Thani 1346/21 October 1927, n. 328/27, R/15/2/130 IOR; minutes by Political Agent Bahrain, 15 November 1932, R/15/2/1896 IOR; Political Resident Bushehr to Bombay Government, 8 February 1905, L/P&S/10/81 IOR; conversation with former residents of Farij al-Jami', Manama, June 2000; al-Khatir, *al-Qadhi al-Ra'is Qasim ibn Mahzah*.

[75] See pp. 153–6.

[76] Oral history collected by 'Ali Akbar Bushehri from 'Abd al-Husayn Muhammad Tahir al-Sharif (b. 1916).

religious patronage differed. Among the Sunnis, the rich Persian and Najdi merchants opened their *majlises* during religious holidays for the distribution of alms to the poor. Among the Shi'is, community life centred upon *ma'tam* congregations as elsewhere on the islands; by 1913 Manama had thirteen buildings where congregations gathered, of which eleven were controlled by the Baharna and two by the Persian community.[77]

The houses of mourning and the organisation of sect

As a testimony of the love for Imam Husayn and as the venues for *'ashura'* celebrations, *ma'tam* congregations and the specialised buildings which hosted them translated individual devotion into demonstrations of collective mourning for the *shuhada' al-Karbala'*, the ill-fated Imam and his family slaughtered in southern Iraq in AD 680. Unlike mosques, *ma'tams* were not under the scrutiny of qadis or imams but were managed by households and groups through consensus. Houses of mourning ranked in popularity and importance in accordance with their ability to organise religious celebrations and to provide religious instruction by sponsoring mullas and preachers who acquired fame by their association with important *ma'tams*. A crucial factor in their success was also their performance as community halls staging funerals, marriages and recreational activities.

The establishment of 'official' houses of mourning as independent buildings at the end of the nineteenth century (as opposed to the informal congregations which had gathered in private residences in the early Al Khalifah period) symbolised the economic and political emancipation of the Shi'i community. The profile of Manama's *ma'tams* became established after 1891 when Mirza Muhammad Isma'il, the local agent for the British India Steam Navigation Company, used his official position to lead the first open air celebration of *'ashura'* in the inner city. This was a momentous event for Manama's Shi'is. People flocked behind a heavily armed Mirza Isma'il who proudly made his way through Manama's streets in defiance of the veto imposed by the rulers on public manifestations of Shi'i devotion.[78]

Ma'tam buildings were also the new architectural manifestation of mercantile wealth engendered by the pearl boom, and offer an indication of patterns of investment in real estate throughout the town. At the turn of the twentieth century Ma'tam al-'Urayyad, which was built around 1870 in the garden of Ibrahim ibn 'Ali al-'Urayyad (a pearl merchant), was

---

[77] Interviews with Tayyebah Hoodi, Khalid al-Bassam and Muhammmad Ishaq 'Abd al-Rahman al-Khan, Manama, 21 and 22 March and 8 April 2004; Sayf, *al-Ma'tam*, vol. I; al-Nabhani, *al-Tuhfah al-Nabhaniyyah*, p. 22.

[78] Interview with 'Ali Akbar Bushehri, Manama, 20 May 2000.

supported by endowments such as shops, land and the large family ware-house, properties acquired by the family in the years following the estab-lishment of the funeral house.[79] The mushrooming of specialised buildings for the celebration of *'ashura'* also explains the changing demog-raphy of expanding Shi'i popular neighbourhoods. After the 1860s, the al-'Ajam al-Kabir and Bin Rajab, the oldest of Manama, were testimony to the presence of large numbers of Persians and Baharna immigrants in the inner city. Similarly, the appearance of the Ma'tam al-Ahsa'iyyin in al-Mukharaqah district in 1895 is an indication of substantial migrations from al-Ahsa', which most likely occurred after the 1850s.[80]

*Ma'tam*s also fostered new uses of urban space. The establishment of specialised buildings and the outdoors celebration of *'ashura'* contributed further to create a new public arena in Manama's neighbourhoods trans-forming them into spaces of popular devotion. Although individual families and small congregations continued to sponsor indoor events, preachers reciting the stories of the *Ahl al-Bayt* during religious holidays gathered large crowds of listeners outside *ma'tam* buildings who were eager to weep and lament their sad fate. Moreover, ritual performances for *'ashura'* became the most heavily attended public events in town. From the seventh to the tenth day of the month of Muharram, congregations marched through the streets of the inner city conducting coordinated rituals of chest beating, sword self-mutilation and the theatrical representation of the battle of Karbala (*al-tamthiliyyah*).[81] In July 1926 Charles Belgrave provided one of the earliest lengthy descriptions of Muharram's celebra-tions from the roof of a house in the vicinity of Manama's Friday mosque:

The sides of the square simply packed with people and all the roofs crowded with women, in black, all howling and crying. The procession really looked like a circus, flags and banners and then all the figures, like a mystery play, from the story of Hussein and Hosein, the corpses, very realistic and covered in blood, one headless corpse, very unpleasant, horses covered in gore, wives, prisoners, Hosein's house, an affair of cardboard and tinsel, and camel and horses etc, etc, really amazing, then thousands of men beating themselves and then, the pièce of resistance, about 50 men carrying swords and cutting themselves across the forehead, dressed in white clothes, simply covered with blood![82]

Patterns of ritual patronage and participation in *ma'tam* congregations reflected the economic position and social standing of their patrons as the

---

[79] al-'Urayyad, *Nafidhah 'ala al-tarikh*, pp. 33–4.
[80] Sayf, *al-Ma'tam*, vol. I, pp. 108–11, 119–23, 133–4; Khuri, *Tribe and State in Bahrain*, pp. 160–2.
[81] Videotape of *'ashura'* procession (Manama, *c.* 1932), BA; P. Thomas, 'The Passion Play at Bahrain', *The Arabian Mission*, vol. II, 65 (April–June 1908), pp. 3–5.
[82] Belgrave Diaries, 21 July 1926, AWDU.

'big men' of the community. The majority of the sponsors of Baharna *ma'tam*s were pearl merchants with fleets who financed expeditions to the pearl banks. Some households like the Ibn Rajabs, Ibn Zabars and al-'Urayyads were owners of agricultural land. Persian *ma'tam*s were supported by general merchants and entrepreneurs, like the Bushehris and the Kazerunis, reflecting the patterns of occupation among the higher echelons of the community. Merchant households used their association with several *ma'tam*s to cement alliances and to bind clientele networks together. The Ibn Rajab and al-'Alawi families, for instance, financed part of the building of Ma'tam al-Madan, while the rich pearl merchants al-Mudayfa' joined the Ma'tam Bin Rajab before they took over the management of their own house of mourning in al-Hammam. While Persian *ma'tam*s were organised mainly along ethnic lines, among the Baharna affiliation to the houses of mourning united segments of artisans and petty traders, providing the platform for the creation of strong corporatist identities. A powerful association of butchers (*jama'ah al-qassabin*) emerged under the umbrella of the Ma'tam al-Madan which had a strong following among the traders of the markets controlled by the Al Khalifah. In al-Mukharaqah district, Ma'tam Bin Aman, originally a congregation supported by fishermen and pearl labourers, maintained a strong connection with its popular base after it became an 'official' house of mourning during the pearl boom. In some cases, *ma'tam*s also served to cement quarter solidarities. The committee of Hajj 'Abbas included families of different social standing and represented the different segments of the population of al-Hammam district.[83]

Donations by affiliates were an important facet of the collective ethos of *ma'tam*s and an integral part of the mobilisation of resources for the organisation of religious celebrations. Direct sponsorship brought personal fulfilment and social reward, regardless of the means of donors. Contributions ranged from labour for the construction, upkeep and repair of the buildings, cooking and serving food during festivities, to commodities such as rice, meat, oil, candles and kitchen utensils. Several examples suggest that offering religious texts and expertise were particularly prestigious gifts, as they nurtured peoples' sentiments towards the *Ahl al-Bayt*. In 1854 Salih Jum'ah al-Khatti gave two books of *hadith* to the recently established Ma'tam al-Bada', and recorded his name in the front page of the manuscript listing his other contributions, several coffee pots and rice containers.[84] Around 1885 one donor, possibly a mulla from Iran,

[83] Sayf, *al-Ma'tam*, vol. I, pp. 99–102, 113, 179–82; interview with 'Abdallah Sayf, Manama, 20 March 2004.
[84] Sayf, *al-Ma'tam*, vol. I, p. 195.

produced his own manuscript for the 'Ajam al-Kabir which included stories of the death of Prophet Muhammad and of Imam 'Ali and Rida. In 1892, Za'ir Mashallah ibn Karim Husayn donated thirty *juzur* of the holy Qur'an to Ma'tam al-'Ajam al-Kabir to be read for *'aza'* Husayn during the month of Muharram. Fifteen years later Za'ir's Qur'an started to be used as a register of deaths for the congregation.[85]

The history of congregations was an integral part of the cult of founders. The strengthening of spiritual feelings towards early donors became one of the *raisons d'être* of Manama's *ma'tam*s. The celebration of individuals and households had a very distinctive flavour as attributes of piety were seldom dissociated from the mercantile milieu. Land grants, community welfare and investment, rather than religious fervour, established the credentials of *ma'tam* lineages. The pearl merchant Ahmad ibn 'Ali al-Nasir who established Ma'tam Bin Zabar is said to have sponsored a purpose built *barasti* in al-Mukharaqah after he donated land to the local community for the celebration of *'ashura'* in the early 1890s. Oral tradition explains his continuous involvement in *ma'tam* affairs in relation to the expansion of his business which allowed him to provide for the construction of a square building with a *shamsiyyah* (parasol), teak-framed windows and a well.[86] The pedigree of Manama's houses of mourning was also subject to fierce contestation which often evolved around disputes over land donations. The Ibn Rajab family still claims to have gifted land to poor Persian immigrants for the establishment of the first building for Ma'tam al-'Ajam al-Kabir, while Persian families attribute the donation to a *sayyid* (religious notable) from Bushehr in the 1870s.[87]

After the collapse of pearling in the late 1920s, houses of mourning ceased to represent the interests of their merchant notables, particularly in the case of Baharna family *ma'tam*s. With the exception of the Bin Rajab and al-'Urayyad, they changed hands when their founders died or lost their fortunes. After 1939 Ma'tam al-Mudayfa' became organised along professional lines with a strong following in Suq al-'Attarah, which sold herbs and herbal medicine. The endowments which supported these houses of mourning started to be placed increasingly under the scrutiny of religious courts, which after 1927 were integrated into the modern administration. Community *ma'tam*s were less affected by the collapse of pearling as they were not so dependent on the prosperity of individual households.[88] From

---

[85] Mss, 3 vols., no title, *c.* 1885, BA.   [86] Sayf, *al-Ma'tam*, vol. I, pp. 90–2.

[87] Sayf, *al-Ma'tam*, vol. I, pp. 170–4; oral history on the Ma'tam al-'Ajam al-Kabir related by Kazim Bushehri (b. 1925).

[88] Sayf, *al-Ma'tam*, vol. I, pp. 25, 90, 99–102, 119–22. In the early 1990s private funds still supported two-thirds of the *ma'tams* in Bahrain.

the detailed information available on the constellation of endowments of the 'Ajam al-Kabir and the al-Ahsa'iyyin, it is clear that both benefitted more consistently from substantial donations from the community, exclusively houses and shops which were endowed by members of the congregations between 1898 and 1924.[89]

Conclusion

As a port town and urban society, nineteenth-century Manama developed as the archetype of a segmentary urban system. The topography of the town of the pearl boom expressed the ideology of entrepreneurship of its settlers and the cosmopolitan make-up of the population. Its ethnically and religiously mixed residential areas are evidence of the openness which had characterised modes of community implantation since the arrival of the Al Khalifah in Bahrain. In contrast, by the early twentieth century the social and political milieus which structured urban life remained strictly communitarian. In this respect, Manama continued to display the features of an immigration unit; even intermarriage between merchant households was restricted to family blocs united by sectarian affiliation, provenance and, among the Shi'i upper class, by their control of *ma'tam*s. Communitarian was also the logic of diffused political authority which structured public life and transformed *ma'tam*s and *majlis*es into centres of 'informal' politics. Sponsorship of religious institutions united Sunni and Shi'i notables in their pursuit of clientele and social prestige, placing them at the head of urban society. The patronage ties which linked Shi'i merchants to the popular classes through membership in *ma'tam* congregations were the single most influential factor in determining the social and political organisation of large segments of urban society. *Majlis*es fulfilled a similar function among the Sunni population, although they lacked the strong collective and participatory ethos of the houses of mourning.

By the early twentieth century the combination of trade profit and wealth from real estate structured the patterns of cooperation between merchants and the ruling family. The markets and the harbour were the venues which brokered relations between the Al Khalifah and the economy of the inner city on the one hand, and the cosmopolitan merchants and the overseas markets on the other. The increasingly complex organisation of the commercial areas and of customs facilities reflected the growing mutual dependence between Bahrain's tribal elites and the

---

[89] 'Daftar ma'tam al-'Ajam al-Kabir', 1342–72 (1929–71); 'Daftar buzurg ma'tam al-'Ajam al-Kabir', 1 Muharram 1351–10 Muharram 1352 (7 May 1932–5 May 1933), BA; Sayf, *al-Ma'tam*, vol. I, p. 123.

town's entrepreneurs. While Shaykh ʿIsa distributed tax-farms in order to maximise revenue, Persian, Indian and Arab merchants were able to consolidate their position in crucial areas of state activity, particularly by taking over the management of the harbour, the customs house and the local markets. As the notable class amassed wealth, they took an active role in processes of urbanisation. Through their sponsorship of rural and overseas migrants they satisfied an increasing demand for labour. In turn, they enlarged their patronage networks which were crucial in the expansion of Manama's residential areas.

The politics of real estate was another act of 'balanced opposition' which sealed the partnership between merchants and rulers. Mercantile wealth was generally invested in the residential areas where revenue from rent and the distribution of properties to clients became an integral part of Manama's politics of patronage. Yet, in spite of the advance of merchant capital, the entrepreneurs of the pearl boom did not break the traditional monopoly over market properties held by the Al Khalifah and their allies. Sectarian cleavages, however, fragmented the merchant class as an interest group bound by land ownership, reflecting the inequalities between Sunnis and Shiʿis. The lucrative properties of the markets continued to be the preserve of Sunnis: members of the Al Khalifah family, Hawala merchants and the Persian Sunni *nouveaux riches* of the trade boom. In contrast, the properties owned by Shiʿi entrepreneurs in the popular neighbourhoods (and the closely knit network of *ma'tam*s which they supported) transformed them into the strongholds of Shiʿi mercantile power and political influence. In this respect, the dual spatial hierarchy of markets and residential areas mapped fairly accurately the Sunni–Shiʿi political divide.

Capitalist expansion, the penetration of foreign (and particularly British) trade in the Gulf and the influence of the Government of India in commercial arbitration accentuated the dependence of merchants on foreign connections, a crucial factor in the progressive weakening of the tribal administration after 1900. The exile of ʿAli ibn Ahmad Al Khalifah, the governor of Manama, in 1905 as a result of the military intervention of the British Navy marked the beginning of the end of the urban order of the pearl boom and foreshadowed the imposition of tighter British control over Manama and Bahrain after 1919.[90] The power vacuum left by the departure of Shaykh ʿAli irreversibly compromised the position of the town within the system of the tribal estates controlled by the Al Khalifah and transformed it into the natural platform for imperial reform and political modernisation in the era of municipal government.

---

[90] See p. 156.

4 Restructuring city and state: the municipality and local government

With the establishment of a municipality in 1919, Manama entered a new era of modernisation and local government. The reorganisation of the town became an integral part of the process of reform which throughout the 1920s supported the creation of a modern state administration under the aegis of the Government of India. As Manama consolidated its position as the lynchpin of British informal empire in the Persian Gulf, it acquired a dual administrative and political personality as the centre of the modern state of Bahrain (*Hukumah al-Bahrayn*) and of a municipal administration (*Idarah al-Baladiyyah*). The merchant elite of the pearl boom effectively took control of local government as members of the town's municipal council (*majlis al-baladiyyah*). While municipal elections and the enforcement of legislation and taxation became the pillars of *baladiyyah* rule and the symbol of a new era of modernisation, the council provided the forum for the continuation of patronage politics cementing the traditional alliance between merchants and rulers.

After 1927 the municipal government survived the collapse of the pearling industry, which caused widespread economic dislocation throughout the Gulf and jeopardised the continuation of the reforms in Bahrain. The *baladiyyah* assisted the development of the town after the discovery of oil in 1932 but its political legitimacy was short-lived. After World War II, in particular, the new social and political forces which had emerged in the first two decades of the oil boom started to challenge municipal government and the old notable class as an integral part of a 'reactionary' *ancien régime*. Between 1951 and 1957, popular mobilisation, sectarian conflict and the rise and consolidation of nationalist politics transformed the *baladiyyah* into one of the symbols of the conservative alliance between the old merchant elite, the rulers of Bahrain and the British imperial order. The collapse of the municipal order in 1957 somewhat ironically coincided with the suppression on the part of the government of the nationalist movement which had antagonised the *baladiyyah* so bitterly during the protests staged throughout Bahrain in the 1950s.

The age of reform

The government which emerged in Bahrain in the 1920s represented a new stage in the evolution of the infrastructure of informal empire which Britain had established throughout the Gulf in the nineteenth century. British involvement in the internal affairs of Bahrain had started in 1816 when William Bruce, the British Resident in Bushehr, established official relations with the Al Khalifah family. Soon after Bruce's visit to the islands the first Indian native agent was appointed in Manama, Sadah Anandadas.[1] In 1861 Muhammad ibn Khalifah was recognised as the independent Ruler of Bahrain under British protection but it was only in 1880 and 1892 that the external relations of Bahrain were placed firmly under British control.[2] That Bahrain was the only principality of the Arab coast to acquire a modern administration before the discovery of oil is testimony to the renewed strategic and economic significance of the islands during and after World War I. In 1914 the Government of India used Manama as a basis for military operations to protect the advance of the British Indian army towards Mesopotamia, then under Ottoman control. The prospects of oil exploitation also played a part in the new trajectories of imperial politics. Although the question of the role played by oil is still open to debate, it is significant that in 1914 the possibility of oil reserves in Bahrain prompted the Bushehr Residency to stipulate the first 'informal' oil agreement with Shaykh 'Isa, which prevented him from undertaking the exploitation of oil resources or entering negotiations with foreign governments.[3] Five years later, the application of the Bahrain Order-in-Council (which was issued in 1913) integrated Bahrain into the sphere of informal empire as an overseas imperial territory and laid the foundations for the establishment of the new administration. Under the provisions of the Order, Bahrain became the lynchpin of the new 'forward' policy advocated by the Government of India in the Gulf following the imposition of British control over Iraq.

---

[1] Onley, *The Arabian Frontier of the British Raj*, p. 138; M. G. Rumaihi, *Bahrain: Social and Political Change since the First World War* (London and New York: Bowker, 1976), p. 10.

[2] The relations between the British government and the Al Khalifah have been studied fairly extensively. For further details see Rumaihi, *Bahrain*, pp. 11–14; T. T. Farah, *Protection and Politics in Bahrain, 1869–1915* (Beirut: American University, 1985), pp. 18–130.

[3] Rumaihi, *Bahrain*, p. 14. For a general discussion of British oil policies in the Persian Gulf in this period see Yapp, 'The Nineteenth and Twentieth Centuries' and 'British Policy in the Persian Gulf' in Cottrell et al., *The Persian Gulf States*, pp. 41–69 (pp. 59–60) and 70–100 (84–6); M. Kent, *Oil and Empire: British Policy and Mesopotamian Oil, 1900–1920* (London: Macmillan, 1976), pp. 117–57; A. Keating, *Mirage: Power, Politics and the Hidden History of Arabian Oil* (Amherst, NY: Prometheus, 2005), pp. 43–88.

The Order granted extensive powers to the British political agent based in Manama. It subordinated the Al Khalifah administration to the Residency of Bushehr, and hence to the Government of India.[4] The establishment of a municipal government in Manama in 1919 inaugurated the new era of political reform which continued apace throughout the 1920s. In 1923 the reorganisation of the customs administration, which the Bushehr Residency had advocated since 1903, represented the first step towards the bureaucratisation of Bahrain's tribal government. Manama's customs house was placed under the control of Claude de Grenier, an Englishman who served as its director between 1924 and 1943. Customs receipts were funnelled into a newly created state treasury and the nine clerks working under his supervision became the first officials on the payroll of the new government.[5] The creation of a Department of Land Registration (*Idarah al-Tabu*) in 1925, the establishment of a system of Civil Courts after 1923 and the reform of the pearling industry initiated in 1924 constituted the pillars of the new imperial regime.[6]

The rationale of British intervention in Bahrain was administrative rather than political. The reforms maintained the native regime in power and minimised formal responsibility of government on the part of the authorities of India. The position of the Al Khalifah family remained unchallenged as Shaykh Hamad headed the reformed administration as regent after the forced abdication of Shaykh 'Isa in 1923 and until his death in 1932. The centrepiece of the reforms was the abolition of *al-'imarah* system and the suppression of feudal rights exercised by the ruling family in urban and rural areas. As administrative authority was progressively devolved to the new departments, positions were no longer allocated to members of the ruling family and to the clients of the Al Khalifah on the bases of tribal patronage, at least in principle. In practice, many of Shaykh Hamad's relatives turned into state employees as they served in the Civil Courts and headed the municipal councils of Manama and Muharraq, the latter established in 1929. Moreover, with the creation of a state treasury and the institution of a Civil List in 1923, the properties

[4] 'The Bahrain Order in Council, 1913', L/P&S/10/248 IOR.
[5] *The Bahrain Government Annual Reports, 1924–1970*, 8 vols. (Gerrards Cross: Archive Editions, 1986): 'Administrative Report for the Years 1926–1937', vol. II, pp. 15–16; 'Revenue and Expenditure for the Year 1354', vol. I, p. 7; 'Annual Report for the Year 1356', vol. II, p. 42; 'Annual Report for the Year 1357', vol. II, p. 50; 'Annual Report for the Year 1358', vol. II, p. 40.
[6] The administrative reforms of the 1920s have been studied in some detail. See as main contributions Rumaihi, *Bahrain*, pp. 167–92; Khuri, *Tribe and State in Bahrain*, pp. 85–117; al-Tajir, *Bahrain, 1920–1945*, pp. 52–103.

6 Charles Belgrave in his office instructing Baluchi policemen as Head
of the Bahrain Police Force, mid 1940s. Standing on his left side is an
officer of Iraqi origin.

controlled by the ruling family were separated from those controlled by
the state.[7]

Between 1919 and 1926 the British agents acted as the executors of the
provisions of the Bahrain Order-in-Council and established the new
administrative bodies. After 1926 Charles Belgrave, formerly of the
Colonial Office, assumed responsibility for the continuation of the
reforms and for the day-to-day administration of Bahrain as the financial
advisor to Shaykh Hamad. Although the appointment of Belgrave
responded to a new imperial vision of 'necessary' interference in the
islands, it effectively separated the political agency from the new state
apparatus. The role of Belgrave was far more prominent than that suggested by his title of financial advisor. After 1926 he controlled the new
administration, and was in charge of key departments such as Land
Registration, Finance and of the newly formed State Police. As the
éminence grise of state formation, Belgrave organised a self-financing and
efficient administration (see Figure 6). As aptly summed up by Glen
Balfour-Paul: 'the progress in administrative disciplines which he

---

[7] Khuri, *Tribe and State in Bahrain*, pp. 89–101, 109–110; al-Tajir, *Bahrain, 1920–1945*,
pp. 52–3.

[Belgrave] succeeded in accomplishing was such that it was regarded by some as unparalleled in the Arab world.'[8]

The profile of Belgrave as state builder was unique in the history of British involvement in the Middle East and his appointment to a position of influence in Bahrain was certainly timely. In the 1950s, the employment of British advisors in Kuwait, Qatar and the Trucial States in fields such as education and public security encountered mixed success partly for their limited scope and partly for the changed political climate which surrounded the British presence in the Arab world.[9] By then, the position of Belgrave in Bahrain had become untenable as a result of the growth of Arab nationalism and of a strong anti-British sentiment which marked the twilight of the British imperial age east of Suez. The growing concentration of power in the hands of the advisor (or *al-mustashar*, as Belgrave became known in Bahrain) attracted criticism from both indigenous activists and from the British Residency, leading to his dismissal by direct intervention of the Foreign Office in 1957 after the nationalist protests.[10] In many respects, the departure of Belgrave sanctioned the end of imperial reform in Bahrain. Before the declaration of independence in 1971 the appointment of new advisors was purely cosmetic, reflecting the progressive devolution of authority to the indigenous administration on the one hand, and the direct control exercised by the British Residency over public security on the other. Belgrave has left an indelible mark on the popular mythology of statehood, if not on the official narrative of modernisation and oil development promoted by the government. While his name and photographs feature very seldom in the displays of Bahrain's national museum and in history books, the memory of Belgrave has lived on in the lively political debates which have characterised the post-independence years.

The changing rhetoric of empire

With reform already on the agenda at the turn of the twentieth century, the political agents who established the new administration between 1919 and 1926 arrived in Manama with instructions to seek the amelioration of local government and to turn public opinion in favour of British rule. In 1919 the enforcement of the Bahrain Order-in-Council encountered

---

[8] G. Balfour-Paul, *The End of Empire in the Middle East: Britain's Relinquishment of Power in Her Last Three Arab Dependencies* (Cambridge University Press, 1991), p. 109.

[9] Balfour-Paul, *The End of Empire*, pp. 108–9.

[10] For an account of Charles Belgrave's life and experiences in Bahrain see C. Belgrave, *Personal Column* (London: Hutchinson, 1960).

opposition throughout the islands, particularly among tribal leaders who perceived it as the first step towards the imposition of a colonial regime. As the men on the spot, political agents carried out policies often at odds with the directives of their superiors, influenced by their training and experience in Iraq. In their minds reform was neither an indigenous adaptation to European models nor a compromise between the old principle of non-interference and the new policy of 'intrusion' advocated by the Government of India. They took upon themselves the civilising mission of empire as a process of regeneration of state and society.

Captain Norman N. E. Bray, appointed as Political Agent in November 1918, famously lamented in an official report that 'British prestige [in Bahrain] rests on entirely false standards, namely on fear and not on respect'. The subtext of his argument is an incisive critique of the aloofness of the British *ancien régime* in Bahrain which had prevented local officials from gaining the trust of the natives. In the same report he also draws some impressionistic sketches of the local population, a testimony to the paternalism and stereotyping which characterised the attitude of British agents in the first decade of the reforms.[11] Bray's portrayal of the indigenous leadership is dominated by irrational psychological attributes such as fear and pride. Moreover, he denies them an active role in any meaningful process of change as a result of their deep-seated ignorance: 'Very few [among the rich and influential] can read and write. Geographical knowledge is appalling, politics of most amazing conception, they cannot understand the simplest measure of administration and reform, incapable of clear statement and dull reasoning, intellectually dull and naturally stupid.'[12]

According to Bray, hostility to British authority was a dangerous local 'disease' which demanded the prompt intervention of the political officer, the doctor who 'must know accurately the medicine required for each of his patients'. As the 'cure' for Bahrain's society, Bray proposed the organisation of weekly meetings with the population in the political agency and the establishment of a special fund for 'rewards for service'. Moving from the figurative to the literal, Bray believed that improvement in health and sanitation was the key means of 'progress' whose benefits could no longer be denied to the indigenous population. The decaying urban landscape of Manama, he wrote, reflected local ignorance and superstition. The municipality, established soon after Bray wrote his account, was invested

---

[11] Captain N. N. E. Bray, 'Note on the Political Situation in Bahrein as Existing at the End of 1919, with Suggestions and Proposals for Improving the Situation' in Political Agent Bahrain to Civil Commissioner Baghdad and Deputy Political Resident Bushehr, 5 January 1920, DN 2A/4/26–27, Dickinson Papers, Middle East Centre, University of Oxford (kindly supplied by James Onley).

[12] Bray, 'Note on the Political Situation', p. 12.

with the task of enforcing a new political and sanitary regime in the town as the antidote to Bahrain's social and political malaise.

Bray's rhetoric inspired his successor, the vigorous Major Dickinson who had also served in Mesopotamia. Familiar with Arab customs, Dickinson transformed the British agency once a week into a tribal *majlis* where notables were seated on carpets and invited to air grievances and discuss matters of public concern.[13] The policy of rewards advocated by Bray also came to fruition. In 1922, Shaykh Hamad, then still heir apparent, and a handful of prominent urban notables such as 'Abd al-'Aziz al-Qusaybi and Yusuf ibn Ahmad Kanu gained the rank of khan bahdar, a honorific title awarded to British Indian Muslims for services rendered to the Crown. Under Dickinson the agency became increasingly involved in the reorganisation of local government in Manama. The new course of policy was inaugurated in 1919 by the temporary dissolution of the *Majlis al-'Urf*, the indigenous council for commercial arbitration, following allegations that Shaykh 'Isa had dismissed one of its members unfairly. When it was reconvened in January 1920, the agency appointed half of its members, a right which was also extended to the new *baladiyyah* in July.[14]

Although reforms were generally understood to be beneficial to British interests, the Bombay Government, the Political Residency in Bushehr and the Foreign Office in London supported the initial modernisation of Bahrain with uncertainty and ambivalence. The vigorous involvement of political agents in local affairs continued apace with Major Daly, who reformed the customs and established the Department of Land Registration. For their part, British government offices continued to question the suitability of reform in the wider context of imperial policies in the Gulf. As early as 1919, the deputy political resident in Bushehr gave an unusually clear-cut assessment of the British presence in the region measured against the uncertain British commitment to the modernisation of Bahrain:

Until very recent times our claims to predominance in the Persian Gulf, though well enough founded on our performances in the role mentioned above [of keeper of the Maritime Truce] were not really much supported by any exertions of ours in the direction of lighting and buoying, although British statesmen were in the habit of assuming this for public consumption ... the fact remains that Great Britain has been the maritime police of the Gulf, and very little more. Is it, or is it not, desirable that we should take a pronounced step further, and assume the

---

[13] 'Bahrain's Political Diary, December 1919' in *Political Diaries of the Persian Gulf, 1904–1958*, 20 vols. (Farnham Common: Archive Editions, 1990), vol. VI, p. 511.

[14] 'Administration Report of the Persian Gulf Political Residency for the Year 1922' in *The Persian Gulf Administration Reports, 1873–1949*, vol. VI, p. 53; Rumaihi, *Bahrain*, pp. 170–3. See R/15/2/12 IOR on the dissolution of the *Majlis al-'Urf*.

responsibility for a gradual education of the Gulf populations on the lines of Western civilisation?[15]

The unease with which the imperial order viewed the social and political modernisation of Bahrain continued to transpire from the correspondence between the various departments of the British government throughout the 1920s. Somewhat ironically, the political residency of Bushehr often defended the position of Belgrave against what continued to be referred to in India and London as the 'excessive westernisation' of the country. In 1927, the Foreign Secretary remarked that 'a British financial adviser, British Police Superintendent [Belgrave] and British customs manager [De Grenier], this is more British than Katal, which is a border state [one of the native states of India].'[16] Two years later, the political resident explained the necessity for the continuation of British involvement to the Indian Government in these terms: 'Mr De Grenier [the customs director] collects the revenue of the state and Belgrave [the financial advisor] preserves them. If the efficient collector and conserver are removed, what is to happen to a state which has become accustomed to a far higher expenditure than ever before in its history?'[17]

In the 1930s and in the 1940s, the debate about what constituted British interference in Bahrain (and Gulf) affairs continued. Yet it was the discovery of oil in commercial quantities in 1932 and the beginning of oil exports in 1934 that provided the political motives and the material resources for the continuation of administrative reforms under Charles Belgrave. Moreover, from the mid-1930s new geopolitical considerations prevailed. Bahrain, alongside Iran and Iraq, became crucial to British planning in preparation for World War II as its oil reserves supplied British imperial possessions east of Suez, including India. As Middle Eastern oil and the defence of imperial interests had become closely connected, the Foreign Office included the islands in the Persian Gulf defence scheme in 1938.[18]

Besides oil reserves, the strategic importance of Bahrain as an air station between Great Britain, India and the Far East reshaped the basis of the British presence in the islands. As these strategic considerations gained the upper hand after the end of World War II, Bahrain was transformed into the harbinger of British power in the Gulf region. In 1947 the Residency was transferred from Bushehr to Manama following the

---

[15] G. H. Bill to Officiating Political Resident Bushehr, 17 June 1919, DN2A/4/26–27, Dickinson Papers, Middle East Centre, University of Oxford (kindly supplied by James Onley).

[16] Quote from Rumaihi, *Bahrain*, p. 183.

[17] Political Resident Bushehr to Secretary of State for India, 29 June 1929, R/15/2/127 IOR.

[18] M. Kent, *Moguls and Mandarins: Oil, Imperialism and the Middle East in British Foreign Policy* (London: Cass, 1993), pp. 157–8.

independence of India. In matters of domestic policy, the British administration gave precedence to the oil and security alliance with the new
government. These concerns limited the scope of imperial intervention in
the internal affairs of the islands to matters concerning extraterritorial
jurisdiction, public order and, naturally, the oil industry.

In ideological terms, a new focus on social advancement and welfare for
the indigenous population supported, and to a certain extent provided a
justification for, the new aims and objectives of informal empire. It also
replaced the moral values of the 'benevolent' imperialism which had
inspired the rhetoric of reform in the 1920s. Not only was the well-being
of the natives a guarantee of public order, particularly after the Egyptian
revolution of 1952 and the emergence of radical Arab nationalism, but it
also fulfilled the moral imperatives which increasingly underpinned the
British imperial enterprise in the Middle East in the era of decolonisation.
Soon after World War II, the focus of the political discussion shifted from
the suitability of supporting Bahrain's modernisation to the entitlement of
individuals to share the benefits of oil revenue. The debate on agriculture,
which continued throughout the 1930s and 1940s, is quite indicative of
this change of emphasis. For instance, the uncertain financial prospects of
Bahrain in the early oil era raised concerns about the future diet of the
population. As oil royalties exceeded customs receipts for the first time in
1936, the British Agent continued to press for the resumption of the
agricultural scheme, which had been abandoned in 1932 as a result of
insufficient funds.[19]

As the unofficial agent of informal empire, Belgrave pursued his own
rhetoric, often distancing himself from the different generations of British
imperial administrators posted in Manama. Remarkably, during his long
career on the payroll of the ruler of Bahrain his strong, but often rigid,
sense of duty seldom created split loyalties in his role as broker between
the agency, the ruler and the population. While displaying some of the
patronising traits of the British agents, he embraced wholeheartedly the
rhetoric of development before it became the established doctrine of
the British imperial order in the 1940s. Since 1926, Belgrave advocated
the emancipation of the local population along modern lines, a belief
which stemmed from his daily contact with individuals from all walks of
life as head of the Land Department, the Courts and the Police. In this
sense, Belgrave's 'civilising mission' was a personal undertaking rooted in
his years of service in the Colonial Office before his arrival in Manama.
Ultimately, however, the advisor remained part of the infrastructure of

---

[19] Political Agent Bahrain to British Resident Bushehr, 17 November 1936, R/15/2/807
IOR. On Bahrain's agricultural development see al-Tajir, *Bahrain 1920–1945*, pp. 162–9.

informal empire and acted as its most influential agent in Bahrain. In
1957, following his removal by the Foreign Office, he also became its most
illustrious victim. In this respect, Belgrave's departure from the islands
brought to a close the very personal relationship which the British Empire
had entertained with Bahrain since the early nineteenth century.

Imperial intervention and state building before oil: the *baladiyyah* and the law

The evolution of municipal government in Manama in the 1920s and
early 1930s marked a new stage in the relationship between the town and
Bahrain's state administration, exemplifying the institutional tensions
which characterised the early period of reform. As the official application
of British extraterritorial jurisdiction after 1919 sanctioned the beginning
of both reform and municipal government, these tensions became most
apparent in the legal sphere. The newly established *baladiyyah*, the political agency and the nucleus of the modern state administration (which
after 1926 was headed by Charles Belgrave) faced complex issues of
jurisdictional authority inside Manama. The application of the law in
force in British India and the parallel development of municipal and
modern state law blurred the boundaries between municipal, imperial
and state authority. By the early 1930s, however, the progressive relinquishment of direct British interference in municipal affairs and of extraterritorial jurisdiction transformed the municipality into a forum of
indigenous legal contestation. In this period the attempts on the part of
the municipal council to obtain independent judicial powers from the
government are evidence of the important role played by the *baladiyyah* in
the initial stages of state building, as well as of the consolidation of the new
municipal regime.

Municipal government was the brainchild of informal empire and constituted the vanguard of British expansion in Bahrain in the aftermath of
World War I. The *baladiyyah* was the centrepiece of the new regime
ushered in by the enforcement of the Bahrain Order-in-Council in
1919. Established under the first legislation issued under the authority
of the Order, municipal government transformed Manama into an overseas imperial territory with a view to maintaining and expanding the
influence of the Government of India.[20] The consolidation of British
extraterritorial jurisdiction in Bahrain's leading port was central to the
new municipal regime. The enforcement of capitulary rights upon foreign

---

[20] 'King's Regulations under Article 70 of the Bahrain Order in Council, 1913, N.1 of
1921', R/15/2/1218 IOR.

7 The Municipality of Manama festooned with British flags on the
occasion of the coronation of King George VI, 1937

residents, the imposition of new legal systems and the reorganisation of
port towns and cities were the hallmark of European expansion overseas in
the nineteenth century (see Figure 7).[21] Developments in Bahrain are
clear evidence of the exponential growth of British interests in the Persian
Gulf and of the importance attached by both India and London to the
safeguard of the loose capitulary rights exercised by the British agents in
Manama, who often offered their services to Indian traders around the
Gulf.

    As discussed in the previous chapter, in the last quarter of the nine-
teenth century native agents were not in a position to enforce *de jure* the
rulings of the courts they presided over in Manama, as the treaties
negotiated by the Indian authorities with the rulers of Bahrain did not
contain specific provisions with regard to the exercise of extraterritoriality.
The Treaty of 1861, for instance, allowed the native agent to settle
commercial disputes which involved British subjects and dependants,

---

[21] For extraterritoriality and municipal government in treaty port systems see Murphey, 'On
the Evolution of the Port City', p. 240.

but the definition of the latter was open to speculation.[22] In 1905, extra-territorial jurisdiction was extended to the Persian community and to all Arab residents who were not subjects of Shaykh 'Isa. However, legal arrangements remained unclear. As explained by the British resident to the High Court of Bombay in early 1918: 'He [the political agent in Bahrain] does not execute decrees rather than his own.'[23] Under the new municipality, the court convened in the British political agency was firmly placed under the criminal and civil law of India which was codified in 1860. British agents also acquired considerable powers over the indigenous judicial system.[24]

Before the arrival of Belgrave in 1926, the agency controlled municipal government and treated it as an appendix of the capitulary system. While British agents effectively vetoed appointments to the Islamic courts and vetted judgements passed by the local qadis, they also adjudicated all municipal offences in the agency court. There is also evidence that they attempted to extend British jurisdiction to the subjects of the Shaykh of Bahrain, particularly to the Baharna population. These attempts did not find favour in either London or India at a time when British commitment to the advance of imperial influence in Bahrain was subject to fierce controversy.[25] After 1926, the British agents adopted a policy of 'limited' interference in municipal affairs, while continuing to adjudicate cases involving foreigners. By the late 1930s the issue of extraterritorial jurisdiction had become conspicuously absent from municipal affairs, reflecting the course of British imperial politics in Bahrain. The agency progressively relinquished jurisdiction over large segments of the urban population, a process which peaked after the issue of the Bahrain Nationality and Property Law in 1937. In the meantime, the consolidation of the independent authority of the *baladiyyah* can be measured by the emergence of a critical mass of municipal subjects. There is ample evidence to suggest, for instance, that both foreigners and Baharna no longer resorted to the Bayt al-Dawlah, as they had done before 1919, to voice their grievances but appealed directly to the municipal council to remonstrate against the agency, the municipal administration and the new

---

[22] Penelope Tuson, 'Introduction to series R/15/3 IOR, Bahrain Political Agency: Political Agent's Court, 1913–1948', p. 124, India Office Library.

[23] Political Resident Bushehr to Foreign Department of the Government of India, 28 August 1929, R/15/2/127 IOR; quote from correspondence British Residency Bushehr to Registrar of the Bombay Court, 7 January 1918, R/15/2/948 IOR.

[24] Article 14 of 'The Bahrain Order in Council, 1913', L/P&S/10/248 IOR; S. A. Al-Arayyed, *Islamic Law as Administered in British India and in Joint British Courts in the Arabian Gulf, 1857–1947* (Manama: al-Ayam Press, 2001), pp. 500–11.

[25] R/15/2/133 IOR: Political Agent Bahrain to Political Resident Bushehr, 17 March 1923, n. 37/C; Political Resident Bushehr to Political Agent Bahrain, 18 March 1923, n. 267.

government. The increasing influence of the *majlis* after 1926 can also be explained by the establishment of modern civil courts which started to adjudicate cases for municipal offences in lieu of the agency. As the municipal authorities started to file suits in the new courts, residents increasingly appealed to both the council and to the judges in order to contest decisions.

Additional factors contributed to the consolidation of the municipal council as the new power broker in town. Reflecting the demography of Manama, the *majlis* was an indigenous institution, at least if compared to the municipal councils of Mediterranean ports such as Tunis, Alexandria and Istanbul, all of which included Europeans.[26] Its members belonged to the mercantile aristocracy of the town and were appointed (and after 1926 partly elected) on the basis of local influence, wealth, foreign connections and, last but not least, previous service in the Al Khalifah administration. The first council formed in July 1920 was representative of these trends. It included prominent merchants, four of whom were British protected subjects such as 'Abd al-'Aziz al-Qusaybi, the Najdi agent of Ibn Sa'ud, and Set Hamindas Diwan, a member of the syndicate of Indian tax-farmers which controlled the customs. The remaining four members represented the Hawala, Baharna and Sunni Arab communities which were under the jurisdiction of Shaykh 'Isa.[27] While appointments to the council followed the principle of communal representation, the *majlis* had jurisdiction over the various districts of the town irrespective of the ethnic, religious or national affiliation of their residents. Further, the *baladiyyah* acquired city-wide administrative powers, in contrast with the municipal administrations of Alexandria, Tunis and Istanbul which were primarily concerned with the districts inhabited by Europeans and other foreigners.

The legislative powers acquired by the *baladiyyah* also reinforced the authority of municipal government. The *majlis* issued legislation in matters of health, building regulations and public security through periodic proclamations to the public (*i'lanat*) which refined and complemented

[26] G. Baer, 'The Beginnings of Municipal Government in Egypt', *Middle Eastern Studies* 4.2 (1968), 118–40; W. L. Cleveland, 'The Municipal Council of Tunis, 1858–1870: A Study in Urban Institutional Change', *International Journal of Middle East Studies* 9.1 (1978), 33–61; S. Rosenthal, 'Minorities and Municipal Reform in Istanbul, 1850–1870' in B. Braude and B. Lewis (eds.), *Christians and Jews in the Ottoman Empire: The Functioning of a Plural Society*, 2 vols. (New York: Holmes and Meier, 1982), vol. I, pp. 369–85.
[27] Resolution dated 3 Dhu al-Qa'dah 1338/20 July 1920 in Belgrave to Political Agent Bahrain, 15 Ramadan 1347/25 February 1929, n. 1068/8, R 15/2/1218 IOR. 'Annual Report for the Year 1365' in *The Bahrain Government Annual Reports, 1924–1970*, vol. III, p. 46. For a brief account of the first sessions of the *majlis* see, 'al-Baladiyyah insha'at bi amr shafahi' lakinnaha kanat tushabbih bi hukumah', *Akhbar al-Khalij*, 23 July 1980.

municipal by-laws, first issued in 1921 and revised in 1929.[28] Yet after 1926, the piecemeal development of an indigenous system of modern civil law which incorporated British Indian Legislation and the ordinances issued by the new departments and by the ruler triggered a fierce contest over the recognition and application of municipal decrees in the new civil courts. Proposals for the draft of a Bahrain Civil Ordinance started to be discussed in 1924, but at the beginning of World War II the courts were still short of a civil code.[29]

As the activities of the *baladiyyah* expanded, the arbitration of the courts in matters concerning taxation and public security became crucial to support the municipal regime. While the public announcement of decrees and the posting of proclamations on the walls of Manama became the most tangible manifestation of municipal authority, judicial proceedings often challenged it. Once residents were summoned to the court room, judges, who were often unfamiliar with municipal regulations, offered both plaintiffs and defendants an opportunity to bypass *baladiyyah* legislation, as often lamented by the municipal secretary. In 1928 the *majlis* appointed a subcommittee in charge of bringing to the attention of the government the deliberations of the municipality so that they could be included in the general law (*al-qanun al-'amm*).[30] On several occasions in the following years, the municipal council attempted with no success to obtain independent judicial authority. In 1938, for instance, it requested the establishment of a *baladiyyah* court.[31] To some extent this reflected the large number of municipal cases which were pending in the civil courts, but also the lack of standardisation of legal practice that allowed councillors to demand more autonomy in the name of the arbitrary legal authority exercised by the central administration.

Between 1923 and 1929 the recognition of municipal law also had strong political overtones, as the decrees issued by the *baladiyyah* were treated as personal deliberations of Shaykh Hamad, who was president of

---

[28] 'Rules and Regulations under Article 70 of Bahrain Order in Council, N.1 of 1921, Municipal Rules and By-laws' in Political Resident Bushehr to Secretary of State for the Colonies, 19 August 1921, L/P&S/10/349 IOR; 'Surah al-qanun li al-baladiyyah al-asasiyyah' in Secretary of Manama Municipality to Belgrave, 6 Ramadan 1347/16 February 1929, n. 910/6 of 1347, R/15/2/1250 IOR.

[29] Political Resident Bushehr to Political Agent Bahrain, 18 March 1924, R 15/2/133 IOR. The file R/15/2/818 IOR deals extensively with the codification of state law which since the 1930s became a major cause of civil unrest. For the evolution of Bahrain's legal system see H. J. Liebesny, 'Administration and Legal Development in Arabia: the Persian Gulf Principalities', *Middle East Journal*, 1 (1956), 37–42 (37–9); N. Brown, *The Rule of Law in the Arab World: Courts in Egypt and in the Gulf* (Cambridge University Press, 1997), pp. 146–8 and al-Tajir, *Bahrain, 1920–1945*, pp. 54–56, 228–48.

[30] MMBM, 14 Safar 1347/1 August 1928, R/15/2/1218 IOR.

[31] MMBM, 13 Rajab 1357/8 September 1938, R/15/2/1924 IOR.

the municipality. Often applied outside Manama, they were de facto recognised as state legislation. In spite of the conundrum faced by Bahrain's modern legal system in the making, it is clear that in the 1920s the municipality acted as one of the key sources of legislation in parallel with the Customs administration and the Department of Land Registration. The agency and Belgrave tended to view 'excessive' municipal influence as evidence of the political ambitions of Shaykh Hamad and of the municipal councillors, the latter often accused of corruption, mismanagement and nepotism. Between 1929 and 1930, the agency and Belgrave dismantled the early municipal regime headed by the regent. After the amendment of the municipal by-laws, the *majlis* was dissolved and Shaykh 'Abdallah, Hamad's brother, was appointed as the new president.[32] The separation of municipal authority from that of regent can be interpreted as a move towards state centralisation which shifted the balance of institutional power from the municipality to the new administration headed by Belgrave.

The collapse of pearling and the chain of debt, 1927–35

Before the oil era the organisation of the municipal administration proceeded at a slow pace. In the inner city, the pillars of the early municipal regime were taxation, the enforcement of health regulations and the management and upkeep of spaces of public utility, particularly the markets. In 1920, the newly formed *baladiyyah* carried out a census of shops and houses for the purpose of taxation in order to support municipal services. Up to the mid 1920s, taxes levied on imports into Bahrain also financed the organisation of the municipal machinery, as rates revenue was insufficient to cover municipal expenses, particularly the payment of the salaries of its employees. In the following years the government continued to subsidise the *baladiyyah* with grants raised by the road tax and customs duties in order to support the growing numbers of *baladiyyah* workers which included tax collectors, clerks, watchmen and inspectors.[33]

Outside Manama's historic neighbourhoods, the boundaries of the control exercised by the *baladiyyah* were extremely fluid. Although the

---

[32] Political Agent Bahrain to Belgrave, 19 February 1929 and Belgrave to Political Agent Bahrain, 15 Ramadan 1347/25 February 1929, R/15/2/1218 IOR; text of speech by Belgrave to Manama Municipal Council, 22 April 1930, R/15/2/1250 IOR; 'Annual Report for the Year 1365' in *The Bahrain Government Annual Reports, 1924–1970*, vol. III, p. 46.

[33] 'Municipalities, General Principles' in Political Resident Bushehr to Secretary of State for Colonies, 19 August 1921, 8, L/P&S/10/349 IOR; MMBM, 14 Jumadi al-Thani 1367/24 April 1948, R/15/2/1932 IOR.

8 Police Fort (Qal'ah al-Diwan) now the Bahrain Ministry of Interior, *c.* 1950

inner city was surveyed in 1926 by the Department of Land Registration, there is no evidence of any mapping of the municipal territory until the late 1940s. As municipal borders remained fairly arbitrary, they became progressively marked by the public buildings which emerged on the outskirts of the town. In the second set of municipal by-laws issued in 1929, for instance, the southwest boundaries of Manama were fixed to the west at Qal'ah al-Diwan, the old Persian fort turned into the headquarters of the new State Police, and to the east at Qasr Shaykh Hamad, the new palace of the regent completed in 1927 (see Figure 8).[34]

The demise of Bahrain's pearling economy after 1927 brought the young municipality on the verge of collapse. The introduction of Japanese cultured pearls onto the world market impoverished all strata of Gulf societies and had a catastrophic effect on Manama. Between 1929 and 1931, Bahrain's pearling entrepreneurs lost two-thirds of their capital as a result of poor returns from the sale of pearls, which was accentuated by the world's economic depression. By 1932 the advances received by

[34] MMBM, 22 Dhu al-Qa'dah 1345/24 May 1927, R/15/2/1218 IOR; file n. 30, IT; 'Manamah City', April 1926 in *Historic Maps of Bahrain, 1817–1970*, ed. by Jarman, map n. 26; 'Annual Report for the Year 1352' in *The Bahrain Government Annual Reports, 1924–1970*, vol. I, p. 4; art. 1 of 'Surah al-qanun li al-baladiyyah al-asasiyyah' in Secretary of Manama Municipality to Belgrave, 6 Ramadan 1347/16 February 1929, n. 910/6 of 1347, R/15/2/1250 IOR.

divers had plummeted. Not only did the financial crisis affect the diving population and the pearling capitalists but it also paralysed the business of merchants and shopkeepers, and brought the pearling and import economies to a standstill.[35] The merchants and the affluent propertied classes resorted to moneylenders to service their debt. In order to avoid starvation workers and artisans were forced to buy on credit from shopkeepers whose fortunes and ability to obtain supplies were dependent on the precarious position of wholesalers and import merchants.

Yusuf ibn Ahmad Kanu, the richest entrepreneur of Manama, went bankrupt in 1935 and many of his closest business associates followed suit. The collapse of Kanu's fortune epitomised the downfall of the town's eclectic entrepreneurial class. His offices in Bahrain and Bombay, the centres of his shipping empire, were used by pearl merchants for money transfers and to deposit income from pearl sales, which financed the following pearling season. As the financial depression and poor returns from his own business stifled Kanu's celebrated cash flow, he could not pay his creditors, including import–export merchants and food dealers. The Bashmi family, for instance, Manama's largest rice importers, went bankrupt after they sold all their stock on credit in 1927. When Yusuf ibn Ahmad died in 1946, his relatives faced considerable financial difficulties.[36]

The *baladiyyah* entered the chain of debt plaguing both rich and poor. As residents could not pay taxes, they became heavily indebted to the municipality, causing its income to halve between 1929 and 1933.[37] Some members of the mercantile elite used their position as municipal councillors to avoid their fiscal obligations, as suggested by the large sums they owed to the treasury in tax arrears by the mid 1930s. In 1935, the *majlis* started openly to discuss outstanding debts and until 1937 Belgrave threatened to dismiss those councillors who continued to refuse the payment of *baladiyyah* tax.[38] The council increasingly resorted to the direct collection of tax arrears from residents who were considered to be relatively well off before the crisis in order to avoid lengthy proceedings in the civil courts and to rescue the municipal treasury from collapse.

[35] For further details on the pearl crisis see pp. 160–3.
[36] Field, *The Merchants*, pp. 275–86; Kanoo, *The House of Kanoo*, pp. 21–4, 43–7; interview with Ibrahim Bashmi, Manama, 18 March 2004.
[37] 'Annual Report for the Year 1365' in *The Bahrain Government Annual Reports, 1924–1970*, vol. III, p. 47.
[38] Report by Municipal Budget Committee, 22 Safar 1354/25 May 1935 and MMBM, 13 Safar 1354/16 May 1935, R/15/2/1922 IOR; Political Agent Bahrain to Belgrave, 4 and 27 June 1932, R/15/2/1920 IOR; MMBM, 26 Muharram 1356/4 April 1937, R/15/2/1923 IOR.

Hierarchies of wealth were, however, turned upside down. Owner-occupiers of small properties were often forced to sell their possessions. During one unsuccessful attempt to exact taxes from a group of artisans and shopkeepers, the municipal secretary noted with disappointment that: 'the *baladiyyah* is wasting time in listing them in its tax registers. These days it is difficult to distinguish rich from poor.' By 1934 the threat of widespread unrest forced the municipality to cancel outstanding tax payments and to exempt from taxation diving communities, artisans and labourers.[39]

In another important respect the pearling crisis tested the new municipal regime; it heightened existing social tensions and popular discontent. Municipal legislation had already caused a measure of resentment soon after the establishment of the *baladiyyah*. The first by-laws issued in 1920 triggered protests from the poorest neighbourhoods of the inner city. The *majlis* was forced to abolish various decrees which fixed punishments for municipal offenders and enforced the report of cases of infectious disease to the authorities. Popular petitions voiced deep-seated fears of the resumption of the old system of *al-fidawiyyah* and expressed the social stigma attached to the exposure of disease in public.[40] After 1927, the reduction of the wages of municipal employees and of the police as a result of the financial crisis favoured corruption and revived a general distrust against the administration. Anxiety over the abuse of municipal authority was to a great extent justified. In an attempt to increase revenue the municipality started to calculate the wages of tax-collectors on the basis of the sums they brought to the treasury. Only in late 1933 the *majlis* started to scrutinise systematically tax registers, following protests staged by residents in front of the headquarters of the *baladiyyah*.[41]

The socio-economic profile of municipal employees contributed to accentuate the weaknesses of the apparatus of urban administration and increased the hardship of the population. Municipal guards (*na'tur*s) often joined the force only for a few months in order to supplement their meagre income as workers in the pearling industry. Together with the police

[39] MMBM, 2 and 30 Jumada al-Thaniyyah 1353/11 September and 9 October 1934, R/15/2/1921 IOR; Political Agent Bahrain to Belgrave, 4 June 1932, R/15/2/1913; I'lan Baladiyyah al-Manamah, n. 9 of 1353, R/15/2/1921 IOR.

[40] R/15/2/1218 IOR: I'lan Hukumah al-Bahrayn, 20 July 1920/3 Dhu al-Qa'dah 1338; I'lan Baladiyyah al-Manamah, 12 Dhu al-Hijjah 1338/27 August 1920, and 8 and 17 Dhu al-Qa'dah 1338/24 July and 2 August 1920; Municipality to Political Agent Bahrain, 24 Ramadan 1347/6 March 1929 and 17 Shawwal 1347/12 April 1929.

[41] Between the years 1348 (1929–30) and 1349 (1930–1) municipal revenue and expenditure almost halved. 'Administrative Report for the Years 1926–1937' in *The Bahrain Government Annual Reports, 1924–1970*, vol. II, p. 43. MMBM, 25 Sha'ban and 16 Dhu al-Hijjah 1353/3 December 1934 and 21 March 1935, R/15/2/1921 IOR.

forces they confiscated goods and pocketed cash, especially from shop-keepers. This practice had become so widespread that the government and the agency were forced to issue several appeals between 1930 and 1932 warning the population that no credit should be given to any municipal worker.[42] Residents responded to these abuses in a variety of ways. Some used their personal connections and sought the help of individual municipal councillors, some asked for compensation directly from the *majlis* and from Belgrave, while others threatened to file suits against them in the courts for theft.

Municipal guards and members of the police force were themselves trapped in the circle of debt. By 1932 some fifty policemen and *na'tur*s on the payroll of the municipality had outstanding cases in the courts for insolvency. The case of Mahbub ibn Mubarak, a pearl diver turned police-man originally from al-Ahsa', is fairly typical of the ways in which debt continued to affect the conditions of public employment in Manama. In 1932, he was brought to the agency court by a Persian trader for a debt contracted three years earlier. The British agent ruled that the sum should be withdrawn from his salary in monthly instalments. As Mahbub was already paying off a boat captain for a diving debt, the court made attempts at recovering some of the money from the sale of his *barasti* which he claimed was mortgaged to the plaintiff. As the sale fell through, he was forced to take a huge cut in salary. He was still paying back his debt in 1937 when he became a worker in the oil refinery.[43]

The case of Mahbub highlights the long-term repercussions of the pearling crisis on the urban workforce. Between 1928 and 1935 many *barasti* dwellers on the outskirts of Manama transferred their properties to Persian traders and shopkeepers living in the inner city. The appropriation of properties by petty merchants and moneylenders increased dramatically the numbers of homeless among the immigrant communities of Manama's shanty towns and created a new class of small property owners who thrived on real estate speculation. The municipality and the government attempted to bring under control the spiralling transfer of properties. In constant need of funds, the *baladiyyah* issued several proclamations which made compulsory the registration of real estate

---

[42] MMBM, 28 Safar 1347/15 August 1928; I'lan n. 11 of 1347, R/15/2/1218 IOR. R/15/2/ 1896 IOR: Belgrave to Political Agent Bahrain, 16 Rabi' al-Awwal 1351/20 July 1932, I'lan Hukumah al-Bahrayn n. 37 of 1349 and n. 33 of 1350; notice n. 1128 of 1932 issued by the Political Agency.

[43] Minutes by Political Agent, 20 July 1932, R/15/2/1896 IOR; Political Agent's Court: *Muhammad Amin Mir Muhammad Shafi' 'Awadhi (Persia)* v. *Muhbub bin Mubarak (Najd)*, 1932–7, R/15/3/33 IOR.

outside the inner city so that houses and land could be taxed.[44] The proliferation of 'illegal' landlords also troubled Belgrave who feared the turbulence of the dispossessed *barasti* residents, notoriously inclined to resort to violence to voice their dissatisfaction. After 1930, the government even attempted to enforce the registration of mortgages in order to provide a degree of legal protection to the most vulnerable sections of the population. These measures encountered opposition from the people they sought to protect, since debtors were generally disinclined to register mortgages as they were traditionally considered private transactions.[45]

The collapse of pearling was a momentous event in the history of Manama. The recession shattered the town's port economy and threatened to undermine both the traditional socio-political order and the young municipality. The flagrant abuse of authority on the part of counsellors, *na'tur*s, tax-collectors and policemen resurfaced to haunt the most vulnerable segments of urban society. For the majority of municipal subjects from the popular quarters of the inner city and shanty towns, it was as if the clock had turned back to the dark days of *al-fidawiyyah*.

Recreating the merchant class in the oil era

By 1936–7 oil started to alleviate rising social and political tensions. The development of the oil industry offered employment to the discontented urban workforce caught in the vicious cycle of debt while reviving the ailing finances of the municipality. Although the *baladiyyah* was never subsidised directly by oil income, it benefitted substantially from the development of Manama's modern service economy. Houses for rent, in particular, became extremely lucrative as foreign firms established their headquarters in the inner city. Income from taxation on houses and commercial premises accounted for the sharp rise in municipal revenue, particularly after World War II.[46] The early oil era also reinstated Manama as a regional trade emporium and enhanced the position of its

---

[44] Political Agent Bahrain to Political Resident Bushehr, 12 January 1935 and Belgrave to Political Agent Bahrain, 29 February 1940, R/15/2/11869 IOR. For other court cases involving the transfer of properties to Persians, see cases n. 303, n. 2241, n. 2291, n.2292, n. 2294 of 1932 and n. 300 of 1933, R/15/2/1896 IOR.
[45] The mortgage of houses which was used to cover the debts was considered an optional or temporary sale (*bai' khiyari*) and treated as a private transaction which was customarily not certified in the religious courts. I'lan Hukumah al-Bahrayn, n. 4 of 1349, R/15/2/1896 IOR; I'lan Hukumah al-Bahrayn n. 2 of 1354 and n. 1 of 1359, R/15/2/1229 IOR; Shaykh Hamad ibn 'Isa ibn 'Ali to Political Agent Bahrain, 13 Sha'ban 1353/21 November 1934 and Belgrave to Political Agent Bahrain, 9 April 1932, R/15/2/1896 IOR.
[46] 'Annual Report for the Year 1365' in *The Bahrain Government Annual Reports, 1924–1970*, vol. III, p. 48.

merchants and entrepreneurs. It is difficult to draw a detailed picture of the urban economy in the 1930s and 1940s as there are no figures on imports into Bahrain. After the relative prosperity of the late 1930s, the trade restrictions enforced during World War II drastically reduced supplies and severely affected private investment in commercial enterprises. By 1948–9, however, the influence of merchant capital peaked as customs revenue from trade reduced the proportion of oil income to approximately one-third of the total state income.[47]

In the early 1950s Manama's import economy was booming following new trajectories of international trade and new patterns of consumption among the urban population. A wide array of consumer goods made their appearance in the markets of the inner city, which also served the increasing numbers of foreign residents, visitors and employees of the Bahrain Petroleum Company (BAPCO). The circulation of modern commodities explains the rise of a new class of Indian and Iranian merchants such as the Ashrafs, Jashmals and Khoshabis, who had links with Europe, Japan and China. Members of the old notability with established international business such as 'Abd al-'Aziz Khunji and Mustafa 'Abd al-Latif (the latter an entrepreneur from Lingah who ranked among the wealthiest in the Gulf) also branched out as agents of a number of Japanese firms, anticipating the trade boom with the Far East in the 1960s.[48]

Faster sea and air links and the material benefits brought about by oil exploitation transformed the portfolios of old entrepreneurs who refashioned their business in line with the modern service industry. While merchant houses amassed fortunes by obtaining the rights to import and distribute Western products in Bahrain and in other Gulf countries, they also acted as local agents for international corporations which were making inroads in the region. Manama's modern entrepreneurial class took more than two decades to become established. After the death of Yusuf ibn Ahmad Kanu in 1946, for instance, the family started to specialise in a wide array of services linked to the oil boom. Although some of his relatives started tanker work for the Saudi government in the 1950s, it was only in the 1960s that Yusuf's grandnephews, Ahmad and Muhammad, were able to rebuild a large fortune, one which far exceeded the family's assets in the days of pearling. They became the agents of Norwich Union, the first insurance company to open a branch in the Gulf, and of the British Overseas Airways Corporation.[49]

[47] F. H. Lawson, *Bahrain: The Modernization of Autocracy* (Boulder: Westview, 1989), p. 55.
[48] Rumaihi, *Bahrain*, pp. 62–3; Lawson, *Bahrain: The Modernization of Autocracy*, pp. 53–6; interview with 'Ali Akbar Bushehri, 25 April 2004.
[49] Kanoo, *The House of Kanoo*, pp. 278–91.

One of the strategies adopted by the old merchant families to rebuild their fortunes was the parcelling up of assets among heirs and close relatives in order to diversify business portfolios. After 1938, the three al-Qusaybi brothers established independent firms taking advantage of the new trade opportunities offered by oil exploitation on the eastern coast of Saudi Arabia and the low re-export tariffs levied by the government. 'Abd al-'Aziz specialised in the provision of food and consumer goods, 'Abdullah imported cars and 'Abd al-Rahman remained in the pearl business which survived as a result of a limited demand for natural pearls in the European and American markets. When 'Abd al-'Aziz died in the early 1950s the family firm was divided into some twenty branches as his relatives had opened import businesses in al-Qatif and al-Hufuf.[50]

A thriving entrepôt economy and private investment, rather than government grants and direct oil subsidies, supported Manama under the municipal administration. Wealth and entrepreneurship, however, no longer guaranteed direct access to the urban political arena, as they had done in the years of the pearl boom. In this respect, a closer look at the workings of the municipal council reveals how municipal government was still supported by the old merchant families.

Inside the *majlis*: old notables as new councillors

Until the early 1950s, the *nouveaux riches* of the oil boom had virtually no access to municipal government, which remained the preserve of Manama's old mercantile elite. The composition of the municipal council reveals a high degree of continuity in urban leadership in the pearl and oil eras. Some of the *a'yan* of the pearl boom sat in the *majlis* for several decades. 'Abd al-'Aziz al-Qusaybi, a member of the first council formed in 1920, served for more than thirty years. Over time merchant families came to view membership as a 'natural' right deriving from their involvement in early municipal affairs. After the death of 'Abd al-Nabi Bushehri in 1938, his seat was taken over by his son Mahmud.[51] After the collapse of pearling, membership of the council allowed some struggling old merchant households to maintain political influence and social prestige. The new resource base for municipal councillors was the electoral system,

---

[50] Interviews with Hasan Khajah, Ibrahim Bashmi and 'Ali Akbar Bushehri, Manama, 18 March and 20 April 2004; Field, *The Merchants*, pp. 236–7.

[51] There are no comprehensive records which detail membership in the municipal council for the period 1920–50; membership has been inferred from available electoral lists and the minutes of council meetings for the years 1927–9 (R/15/2/1923 and 1218 IOR), 1934–45 (R/15/2/1921 to 1931 IOR), 1946–50 (R/15/2/1932 IOR). I'lan Hukumah al-Bahrayn n. 7 of 1357, R/15/2/1252 IOR.

9 Manama municipal council, photo taken before 1938. Front row: first from the right 'Abd al-Nabi Bushehri, the Persian merchant, and last 'Abd al-'Aziz al-Qusaybi, the Najdi entrepreneur and representative of Ibn Sa'ud in Bahrain

taxation and the provision of services to the population, all of which provided the framework for the continuation of old style patronage politics under the *baladiyyah* (see Figure 9).

Government appointments to the *majlis* and municipal elections formalised the patterns of political representation along communal and sectarian lines in force before the reforms. After 1926, when half of the members of the council started to be elected by popular vote, the *majlis* was progressively extended from eight to twenty-four members and each community obtained a fixed number of seats: the Arab subjects of the Shaykh of Bahrain and the Persians were divided between Sunnis and Shi'is, Indians between a Muslim and Hindu constituency, while Najdis, Jews and Iraqis acquired separate representation. Communities cast their votes separately according to a strict timetable which was issued by the government before the ballot, reinforcing traditional cleavages.[52] The introduction of elections did not break the dominance that the members of the old elite had established in the first years of the municipal regime,

[52] 'Surah qanun al-Baladiyyah', *c.* 1929, R/15/2/1250 IOR; I'lan Hukumah al-Bahrayn n. 66 of 1356, R/15/2/1924 IOR; I'lan Hukumah al-Bahrayn n. 30 of 1353, R/15/2/1229 IOR; Belgrave Diaries, 26 September 1927, AWDU.

when councillors were appointed directly by the British agent and by the ruler of Bahrain. Although British rhetoric of reform hailed municipal elections as the beacon of Bahrain's path towards social and political modernisation, the electoral system in force until 1945 galvanised old clientelist networks. While government appointees (who after 1926 made up half of the councillors) continued to be predominantly members of the old merchant class, ballots contributed to favouring existing office holders. As the electorate could choose any member of their community who fulfilled the criteria fixed by the government (that is ownership of real estate within municipal boundaries), many votes were lost and new candidates disadvantaged.

With the introduction of electoral lists in the early 1930s, the administration accepted electoral candidates on the basis of petitions and testimonies by their followers, thus favouring individuals who could mobilise a vast network of supporters. Further, as the new system restricted the pool of candidates, influential notables started to canvass their constituencies more systematically, often recruiting voters from outside their close circle of affiliates.[53] Popularity among the electorate was not a decisive factor in organising hierarchies of authority inside the *majlis*. Government nominees continued to enjoy more prestige than elected representatives, who often sought to gain the favour of the authorities for the following round of appointments. Only the position of municipal secretary, which was filled in by a government appointee, was monopolised by clerks recruited from the lower ranks of Manama's mercantile communities. The relationship between secretaries and councillors epitomised the growing social tensions between the emerging state bureaucracy and the old political class. Between 1930 and 1935, at the peak of the pearl crisis, several secretaries were dismissed by the council as a result of disagreements over matters of procedure, personal conduct and their alleged excessive interference in deliberations.[54]

As a key area of municipal activity, taxation allowed the members of the *majlis* to act as the custodian of their own interests and of those of the propertied classes. By the late 1930s the benefits of the pearl boom of the late nineteenth century had become fully apparent as merchants and entrepreneurs owned more than 80 per cent of properties for residential

[53] *The Bahrain Government Annual Reports, 1924–1970*: 'Administrative Report for the Years 1926–1937', vol. II, p. 42; 'Annual Report for the Year 1365', vol. III, p. 46. I'lan Hukumah al-Bahrayn n. 66 of 1356, R/15/2/1924 IOR; Belgrave to President of Manama Municipality, 24 February 1946, R/15/2/1252 IOR.
[54] 'Annual Report for the Year 1353' in *The Bahrain Government Annual Reports, 1924–1970*, vol. I, pp. 546–7; MMBM, 17 Muharram 1355/10 April 1936, R/15/2/1923 IOR.

use.[55] After the collapse of pearling some merchant families such as the al-
'Urayyads, Ibn Rajabs, al-Mudayfa's and Bushehris lived off their investments in urban real estate, often using revenue from these properties to
launch new enterprises. The al-Mudayfa's, for instance, moved into general trade, started to import textiles and set up a jewellery shop, initially to
market unsold pearl stocks. Councillors maximised the benefits of taxation by enforcing collections from tenants rather than from landlords. In
the dire economic climate of the late 1920s and early 1930s, house taxes
dominated the agenda of the meetings of the municipal council and
provoked heated discussions between Belgrave and some members of
the *majlis*. At the height of the crisis in 1932, the advisor briefly succeeded
in enforcing collections from landlords as a result of the devastating effects
of the crisis on artisans, shopkeepers and labourers, which represented the
majority of Manama's tenant population. But after only ten months, tax
officials were instructed by the municipal secretary to revert to tenants
following the bitter opposition of the majority of the councillors who were
large property owners.[56]

By imposing a tight control over the fiscal policies of the *baladiyyah*,
councillors were also able to assuage the sensibilities of residents and to
guarantee for themselves steady profits from rents. For instance, they
tended to keep house taxes low irrespective of the value of real estate.
Belgrave was still pressing for higher house taxes after the end of World
War II when the prices of housing and land started to grow exponentially
as a result of a construction boom. In order to make up for the deficit of
the municipal treasury, the *majlis* continued to appeal to the government
for more subsidies; demands ranged from a direct share in oil income to
new entitlements from customs duties.[57]

The continuous tension between the personal interests of the old notables turned councillors and their official duties shaped the outlook of
municipal government in the residential areas. For more than two

---

[55] In 1935 out of 3,186 properties for residential use registered in the municipal ledgers only
fifty-six belonged to the Government. The rest were mainly private property. There is
no evidence of the Al Khalifah owning any houses. Belgrave to Political Agent Bahrain,
21 June 1935, R/15/2/1922 IOR.
[56] R/15/2/1922 IOR: Belgrave to Political Agent Bahrain, 21 June 1935; 'House tax in the
Municipalities of Manama and Muharraq', note on a conversation between the Political
Agent Bahrain, Shaykh 'Abdallah ibn 'Isa Al Khalifah, Belgrave and Muhammad Salih
al-Shutur (Secretary of the Municipality), 18 July 1935; minutes by Political Agent
Bahrain, 22 May 1935; MMBM, 13 Safar 1354/16 May 1935.
[57] Report by Political Agent Bahrain, 29 June 1929, R/15/2/127 IOR; MMBM, 18 Dhu
al-Qa'dah 1369/1 September 1950, R/15/2/1932 IOR. R/15/2/1218 IOR: Secretary of
Manama Municipality to Political Agent Bahrain, n. 247/5 of 1347; MMBM, 29
Muharram 1347/1 April 1938. 'Annual Report for the Year 1368' in *The Bahrain
Government Annual Reports, 1924–1970*, vol. IV, p. 29.

decades, for instance, they were reluctant to appoint officials in charge of the administration of neighbourhoods, fearing to lose authority in their traditional strongholds. Only in connection with the national census of 1941 was the town divided into eighteen districts presided over by *mukhtar*s, census officials directly appointed by the government. After World War II when Manama's census wards were transformed into electoral districts following changes in the municipal electoral system, *mukhtars* started to serve the municipality as registration officers.[58] The treatment of the *barasti* population also offers an illuminating example of how council deliberations could contravene the principles of urban regeneration which had inspired the establishment of municipal government. When in 1927 some residents complained about the hygiene standards of several hut compounds located in the inner city, asking the council to make landlords accountable for their upkeep, the *majlis* dismissed their request on the grounds that 'owners cannot be held responsible for their tenants' behaviour.'[59]

Councillors also sought to further their profile as private benefactors by taking advantage of the role of the municipality as the new body in charge of dispensing state patronage to the urban population. Donations were channelled towards urban services previously controlled by the notable class, which were integrated into new administrative networks. Through the council the *baladiyyah* supported old charitable enterprises (*al-'imal al-khayriyyah*) such as the distribution of meat during Ramadan, the maintenance of graveyards and the provision of shelter for the poor. When the government granted a monthly subsidy for the distribution of food to the needy soon after the outbreak of World War II, council members unanimously increased it by one-third out of the municipal treasury.[60] Through the *majlis*, notables continued to establish, sponsor and support religious services. In 1933, Muhammad Tayyib Khunji, a relative of the renowned Persian philanthropist 'Abd al-'Aziz Lutf 'Ali, received municipal land to build a mosque on the outskirts of Manama. Some notables also used the *majlis* as a platform to voice popular concerns to protect spaces of religious devotion from the often random growth of the inner city. In 1937 'Abd al-Nabi Bushehri successfully contested plans for the expansion of the American Mission Hospital which threatened to affect the Shi'i cemetery. The contributions of *majlis* members also

---

[58] MMBM, 1 and 24 Safar 1360/28 February and 23 March 1941, R/15/2/1925 IOR; MMBM, 1 Dhu al-Hijjah 1369/15 August 1950, R/15/2/1932 IOR.

[59] MMBM, 18 Dhu al-Hijjah 1346/7 June 1928, R/15/2/1923 IOR.

[60] R/15/2/1925 IOR: 'List of Projects Undertaken by the Baladiyyah of Manama in 1360–61 (1941–43)'; MMBM, 4 Jumada al-Ula 1360/31 May 1941.

allowed the municipality to repair mosques, and to take on some of the duties of the new Departments of Pious Foundations (*Idarah al-Awqaf*) which supervised endowments and religious buildings.[61]

The provision of water was another area of municipal intervention which overlapped with the services offered by influential members of the community. The majority of shallow wells which served the popular classes of Manama were charitable enterprises (*al-'abar al-khayriyyah*) sponsored and maintained by notables. For instance, Muqbil al-Dhakir, the powerful pearl merchant of Najdi origin, controlled a large portion of Manama's water supplies until the late 1920s through his large well in the al-Fadhil district which was located in an open ground on his property.[62] With no legal rights on public water until a system of pipes started to be fitted in the 1930s, residents drew water from these wells unless they could afford the drinking water sold in the markets. When after 1925 wells started to be registered in the name of their sponsors, they were placed under strict municipal supervision and vetted by health inspectors.[63] Owners were required to provide for their upkeep in line with municipal regulations, but the level of responsibility was often unclear. They recognised in public the important role played by the municipality in ensuring essential water supplies to the population, but were not prepared to renounce their rights. In 1941 following complaints by the residents of Farij al-Dawawdah, the *majlis* repaired one of the wells of Yusuf ibn Ahmad Kanu, built in 1927. In a letter to the municipality he vehemently accused the institution of violating his private property and of undermining local contributions to public welfare.[64]

The politics and economics of such an essential urban service were ultimately dependent on Manama's decreasing underground water resources, which eventually undermined private contributions. In the late 1920s, artesian wells became an opportunity for business and a sought-after status symbol for both councillors and residents. In 1927,

---

[61] 'List of Projects Undertaken by the Baladiyyah of Manama in 1352 (1933–34)', R/15/2/1921 IOR; MMBM, 28 Dhu al-Hijjah 1355 and 26 Muharram 1356/12 March and 8 April 1937, R/15/2/1923 IOR; MMBM, 19 Rabi' al-Awwal and 2 Jumada al-Ula 1367/31 January and 13 March 1948, R/15/2/1932 IOR.

[62] Lorimer, *Gazetteer*, vol. II, p. 1161.

[63] I'lan Hukumah al-Bahrayn, n. 793/17 of 1348 and n. 48 of 1351, R/15/2/1228 IOR; MMBM, 19 Rabi' al-Thani 1360/16 May 1941, R/15/2/1925 IOR.

[64] MMBM, 21 Rabi' al-Awwal, 7 Rabi' al-Thani and 16 Jumada al-Thaniyyah 1360/18 April, 4 May and 11 July 1941, R/15/2/1925 IOR. It seems that the contest for the control of wells between the Municipality and private individuals continued at least until the end of the 1940s as suggested by the case of 'Abdallah Fakri who in 1948 claimed ownership of his father's well which the Municipality had taken over in 1939 in order to undertake repairs. MMBM, 2 Jumada al-Ula 1367/13 March 1948, R/15/2/1932 IOR.

two members of the *majlis*, Khalil ibn Ibrahim Kanu and Muhammad Yatim, entered into competition with the Eastern and General Syndicate, a British consortium digging artesian wells in Bahrain, and started several water borings in Manama. After 1929, when the government placed drilling under strict licensing as a result of diminishing water supplies, some entrepreneurs attempted to enter a partnership with the municipality which controlled several of the new wells, envisaging the imposition of a water tax. As the direct supply of water to private houses had become extremely popular, residents often had wells drilled in their courtyards at municipal expense as a compensation for properties which the *baladiyyah* had demolished to widen the roads of the inner city.[65] When the government took over control of Manama's water distribution system in 1948, artesian wells had become obsolete given the exhaustion of the underground reserves. In the modern city private sponsorship of water supplies was progressively limited to few projects of public utility financed by the *baladiyyah*, particularly new spaces for recreation and leisure such as the various gardens which dotted the landscape of emerging modern Manama.[66]

The making of municipal markets

As income from shops and warehouses constituted a large proportion of municipal revenue, the control of the markets was central to the survival of the *baladiyyah*. Their economic importance grew exponentially after the collapse of Bahrain's traditional economy when the markets became the hub of Manama's new service industry. Politically, the market place was the venue where the municipality negotiated new alliances with the propertied classes, particularly the old merchant elites and the rulers who not only owned a considerable portion of real estate but had also provided essential services before the reforms. As explained in the previous chapter, before World War I control over the markets sealed the political and economic partnership between the Al Khalifah and Manama's entrepreneurial classes. In the municipal era, while the government essentially upheld the old property regime, the *Baladiyyah* was forced to find a modus vivendi with old property owners, as was the case in the residential

---

[65] Kanoo, *The House of Kanoo*, pp. 36–7; MMBM, 4 Rabi' al-Awwal and 16 Jumada al-Thaniyyah 1360/1 April and 11 July 1941, R/15/2/1925 IOR; Secretary of Manama Municipality to Political Agent Bahrain, 24 Muharram 1353/8 May 1934, R/15/2/1923 IOR; MMBM, 19 Rajab 1354, R/15/2/1922 IOR. For artesian wells and improvements of water supplies between 1932 and 1950 see files R/15/2/1267, 1307 and 833 IOR.
[66] MMBM, 7 Jumada al-Ula 1356/16 July 1937, R/15/2/1924 IOR; MMBM, 15 Jumada al-Ula and 27 Jumada al-Thaniyyah 1359/21 June and 2 August 1940, R/15/2/1925 IOR.

districts. As the new tax-collector, supervisor and enforcer of public security, the municipality faced particular resistance in the local markets which were the traditional fiefdom of the Al Khalifah family.

The import markets

In the old markets dealing with foreign goods, the advance of merchant capital continued apace, facilitated by the fixation of rights of private property implemented by the Department of Land Registration after 1925. After 1937, those Persian merchants who had acquired Bahraini nationality continued to invest in shops, as they had done so conspicuously in the previous decades. Further, in the interwar period small scale properties were acquired by petty traders of foreign descent as suggested by the large numbers of shops occupied by Persians and Indians by the early 1950s.[67] The large pool of properties owned by the former qadi Qasim al-Mahzah was put up for auction in the 1930s and early 1940s as their ownership and unclear status as *awqaf* had become the subject of complex court cases.[68] Family *awqaf* remained in the hands of their original owners. It seems that even at the peak of the pearl crisis only a few large properties were sold, most notably the large warehouse of Yusuf ibn Ahmad Kanu which was bought by the Kuwaiti merchant Hilal al-Mutayri in 1934. The retention of these properties rescued some of the old merchant families from financial collapse. Warehouses in particular provided one of their main sources of revenue in the early oil era once they were converted into apartments and offices in order to accommodate new businesses and foreign firms.[69]

As the old import markets became the centre of the modernising service economy of Manama, the port regime continued to favour merchants and retailers dealing with overseas commodities. After the reorganisation of customs in 1923, import duties were fixed by the government at a modicum 5 per cent, a tariff which was not increased substantially until the 1960s. Until the late 1930s, however, the Directorate of Customs faced

---

[67] Lawson, *Bahrain: The Modernization of Autocracy*, pp. 55–6.
[68] Between 1942 and 1943 Husayn 'Ali Kazim Bushehri (the son of the famous Persian merchant) bought several shops in Suq al-'Ajam, which were previously under the control of the Sunni qadi. 'Annual Report for Year 1362' in *The Bahrain Government Annual Reports, 1924–1970*, vol. III, p. 25; I'lan Hukumah al-Bahrayn, n. 38 of 1350 and n. 2 and 51 of 1351, Belgrave to Political Agent Bahrain, 25 Rabi' al-Thani 1347/9 October 1928, R/15/2/130 IOR; 'Daftar Husayn 'Ali Kazim Bushehri, 1939–1951', BA; minutes by Belgrave, 15 January 1933, R/15/2/1228 IOR; Belgrave to Political Agent Bahrain, 5 November 1932, R/15/2/1896 IOR.
[69] Interviews with 'Abd al-Rahim Muhammad and Hasan Khajah, Manama, 20 and 25 April 2004.

the stiff competition of the *baladiyyah* for the control of imports at the point of entry into Bahrain. This contest reflected the unclear division of responsibilities between the new government departments and the municipality which typified the early stages of the reforms. Officials from both sides enforced lengthy inspections in the harbour causing considerable delay to the delivery of perishable goods to Manama's warehouses. In the wake of the pearl crisis in 1929 municipal collectors started to levy their own import duties on tobacco from Oman in order to finance the activities of the *baladiyyah* in the inner city.[70] Only during World War II did the authority of the municipality in matters of imports become firmly subordinated to that of the Directorate of Customs. As provisions started to be rationed, municipal officials took charge of the distribution of rice, sugar and other essential commodities to authorised shops under the supervision of the Customs Director who was appointed by Belgrave as Food Controller.[71]

One of the most notable developments of the early municipal era was the gradual decrease of the influence of Indian merchants and wholesalers, the traditional British protégés. This partly reflected the demise of the British agency as the supreme arbiter in trade disputes. Between 1926 and 1929, for instance, a group of Indian rice importers and textile dealers were fined several times by the municipality and by the Directorate of Customs for having marketed rice, cotton cloth and silk textiles short of the weight and length advertised. Although the agency made consistent efforts to contest municipal legislation which affected its protégés, by 1929 Indian merchants were advised to resort to the courts to overturn the decisions of the *majlis*.[72] The consolidation of a powerful lobby of Arab and Persian merchants with connections to the municipality undermined further the position of the Indian trading community. Although the inflow of goods from India continued to dominate Manama's and Bahrain's import economy,[73] it was only in 1940 that Manama's Indians

---

[70] Belgrave to Political Agent Bahrain, 17 October 1929, and Director of Customs to Political Agent Bahrain, 5 November 1929, R/15/2/1208 IOR; Iʻlan Hukumah al-Bahrayn – Daʼirah al-Gumruk, 26 Jumada al-Ula 1348/29 October 1929, R/15/2/1228 IOR.

[71] al-Tajir, *Bahrain, 1920–1945*, pp. 252–6.

[72] R/15/2/1218 IOR: Secretary of Manama Municipality to Political Agent Bahrain, 25 Rajab 1347/12 August 1928; minutes by Belgrave, 4 January 1929; Iʻlan Baladiyyah al-Manamah, n. 15 and 16 of 1347 and n. 1 of 1348; Political Agent Bahrain to Belgrave, 1 July 1929; Belgrave to Political Agent Bahrain, 8 July 1929; petition by Indian merchants to Political Agent Bahrain, 31 July 1929; Political Agent Bahrain to President of Manama Municipality, 1 Rabiʻ al- Awwal 1348/7 August 1929.

[73] In 1929–30 72.5 per cent of Bahrain's imports came from India. Rumaihi, *Bahrain*, p. 61.

acquired formal representation in the *majlis*, partly as a result of their traditional reluctance to engage in local politics.

Contest over the local markets

As the markets which sold local produce remained part of the family estate of the Al Khalifah, customary practice continued to regulate the transfer of properties from the ruler to his relatives. In 1927, the control of the fish and vegetable markets was given by Shaykh Hamad to his son Salman as heir apparent. When he succeeded in 1942, the fish market came under the control of his brother, Da'ij, who resided in Manama and served as judge in the Bahrain Court. Moreover, as the ruling family continued to be the largest owners of real estate, municipal taxes on shops and ware-houses were strictly enforced upon tenants. There was no question to impose taxation upon the Al Khalifah shaykhs. They were notoriously reluctant to abandon the privileges they had enjoyed before the reforms, as suggested on several occasions by Belgrave.[74]

After the collapse of pearling, the shaykhs refashioned themselves as market entrepreneurs under the aegis of the *baladiyyah*. In 1937 Shaykh Hamad transformed the open market which was used by occasional sellers of agricultural produce into a new commercial complex. While members of the ruling family continued to collect rent and invest in the modernisa-tion of market facilities, the municipality supported their monopolistic policies in order to establish its fiscal rights. During the pearl recession the *baladiyyah* started to fix prices and to enforce strict supervision over the workforce. From 1931 the sale of local produce such as fruit and fish outside the Al Khalifah markets was banned by municipal decree. Overseas and local suppliers of meat, a commodity which continued to bring considerable revenue to Shaykh Hamad, were also placed under close municipal scrutiny.[75] In the first years of municipal government the Al Khalifah continued to appoint their own tax-farmers and brokers (*al-dallalun*) in the meat, vegetable and fish markets in order to collect

---

[74] British Resident Bahrain to Foreign Office, 2 June 1951, FO 371/91264 Public Record Office (hereafter PRO); Belgrave to Political Agent Bahrain, 22 June 1935, R/15/2/1922 IOR.

[75] 'Administrative Report for the Years 1926–1937' in *The Bahrain Government Annual Reports, 1924–1970*, vol. II, p. 45; I'lan Baladiyyah al-Manamah, n. 11 of 1353, R/15/2/1921 IOR; I'lan Baladiyyah al-Manamah, n. 369/17 of 1346, R/15/2/1208 IOR; I'lan Hukumah al-Bahrayn, n. 1430 of 1347, R/15/2/1227 IOR and I'lan Hukumah al-Bahrayn n. 49 of 1356, R/15/2/1229 IOR; MMBM, 17 Rabi' al-Thani, 1357/16 June 1938, R/15/2/1924 IOR; petition from Zayer Abbas ibn Zayer Muhammad Dashti to Political Agent Bahrain, 13 November 1937 and Belgrave to Political Agent Bahrain, 23 November 1937, R/15/2/1896 IOR.

rents and taxes, which continued to be levied as a percentage of the value of sales. In theory, the employees of the Al Khalifah were also in charge of collecting *baladiyyah* dues. In practice, the municipality was progressively forced to buy old tax-farming rights from Shaykh 'Isa and his relatives in order to collect revenue and to assuage the sensibilities of Baharna retailers who increasingly resorted to the *majlis* to voice their grievances against the ruling family.

The meat market became the centre of fierce disputes. In an unprecedented move in 1921, a group of butchers (*al-qassabun*) raised the price of meat. They appealed to the municipal council, complaining that the margin of profit was too narrow to make ends meet as a result of the high rent of market stalls. They also voiced their dissatisfaction against Shaykh 'Isa, still the ruler of Bahrain, who imposed excessive taxation upon the butchers working in the slaughterhouse (*al-muhawsi*).[76] After a municipal delegation entered negotiations with the ruler, Shaykh 'Isa lowered the tax on meat imports in order to ease the burden of the butchers, and granted the municipality the rights to enforce collections on sheep skins and leather, which was the main bone of contention in the slaughterhouse.[77] This episode is significant as the first documented instance of the appropriation on the part of the *baladiyyah* of the customary system of taxation enforced by the Al Khalifah. A poignant statement recorded by the secretary sealed the decision of the *majlis*: 'after having removed the causes of dissent and injustice the interests of the ruler continue to be respected while the municipality gains material benefit and moral reward.'[78]

This rhetoric of common good sealed the new partnership between the ruler and municipal councillors, particularly notables like 'Abd al-Nabi Bushehri and Ahmad ibn Sallum who were still serving as tax-farmers and contractors for Shaykh 'Isa. Eleven years later fresh complaints from *al-qassabun* suggest that municipal authority had not yet become fully established. The Al Khalifah, the butchers claimed, were still sending their own employees to the meat market and forced many of them to hand over a quarter of their profit on meat sales. When the case was brought again to the attention of the council in March 1933, the *majlis* firmly upheld its exclusive rights to appoint brokers. Yet the councillors turned a deaf ear to the activities of the ruler's collectors as long as the

---

[76] MMBM, 2 and 17 Muharram and 24 Jumada al-Thaniyyah 1340/5 and 20 September 1921 and 21 February 1922, R/15/2/1921 IOR.
[77] R/15/2/1921 IOR: MMBM, 15 and 29 Rajab 1340/17 and 31 October 1921 and 12 and 27 Sha'ban 1340/10 and 25 April 1922; Secretary of Manama Municipality to Shaykh 'Isa bin 'Ali Al Khalifah, 28 Sha'ban 1340/26 April 1922.
[78] MMBM, 27 Sha'ban 1340/25 April 1922, R/15/2/1921 IOR.

municipality got its share. In a similar fashion, when the butchers asked the municipality to lower the rent of their stalls (which started to be fixed by municipal decree in June 1928), the council turned their plea directly to Shaykh Salman, the owner of the premises. In 1934, the butchers took drastic action. In defiance of *baladiyyah* regulations, for two days they sold meat outside the market, fixing their own price. After some negotiations, *baladiyyah* officials confiscated the meat while large numbers of *al-qassabun* were taken to court and fined heavily, with no right of appeal.[79]

Claims to old feudal entitlements also continued to hinder attempts by the *baladiyyah* to control the meat trade into the 1930s. The control of the slaughterhouse continued to be the subject of a dispute with Shaykh Salman, who invoking tribal custom argued that any right enjoyed by the municipality was a personal concession (*hibah*) which he could revoke at any moment. As Belgrave intervened in 1933, the municipality issued a statement to the effect that the new slaughterhouse was rebuilt at municipal expenses in 1927 and as such it had de facto come under municipal control. But it was only with the programme of food rationing enforced during World War II that the *baladiyyah* was able to consolidate its position in the meat market. The fixing of prices triggered another series of strikes by the butchers in 1945, forcing the *baladiyyah* to sell meat directly to the public. After this episode, the imposition of a direct tax on butchers recognised their status as a professional group under municipal supervision in the same way as bakers, peddlers, porters and builders, all of which started to be licensed in 1931.[80]

Besides the resilience of tribal custom and privileges, a complex network of old and new commercial intermediaries constrained the centralisation of the collection of revenue. As the municipality acquired tax-farming rights on the fish and vegetable markets after 1939, a new class of municipal brokers became established. Independent *dallalun*, however, continued to demand their fees. Moreover, attempts by the municipality in the 1940s at doing away with the brokerage system altogether in order to enforce direct collections encountered fierce resistance on the part of licensed brokers. The case of the wood trade is emblematic. Until 1934, the official municipal broker Qutb al-Din Ibn Jalal paid yearly advances to the *baladiyyah* in the form of a licence fee, also

[79] MMBM, 7 and 22 Dhu al-Qaʻdah 1351/4 and 19 March 1933, R/15/2/1921 IOR; minutes by Assistant Political Agent Bahrain, 26 November 1934, R/15/2/1920 IOR.
[80] R/15/2/806 IOR, particularly Belgrave to Political Agent Bahrain, 16 September 1933. MMBM, 19 Safar 1359 and 13 Shaʻban 1362/28 March 1940 and 15 August 1943, R/15/2/1925 IOR; Article n. 52 'Surah Qanun al-Baladiyyah', *c.* 1929, R/15/2/1250 IOR. 'Annual Report for the Year 1365' in *The Bahrain Government Annual Reports, 1924–1970*, vol. III, p. 84.

supplementing his personal income with a percentage on sales. As control of the market proved to be extremely problematic, the Directorate of Customs and the municipality issued licenses to several individuals in order to ensure the payment of *baladiyyah* tax. Qutb al-Din and his son, who took over the business after his father's death in 1949, continued to campaign relentlessly for their rights, making frequent appeals to the council.[81]

By the end of World War II the local markets had remained economically and politically the stronghold of the Al Khalifah in the inner city. If on the one hand the merchants sitting in the *majlis* endeavoured to consolidate municipal authority in order to raise revenue, on the other the council secured the old partnership between the merchant class and the rulers. The impact of this alliance on the workforce was mixed. While the municipality advanced fairly successfully the centralisation of tax-collection, the position of middlemen and brokers became increasingly precarious. At the same time municipal intervention provided a degree of protection to Baharna artisans and retailers and eventually contributed to the awakening of their political consciousness.

Elections and the market place: urban conservatism, nationalist politics and the collapse of the municipal regime

By the late 1930s the local markets became an arena where sectarian grievances against Al Khalifah landlords intersected with emerging class solidarities. Both, moreover, began to be expressed in the form of labour mobilisation. Opposition to the municipality became part of a repertoire of popular dissent which relied on informal networks of political representation. After 1931, the creation of new professional groups under the aegis of the *baladiyyah* through the issue of licences contributed to increasing the influence of informal associations of Shi'i workers, some of which gravitated around the funeral houses of the inner city. Bakers lobbied the *majlis* throughout the 1930s and 1940s to reduce the price of flour, and on several occasions raised the price of bread. Even municipal employees, many of whom were Baharna, staged a general strike in 1948, demanding higher wages. The labour effervescence of the municipal era

[81] R/15/2/1921 IOR: Acting Secretary of Manama Municipality to Shaykh 'Abdallah ibn 'Isa Al Khalifah, 5 Safar 1353/19 May 1934; Political Agent Bahrain to Director of Customs, 20 Safar 1353/3 June 1934; MMBM, 22 Safar 1353/5 June 1934; Municipal Council to Political Agent Bahrain, 8 Rabi' al-Awwal 1353/20 June 1934; minutes by Assistant Political Agent Bahrain, 20 May 1934. MMBM, 7 Jumada al-Ula 1356/16 July 1937, R/15/2/1924 IOR; MMBM, 19 Safar 1359/28 March 1940, R/15/2/1925 IOR.

was epitomised by the butchers whose activism and protracted struggles were also supported by their high status, which stemmed from the ritual importance of meat in the Muslim culture of Manama. Under the leadership of Yusuf Zulaykh, a butcher from al-Mukharaqah district, who campaigned for workers' rights by appealing to egalitarian ideas of social emancipation, they earned the nickname of 'bolshies' in British official circles.[82]

The presence of the municipality did not ease sectarian antagonism. In the eyes of the popular classes the *baladiyyah* remained closely identified with the interests of the Al Khalifah and with those of the Manama Sunni community. During the strike staged by the butchers in 1934, for instance, they bitterly resented the municipal officials who confiscated their meat as *al-fidawiyyah al-jadidah*, the new employees of the Al Khalifah. Moreover, the municipal electoral charter in force until the late 1940s excluded from the electoral process a large proportion of the Shi'i population, particularly labourers, artisans and tenants of small properties. As only male residents who paid 8 rupees a year in municipal tax were entitled to vote, it favoured more affluent groups. Until 1935, for instance, Sunni Arabs were entitled to more seats than their Shi'i counterparts. Among the Persians, the two sects were equally represented although in both groups Shi'is formed the majority.[83] Fuelled by the growing disputes in the markets between the Al Khalifah and Baharna retailers, in 1934 Shi'i municipal councillors, religious leaders and representatives of Manama's *ma'tam*s started to campaign for equal representation in the municipality. The following year the government increased the number of Baharna seats in the municipal council and reduced the franchise qualification from 8 rupees to 3 rupees. Yet, the results of the 1935 elections clearly suggest that Baharna residents were disinclined to resort to the ballot box, preferring to appeal directly to their community leaders.[84]

---

[82] R/15/2/1922 IOR: Interview with 'Abdallah Sayf, Manama, 14 April 2004; MMBM, 17 Sha'ban 1354/14 November 1935. MMBM, 14 Dhu al-Hijjah 1355/26 February 1937, R/15/2/1923 IOR. R/15/2/1925 IOR: MMBM, 24 Sha'ban 1359/27 September 1940; petitions from bakers dated 13 Sha'ban and 2 Dhu al-Hijjah 1359/16 September 1940 and 11 January 1941 and 25 Rabi' al-Thani 1361/11 May 1942; MMBM, 6 Shawwal 1360/27 October 1941. MMBM, 3 Dhu al-Qa'dah 1367/7 September 1948, R/15/2/1932 IOR.

[83] 'Surah Qanun al-Baladiyyah', *c.* 1929, R/15/2/1250 IOR. R/15/2/1252 IOR: Belgrave to Political Agent Bahrain, 5 Shawwal 1348/6 March 1930; Political Agent Bahrain to Hindu Community, 9 March 1930. Belgrave to President of Manama Municipality, 21 Sha'ban 1356/26 October 1937, R/15/2/1924 IOR.

[84] A comparison of the electoral results with the municipal census of 1930 is revealing. Successful Sunni Arab candidates totalled 331 votes out of 463 households eligible to go to the polls, while only 175 votes were cast for Baharna counsellors who appealed to an

By the early 1950s the sectarian divide which had inspired Shi'i demands in the mid 1930s came to the fore in a spectacular fashion, leading to the disintegration of the municipal order and to the demise of the old merchant classes that had supported it. After 1945, the institution of municipal representation based upon electoral districts reshaped the secure, albeit contested, boundaries of communal politics. For the first time in municipal history, however, the elections of May 1950 became bitterly contested. The new electoral criteria were undoubtedly more inclusive as women were allowed to vote, but the Shi'i population bitterly criticised the new electoral wards for continuing to favour the Sunni community. Although the new council became dominated by Sunni Arabs, it seems that their success was due as much to a higher Sunni turnout at the ballot boxes as it was to the inequalities of the new electoral system. By granting only three representatives out of twelve to the predominantly Sunni districts of al-Fadhil and Kanu, the new wards effectively favoured the Shi'i electorate as they also grouped the large Shi'i popular neighbourhood of Ras Rumman with the affluent Persian Sunni al-'Awadiyyah.[85]

After 1950, the abolition of communal representation in the municipal council also allowed a young group of Arab nationalist activists recruited from the middle ranks of Manama's commercial classes to use municipal elections as a platform for the promotion of cross-sectarian interests. With the new instruments of nationalist propaganda, particularly loudspeakers and leaflets, they were able to organise very effective electoral campaigns and to rally the support of the market population in order to gain access to the municipal council.[86] The dramatic political and social changes that transformed Manama into a hotbed of Arab nationalist mobilisation will be examined in more detail in the following chapter. It can simply be noted here that the municipal council became the first institutional arena where the divisions of Bahrain's national movement were played out. On the one hand, the young counsellors started to contest the monopoly of the old notable class on the grounds that the latter embodied the conservative agenda of Belgrave, of the Al Khalifah and of the British imperial

---

electoral constituency of over 550. Political Agent Bahrain to Political Resident Bushehr, 18 January 1935, R/15/2/1921 IOR; 'Annual Report for the Year 1353' in *The Bahrain Government Annual Reports, 1924–1970*, vol. I, pp. 545–6; Belgrave to Political Agent Bahrain, 5 Shawwal 1348/6 March 1930, R/15/2/1252 IOR; I'lan Hukumah al-Bahrayn, n. 30 and 33 of 1353, R/15/2/1229 IOR.

[85] Belgrave to President of Manama Municipality, n. 455 of 1365/24 February 1946 and I'lan Hukumah al-Bahrayn, n. 17 of 1369, R/15/2/1252 IOR; Political Residency Bahrain to Secretary of State for Foreign Affairs, 2 June 1951, n. 73 and enclosures, FO 371/91624 PRO.

[86] 'Annual Report for the Year 1369' in *The Bahrain Government Annual Reports, 1924–1970*, vol. IV, p. 31.

order. On the other, sectarian tensions assumed a new nationalist dimension as the rights of 'Arab nationals' entered the vocabulary of sectarian grievances. In March 1951, as a result of a quarrel over the demolition of a number of shops, five Baharna counsellors resigned and appealed directly to the government on behalf of the workforce. They accused Shaykh Salman, the owner of the shops, of acting against national interests by letting the premises to 'foreigners', particularly to Indian retailers.[87]

After this episode the government was forced to dissolve the municipal council. Despite several calls for fresh elections in the following years, the Municipality, which continued to be boycotted by both Baharna leaders and national activists, was run by a close circle of Sunni nominees.[88] In this period the *baladiyyah*, along with other government institutions and foreign enterprises, became the target of a new type of popular militancy. During the nationalist demonstrations in Manama between 1951 and 1957 (which will be examined in the next chapter) the municipality was attacked by demonstrators. The markets, meanwhile, continued to be the focus of labour disputes. In March 1956, the municipal building was besieged by a crowd of protesters who demonstrated against a tax-collector who had forcibly removed a villager for selling his merchandise outside the designated areas (see Figure 10).[89]

Ultimately nationalist mobilisation combined with the grievances of the Shi'i workforce sealed the fate of municipal government. After 1953 *al-Ha'yah al-Tanfidhiyyah al-'Uliya* (The High Executive Committee), the populist cross-sectarian organisation based in Manama which led the nationalist movement throughout Bahrain, became the fiercest critic of the municipal order. The orchestration of electoral boycotts was an integral part of the activities of *al-Ha'yah*, whose communiqués to the population depicted the *baladiyyah* as an instrument of reactionary government policies.[90] After the disbandment of the nationalist movement in 1957, the municipality continued to be run by government appointees. The first local elections were attempted in 1965 but only 380 people out of 5,000 eligible to vote went to the polls.[91] In the era of

[87] Political Residency Bahrain to Secretary of State for Foreign Affairs, 2 June 1951, n. 73 and enclosures, FO 371/91624 PRO; 'Abd al-Rahman al-Bakir, *Min al-Bahrayn ila al-manfa*, 2nd edn (Beirut: Dar al-Kunuz al-'Arabiyyah, 2002), pp. 40–2.

[88] *The Bahrain Government Annual Reports, 1924–1970*: 'Annual Report for the Year 1370', vol. IV, p. 31; 'Annual Report for the Year 1371', vol. IV, p. 29; 'Annual Report for the Year 1372', vol. V, p. 30; 'Annual Report for the Year 1955', vol. V, p. 37; 'Annual Report for the Year 1956', vol. V, p. 82.

[89] Belgrave Diaries, 17 March 1956, AWDU; al-Bakir, *Min al-Bahrayn*, p. 104.

[90] For one of these communiqués see al-Bakir, *Min al-Bahrayn*, p. 131.

[91] Minutes, 19 December 1957, FO 371/126897 PRO; Political Agent Bahrain to Foreign Office, 16 August 1965, FO 371/179790 PRO.

10 Police vans cordoning off the Municipality (the arched building in the background) in March 1956. Shopkeepers and market sellers are protesting in front of the building

tight government control which followed the nationalist agitations of the 1950s, the political profile of the *baladiyyah* became increasingly insignificant. As local government was considerably weakened, the age of urban reform initiated in 1919 came to a close.

Conclusion

The British rhetoric of reform and 'rational' government which supported the creation of the municipality in 1919 inspired the reorganisation of the state administration in the following decades. The reforms of the interwar period left a strong institutional legacy to Bahrain. They supported the legal and financial reorganisation of the state, the creation of a new judicial system and of a security apparatus. Moreover, these institutional developments fostered the separation of the indigenous administration from the political agency as the new government came effectively under the control of Charles Belgrave.

Manama's municipality institutionalised coercion, finance and jurisdiction, functions which before 1919 were exercised by the tribal administration. Although the arbitrary practices of the Dar al-Hukumah were ostensibly removed, urban reform proved to be an ambivalent instrument of political and social modernisation. The transition from the tribal to the municipal administration was not always smooth. Until the end of World War II, the *baladiyyah* strengthened traditional chains of political authority and social power. Membership in the council guaranteed the merchant families of the pearl era and the ruling Al Khalifah family continued access to decision-making and local influence. The position of merchants in urban politics became much more dependent on pedigree and government support than on foreign connections and wealth, as had been the case before the reforms. With the connivance of the government, they used to their advantage essential services provided by the municipality such as elections, taxation and welfare.

Until 1957 local government was the bastion of the old propertied classes, uniting merchants and rulers in a new institutional alliance. In contrast with developments in Kuwait Town, where since 1938 old merchant families used their monopoly over the *baladiyyah* in order to gain political leverage against the Al Sabah, in Manama the municipality did not provide merchants with an active forum of opposition to the ruling family.[92] In an important sense the political quiescence of the old merchant class in Bahrain is evidence of successful state centralisation in the 1930s and 1940s. Yet in the aftermath of World War II the conservative alliance between the old notable class, the Al Khalifah and Belgrave was no longer viable as Manama became the centre of Bahrain's nationalist movement. As patronage politics and sectarian divisions started to be played out in the arena of nationalist and labour mobilisation, the shortcomings of the municipal regime became apparent on the backdrop of the social and political effervescence of the oil era. Changes in the municipal electoral system, for instance, can be viewed as a symptom of the decline of notable politics and as an attempt on the part of the government to co-opt a nationalist class in the making. Further, municipal intervention in the markets was instrumental in channelling the resentment of the Baharna population towards a new class struggle which was fuelled by the populist propaganda of *al-Ha'yah*. In this respect, rather than acting as a catalyst for political change, the municipality opened a window of opportunity to the rising tide of discontent against the government, Belgrave and the old notability. In doing so, it served as the platform for the consolidation of modern political mobilisation throughout Bahrain.

---

[92] In Kuwait the municipality also served as the platform for the *Majlis* movement which advocated administrative reforms. See Crystal, *Oil and Politics in the Gulf*, pp. 46–55.

5   'Disorder', political sociability and the evolution of the urban public sphere

The previous two chapters have explained the evolution of politics and society in Manama before and after the discovery of oil, focussing on the role of networks of patronage, of imperial and overseas connections and, after 1919, of municipal government. This chapter traces the evolution of urban political sociability in the same period through the lens of civic strife, popular politics and ideological contestation. These were the 'unruly' activities which reshuffled power between urban groups, and between them and the state. Key episodes of unrest and the performance of Muharram rituals are analysed as contexts of public engagement and as evidence of the changing relationship between the body politic of Manama and the government of Bahrain. Not only did they bring new leaders, social groups and political allegiances into the arena of urban politics but also fostered the growth of new forms of community and public consciousness. Muharram rituals, in particular, marked the evolution of Shi'i popular politics throughout the period. The lower classes of Manama used them as venues to express values and symbols which addressed issues of power, authority and class in the public arena.[1]

Episodes of unrest in Manama also marked crucial junctures in the process of nation and state building, a further testimony to the importance of urban activism in reshaping Bahrain's political and social orders. The clashes between Persians and Arabs which engulfed the town in 1904 and in 1923 were closely related to the commercial and political competition engendered by growing British influence and, in the latter case, by the establishment of municipal government. The riot staged by pearl divers in 1932 was triggered by the economic crisis but also by the reforms of the pearl industry which throughout the 1920s activated nascent class solidarities among the workforce. Since the late 1930s, the organised demonstrations and strikes which gradually transformed Manama into a forum of

---

[1] The role played by popular activism, ritual expression and ideological contestation in shaping public arenas in a colonial context is discussed in S. Freitag, *Collective Action and Community*.

Arab nationalist mobilisation (and led to the demise of the municipality) reflected the combined influence of Great Britain and oil as 'state makers'. The explosion of popular nationalism as a movement of anti-colonial resistance after World War II is the most illuminating example of the success of this combined influence. The disturbances during Muharram in 1953 which triggered the nationalist and labour agitations of 1954–6 represented a turning point in the consolidation of a modern political community in Manama and Bahrain. They signposted the enduring role played by ritual and Shi'i culture in providing the framework for grassroots mobilisation and a referent for nationalist politics. At the same time, they functioned as the catalyst for the establishment of *al-Ha'yah al-Tanfidhiyyah al-'Uliya* (The High Executive Committee), the cross-sectarian political organisation which took the lead in the nascent nationalist and labour movements.

Communal violence and 'foreigners', 1900–23

In pre-modern Manama the fragmentation of popular politics along lines of community, patronage and locality effectively prevented any large-scale mobilisation against the tribal government. In the town of the pearl boom, the urban population did not stage the tax or food riots which routinely shook Middle Eastern and Indian provincial capitals in the late nineteenth and early twentieth centuries. While the clientelist system effectively defused popular discontent, the informal professional associations focussed on the houses of mourning did not serve as avenues of political dissent. Until the consolidation of the municipality in the 1920s and the rise of nationalist politics in the early 1950s, these associations lacked the independent economic base and the ideological drive to develop as politically conscious organisations. With no central control over goods, services and membership, they did not enjoy the corporate autonomy of traditional Middle Eastern guilds. Moreover, they did not function as administrative or fiscal units, a feature which had allowed guild leaders in major centres such as Cairo or Istanbul to acquire considerable influence with the government.[2]

---

[2] Literature on Middle Eastern guilds is vast. The classic studies are G. Baer, *Egyptian Guilds in Modern Times* (Jerusalem: Israel Oriental Society, 1964) and A. Raymond, *Artisans et commerçants au Caire au XVIIIe siècle* (Damascus: Institut Français, 1973–4). For a revisionist study on the political and economic transformation which affected crafts and service workers in Egypt in the nineteenth and early twentieth centuries see J. T. Chalcraft, *The Striking Cabbies of Cairo and Other Stories: Crafts and Guilds in Egypt, 1863–1914* (Albany: State University of New York Press, 2004).

The elusive nature of the urban administration was an additional factor which contributed to weaken resistance to public authority. The methods employed by the Al Khalifah to rule the town were often at odds with the aspirations, ideals and commercial practices of traders, artisans and workers. Yet residents were not in a position to appeal to a hierarchy of officials to voice their grievances or to bypass their leaders. Nor they could turn to government offices in order to seek justice against abuses. In their worldview the rule of the Dar al-Hukumah of Muharraq was highly personalised. *al-Shuyukh*, the term commonly used to refer to the ruler and by extension to the tribal administration, was suggestive of the coercive and arbitrary authority exercised by the Al Khalifah family.

Outbreaks of disorder tended to be sudden and sporadic, often sparked by tribesmen, pearl divers and occasional visitors who poured into the markets. Random acts of violence could easily ignite intercommunal conflict and elite factionalism, revealing the Janus-faced character of Manama's patronage system.[3] The disturbances of 1904 between the Persians and the entourage of Shaykh 'Ali, the Al Khalifah governor of Manama, are a case in point. A band of tribesmen of unknown origin came to blows with a servant of 'Abd al-Nabi Kazeruni, the leader of the Persian community, in central Manama in the presence of some of the bodyguards of Shaykh 'Ali. Armed with sticks the tribesmen, whose numbers ranged from 50 to 200 according to eyewitness accounts, attacked Persian shops and residents. When news of the aggression reached 'Abd al-Nabi Kazeruni, he rushed to the market with members of his entourage to coordinate the resistance of the shopkeepers. Caught by some members of Shaykh 'Ali's *al-fidawiyyah*, he was beaten and chased by an infuriated mob of Al Khalifah loyalists.[4]

The dynamics of this incident display some of the features which characterised communal violence in the inner city. Residents, in this case the Persians, were victims rather than offenders as they became involved in confrontations in order to defend their lives and property.

---

[3] This point is applicable more generally to the patron–client networks which organised political life in other pre-modern Middle Eastern cities. For a general overview of their role in urban unrest see G. Denoeux, *Urban Unrest in the Middle East: A Comparative Study of Informal Networks in Egypt, Iran and Lebanon* (Albany: State University of New York Press, 1993), pp. 45–54.

[4] The disturbances are described in great detail from the perspective of British policy in Farah, *Protection and Politics*, pp. 131–49. Political Agent Bahrain to Political Resident Bushehr, 17 November 1904, enclosure n. 1, Political Resident Bushehr to Government of India, 17 December 1904, L/P&S/10/81 IOR; Hajj Abdul Nabi-bin-Kal Awaz, statement n. 2 in enclosure n. 27, 'Statements by Persian subjects' in 'Correspondence Respecting the Affairs of Arabia' in *The Affairs of Arabia, 1905–1906*, ed. by Robin Bidwell, 2 vols. (London: Cass, 1971), vol. I, pp. 116–17.

To refer to the distinction made by Charles Tilly with regard to collective popular movements, their use of violence was 'reactive' rather than 'proactive'.[5] Further, as Shaykh 'Ali and 'Abd al-Nabi Kazeruni mobilised their entourages, segments of the population became involved in a domino effect. Easily recognised by their clothing, physical traits and weaponry, Persians and Arab tribesmen were targeted indiscriminately as members of each group. The animosity against the Persians displayed by the Al Khalifah governor and by his followers was not circumstantial but a reflection of the increasing protection offered by British agents to the community after 1900, when officials from the Government of India had started to replace native agents. In fact, the hidden *casus belli* seemed to have been the detention of some members of Shaykh 'Ali's clique in the agency a few months before the disturbances after they had confiscated several of Kazeruni's boats in the harbour.[6]

The confrontation between Persians and Arabs continued to plague Manama in the early municipal era. A quarrel between a Najdi immigrant and Persian labourer in April 1923 led to a scuffle which set the stage for large-scale disturbances the following month, sparking off a prolonged wave of assaults on Persian shops. On one occasion, the agency was forced to send a detachment of guards to the coast as a menacing crowd of Najdi divers set sail to Manama from Muharraq threatening to besiege the markets.[7] The subtext of narratives by residents and British officials which recounted the factional violence of 1904 and 1923 highlights two important themes of the urban political culture of Manama. The first is the depiction of 'outsiders' as the main source of intercommunal conflict; the second is the almost constant representation of the tribal hinterland as a place of sedition and disruption of communal life. In the aftermath of both disturbances, the testimonies of eyewitnesses and British reports recounted a scenario of almost axiomatic confrontation between primitive tribal folk and town dwellers, the latter epitomised by the sophisticated Persians. Further, regardless of their ethnic and confessional affiliation, the residents of the inner city readily identified the offenders on the Arab side as *'Arab* or *qabali* (tribal Arabs), suggesting that these terms carried

[5] C. Tilly, 'Revolutions and Collective Violence' in F. I. Greenstein and N. W. Ponsby (eds.), *Handbook of Political Science*, 8 vols. (Reading Mass., 1975), vol. III, *Macropolitical Theory*, pp. 503–25 (p. 507).
[6] Political Agent Bahrain to Political Resident Bushehr, 18 December 1904, L/P&S/10/81 IOR; Enclosures n. 11 and n. 17 in 'Correspondence Respecting the Affairs of Arabia', Wonkhaus to Political Agent, 5 November 1904, and Political Agent Bahrain to Political Resident Bushehr, 17 November 1904, *The Affairs of Arabia, 1905–1906*, vol. I, pp. 101–4.
[7] Political Agent Bahrain to Political Resident Bushehr, 22 April 1923, R/15/2/101 IOR; Political Agent Bahrain to Political Resident Bushehr, 13 May 1923, R/15/2/86 IOR; Statement of Mr McKie, 63/AC, 12 May 1923, R/15/2/848 IOR.

the connotation of 'readiness to resort to arms', rather than being strict indicators of tribal and ethnic affiliation.[8]

The disturbances of 1923 present striking similarities with the events of 1904, illustrating the importance of migrant marginal groups in providing the muscle for urban unrest. The tribesmen who joined the militias of Shaykh 'Ali in 1904 were occasional visitors in search of loot, a frequent occurrence in Manama. The protagonists of the 1923 disturbances were dock workers, seasonal labourers and pearl divers from Najd, and Persians from *barasti* communities, the most restless segments of the town's lower classes. While the Persian population had steadily increased since the last quarter of the nineteenth century, the number of Najdis arriving in Manama soared after the Wahhabi conquest of al-Ahsa' in 1913. By the early 1920s the labour force from Najd outnumbered the Persians as a result of the embargo imposed by Ibn Sa'ud on Kuwait, which served to consolidate the position of Bahrain as the entrepôt centre for Eastern Arabia.[9]

Besides increasing economic competition, migration gave impetus to patronage politics which in turn fuelled factionalism among urban notables. Shaykh 'Ali clearly took advantage of the spontaneous outbreak of violence in 1904 to target Kazeruni and his business in the harbour. In 1923 Najdi and Persian notables were important players in the conflict on the side of their protégés, acting as intermediaries with the Municipality and with the British agency.[10] For some years, they had been the upcoming mercantile lobbies of the town. The appointment of 'Abd al-'Aziz al-Qusaybi as the representative of Ibn Sa'ud in Bahrain soon after 1913 allowed his family to acquire a virtual monopoly on the trade towards Eastern Arabia.[11] Among the Persians, the wealthy Sunni community had risen to commercial and political prominence as a result of the demise of

[8] Enclosure n. 20 in 'Correspondence Respecting the Affairs of Arabia', Political Resident Bushehr to Government of India, 17 December 1904, *The Affairs of Arabia, 1905–1906*, vol. I, pp. 104–5; Political Agent Bahrain to Political Resident Bushehr, 22 April 1923, R/15/2/101 IOR.

[9] Political Agent Bahrain to Political Resident Bushehr, 7 April 1929, n.C-50 of 1929, L/P&S/10/1045 IOR; Political Agent Bahrain to Secretary of Political Resident Bushehr, 2 June 1931, R/15/2/101 IOR.

[10] In April 1923 'Abdallah al-Qusaybi, one of the brothers of 'Abd al-'Aziz, negotiated the release of some of the Najdi ringleaders with the political agency by producing a *kifalah*, a document guaranteeing their future good behaviour. In May, as the headquarters of the family firm was the scene of the first clashes, 'Abdallah placated the vehemence of the rioters, gaining the confidence and support of the Bayt al-Dawlah. See R/15/2/101 IOR in particular Political Agent Bahrain to Political Resident Bushehr, 22 April 1923.

[11] Political Agent Bahrain to Secretary of Political Resident Bushehr, 2 June 1931, R/15/2/101 IOR.

Lingah as the main regional port on the Iranian coast after the Qajar government had established a customs administration there in 1900.

The disruption of public order in 1904 and 1923 had far-reaching repercussions for British policy in Manama at a time when concerns with the protection of trade and the extension of extraterritorial jurisdiction were paramount. The exile of Shaykh 'Ali to India in 1905 after the British Navy bombed his residence irreversibly changed the position of the Al Khalifah in the town, effectively placing Manama under the control of the agency some years before the establishment of the municipality.[12] It is significant that *al-fidawiyyah* of Shaykh 'Ali survived him and became the first nucleus of the future municipal police under the supervision of the agency. Further, the Government of India extended the capitulary regime by granting semi-official privileges of protection to residents who were not imperial subjects, particularly Persians.[13] Similarly, the breach of public order in 1923 raised the vexed issue of the position of the agency as the protector of Najdi immigrants. The agency questioned the rights claimed by Shaykh 'Isa ibn 'Ali, the ruler of Bahrain, which he had received from Ibn Sa'ud in 1913 but which the Sultan of Najd had transferred to the political agent in 1920 in exchange for political support for his Arabian campaign.[14]

By 1923 the debates on entitlement to British protection combined with the beginning of reform had revolutionised the political landscape of Manama. As urban groups rallied around the agency as the new power broker in town, the large Baharna community started to challenge the traditional privileges enjoyed by the ruling family. Appealing to their rights as the 'indigenous' inhabitants of Bahrain (*al-asliyyin*), they demanded fair taxation and administration of justice led by several of their notables.[15] It is against the backdrop of these developments that the confrontation between Persians and Najdis became an integral part of the formation of modern political identity. During the turbulent 1920s this unrest was instrumental in the emergence of new ideas of nation and

---

[12] Reports by H. M. S. Fox at Bahrein, 2 March 1905, and by H. M. S. Fox at Bombay, 10 March 1905 in *Persian Gulf and Red Sea Naval Reports, 1820–1960*, ed. by Anita Burdett 15 vols. (Slough: Archive Editions, 1993), vol. VII, pp. 492–500.

[13] British Resident Bushehr to Foreign Department, Government of India, 17 December 1904, n. 421, L/P&S/10/81 IOR.

[14] 'Abd al-'Aziz Ibn Sa'ud Rahman al-Faysal al-Sa'ud to Political Resident Bushehr, 5 Shawwal 1341/22 May 1923; British Residency Bushehr to 'Abd al-'Aziz Ibn Sa'ud Rahman al-Faysal al-Sa'ud, 14 June 1923, R/15/1/341 IOR; 'Note on the Persian Communities at Bahrein', 4 November 1929, in Political Agent Bahrain to British Resident Bushehr, 7 April 1929, L/P&S/10/1045 IOR. al-Tajir, *Bahrain 1920–1945*, pp. 22–3.

[15] al-Tajir, *Bahrain 1920–1945*, pp. 60–2.

national community in response to the new challenges and opportunities offered by municipal reform and by the reorganisation of Bahrain's state administration under the aegis of the British agency.

The baladiyyah *affair: the emergence of Arab sentiment*

The 1923 clashes between Persians and Arabs form the centrepiece of the early nationalist mythology of Bahrain. At the end of the hostilities Shaykh 'Isa was deposed by the Government of India so that the agency could pursue the institutional reforms initiated with the establishment of the *baladiyyah*. The official announcement of the formal abdication of the ruler triggered competing political visions for the future of Bahrain. Loyalists of Shaykh 'Isa, including a group of young Sunni intellectuals and aristocrats from Muharraq, affirmed the legitimacy of his government and started to promote new ideas of self-determination against British rule. In contrast, the plans for administrative modernisation pursued by the Government of India relied on the cooperation of the regent Shaykh Hamad, Shaykh 'Isa's eldest son and successor.[16] As Muharraq became the stronghold of the supporters of Shaykh 'Isa, they started to see it as the centre of a new 'Arab national' government in opposition to Manama, whose 'foreign' settlers and municipality became construed as the lynch-pin of British domination. In other words, under the escalating threat of British imperialism Bahrain began to be imagined as a political and territorial entity, united by Arab solidarities, by the very elites who con-stituted the pillars of the old tribal regime.

During the 1923 disturbances one episode in particular became bitterly contested: the confrontation between the municipal police and Najdi rioters in the markets. The bone of contention was the composition of the police forces, mostly Persians, who opened fire in the market, killing several rioters. The involvement of the newly established *baladiyyah* placed the agendas of urban factions within a new framework. 'Abdallah al-Qusaybi, the brother of 'Abd al-'Aziz, rushed to the British agency, accusing the security forces of having targeted his followers at the instiga-tion of the Persian secretary of the municipality, Muhammad Sharif. The secretary, himself an immigrant who had arrived in Bahrain around 1915, became the self-appointed defender of Persian interests. He launched a campaign against the al-Qusaybis in the municipal council, accusing the family of having instigated the riots in order to undermine civic

---

[16] For a detailed account of the events which led to the deposition of Shaykh 'Isa and its aftermath see Rumaihi, *Bahrain*, pp. 176–80 and al-Tajir, *Bahrain 1920–1945*, pp. 42–6.

harmony.[17] Evidence on the incident is far from conclusive and is col-
oured by partisan feeling. al-Khayri, a local Arab historian writing soon
after the events, maintains that Muhammad Sharif supplied policemen
with rifles and instructed them to fire upon the Najdis. Significantly,
British reports did not mention the episode in any detail although the
dismissal of some municipal guards suggests that they may have been
involved in acts of factional violence.[18]

This episode inflamed the young loyalists of Shaykh ʿIsa who were
conversant with modern political ideas stirred by the anti-colonial struggle
unfolding in India, where many of Bahrain's aristocrats of tribal descent
had received their education. In October 1923, they formed an organisation called the Bahrain National Congress inspired by the ideas of con-
stitutionalism and representative government championed by the Khilafat
movement and by the Indian National Congress. Led by ʿAbd al-Wahhab
al-Zayyani, the scion of a prominent pearling family, this organisation
demanded the establishment of a legislative council (al-Jamʿiyah al-
Tashriʿiyyah) under the guardianship of Shaykh ʿIsa as the rightful leader
of the people of Bahrain.[19] Further, as reported by Amin al-Rihani, the
Lebanese American traveller and Arab activist who visited the islands after
1923, Muharraq was developing as the centre of an Arab 'revival' also
under the influence of Pan-Islamism and Islamic modernism which since
the 1890s had monopolised the intellectual life of the town's Sunni
religious circles.[20]

The confrontation between the 'Persian' police and the 'Arab' rioters in
Manama inspired a new vocabulary of 'national' rights pioneered by the
Bahrain National Congress (which was prematurely dissolved in late 1923)
and popularised by intellectuals and activists in the following years. This
vocabulary denounced municipal government as 'illegitimate' and celebrated the common good of the nation (al-maslahah al-wataniyyah) as the
rallying cry against the dominance of foreigners, particularly in the baladiyyah. In a letter to Shaykh ʿIsa around 1927 ʿAbdallah al-Zaʾid, a young
intellectual from Muharraq, bitterly dismissed the spurious municipality as
a government within the government (al-hukumah al-munaddimah) and as a

---

[17] R/15/2/86 IOR: Political Agent Bahrain to Political Resident Bushehr, 13 May 1923;
Statement of Mr McKie, 63/AC, 12 May 1923.
[18] ʿAbd al-Rahman ibn ʿAbdallah al-Khayri, Qalaʾid al-nahrayn fi tarikh al-Bahrayn
(Manama: al-Ayyam, 2003), pp. 323–5; Political Resident Bushehr to ʿAbd al-ʿAziz Ibn
Saʿud Rahman al-Faysal al-Saʿud, 20 June 1923, R/15/1/341 IOR.
[19] Rumaihi, Bahrain, pp. 161–2; al-Tajir, Bahrain 1920–1945, p. 62.
[20] Amin al-Rihani, al-Muluk al-ʿArab, 2 vols. (Beirut: al-Muʾassasah al-ʿArabiyyah li al-
Dirasat wa al-Nashr, 1970), vol. II, pp. 282–93; Mubarak al-Khatir, al-Muntada al-Islami:
Hayyatihi wa atharihi, 1928–1932, 2nd edn. (Manama: al-Matbaʿah al-Hukumiyyah li
Wizarah al-ʿIlam, 1993), p. 17.

stronghold of foreign interests.[21] The currency of these new ideas also transpires from Amin al-Rihani who reported that Bahrain was divided between a national government led by Shaykh 'Isa, and a foreign administration controlled by the British agency and by the *baladiyyah* in Manama.[22]

The eloquent polemics of 'Abdallah al-Za'id also illustrates how Sunnis and Shi'is entered the nationalist discourse as modern political communities. His interpretation of the *baladiyyah* affair of 1923 follows a traditional rhetoric of communal antagonism. In the same correspondence with Shaykh 'Isa he dismissed the role of the British agency, focussing instead on Muhammad Sharif and the 'Persian' police. He accused the former of fomenting rebellion against the Al Khalifah by popularising the idea that Bedouin tribes and rulers were alien to the body politic of Manama. By denouncing the *baladiyyah* and its Persian secretary, al-Za'id provides a novel definition of the familiar theme of 'foreigners'. He portrays the Persians as a non-indigenous 'other', in contrast to the authentic patriots (*al-wataniyyun*) of the town, the Baharna population. As the majority of Arab residents under the jurisdiction of the Al Khalifah, the Baharna became legitimate political subjects whose rightful aspirations were crushed by the arbitrary justice dispensed by the municipality. That al-Za'id was attempting to win their loyalty by appealing to traditional grievances is evident from the language of oppression (*zulm*) he used to describe the condition of the Baharna, which echoes the vocabulary employed by Shi'i religious leaders and laymen to denounce Al Khalifah rule.[23]

It is not surprising that by the end of the 1920s al-Za'id's partisan analysis identified the Persians as the major threat to the tribal order of Bahrain. As the Iranian government renewed its claims over the islands, Manama's Iranian Union School (an offspring of Ma'tam al-'Ajam al-Kabir) disseminated Pahlavi propaganda through its curriculum and recreational activities.[24] Further, the extension of British extraterritorial

---

[21] 'Abdallah al-Za'id to Shaykh 'Isa ibn 'Ali Al Khalifah, *c.* 1927, BA.

[22] Rihani, *Muluk al-'Arab*, vol. II, p. 285.

[23] 'Abdallah al-Za'id to Shaykh 'Isa ibn 'Ali Al Khalifah, *c.* 1927, BA; Ibrahim 'Abdallah Ghulum, *'Abdallah al-Za'id wa ta'sis al-khitab al-adabi al-hadith: Jaridah al-Bahrayn, 1939–1944* (Muharraq: Dar al-Tiba'ah wa al-Nashr, 1996), pp. 16–19; Mubarak al-Khatir, *Nabighat al-Bahrayn: 'Abdallah al-Za'id* (Manama: Matbu'at Banurama al-Khalij 1996), pp. 23–24.

[24] Fuccaro, 'Mapping the Transnational Community', pp. 52–3; 'Ali A. Bushehri, 'National Union School', typescript, 17 pages, n.d., pp. 3–4, BA. After the incident in the suq the Persian Shi'is sent their remonstrations to Teheran while the Sunnis appealed to the agency through the intercession of Muhammad Sharif. Ma'tam al-'Ajam al-Kabir and

jurisdiction after 1904 had brought considerable advantages to the community, which became a prominent symbol of the fragmented political arena of Manama. al-Za'id expressed the fears of Bahrain's tribal aristocracy when (in connection with the *baladiyyah* affair) he deliberately asked Shaykh 'Isa if he expected any member of his own family to be judged by a court presided over by Muhammad Sharif in the near future.[25] The testimony of al-Za'id is a poignant reminder of the importance of intercommunal conflict in Manama in the emergence of a new national narrative against British rule. It also points to the unprecedented threat posed to the indigenous government by British intervention in the early 1920s. This threat resurfaced later in the decade when the combination of the pearling reforms and the decline of the industry contributed to undermine the economic foundations of the old order and the power base of its aspiring national leaders.

The pearling riots: challenging old and new orders

In late December 1926, some 300 foreign divers assembled in front of the office of Charles Belgrave in Manama and marched on to the palace of al-Sakhir in central Bahrain to appeal to the regent against the reduction of the advances announced by the government for the next pearling season. Not having received satisfaction they regrouped in front of the customs house and began to attack the markets. They then crossed to Muharraq, looted the warehouse of an unpopular merchant and burnt his ledger books, thus destroying evidence of his long list of debtors.[26] After this episode the workforce started a systematic boycott of the pearl banks, an action which impacted upon the most powerful capitalists in the industry. In 1930 seventy men employed by Jabir ibn Al Musallam, the largest boat owner of Muharraq, took their advances but refused to board the ships. Several boats owned by 'Abd 'Ali ibn Rajab, one of the wealthiest pearl merchants of Manama, were forced to return ashore after their crews initiated a mutiny.[27]

Turmoil among Bahrain's diving communities was nothing novel. As the fluctuation of the price of pearls determined the divers' income, the beginning and the end of the pearling season were particularly critical moments for the markets. Foreign divers were in a unique position to

Persian School, 1913–57, BA: Telegram Ahali Bahreyn to the Iranian Prime Minister, Minister of War and of Foreign Affairs in Teheran, 1 Khordad 1302/21 May 1923; telegram Ahali Bahreyn to Prime Minister Teheran, 8 Khordad 1302/28 May 1923.
[25] 'Abdallah al-Za'id to Shaykh 'Isa ibn 'Ali Al Khalifah, *c.* 1927, BA.
[26] Belgrave Diaries, 30 December 1926 and 19 May and 25 August 1930, AWDU.
[27] Political Agent Bahrain to Political Resident Bushehr, 1 January 1927, R/15/1/349 IOR.

resort to violence; neither ties with local patrons nor family connections in Bahrain could restrain their unruly behaviour. Many of them were former slaves of African origin who had been manumitted by British agents based in Gulf ports since the early 1850s.[28] The human and economic impact of foreign divers on Bahrain cannot be overestimated. In the 1920s the seasonal diving population was approximately 15,000, one-fourth of the population of Manama and Muharraq and one-tenth of the labour force employed around the entire Gulf.[29] The events of December 1926 anticipated a new phase in the history of the mobilisation of divers triggered by the pearl crisis and by the reforms initiated by the government two years earlier, which weakened the ties between the labour force and the higher echelons of the industry. In fact, the dynamics of the protests staged in Manama and Muharraq reveal that the rioters challenged pearling entrepreneurs while simultaneously identifying the new government as an integral part of the apparatus of exploitation.

The system enforced after 1924 centred on the fixing of the amount of *salaf* and *tiqsam*, the cash given to the crews before and after the pearling season. Traditionally the quota was set by the *Majlis al-Salifah*, the diving council which included representatives of Muharraq's tribal aristocracy. In theory, the new system should have sheltered divers from customary abuses. In practice, the depression of the late 1920s impoverished them alongside the upper echelons of the industry. By the early 1930s, the majority of handsomely dressed and corpulent *nakhudah*s (boat captains), and pearl merchants faced the real prospect of bankruptcy as falling returns from the sale of pearls drained their capital resources. As they became heavily indebted, they started to mortgage their houses and lands to make ends meet, thus rendering largely ineffective the efforts of the government to fix the amount of advances by decree in order to protect the ratio investment return.[30]

When in 1932 the amount of *salaf* reached the absolute minimum in living memory, violence intensified and the boycott of the pearl banks started to take the form of organised strikes. In the most famous episode of

---

[28] The official manumission programme was set up only in 1897 following an enquiry into slavery in the Gulf commissioned by the House of Commons. Khalifa, 'Slaves and Musical Performances in Dubai', pp. 92–3, 103.

[29] 'Note by Belgrave on Pearl Fisheries', c. 1931, R/15/1/349 IOR; Belgrave Diaries, 15 May 1930, AWDU; Political Agent Bahrain to India Office London, 9 January 1927, R/15/1/349 IOR.

[30] *The Bahrain Government Annual Reports, 1924–1970*: 'Administrative Report for the Years 1926–1937', vol. II, pp. 48–50; 'Annual Report for the Year 1350', vol. I, pp. 260–4. R/15/1/349 IOR: Political Agent Bahrain to Political Resident Bushehr, 20 November 1925; Political Agent Bahrain to Political Resident Bushehr, 24 May 1930. al-Tajir, *Bahrain: 1920–1945*, p. 120.

unrest a crowd of about 1,500 foreign divers set sail from Muharraq to Manama, heading to the police station where some of their comrades were detained on charges of sedition and theft. Armed with wooden bars and boat fittings, they paraded angrily along the sea road, surrounded the building and freed one of the captives. The demonstrators were eventually driven back into the sea by policemen lined up along the seafront after fierce hand to hand combat.[31] The scale of the demonstrations of 1932 shows an unprecedented degree of class solidarity. Muharraq's diving lodges (*al-dur*), where most of the foreign divers resided, played a crucial role in coordinating the riot, and were burnt down by the police afterwards. Labour boycotts were organised by experienced leaders who presented the demands of the workforce to Belgrave and to the regent. In some cases ethnicity played a role in mobilising resources. At the end of the 1930 season, for instance, pearl divers from the Iranian coast asked to be released from the fees which they were due to pay to enter Bahrain the following year.[32] Boat captains displayed an ambivalent attitude towards the tide of discontent. Some used the dissatisfaction of the divers in order to put pressure on the authorities, launching vigorous petition campaigns in order to revert to the old system of fixation of diving quotas. Others joined the protests in order to antagonise rivals and to gain the favour of their crews.

Although the reforms of the pearl industry had a very limited effect in easing the hardship of the divers, they undoubtedly strengthened their class solidarities by fostering the development of an increasingly independent labour force. As the transfer of debts from father to son was declared illegal, workers no longer constituted a transferable commodity to be used in dealings between financiers, captains and pearl merchants, some of whom released increasing numbers of divers. By 1934 the gradual shift from *al-salafiyyah* to *al-khammas* diving system suggests that labourers could sell their services in an increasingly free market. Under the established *al-salafiyyah*, divers were bound year after year to particular boat captains, who relied extensively on merchants to finance expeditions. In contrast, no cash advances were offered to divers who worked under the *al-khammas* arrangement and no chain of creditors was involved, as *nakhudah*s generally equipped their own boats. Returns were shared at the end of each season, after which divers were free to choose another employer.[33] After 1926, the new government also enforced a degree of

---

[31] Political Agent Bahrain to Political Resident Bushehr, 30 May 1932, R/15/2/848 IOR; Belgrave Diaries, 26 May 1932, AWDU.

[32] Belgrave Diaries, 30 December 1936, 4 October 1930 and 26 May 1932, AWDU.

[33] *The Bahrain Government Annual Reports, 1924–1970*: 'Administrative Report for the Years 1926–1937', vol. II, pp. 48–9; 'Annual Report for the Year 1352', vol. I, p. 440.

reciprocity of rights and duties. Divers working under the *al-salafiyyah* system could resort to the courts for arbitration while they became liable to prosecution if they refused to comply with their obligations. The mobilisation of the workforce also opened up new avenues of participation. After the troubles of 1926 the government was forced to reinstate the *Majlis al-Salifah*, the old diving council which had been abolished in 1924, and to appoint a leading diver to oversee the interests of the community. Divers could also scrutinise the accounts of their masters and contest sale prices, although it seems that they were seldom able to exercise these new rights. The majority of them were in fact illiterate and the leaders of the industry continued to negotiate deals in secret.[34]

The gradual employment of workers in the oil industry from 1936 led to the virtual disappearance of pearl diving. With it vanished the old order of Manama as well as that of Muharraq, al-Hidd and al-Budayya', the traditional centres of pearl production. The divers' protests of the 1920s and 1930s combined elements of old and new, marking a crucial stage in the transition to the oil era. This combination is epitomised by the public ceremony organised in Muharraq for the punishment of the ringleaders of the 1932 riot. Prisoners locked in cages were exhibited to large crowds in the main square, with policemen and municipal guards lined up to pay their respects to Belgrave and to the rulers. Following the tradition of public flogging for criminal offenders, one by one the prisoners were laid on the ground, beaten with a heavy cane and then sent off to their boat captains to dive. Yet the governor of Muharraq, deputising for Shaykh Hamad, delivered a long speech which defended their punishment on the grounds that their attack upon the police station during the riot was an outrage against a 'sacred' institution of government.[35] For the first time a public event was orchestrated as the showcase of the disciplinary powers of the reforms and as a platform for the new rhetoric of state centralisation.

'Ashura' as a public performance

Unlike pearl divers, Shi'i mourners constituted a critical mass of public actors who resided in the inner city and continued to mobilise as a cohesive group after the discovery of oil. Since the first public performance of 'ashura' in 1891, Manama's houses of mourning became key

---

[34] R/15/1/349 IOR: Political Agent Bahrain to Political Resident Bushehr, 1 and 9 January 1927; 'Note by Belgrave on Pearl Fisheries', *c.* 1931. 'Administrative Report for the Years 1926–1937' in *The Bahrain Government Annual Reports, 1924–1970*, vol. II, p. 49.

[35] Belgrave Diaries, 29 May 1932, AWDU.

urban landmarks, and Imam Husayn the town's unofficial patron saint. The outdoor celebrations sponsored by the *ma'tams* in the month of Muharram became a window onto the political and social cleavages of the Shi'i population. The processions were the venues where a large proportion of the residents of the inner city exhibited and dramatised their allegiances to urban patrons and engaged with the government. In the oil era, the performance of Muharram rituals continued to be the platform for the affirmation of political loyalties and social solidarities. Yet the old merchant class no longer acted as champions of popular Shi'ism, as their influence as patrons of houses of mourning and sponsors of performances waned. By the early 1950s Muharram had become part of a popular repertoire of nationalist mobilisation, a symbol of, and a venue for, the expression of political dissent against the state.

Ritual behaviour and communal hierarchies

The ceremonial performance and textual tradition of *'ashura'* contributed to the distinctive character of Shi'ism in Manama. Although evidence from the first decades of the twentieth century is scanty, celebrations evolved around the organisation of the procession and of the memorial services, the *majalis al-ta'ziyah* which featured the *qira' al-husayniyyah*, the reading of the stories of the family of Imam Husayn. It seems that the passion play (*al-tamthiliyyah*) which dramatised the battle of Karbala began to be staged as a separate performance only after World War I. The name *ma'tam* (most likely from the Arabic word for funeral) which was used for the congregation and for the building which hosted it suggests an emphasis on bereavement.[36] Manama's houses of mourning were primarily venues for sorrow and condolences. They did not host cultural and literary activities, nor did they exhibit the architectural splendour of the *imambaras* of Lucknow in India sponsored by the Nawabs of Awadh, where the term *matam* defined the lamentation which accompanied the readings of the Karbala stories in private houses. Neither did the ritual behaviour of Manama's congregations display the strong tribal ethos and the cult of saints of Iraqi Shi'ism, which emphasised manhood and honour. Performances were simple dramatisations whose theatrical qualities

---

[36] P. Thomas, 'The Passion Play at Bahrein' in *The Arabian Mission*, vol. II, 65 (April–June 1908), pp. 3–5; P. W. Harrison 'The Feast of Muharram' in *The Arabian Mission*, vol. IV, 107 (Oct.–Dec. 1918), pp. 13–14 ; F. Lutton 'Moslem Women's Meetings in Bahrein' in *The Arabian Mission*, vol. III, 84 (Jan.–March 1913), pp. 14–18; photographic evidence on *'ashura'* in Manama (1930s and 1940s) and video of procession (*c.* 1932), BA. See Sayf, *al-Ma'tam*, vol. I, pp. 38–49 and 53–74 for recent examples of performances and texts of Karbala stories.

were much less sophisticated than those of the Iranian *ta'ziyah*. Several episodes which rehearsed the vicissitudes of the *Ahl al-Bayt*, the family of Imam Husayn, were enacted during the procession, particularly the beating and desecration of the coffin of the Imam which provoked universal sobbing and excitement.[37]

'Ashura' in Manama mirrored the cultural and political divisions between Arabs and Persians. The two communities differed in the nomenclature of performances, their style of chest beating and in the *marasim al-'aza'*, the protocol of mourning. As hiring preachers for the *qira' al-husayniyyah*, the readings of the stories of Imam Husayn, was an integral part of the seasonal recruitment of labour overseas, the Baharna drew extensively on the Iraqi *ta'ziyah* tradition while the Persians relied on those of Dashtistan and Fars. Different world views were also at play in the versions of the stories of Karbala recounted in the *majalis al-ta'ziyah*, the memorial services. While the Baharna emphasised their condition of oppression, mourning brought the hope of redemption and rewards in the hereafter to Persian devotees.[38] Episodes of violence between Arabs and Persians during Muharram often evolved around contestation over the right of *ma'tam* affiliates to appropriate the sacred space of Imam Husayn during the processions, symbolised by the route followed by the mourners.

This occurred increasingly frequently after 1925 when the parades (*mawakib al-'aza'*, sing. *mawkib*) became carefully choreographed events organised by a procession committee which included the heads of Manama's houses of mourning. As a strict timetable regulated the flow of mourners who reached the procession route from their *ma'tam*s, each parade, whose boundaries were clearly demarcated by a standard, flags and banners, had to complete a round of performances along the route to pay homage to Imam Husayn. During Muharram 1942, for instance, the accidental rerouting of the procession of Ma'tam Bin Rajab (the largest Arab house of mourning of Manama) by a police inspector triggered a reaction by the followers of the Persian *ma'tam*. As Baharna mourners forced their way into the alleys where the Persians were marching, the police fired shots in the air in an attempt to separate the two parties. Out of a sense of outrage at the violation of the order and hierarchy of the

---

[37] Freitag, *Collective Action and Community*, pp. 256–8; J. R. Cole, *Roots of North India Shi'ism in Iran and Iraq: Religion and State in Awadh, 1722–1859* (Berkeley: University of California Press, 1988), pp. 92–119; Y. Nakash, *The Shi'is of Iraq* (Princeton University Press, 1994), pp. 141–54; K. S. Aghaie, *The Martyrs of Karbala: Shi'i Symbols and Rituals in Modern Iran* (Seattle: University of Washington Press, 2004), pp. 15–29.

[38] Interviews with 'Ali Akbar Bushehri and 'Abdallah Sayf, Manama, 3 and 15 September 2004.

procession, Persian residents started to throw chairs and household utensils out of the windows. As the torches and lamps which illuminated the procession were hurled to the ground and caught fire, mourners, spectators and the police forces engaged in bitter fighting.[39]

In spite of such communal divisions, Muharram processions were not marked by quarter competition, a feature which distinguished the celebration of religious events in major Iranian cities like Teheran and Bushehr, where neighbourhoods sponsored their own performances.[40] As an indication of the overarching solidarity which united the Shi'i population, the route was shared by all the parades and crossed the quarters where the largest *ma'tam*s were located. In common with the establishment of the funeral houses themselves, the emergence of autonomous processions reflected the progressive consolidation of urban communities. In the early years of the establishment of Ma'tam al-'Ajam al-Kabir, for instance, its followers joined the procession of the Bin Rajab. At the turn of the century Arab and Persian parades parted company once the number of Persian devotees increased and their *ma'tam*s acquired sufficient funds through donations.[41]

The composition of the parades expressed hierarchies of prestige based upon the seniority and following of the houses of mourning. The large *ma'tam*s established before World War I have continued to monopolise the Muharram celebrations to the present day. Among the *ma'tam*s established after the collapse of the pearl industry, only al-Safafir in 1954 began to stage its own procession. Ritual performances also celebrated those houses of mourning associated with the mercantilist era of the pearl boom, and the families which had supported them. According to a meticulously defined choreography, the chest beaters (*halqat al-sanqal*) who opened the parades performed outside and inside the old *ma'tam*s to salute their leaders and devotees. By the 1950s the chest beaters of al-'Ajam al-Kabir stopped in front of the building of the *ma'tam* named after Sayyid Ja'far Agha as a token of respect for its pious founder, who had contributed to the establishment of this small house of mourning several decades earlier.[42]

---

[39] Belgrave Diaries, 27 and 28 January 1942, AWDU; Belgrave, 'Report on Muharram Disturbances', 30 January 1942, R/15/1/345 IOR.

[40] Aghaie, *The Martyrs of Karbala*, pp. 34–5; interview with 'Ali Akbar Bushehri, Manama, 20 May 2000.

[41] Interviews with 'Abdallah Sayf and 'Ali Akbar Bushehri, Manama, 3 and 12 September 2004.

[42] Sayf, *al-Ma'tam*, vol. I, pp. 77–9; interviews with 'Abdallah Sayf and 'Ali Akbar Bushehri, Manama, 3 and 12 September 2004.

Muharram and the state

These flamboyant performances of suffering set the rhetoric, imagery and vocabulary which informed relations between the Shi'i popular classes and the government. Further, as Muharram celebrations were the most important public event staged in Manama, they provided a shared experience of religiosity for both performers and spectators.[43] Regardless of sect and ethnicity, residents experienced a world of ritual which spoke of universal concepts such as justice and injustice, and heroism and oppression. Until the rise of nationalist politics, the ritual world of Manama's Shi'ism was not overtly subversive. *'Ashura'* dramatised political allegiances and displayed them to the audience but did not advocate outright political protest. Yet Shi'i devotion carried a strong populist message, as rituals portrayed political power in reverse. They emphasised relations between power holders and ordinary people and exemplified the community's interpretation of justice. Symbols of domination featured as subjects of mockery and entertainment, disguising distrust for constituted authority which appealed to all segments of Manama's lower classes. During the performance of *al-tamthiliyyah* in 1932, for instance, the actor playing Ibn Zayd, the hated commander of the army which killed Imam Husayn, was dressed as a soldier of the British Indian army. Holding a bottle of whisky, he was made into a caricature of the dubious morality of the foreign servicemen who served as agency guards and policemen.[44]

Before the reforms, the performances offered the Baharna population collective redemption and release from the order supported by the Al Khalifah. Settings and protocol emphasised their condition of misery (*al-masakin*) without making explicit reference to tribal oppression. Camels and horses were often borrowed from the rulers by Arab *ma'tam*s for the occasion. Swords, the symbol of tribal authority par excellence, were used only by the Persians for the ceremony of self-mutilation (*halqat al-suyuf/al-haydar*), the most violent form of flagellation. Contravening the ban imposed by the rulers on the ownership of swords, the Persian *ma'tam* (al-'Ajam al-Kabir) relied on the protection of the agency as suggested by the registration of forty-six swords for *'ashura'* in 1937.[45]

---

[43] As suggested by Sandria Freitag in her study of communal politics in northern India during the colonial period, in Manama ceremonies of religious nature set 'the patterns for all public activities', at least until the 1950s. Freitag, *Collective Action and Community*, p. 25.
[44] Photographic evidence, Manama, c. 1930, BA.
[45] Licence 0002 issued by the British agency, 10 May 1937, BA; Sayf, *al-Ma'tam*, vol. I, p. 102.

The Muharram festivities also reinforced Manama's tradition of autonomy from Muharraq. Despite being the most important public occasion of the year, the celebrations for *'ashura'* did not involve any official protocol. The shadow of the tribal government was felt mainly through the presence of guards and watchmen deployed along the route and across the inner city to enforce public security. While the patrons and sponsors of the *ma'tam*s took centre stage, religious leaders did not play a significant role as censors and regulators of performances. *Fatwas* (legal opinions) from leading *mujtahids* had been reaching Bahrain from Iraq and Iran since the death of the last *shaykh al-ra'is* of Bahrain in 1801. Yet overseas preachers hired to perform the *al-qira' al-husayniyyah* (the readings of the stories of Imam Husayn) continued to function as the main religious intermediaries between the islands and the main centres of Shi'ism.

In the age of reform, the impact of ritual as a platform for the mobilisation of Shi'i interests continued to be limited. The rhetoric of development which inspired nation building in Bahrain underplayed sectarian divisions, as exemplified by the institutionalisation of both a Sunni and a Shi'i court system after 1927. The Baharna community also lacked the independent power base, hierarchical religious organisation and learned tradition which characterised their Iraqi and Iranian counterparts under the Hashemite monarchy and the Pahlavi dynasty respectively.[46] A number of factors restricted the political effectiveness of Muharram in Manama. With the collapse of pearling, ritual patronage lost momentum as a means of promoting social status among the old merchant classes (as explained in Chapter 3), and the moneyed elites and senior bureaucrats of the early oil era no longer invested in the houses of mourning. In contrast with Pahlavi Iran, where those in charge of *awqaf* controlled the opposition to the Shah's regime, the historic monopoly held by the Al Khalifah and by the Sunni Hawala community over market endowments precluded the consolidation of *ma'tam*s as political organisations able to compete with the government. Last but not least, the management of *ma'tam*s became increasingly integrated into institutional networks. While the authorities appointed a committee in charge of overseeing the procession in 1925, many of the endowments which supported the oldest houses of mourning were taken under the control of the *Idarah al-Awqaf al-Ja'fariyyah*, the Department of Shi'i Pious Foundations established in 1927.

---

[46] For developments in Iraq and Iran see Nakash, *The Shi'is of Iraq*, pp. 157–62; Aghaie, *The Martyrs of Karbala*, pp. 47–66; N. Keddie, 'The Roots of 'Ulama Power in Modern Iran' and H. Algar, 'The Oppositional Role of the Ulama in Twentieth-Century Iran' in N. Keddie (ed.), *Scholars, Saints and Sufis: Muslim Religious Institutions in the Middle East since 1500* (Berkeley: University of California Press, 1972), pp. 211–30, 231–56.

In both the pearl and oil eras ritual behaviour reflected important shifts in the relations between Shi'i groups and the government, most importantly the progressive emancipation of the Shi'i population of Manama. The first outdoor procession in 1891, led by Mirza Muhammad Isma'il, the local agent for the British India Steam Navigation Company, marked the beginning of the protection granted by the British agency to the Baharna community, protection which was dispensed on an unofficial basis as they were *de jure* subjects of Shaykh 'Isa.[47] In 1907, the Persians, encouraged by the enforcement of British extraterritorial jurisdiction, raised the imperial flag of Iran at the opening of the parade, a clear statement of their allegiance to the Qajar government under threat from the constitutional movement. By the 1950s, when Ma'tam Ras Rumman marched chanting nationalist slogans preceded by the banner of Nasser's Egypt, the road became open to a new type of popular politics which transformed some of the Arab congregations into hotbeds of nationalist propaganda. Fuelled by anti-British sentiment, this development attests to the dramatic changes in urban political life since 1891.[48] In the first two decades of the oil era, the participation of new congregations in the procession showed the emergence of new solidarities among the workforce. This process continued after Bahrain achieved independence, as shown by Fuad Khuri in his study of *ma'tams* in the 1970s.[49]

In the town of the pearl boom the processions had empowered immigrant communities and occupational groups, allowing them to enter the public arena under the protection of their merchant patrons. By the 1940s and 1950s, religious devotion became a conduit for the expression of the class sentiments beginning to unite oil workers, professionals and government employees. Processions also became bitterly divided along political lines. For instance, Ma'tam al-Shabab gathered many of the young Persian employees of BAPCO (The Bahrain Petroleum Company), who became renowned for their subversive political inclinations and used *'ashura'* as a platform to voice their resentment against the Pahlavi regime. Pro-shah and pro-Musaddiq rival groups engaged in bitter wars of slogans while marching through the streets of Manama after the nationalisation of the oil industry in Iran in the early 1950s. Arab *ma'tams*, meanwhile, had to come to terms with the new nationalist tide unleashed by devotees belonging to the poorest strata of the urban population now employed in the oil industry. Contestation during *'ashura'* became symptomatic of the decadence of the traditional Arab notability who had controlled the houses of mourning before the collapse of pearling, and of the emergence

---

[47] Oral history from the Bushehri family.   [48] P. W. Harrison, 'The Feast of Muharram'.
[49] Khuri, *Tribe and State in Bahrain*, pp. 169–70.

of progressive social forces, as will be explained in the discussion of the nationalist movement.[50]

Fitnah al-Muharram, *September 1953*

The emergence of new social groups employed in the private and public sectors of Bahrain's modern economy, the working class, the bureaucracy and young white-collar professionals, contributed to the decline of religious solidarity as the basis for the politicisation of the Baharna residents of Manama. From the 1940s until independence in 1971, Muharram celebrations functioned as an increasingly inclusive socio-political space in the new arena of Arabism and nationalism. The outbreak of sectarian violence during Muharram 1953 transformed ritual and popular practice into a powerful symbol of political communication, a 'public connector' which provided an arena of encounter between the state and urban residents.[51] This momentous episode, which became known as *Fitnah al-Muharram* (the dissent of Muharram), allowed the nationalist movement to make use of the disturbances in order to forge a new political consensus between Sunnis and Shi'is and to recompose the sectarian tensions which had led to the dissolution of Manama's municipal council in 1951.[52]

The violence which erupted during *'ashura'* of 1953 was of a different order from earlier conflicts, since it developed into a sectarian confrontation which spread throughout Bahrain. Fighting initially spread out along the procession route in central Manama, allegedly sparked off by the intrusion into the procession of the car of Shaykh Da'ij ibn Hamad Al Khalifah, the brother of the ruler Shaykh Salman, who had succeeded Hamad in 1942. Sunnis attacked Shi'is, spectators retaliated against performers, residents targeted villagers and the police forces beat up rioters indiscriminately, opening fire at intervals in an attempt to restore order. As news of the incident circulated outside Manama, bands of oil workers from Muharraq started to attack their Baharna counterparts. They pulled them off the oil company buses and beat them severely. The following day, as rumours circulated that Sunnis were being slaughtered, angry protesters hijacked buses in Muharraq and Awali, the new

[50] Interviews with 'Ali Akbar Bushehri and 'Abdallah Sayf, Manama, 4 April and 3 September 2004; Political Agent Bahrain to Political Resident Bahrain, 5 October 1953, FO 371/104263 PRO.

[51] For a general discussion of how popular practices function as a sphere of public engagement see J. L. Brooke, 'Reason and Passion in the Public Sphere: Habermas and the Cultural Historians', *Journal of Interdisciplinary History*, 29.1 (1998), 43–67 (43–4).

[52] On the dissolution of the council see pp. 147–8.

headquarters of the oil industry, planning to besiege Manama. Police patrols blocked roads in and out of the town but the government imposed a curfew only after rioters began to attack villages. In the residential areas of Manama guards protected the Shiʻi population which had sought sanctuary in their *maʻtam*s. Seventy people were injured in two days of disturbances. Although the security forces managed to restore order, tension continued to escalate in the following months, particularly in the oil refinery located in the island of Sitrah where one Sunni was killed and several Shiʻis injured in June 1954.[53]

The riot, which became one of the most fiercely contested events in the history of modern Bahrain, displayed some established features of earlier sectarian strife. Shiʻis still apportion blame to the Al Khalifah family. In their eyes the violation of the procession by Shaykh Daʻij was one of the several acts of injustice which characterised the tyranny of Bahrain's Sunni rulers. As the shaykh was reported to be in the company of a prostitute, it also offered an example of their moral degeneracy which had become legendary among many Manamis.[54] The British agent reported to the Foreign Office that the commotion had started before the arrival of the car and that the violence was sparked by a series of simultaneous incidents: a verbal quarrel between spectators, the intervention of agency guards, and last but not least, the arrival of Persian mourners covered in blood after they performed *al-haydar*, the ritual of self-mutilation with a sword.[55]

Whatever the involvement of Shaykh Daʻij in triggering the disturbance, it was clearly not premeditated, contrary to the accounts provided by the various parties involved. The police proved to be very ineffective, thus reinforcing the general distrust of public authority. The gendarmes acted almost as a third party in the contest, fuelling episodes of random violence from all sides.[56] After the tragic events in the oil refinery in July 1954, Shiʻi villagers assembled in one of Manama's mosques and staged a protest in front of the police fort where a military court had tried the Shiʻi culprits. As the police opened fire on the demonstrators, killing several of them, protesters sought sanctuary in the British agency. Determined to sanctify their dead following the Shiʻi tradition of martyrdom, they grabbed a

[53] Political Agent Bahrain to British Resident Bahrain, 5 October 1953 in British Resident Bahrain to Foreign Office, 13 October 1953, FO 371/104263 PRO; Belgrave Diaries, 20 and 21 September 1953, AWDU.
[54] Interviews with Muhammad Jaʻfar Muhsin al-ʻArab and Mirza al-Sharif, Manama, 10 and 19 April 2004; al-Bakir, *Min al-Bahrayn*, p. 48.
[55] Political Agent Bahrain to British Resident Bahrain, 5 October 1953 in British Resident Bahrain to Foreign Office, 13 October 1953, FO 371/104263 PRO.
[56] Belgrave Diaries, 20 September 1953, AWDU.

British flag and wrapped it around the body of one of the deceased as a makeshift symbol of *al-kafan*, the white linen symbolising the ordeal of the family of Imam Husayn. Before proceeding to the graveyard to bury their dead as *shuhada'* (martyrs), they asked the agent to intercede on their behalf with the ruler, rehearsing familiar patterns of protection politics.[57]

Although traditional grievances played a role in the events of 1953–4, the foundations of popular activism had become cast in a new mould as a result of two decades of state building and oil. By 1953 industrial labour had entered the political scene as BAPCO became the country's largest employer. Oil workers provided the muscle of urban unrest, the spread of which was heightened by fast new road links between Manama, Muharraq and the centres of the industry. Buses belonging to the oil company became part of a new repertoire of dissent. Many were hijacked and torn apart after they reached their destination, with demonstrators brandishing iron bars as weapons. Mobilisation displayed elements of coordinated protest which united different strata of the Shi'i population. Considerable numbers of civil servants and BAPCO employees abstained from work during the disturbances as the government prohibited public assemblies and launched a censorship campaign in the press.[58]

Fitnah al-Muharram marked a further step in the construction of Sunnis and Shi'is as a modern political community, a process which had begun with the clashes between Persians and Najdis in 1923. Thirty years later, the violence mobilised a younger generation of activists. The government, particularly Charles Belgrave, continued to support traditional channels of consultation with municipal councillors and notables, treating them as the representatives of the population. Yet Bahrain's new nationalist class appealed directly to the grass roots in opposition to sectarian divisions, urban conservatism and imperialist encroachment. These were themes which had started to monopolise the discursive field supporting Arab emancipation in Bahrain since the 1930s and which had much resonance in the troubled evolution of municipal politics in the late 1940s and early 1950s.[59] These enlightened leaders were to guide the masses into a new public arena as rational and modern subjects. As suggested by 'Abd al-Rahman al-Bakir in his autobiography:

---

[57] Correspondence from Husayn 'Ali Kazim Bushehri to Habib 'Ali Kazim Bushehri, 2 Dhu al-Qa'dah 1373/3 July 1954, BA; Belgrave Diaries, 1 July 1954, AWDU; interview with 'Abdallah Sayf, Manama, 20 March 2004; Political Agent Bahrain to British Resident Bahrain, 5 October 1953, FO 371/104263 PRO.

[58] Political Resident Bahrain to Foreign Office, 13 October 1953, FO 371/104263 PRO.

[59] Political Agent Bahrain to British Resident Bahrain, 5 October 1953 in British Resident Bahrain to Foreign Office, 13 October 1953, FO 371/104263 PRO; Khuri, *Tribe and State in Bahrain*, pp. 199–201; al-Bakir, *Min al-Bahrayn*, pp. 49–62.

Regrettably, faced with *al-Fitnah* many youths became oblivious of their national duty, abandoned their beliefs and views. Especially some of the intellectuals from Muharraq who started to be drawn towards sectarian feeling, and appealed to partisan loyalties by using terminology such as Muharraqi and Manami ... I had witnessed in Bombay how the English ignited sectarian strife between Hindus and Muslims and I felt I had a major responsibility. If sectarian strife had continued [in Bahrain], what would have been the result? Bloodshed![60]

After the riots, al-Bakir became one of the main promoters of *al-Ha'yah al-Tanfidhiyyah al-'Uliya* (The High Executive Committee), the populist organisation based in Manama which by 1956 became the first political association recognised by a Gulf government.

Urban and national politics as a 'mass subject', 1932–57[61]

Between 1932 and 1957 Manama emerged as the principal arena of Arab nationalism in Bahrain. In this period, three elements contributed to the gradual consolidation of mass politics in what by the early 1950s had become the city of Bahrain's oil boom. The first was the propagation of the political language of Arabism, which the supporters of Shaykh 'Isa had introduced in the 1920s, as a 'subject' of popular mobilisation. The new rhetoric condemned loyalty to sect, patron and locality, particularly after *al-Fitnah*, which marked the beginning of Bahrain's second national 'revival' after the intercommunal violence of 1923. The second element was the emergence of new urban leaders. Although appeals to traditional solidarities continued to command the support of the grass roots, a group of young Arab activists imbued with nationalist ideals gradually replaced the merchant patrons of the pearl era. The demise of the municipal government in 1951 sealed the transition between the old and new leadership. Many of the new activists participated in the agitations which led to the dissolution of the *majlis*, thus contributing to undermining the last bastion of the urban order identified with the old merchant classes. The third element was the creation of *al-Ha'yah*, a modern political organisation whose ethos was instrumental in reorganising popular militancy in accordance with anti-British nationalist sentiment.

---

[60] al-Bakir, *Min al-Bahrayn*, p. 49 (my translation).
[61] The expression 'mass subject' is borrowed from Michael Warner's discussion of the creation of public subjectivity through print culture, ideology and publicity. M. Warner, 'The Mass Public and the Mass Subject' in C. Calhoun (ed.), *Habermas and the Public Sphere* (Cambridge, MA: Massachusetts Institute of Technology Press, 1999), pp. 377–401.

The emergence of a new nationalist class in the interwar period

The 1930s and 1940s were crucial decades for the evolution of modernist elites, and laid the foundations for the explosion of popular politics under *al-Ha'yah*. The angry young men who started to populate the nationalist landscape of Manama articulated the social interests of the middle ranks of the town's commercial classes whose economic position was greatly enhanced by the boom in the trade and service economy of the late 1940s.[62] Although still divided along communal lines, the two types of 'political agitator' which emerged in the 1930s violated the conventions and venues of traditional elite politics and no longer sat at the feet of their elders in *majlis*es and *ma'tam*s. The radical young Sunni Hawala became conversant with nationalist ideals and imbued with a new class consciousness as a result of his associations with the outside world. Exposed to the Iraqi, Syrian and Egyptian nationalist press, his nationalism was strengthened by easier travel and faster business links. Keenly political and generally better educated than his peers, he epitomised the figure of the Manama national activist. The Shi'i militant pursued modern ideas of social justice more pragmatically, and appealed to the sectarian solidarities of the traditional constituencies of merchant patrons.[63]

'Abd al-Rahman al-Bakir belonged to the first group. Inspired by the ideas of Pan-Arabism and by Nasserism after the Egyptian revolution of 1952, he made use of the overseas contacts and entrepreneurial spirit which had brought the Hawala community commercial success before oil. After the collapse of his family business in 1933 he left Manama, returning to Bahrain three years later to take up a job as a translator in the oil company. While employed in BAPCO, he played a role in the first labour agitation of 1938 as the promoter of a sports and cultural club which gathered together young employees. In 1941, after he joined the oil company in Qatar, al-Bakir established a successful import–export firm in Dubai with links to East Africa. When he returned to Bahrain in 1948 his career as a journalist and propagandist became closely connected to the establishment of *al-Ha'yah*.[64]

Hawala activism set the stage and pace of the urban political arena in the oil era. In 1938, underground organisations such as *Shabab al-Ahrar*

---

[62] See pp. 131–2.

[63] For a cogent reading of the national movement from the perspective of Bahrain's political economy and class alliances, see Lawson, *Bahrain: The Modernization of Autocracy*, pp. 58–62; Belgrave to Political Agent Bahrain, 17 February 1948, D.O. n. 782, R/15/2/485 IOR. On the Hawala as the progressive segments of modern Gulf societies, see A. Dessouki, 'Social and Political Dimensions of the Historiography of the Arab Gulf', pp. 96–112.

[64] al-Bakir, *Min al-Bahrayn*, pp. 28–35.

(Free Youth) and *Shabab al-Ummah* (Islamic Youth) introduced ideas of national rights inspired by the establishment of a legislative council in Kuwait (*Majlis al-Ummah al-Tashri'iyyah*) in that year. Their members, who also included young Hawala from Muharraq, promoted a new type of political literacy which targeted the grass roots directly. Graffiti and anonymous notices started to appear on the walls of Manama. One of their favourite targets was the Bahraini Court, the highest judicial authority in the country, which they considered the symbol of Bahrain's flawed legal system under Belgrave and the Al Khalifah. Leaflets circulated inciting popular militancy against the government. They ordered the 'noble Arab nation' to go on strike and to boycott cinemas and modern amenities in order to devote its energy to the struggle against the corruption of the government and the despotism of the advisor.[65] If 1938 became known in Kuwait as the 'year of the *Majlis*', in Bahrain it started a new era of political contestation under the aegis of these youth organisations. After a series of political meetings led to the arrest of a number of activists, the clerks employed in the oil refinery joined forces with oil workers and went on strike. The agitation was suppressed by the police, and the Hawala leaders were exiled in what was a dress rehearsal for the tragic events which would involve *al-Ha'yah* almost twenty years later.[66]

Among the Baharna, the 'political agitator' was concerned with the grievances of the Shi'i lower classes. He addressed these grievances in a traditional setting, often using his connections with the increasingly militant labour force of the markets, and displayed a vociferous populist rhetoric and distaste for hierarchy and authority. In 1932 'Abd 'Ali al-'Alawayt, a young trader from al-Mukharaqah district and a future militant in *al-Ha'yah*, stormed into the *majlis* of Shaykh Hamad with a crowd of petty shopkeepers and butchers. The thirty-strong group had assembled to protest against the enforcement of the compulsory registration of the estates of minors with the government which had triggered unrest throughout Bahrain. The Shi'i delegation blatantly violated the rigid protocol which guided deputations to the regent, who was subjected to a long and vehement speech delivered by al-'Alawayt on the subject of

---

[65] Muhammad 'Abd al-Qadir al-Jasim and Sawsan 'Ali al-Sha'ir, *al-Bahrayn: qissah al-sira' al-siyasi, 1904–1956* (Manama: [n.pub.], 2000), pp. 175–200. R/15/2/176 IOR: Political Agent Bahrain to Political Resident Bushehr, 12 November 1938; Belgrave to Political Agent Bahrain, 22 November 1938; leaflets and letters by *Shabab al-Ahrar, Shabab al-Ummah* and *Shabab al-Watani*; minutes by Political Agent Bahrain, 3 November 1938. On the *Majlis* in Kuwait see Crystal, *Oil and Politics in the Gulf*, pp. 47–55.

[66] Khuri, *Tribe and State in Bahrain*, pp. 197–8; Political Agent Bahrain to Political Resident Bushehr, 12 November 1938, R/15/2/176 IOR; 'Annual Report for the Year 1357' in *The Bahrain Government Annual Reports, 1924–1970*, vol. II, pp. 29–30.

government corruption. Brandishing a popular petition, he was applauded loudly by his supporters at intervals.[67] Young activists like al-'Alawayt also acquired a popular base by joining merchant notables and religious leaders who after 1934 used their connections to find employment in the oil fields for impoverished villagers.[68]

Throughout the 1930s and early 1940s, community leaders and members of the old notability adapted to the new climate of mounting populist militancy which was becoming the hallmark of the young nationalists. In parallel with the efforts of the youth organisations, progressive individuals initiated intersectarian cooperation and introduced a new official language of popular representation and of rights for the 'national' labour force. In a petition sent to Shaykh Hamad in November 1938 Sunni, Shi'i and Hawala merchants from Manama and Muharraq demanded the formation of a labour committee and the appointment of Bahraini subjects instead of 'foreigners' to the *majlis al-baladiyyah*, while requesting the formation of an elected body of merchants to represent the urban residents.[69]

The making of a new public opinion

In the 1940s and 1950s, Arab nationalism gradually became the terrain of both elite and popular contestation. As an ideology of political emancipation, nationalism nurtured Bahrain's independence movement against British control. In social terms, it reclaimed popular sovereignty from the Al Khalifah family as the 'natural' right of newly born modern citizens.

Two crucial developments promoted consensus across the broad spectrum of localised allegiances which characterised the Arab residents of Manama. The first was the role which national solidarities had increasingly assumed in the propagation of ideas of political and social regeneration. The 'Arabisation' of Manama was proposed as an antidote to the 'Indianisation' of Bahrain, that is, the imperial ideology which had placed the islands under the control of the Government of India in 1919. The second was the consolidation of new notions of citizenship. Following the

---

[67] 'Annual Report for the Year 1350' in *The Bahrain Government Annual Reports, 1924–1970*, vol. I, pp. 278–81; Belgrave Diaries, 9 and 12 February 1932, AWDU.

[68] Confidential note by Belgrave, January 1935 and Belgrave to Political Agent Bahrain, 28 January 1935, R/15/2/176 IOR.

[69] Memorandum dated 19 Ramadan 1357/12 November 1938 to Shaykh Hamad ibn 'Ali Al Khalifah, petition from the people of al-Hidd to Shaykh Hamad ibn 'Ali Al Khalifah, 24 Ramadan 1357/17 November 1938 in Political Agent Bahrain to Political Resident, 19 November 1938, R/15/1/343 IOR; Belgrave to Political Agent Bahrain, 27 Dhu al-Qa'dah 1357/18 January 1939, R/15/1/344 IOR.

promulgation of the Bahrain Nationality and Property Law in 1937, a segment of the foreign population became a new focus for dissent. As non-Arabs and non-nationals, British officials, European residents and the Indians and Persians employed in the modern sector of the economy were increasingly construed as instruments of state oppression, threatening the welfare of the nation and hindering its political maturity. The currency and strength of these feelings are described by an academic observer who visited Bahrain in 1952–3:

[Nationality] manifests itself in two ways: first, negatively in a desire to expel the foreigner (this has a considerable appeal: it is concrete, intellectually easy to grasp, can be used as a rallying cry, and above all does not conflict with established social patterns); and second, positively in a confused ideal of Pan-Arab and Pan-Islamic union. No clear distinction is drawn between the two last concepts and the terms are used interchangeably ... through this *intellectual device* the two groups [Sunnis and Shi'is] can now present a common front against foreigners to protect their rights and interests, whether real or imaginary. (my emphasis)[70]

As the new 'intellectual device' which shaped the political imagery of ordinary citizens, Arab nationalism was obviously defective, as shown by the resurgence of sectarian animosity during *Fitnah al-Muharram* of 1953. Yet novel forms of communication and association allowed increasing numbers of people to participate in, and incrementally redefine, the political culture of Manama as the centre of a modern Arab nation in the making. After World War II in particular modern education, the press, and cultural and sports clubs transformed the town's public life.

The proliferation of associations promoting cultural, educational and sports activities served as crucial venues for political socialisation. They became the training ground for modernist elites and enlarged the rank and file of the nationalist class, which now came to include entrepreneurs, traders, civil servants and professionals.[71] Although clubs were not established as political organisations, they played a crucial role in the articulation and circulation of political opinions. *Nadi al-'Urubah* (The Arab Club) established in 1938, Manama's most influential club, inherited the mantle of the intellectual circles which had first raised the banner of Arabism in Muharraq in the first three decades of the twentieth century. Most importantly, *al-'Urubah* along with *Nadi al-Bahrayn* (The Bahrain Club) in Muharraq followed the footsteps of the movement championed

---

[70] F. I. Qubain, 'Social Classes and Tensions in Bahrain', *The Middle East Journal*, 9.3 (1955), 269–80 (273).
[71] Clubs as venues of political socialisation are discussed in Khuri, *Tribe and State in Bahrain*, pp. 174–83 and E. Nakhleh, *Bahrain: Political Development in a Modernising Society* (Toronto and Massachusetts: Lexington Books, 1976), pp. 41–58.

by the Hawala activists in 1938. Both associations promoted increasing cooperation between activists from Manama and Muharraq and intersectarian interests, although until 1950 their membership remained confessional, Shi'i and Sunni respectively.

These new societies were able to acquire followings among different strata of the urban population also thanks to the development of modern education. First, with the introduction of physical activities in the curriculum of modern schools which started to be established in 1919, the value of sport as a tool for moral education and political indoctrination became apparent. As football gained widespread popularity, clubs started to sponsor their own teams, attracting increasing numbers of young men. After 1957 the Bahrain football association included eleven teams which were all attached to mainstream clubs.[72] Second, clubs endorsed the figure of the public intellectual whose role was to promote a new consciousness by engaging in a 'conversation' with society (*mukhatibah al-mujtami'*). In Manama, *Nadi al-'Urubah*, which was established as a youth society, opened a branch in one of the primary schools and appointed teachers as honorary members. Although most of the club affiliates were Shi'i, the programme of public lectures and discussion forums which it organised advocated a new relationship between individual, community and society within the framework of the emerging nationalist ethics. In a speech to the central committee of the club in February 1939, Hasan Jawwad al-Jishi, the headmaster of the affiliated primary school, declared that the recognition of the indivisible personality of the Arab nation of Bahrain was a precondition of the country's aspiration to nationhood.[73]

The growth of a polemical press and rising literacy also facilitated the popularisation of Arab nationalism. After 1952 the publication of independent weeklies such *al-Qafilah* and *al-Watan* became part of an orchestrated press campaign which extended from Manama to the remotest villages of Bahrain. *al-Qafilah*, which was published between 1953 and 1956, had a weekly circulation of more than 4,000 copies.[74] 'Abdallah al-Za'id, the pioneer of Bahrain's political writing in the late 1920s,

---

[72] Bushehri, 'National Union School', pp. 7–8; *Nadi al-Muharraq: ra'id al-nahdah al-riyadiyyah* (Manama: Commemorative pamphlet, c. 1981); *Nadi Ras Rumman: thalathun 'am 'ala ta'sis* (Manama: Commemorative pamphlet, c. 1986). For a history of modern education in Bahrain based on local sources see Mayy Muhammad Al Khalifah, *Mi'ah 'am min al-ta'lim al-nizami fi al-Bahrayn: al-Sanawat al-ula li al-ta'sis* (Beirut: al-Mu'assasah al-'Arabiyyah li al-Dirasat wa al-Nashr, 1999).

[73] Taqi Muhammad al-Baharna, *Nadi al-'Urubah wa khamsun 'am*, 1939–1989 (Manama: Ministry of Information, 1991), pp. 23, 48–9.

[74] Nakhleh, *Bahrain*, p. 65.

continued his activities into the new era of nationalist agitation as the editor of *Jaridah al-Bahrayn* (The Bahrain Gazette), a weekly sponsored by the British agency. Despite the censorship of the British authorities, he skilfully used his position to raise issues of political concern. In a series of articles published anonymously in 1941 under the title 'The New Democratic Order' he discussed democracy and individual rights in several Western countries.[75] After his premature death, al-Za'id's legacy continued with the publication of *Sawt al-Bahrayn*, the first independent monthly issued between 1950 and 1954, which served as a launching pad for *al-Ha'yah*. Its editorial board included members of *Nadi al-'Urubah* and *Nadi al-Bahrayn*, including 'Abd al-Rahman al-Bakir and 'Abd al-'Aziz Shamlan, an employee of the British Bank of the Middle East, who became one of the leaders of *al-Ha'yah*.[76]

It was this journalism which promoted Arabism as a progressive ideology. The press encouraged ideas of social justice and equality as the historic rights of nationals deriving from their membership in the concert of Arab nations. In championing the cause of the indigenous workforce, it gained the support of the lower strata of both urban and rural society. By 1956 approximately 41 per cent of the manual labourers employed in the oil industry and building firms were foreign. Further, the average wages of oil workers and of the artisans and labourers employed by the Department of Public Works were low even in comparison with those of their counterparts employed by private building firms.[77] To a large extent the efforts by BAPCO and the government at 'nationalising' and 'Arabising' the labour force after World War II played into the hands of the populist rhetoric of the national movement. Immigrants from Arab countries started to be regarded by the indigenous population as *awlad al-'amm* (cousins), a term which conveyed the emotional overtones of family life and of the blood ties linking the nation. In his articles 'Abd al-Rahman al-Bakir also supported the nascent labour movement in neighbouring Saudi Arabia.[78]

The press also deployed a new vocabulary of militancy against the government, depicting the nationalist struggle as one against the forces

[75] Ghulum, *'Abdallah al-Za'id*, pp. 17–18 and 42–56; *Jaridah al-Bahrayn*, ns. 128/129/130, Rajab 1360/August 1941, AWDU.

[76] Rumaihi, *Bahrain*, pp. 209–11; *Sawt al-Bahrayn: Majallah 'Adabiyyah wa Ijtima'iyyah*, 4 vols. (Beirut: al-Mu'assasah al-'Arabiyyah li al-Dirasat wa al-Nashr, 2003); al-Bakir, *Min al-Bahrayn*, pp. 36–9; Nakhleh, *Bahrain*, pp. 63–6.

[77] W. A. Beiling, 'Recent Developments in Labor Relations in Bahrayn', *The Middle East Journal*, 13.2 (1959), 156–69 (159–60); 'Annual Report for the Year 1954' in *The Bahrain Government Annual Reports, 1924–1970*, vol. V, p. 67; D. Finnie, 'Recruitment and Training of Labor: The Middle East Oil Industry', *Middle East Journal*, 12.2 (1958), 127–43 (129–30).

[78] Qubain, 'Social Classes and Tensions', 278; al-Bakir, *Min al-Bahrayn*, pp. 37–8.

of social conservatism. Allegiance to tradition, community and to 'nat-ural' hierarchies defined by kin ties, sect and patronage disrupted the historical homogeneity of the nation. The tribal loyalties which bound the Al Khalifah to their allies, including the British authorities, and the old politics of patronage which dominated the municipal council of Manama, were construed as the major source of sectarian division and primordial conflict. Significantly, an editorial in *Sawt al-Bahrayn* condemned sec-tarianism as 'the deadliest of our diseases'.[79] Moreover, the portrayal of British imperialism as the mother of all the forces of reaction gained momentum as a quest for solidarity with the Palestinians during the revolt of 1936–9 and again during the Arab–Israeli wars which followed the establishment of Israel in 1948.

al-Ha'yah: *organising popular militancy, 1954–6*

In October 1954 the creation of *al-Ha'yah* revolutionised the political landscape of Bahrain. Based in Manama, the organisation provided cru-cial links between the young nationalists and the popular base across the country, with an executive committee of eight members assisted by a network of 120 individuals recruited from both urban and rural areas. The social composition of the leadership reflected the growth of the nationalist movement since the 1930s. A majority of professionals and traders led local committees while the *nouveaux riches* of the economic boom of the late 1940s and early 1950s abstained from engaging overtly in political activities. Very few individuals from the old notable class joined the organisation, usually from families which had not regained their fortunes after the collapse of pearling.[80]

The mass appeal of *al-Ha'yah* can be readily explained by the *raison d'être* of the organisation, the mobilisation of the labour force to redirect local grievances towards national concerns. As labour relations became central to the quest for national self-determination, the creation of *al-Ha'yah* was part of a new populist strategy aimed at challenging the government and foreign interests. Soon after the establishment of the first labour union under the aegis of *al-Ha'yah* in 1955, the union claimed some 6,000 members from BAPCO and government offices and forced

---

[79] Khuri, *Tribe and State in Bahrain*, pp. 198–9; al-Bakir, *Min al-Bahrayn*, pp. 37–8; *Sawt al-Bahrayn*, vol. I, p. 1369.

[80] al-Bakir, *Min al-Bahrayn*, pp. 65–7. On the political activities of the organisation see al-Bakir, *Min al-Bahrayn*, pp. 63–116 ; al-Jasim and al-Sha'ir, *al-Bahrayn: qissah al-sira'*, pp. 327–42; Khuri, *Tribe and State in Bahrain*, pp. 199–217; Rumaihi, *Bahrain*, pp. 212–21; Lawson, *Bahrain: The Modernization of Autocracy*, pp. 58–68.

the government to open negotiations on a labour law.[81] It is also significant that popular mobilisation was initiated with the establishment of
cross-sectarian cooperative institutions (*al-mu'assasat al-ta'awuniyyah*)
such as the Drivers' Association (*Jam'iyyah al-Sawwaqin*) which functioned as a compensation bureau and insured drivers for a relatively low
membership fee.[82] Despite preaching new national and class solidarities
to the grass roots, the movement capitalised on traditional networks. With
no committees established at a local level in Manama until 1955, when
branches of the labour federation were established in the inner city,
activists capitalised on personal and family contacts. 'Abd al-Rahman al-
Bakir had a hard core of supporters in al-Fadhil, his native quarter. 'Abd
'Ali al-'Alawayt, the vociferous Shi'i trader of al-Mukharaqah who
became a member of the executive committee, liaised with the *ma'tams*.
Employees of BAPCO coordinated the mobilisation of oil workers
throughout the town, particularly the hot-blooded *al-shabab* (youths)
who populated the poorest outskirts.[83]

Religious institutions and festivals took centre stage in the new political
geography of the city. Like the Communist gatherings in Iraq in the last
years of the monarchy, *al-Ha'yah* commandeered mosques, houses of
mourning and religious celebrations. As places of encounter between
activists and ordinary people, spaces of religious devotion became the
operational bases of the movement, where competing claims of authority
were made in the name of the direct delegation of power from the grass
roots. After the establishment of the organisation, thousands assembled
in Masjid al-Mu'min, the oldest Shi'i mosque in Manama, during the
celebration of the fortieth day of mourning for Imam Husayn (*al-arba'in*)
and in Masjid al-'Id, the large Sunni open-air mosque.[84] Gatherings also
underlined the importance of Islam as a unifying factor in the national
struggle. The establishment of *al-Hay'ah* in October 1954 was preceded
by a meeting in the al-Khamis mosque, the historical symbol of the Islamic
past of Bahrain revered by Sunnis and Shi'is alike. Leaders delivered
fiery speeches and announced the impending formation of an organised
popular front. Political rallies were carefully orchestrated, emphasising

[81] Beiling, 'Recent Developments in Labor Relations in Bahrayn', 161.
[82] al-Bakir, *Min al-Bahrayn*, pp. 60–1; Belgrave Diaries, 25 September and 16 October
1954, AWDU; Rumaihi, *Bahrain*, p. 216.
[83] Interviews with Muhammad Ja'far Muhsin al-'Arab, Khalifah Ahmad Sulaybikh and
Murad Jasim, Manama, 10, 17 and 18 April 2004; al-Bakir, *Min al-Bahrayn*, pp. 86–7;
Khuri, *Tribe and State in Bahrain*, p. 210; Sulaybikh, *Hikayat min al-Hurah*, pp. 29–30.
[84] al-Bakir, *Min al-Bahrayn*, pp. 71–3; Belgrave Diaries, 18 October 1954, AWDU; interview
with 'Ali Rabi'a, Manama, 1 April 2004; Khuri, *Tribe and State in Bahrayn*, pp. 203–4;
Nakash, *The Shi'is of Iraq*, p. 161.

the new egalitarian, participatory and cross-confessional character of the movement. Ordinary people from all walks of life from the villages and towns of Bahrain addressed crowds in the mosques and *ma'tam*s of Manama on matters of national concern.[85]

The autonomy of civil society was further underscored by the creation of popular arenas where *al-Hay'ah* influenced public opinion. The leaflets and bulletins circulated by the organisation affected the life of ordinary Manamis to an unprecedented extent. Bulletins became part of public policy, distributed simultaneously to the population and to the government. Announcements by the central committee were drafted, circulated and read aloud in the streets by *al-kashshafah* (boy scouts), which functioned as the right arm of the movement. Manama's boy scouts became instrumental in the organisation of strikes by canvassing popular support house to house and by inciting shopkeepers to close their business in the markets. Their white uniforms became the symbol of the peaceful credentials of the nationalist cause until they were constituted as a paramilitary organisation in June 1956.[86]

After the Egyptian revolution of 1952, radio became another form of egalitarian political acculturation. The broadcasts of *Sawt al-'Arab* from Cairo propagated the anti-imperialist message of Nasser, the iconic Pan-Arab leader who also started to target Belgrave and British imperialism in Bahrain directly. Regardless of status and education, Nasserist propaganda entered the heart and minds of Arab residents. Manama's coffee shops gathered large crowds of listeners, and in poor Sunni neighbourhoods with no public facilities radio broadcasts increasingly shaped the activities of the *majlis*es of influential members of the community. In al-Hurah, one of the new popular quarters of Manama, personal consultation and collective gatherings in affluent houses started to be defined by the times of broadcasts as radio sets made their appearance in both outdoor and indoor reception areas (see Figure 11).[87]

With organised protests, political rallies and labour boycotts, a new culture of urban violence emerged, particularly among Shi'i youths. This culture expressed the social alienation and economic dislocation of a poorly paid or unemployed workforce. It is worth noting that until the 1960s the modern educational system offered inadequate technical

---

[85] al-Bakir, *Min al-Bahrayn*, pp. 62–3; Khuri, *Tribe and State in Bahrain*, pp. 201–2.

[86] Interviews with Muhammad Ja'far Muhsin al-'Arab and Khalifah Ahmad Sulaybikh, Manama, 10 and 17 April 2004; interview with Rashid al-'Urayfi, Muharraq, 12 April 2004; Belgrave Diaries, 15 August and 8 November 1956, AWDU.

[87] Interview with Khalifah Ahmad Sulaybikh, Manama, 17 April 2004; interview with Rashid al-'Urayfi, Muharraq, 12 April 2004.

11 Popularising radio sets: advertising for the new model of PHILCO radio, 1937

training to Bahraini nationals.[88] Although violence was localised and erratic, by 1956 the successful nationalist indoctrination redirected resentment against the symbols and interests of British power and foreign capital. Arson, the stoning of cars and attacks on government buildings became familiar tactics on the part of bands of youngsters who disrupted the protests and strikes organised by *al-Ha'yah*. As noted by a British

---

[88] It was only in 1948 that BAPCO initiated a programme providing summer placements in the oil company for secondary school students. Finnie, 'Recruitment and Training of Labor', 138.

observer, there was a fine line between 'old fashioned riots' and the new nationalist demonstrations.[89]

Activists were divided with regard to the issue of civil unrest, although they often had no means of imposing order during marches. After a crowd of protesters assaulted the convoy of Selwyn Lloyd, the British Foreign Secretary, during an official visit to Bahrain in March 1956, al-Bakir publicly denounced some of these actions as 'hooliganism'. 'Abd al-'Aziz Shamlan, in contrast, was reported to have delivered inflammatory anti-imperialist speeches to the mob.[90] Demands from the popular base created a rift between al-Bakir and al-'Alawayt which was accentuated by the evolution of opposing ideological positions. While al-Bakir had become the custodian of Pan-Arabism by pursuing contacts with Nasserist Egypt, and was a staunch supporter of the peaceful credentials of *al-Hay'ah* as a populist organisation, al-'Alawayt had to come to terms with the turbulence of many followers of Manama's *ma'tam*s who represented his power base (see Figure 12).[91]

The potential for political dissidence embedded in Shi'i political culture and ritual resurfaced under the shadow of the new nationalist rhetoric. Many of the young, the unemployed and the disaffected used Muharram celebrations to mobilise against the government, the supporters of the Arabist secular line promoted by al-Bakir and, in some cases, even against the old notable class. By 1956 many of the followers of al-'Alawayt, often inflamed by *ma'tam* preachers, started to support a 'righteous' revolution against the Al Khalifah, Belgrave, British imperialism and the urban 'reactionaries'. The turbulence of devotees started to define the nationalist credentials of houses of mourning such as Ma'tam al-Qassab, Hajj 'Abbas, al-Madan and Ras Rumman, which were drawn into the nationalist orbit by the activism of their followers.[92] Only in a few cases were old merchant families still able to influence the political orientation of congregations. The most notable were the Ibn Rajabs, who sided with the government following a tradition which dated back to the second half of the nineteenth century.[93]

Three days of intense rioting which engulfed Manama in November 1956 marked the breakdown of the idea of peaceful civil protest advocated

---

[89] R. A. Read, 'Report on Strikes and Riots in Bahrain', 12 March 1956, FO 371/120545 PRO.

[90] Belgrave Diaries, 2 March 1956, AWDU; Khuri, *Tribe and State in Bahrain*, pp. 207–8; al-Bakir, *Min al-Bahrayn*, p. 105.

[91] al-Bakir, *Min al-Bahrayn*, pp. 58–9; Khuri, *Tribe and State in Bahrain*, pp. 210–13.

[92] Interviews with Muhammad Ja'far Muhsin al-'Arab and 'Abdallah Sayf, Manama, 10 and 20 April 2004; al-Bakir, *Min al-Bahrayn*, pp. 54–5.

[93] See p. 100.

12 The Egyptian 'connection': Vice-President Anwar al-Sadat, a close confidant of Nasser, delivering a speech in Manama for Bahrain's radio station, 1956

by the progressive cadres of *al-Ha'yah*. Triggered by the second Arab–Israeli war and by the British occupation of the Suez Canal, unrest began with the disruption of a peaceful demonstration organised in central Manama. The parade, whose route had been agreed upon with the government and which gathered a majority of the followers of al-Bakir, was disrupted by rioters, leading to widespread chaos. As unrest continued, private property owned by foreigners, government buildings, British enterprises and the Catholic Church in Manama were burnt or severely damaged. British and European residents were evacuated from the market area, while petrol stations were targeted and menacing crowds marched in front of the British political residency and of Belgrave's office shouting anti-British slogans.[94]

By the end of 1956 mob violence and sectarian resurgence had become enmeshed with the potent nationalist and anti-imperialist rhetoric of *al-Ha'yah*. In this respect, the organisation was fairly effective as a broad-based movement of urban political protest. Yet the front of popular mobilisation was clearly divided and violence had become an essential tool for political protest. These divisions limited the effectiveness of *al-Ha'yah* as a modern political organisation and contributed to seal its fate in November 1956.

The limits of national space

In the tense climate which characterised British imperial politics in the Arab Middle East during the Suez crisis, the riots of 1956 precipitated British military intervention in Bahrain and the disbanding of *al-Ha'yah*, only a few months after the organisation had received official recognition from the government. Members and followers of *al-Ha'yah* still attribute the collapse of national 'resistance' to the evils of military intervention as British troops entered Manama in November 1956. British intervention gave further credit to a long-standing tradition in Manama's political culture, that of blaming 'foreigners' for the evils which befell the town. It is true that in the following decades British support allowed the government to create a 'national security' sphere which posed severe constraints on the activities of clubs and political associations.[95] Yet the nationalist and anti-imperialist lore which surrounds the turbulent popular politics of 1954–6 has tended to underplay the shortcomings of Arabism and Pan-Arabism as ideologies of popular mobilisation able to appeal to the cosmopolitan and communitarian tradition of Manama.

The archetypal nationalist logic of the ideologues of *al-Ha'yah*, particularly that of al-Bakir, shows the limits posed by Arabism in transforming Manama into a cohesive national space. While claiming to champion the interests of Bahraini nationals (*al-wataniyyun*), the political community

---

[94] Political Resident Bahrain to Foreign Office, 4 March 1956, FO 371/120544 PRO; al Bakir, *Min al-Bahrayn*, pp. 105, 116; Belgrave Diaries, 2 March and 1–3 November 1956, AWDU; Khuri, *Tribe and State in Bahrain*, p. 104.

[95] al-Bakir, *Min al-Bahrayn*, pp. 112, 189–90 and 125–50; Khuri, *Tribe and State in Bahrain*, p. 104; Interview with Murad Jasim, Manama, 18 April 2004; Rumaihi, *Bahrain*, pp. 220–29.

they envisaged was exclusive to Arabs. Persian Shi'is, for instance, boy-cotted the movement on the grounds that *al-Ha'yah* had betrayed its claims to patriotism (*al-wataniyyah*) by supporting the supremacy of the Arabs as a political community (*al-qawmiyyah*). The secular Arabism advocated by al-Bakir was inevitably a narrowly defined discourse of political emancipation which serve to trigger the emergence of competing ideologies. This is also suggested by the evolution of the *ma'tam*s, whose followers provided their own religiously oriented interpretation of Arabism as a struggle against oppression (*zulm*) informed by divine jus-tice. Some Shi'i factions which operated within *al-Ha'yah* even came to political maturity under a splinter group called the National Pact shortly before the disbandment of the organisation.[96]

In the age of nationalist upheaval Persian Shi'is formed their own societies and political organisations. Clubs and football associations emerged after World War II under the umbrella of the Iranian Union School. The *Firdawsi* club, established in 1946, continued its relentless promotion of Iranian culture and maintained strong connections with the oil company, which absorbed the largest proportion of the Persian labour force.[97] An underground organisation influenced by the Iranian Communist party (*Tudeh*) started to operate in Manama under the name of *Hizb-i 'Adalat* in the early 1950s, while pictures of Musaddiq were displayed in the shops in support of the nationalisation of the Iranian oil industry. By 1956 community leaders were petitioning Belgrave for permission to form their own national committee modelled on *al-Ha'yah*.[98]

The nationalist press also provides evidence of the exclusive nature of the political discourse propagated by the intelligentsia of the national movement. Images of aloof but threatening Persians, Indians and Jews featured prominently in editorials and cartoons. After the establishment of Israel the position of many Jews became precarious, both socially and economically, and in 1947 protesters had targeted the Eastern Bank, which employed many members of the community.[99] Indians, who rep-resented a large proportion of the professional and clerical classes by the

---

[96] Interview with 'Ali Akbar Bushehri, Manama, 20 April and 15 September 2004; Khuri, *Tribe and State in Bahrain*, p. 209.

[97] Constitution of the *Firdawsi* club, 17 June 1946, BA; Khuri, *Tribe and State in Bahrain*, pp. 177–8.

[98] Interview with 'Ali Akbar Bushehri, Manama, 20 April and 15 September 2004; Belgrave to Political Agent Bahrain, 17 February 1948, R/15/2/485 IOR; Qubain, 'Social Classes and Tensions', 275; Belgrave Diaries, 4 September 1956, AWDU; Beiling, 'Recent Developments in Labor Relations in Bahrayn', 157.

[99] Belgrave Diaries, 2 December 1947, AWDU.

early 1950s, bore the full brunt of the anti-Indian sentiment of the labour movement. In January 1953 *al-Qafilah* published a letter from a reader which sums up the causes of the widespread resentment against Indian clerks and the strength of the Arab feeling of the readership:

It is strange that this department [the Post Office] continues to employ clerks who do not understand the language of the country. In this connection, I remember that a short time ago I sent my servant with a piece of paper on which I had written in Arabic the quantity of stamps I wanted of each denomination. Shortly afterwards he came back very angry. He told me that the clerk threw him out of the building and ordered him to "tell [your master] to write in Indian, Persian, or English ... We are not Arabs".[100]

If the ideological orientation of *al-Ha'yah* was at odds with the multi-cultural ethos of old communitarian Manama, its political legacy attests to the importance of the organisation in forging powerful tools of statecraft. After 1957 many of its members were co-opted into the bureaucracy, and acquired political offices and wealth. Although al-Bakir died in exile in Lebanon and al-'Alawayt in Iraq after both were tried for high treason in Bahrain, 'Abd al-'Aziz Shamlan became the vice president of the Constitutional Congress in 1971 and subsequently served as Bahrain's ambassador to Egypt. The old nationalist elites came to form a new political class, dependent on the government, which allowed the state to appropriate the ideological apparatus of Arabism.

Conclusion

Civic strife, popular politics and ideological contestation underscored the transformation of Manama's political life and public sphere in the transition between the pearl and the oil eras. In the fast expanding town of the pearl boom and well into the 1920s, networks of patronage and interfactional conflict were central to public life. As shown by the dynamics of the clashes between Persians and Arabs in 1904 and 1923, the tribal administration, the British agency and the municipality were an integral part of the apparatus of patronage. The political arena of the town was fragmented, dominated by the tension between British-protected communities and the subjects of the Shaykh of Bahrain, as well as between mercantile groups, tribesmen and immigrants. In the oil era, two key elements transformed the arena of urban politics and reshaped public life. The first was the cumulative popular experience of nationalism accrued through participation in a variety of activities: political rallies,

---

[100] Qubain, 'Social Classes and Tensions', 277.

strikes, demonstrations, Muharram celebrations, and membership of cultural clubs, sporting and youth associations. The second was the modernist project of popular representation and labour rights which the nationalist class pursued as an integral part of the anti-colonial movement. The press, radio and propaganda literature articulated a new web of public communication which connected activists, the new professional groups and the mercantile classes to oil workers, artisans and shopkeepers.

The transition from notable to nationalist politics was relatively smooth. After 1932, the demise of Bahrain's pearling economy gradually undermined the position of the old notables as popular leaders. The appeals to national and class solidarities launched by the young nationalists starting with the strikes of 1938 served to alienate the notables from their popular base in contrast with contemporary developments in the Arab Middle East during the period of the British and French mandates. In Damascus, for instance, the urban landowners who had risen to prominence in the second half of the nineteenth century carried forward the banner of Arab nationalism against the French occupation of Syria.[101] Partly because they became identified with the British imperial order in Bahrain, the a'yan of Manama were no longer in a position to act as a cohesive political force. By the late 1930s, they were unable to form an alliance with rising groups of middle-class professionals, intellectuals and bureaucrats. The incongruity between accelerating socio-economic modernisation precipitated by oil revenue and the conservatism of the process of nation building explains the peculiarity of the case of Manama. The expectations and popular demands of the young nationalist class were not matched by the development of representative institutions under the aegis of the reformed administration. In other words, Bahrain did not have a parliament sponsored by the mandatory power as in Syria or Iraq, where urban notables could pursue their political interests and satisfy the demands of their clientele. It is not surprising, as perceptively noted by Fuad Khuri, that at the peak of its popularity al-Ha'yah gathered popular consensus and pursued its political agenda largely 'as a de-facto [independent] government opposing the [imperial] regime'.[102]

By the early 1950s, the strong populist rhetoric of the young nationalist class had succeeded in forging new bonds among different strata of Manama's Arab society. Episodes of violence such as the baladiyyah episode in 1923, Fitnah al-Muharram of 1953 and the riots of November 1956 contributed to the transformation of communalism and sectarianism into

---

[101] These developments are discussed by Philip Khoury in his *Urban Notables and Arab Nationalism* and *Syria and the French Mandate*.
[102] Khuri, *Tribe and State in Bahrain*, p. 212.

key elements in the evolution of modern political identity. The nationalist discourse condemned communal and sectarian cleavages as a curse brought upon the nation by the forces of backwardness. As an ideology of popular militancy, Arabism opened up new communitarian spaces which united Sunnis and Shi'is. As the basis for political mobilisation, however, it did favour the resurgence of ethnic and sectarian particularism as suggested by the political inclinations of the Persians and of large segments of the *ma'tam* population in the era of *al-Ha'yah*.

As the outbreaks of unrest continued to mark crucial historical junctures, Bahrain's leading port retained the character of a 'border' town and of an unstable frontier society. In this respect, it is significant that 'foreigners' provided a constant focus of contestation and civic strife in times of conflict even after the discovery of oil. In fact, the changing meaning of this term in public discourse reveals the influence of nation building and state centralisation in reshaping the definition of 'outsiders' and 'insiders' to the town. In the early twentieth century, the aliens were Bedouin tribesmen, the Al Khalifah family and their entourage and the British-protected migrant communities, often viewed as instruments of imperial 'intrusion'. By the early 1950s, 'foreigner' had become synonymous with non-Arab and non-national, and the symbol of the new face assumed by British imperialism in the oil era as the agent of the economic exploitation of the national population.

6   City and countryside in modern Bahrain

This final chapter examines the making of Manama as an oil town and capital city. The focus is the impact of state intervention on the built environment and on urban life, and the contrast between these developments and those in the agricultural hinterland of Bahrain. The impact of oil did not trigger a new dialect of urbanisation, in the sense that it did not radically transform the patterns of settlement which had become apparent in the nineteenth century. Cultivators, turned into oil workers, continued to reside in their ancestral towns and villages, some of which were absorbed into Manama's metropolitan area after the oil boom of the 1970s. Awali, the first modern oil town (*madinah al-naft*) in the Gulf, built in 1937 by the American-owned BAPCO, developed as a 'neocolonial' settlement, a gated community which housed a new class of European and American technocrats who run the industry.

Oil revenue and state centralisation did not efface the traditional political and socio-economic differences between Manama and the rural areas inhabited by the indigenous Shi'i population. Rather, they enforced a new set of inequalities. In the oil era, historical legacies and inequalities continued to be enshrined in built environments and social landscapes, as they had been in the days of pearling. Manama became the harbinger of Bahrain's modernity as well as that of the entire Persian Gulf. The capital of the region's first modern state and its first 'metropolis' in the making, its position was consolidated by the transfer of the British Political Residency from Bushehr to Manama in 1947 after the independence of India. Urban development and the modernisation of urban life became the centerpieces of the new national project pursued vigorously by Belgrave and by the Government. In contrast, the agricultural hinterland of Manama developed at a different pace. Rural areas fell short of private and public investment and were penalised by the land regime enforced after 1925, while traditional rural life was fatally undermined by the decline of Bahrain's agriculture.

Organising Manama as a modern capital

The government supervised the infrastructural development of Manama under the directives of the Department of Land Registration (*Idarah al-Tabu*) and of Public Works (*Idarah al-Ashghal*), which until 1957 were controlled by Belgrave. Changes in the built environment, European influence and technological innovation were already apparent in 1937, as clearly suggested by the advisor:

a person returning to the country [after ten years] would notice [in Manama] the wider streets, better buildings, and a decrease in straw huts, trees, gardens and more vegetation, large shops selling European goods, motor traffic, European dress worn by natives, increasing use of machinery, partly owing to the installation of electric power, knowledge of English language, and a far greater interest taken in outside world affairs.[1]

Manama's modern outlook in the wake of the oil boom is testimony to the progress made by municipal government in the 1920s and early 1930s. Yet, in spite of the continuous efforts of the municipality and of the Department of Public Works, Manama did not grow organically in the following decades. The reorganisation of the inner city was sketchy and capricious at best. While the government modernised the waterfront and the port facilities, the old markets and the residential neighbourhoods became extremely congested with few open spaces left for construction. On the outskirts of the town, the Department of Land Registration and the municipality encouraged the permanent settlement of *barasti* communities. Only in 1968 was a committee appointed to devise a master plan for the city, although Belgrave had been pressing the municipality in that direction well before World War II.[2] This plan was enforced with mixed results after independence in 1971.

Mapping state intervention: the port and the inner city

Developments which affected Manama's waterfront were the most tangible manifestation of the control exerted by the government over the political, economic and social modernisation of Bahrain. The maritime landscape, however, did not enforce the visual separation between the new city and the old town. The architecture of the old neighbourhoods and of *barasti* conglomerates blended in organically with the new port

---

[1] 'Administrative Report for the Years 1926–1937' in *The Bahrain Government Annual Reports, 1924–1970*, vol. II, p. 56.

[2] Interview with anonymous informant, Manama, 5 April 2004; MMBM, 10 Sha'ban 1359/ 13 September 1940, R/15/2/1925 IOR; 'Annual Report for the Year 1368' in *The Bahrain Government Annual Reports, 1924–1970*, vol. IV, p. 33; J. W. Cummins, 'Report of an Inquiry into the Working of the System of Government in Bahrain and the Structure of the Bahrain Civil Service', 1957, Part I, FO 371/126897 PRO.

facilities and with the large buildings lining the seafront. By the 1950s Manama's warehouses had become the largest in the Gulf, serving Bahrain as well as the oil companies in Qatar and Saudi Arabia, and international firms began to establish branches in Bahrain. New wealth brought modern building materials into Bahrain, particularly cement. Yet in 1941 thatched huts still represented more than half of Manama's dwellings, and these survived well into the 1970s.[3] Government investment was concentrated on new customs services, official buildings and landing facilities. As modern technology was mobilised in the service of the expanding entrepôt economy, new urban landmarks bridged land and sea in novel ways (see Figure 13).

Belgrave was the *deus ex machina* of Manama's waterfront renewal, which was implemented in successive stages through land reclamation. His brainchild was Bab al-Bahrayn which he designed in 1945 as the seat of government, part of a complex which was built in front of the harbour after 1939. This rectangular building was conceived as the 'gateway' into modern Bahrain, and most likely inspired by the Gateway to India built by the British in Bombay harbour between 1913 and 1924. Its arched entrance overlooked the Customs Square (Maydan al-Gumruk or Maydan Shaykh Salman), which became the centre of modern Manama and provided access from the harbour to the city. Devoid of the orientalised classicism of its counterpart in Bombay, the building introduced to the overseas visitor the new architectural style of Manama, fusing the modernist lines of British colonial public architecture which developed in the interwar period with indigenous features.[4]

Rather than symbolising metropolitan authority and colonial hegemony, Bab al-Bahrayn affirmed the dynamism and the political primacy of Manama as the new capital of Bahrain. Moreover, the architectural language of the new seat of government, which also accommodated the personal office of the ruler, became a landmark in the process of

---

[3] In 1920 Manama included 2,240 dwellings for residential use with a very large proportion of *barastis*. By 1941 the number of dwellings had grown to approximately 4,000. Appendix to Manama Municipal Regulations, 1921, L/P&S/10/349 IOR; 'Annual Report for the Year 1359' in *The Bahrain Government Annual Reports, 1924–1970*, vol. II, p. 38.

[4] Belgrave, *Personal Column*, p. 135; 'Annual Report for the Year 1368' in *The Bahrain Government Annual Reports, 1924–1970*, vol. IV, pp. 44–5; interview with 'Abd al-Rahim Muhammad, Manama, 17 April 2004. For the Customs Square scheme, see 'Annual Report for the Year 1365' in *The Bahrain Government Annual Reports, 1924–1970*, vol. III, pp. 80–1 (with map). M. Crinson, *Modern Architecture and the End of Empire* (Aldershot: Ashgate, 2003). On the Gateway of India see P. H. Davies, *Splendours of the Raj: British Architecture in India, 1660–1947* (London: Murray, 1985), pp. 180–1 and T. R. Metcalf, *An Imperial Vision: Indian Architecture and Britain's Raj* (New Delhi, Oxford University Press, 1989), p. 231.

13 Aerial view of Manama from the port in the early 1950s with Bab al-
Bahrayn and the Customs Square at the centre. The marshland and the
barasti settlements to the south of the city are visible in the background

Arabisation of urban culture. The 'Arab' character of its wooden panels,
balustrades and doors undermined the cosmopolitan influences which
had characterised Manama's residential architecture before oil.[5] As the
harbour continued to be the political and economic hub of the city, Bab al-
Bahrayn provided continuity with the urban layout of the nineteenth
century. Only following the announcement of British withdrawal from
the Gulf in 1968, the government redesigned the waterfront. The port was
transferred to the south of the city in Mina' Salman and the government

[5] 'Annual Report for the Year 1368' in *The Bahrain Government Annual Reports, 1924–1970*,
vol. IV, pp. 44–5.

14 a Bab al-Bahrayn (north side) with the Customs Square, 1948–9
b Bab al-Bahrayn (south side), *c.* 1958

offices were relocated to a large compound on reclaimed land on the
northeastern coast (see Figure 14a and Figure 14b).

Policies on health and sanitation promoted the new civic spirit of
modernity. The first modern medical facilities were established at the
beginning of the twentieth century by the American missionaries and by
the British agency, which had subsidised the construction of the Victoria
Memorial Hospital in 1904. The government-built al-Na'im and al-
Salmaniyyah hospitals were added on the outskirts of town, in 1937 and
1959 respectively. Dramatic improvements in sanitation reflected the
achievements of the *baladiyyah*. Streets in the markets were widened in

order to open dead ends which were notorious rubbish dumps, while medical dispensaries initiated a programme of vaccination against small-pox and typhoid in the late 1920s. After 1924 land reclamation also became part of the new 'cosmetics' of urban modernisation, as refuse started to be used systematically for the construction of the motor road along the seafront and of the causeway which linked Manama to Muharraq.[6]

The fear of disease promoted a new morality which relegated social outcasts at the margins of the inner city by government decree. In the early 1920s when the British agency supervised closely municipal affairs, destitute Persians and the growing numbers of emancipated slaves living in the city were moved en masse from upmarket Kanu to an agricultural allotment south of the town. Their appalling living conditions, notoriously summed up in the name of their hamlet (Zulmabad, the land of oppression), were the main cause of the epidemics which had long plagued the urban population.[7] After 1937, the male and female prostitutes from India, Oman, Iran and East Africa who crowded the harbour and the markets were transferred to Garandor, an area located on the western outskirts of the inner city. The sale of sexual favours, which was an integral part of Manama's traditional overseas economy, became the subject of a relentless government campaign which denounced prostitution as a source of disease and superstition, the latter with reference to widespread practices of exorcism, particularly *zar*.[8]

Modern transport and technological innovation underpinned the fast-growing entrepôt economy of the city, nurtured by the speedier sea links and the new air facilities which consolidated the position of Bahrain at the centre of global routes. BOAC (British Overseas Airways Corporation) operated regular flights from Bahrain and in 1950 a local company was formed by a former Royal Air Force serviceman.[9] The construction and maintenance of roads absorbed a large part of the municipal budgets.

---

[6] *The Persian Gulf Administration Reports, 1873–1947*, vol. VII, pp. 48, 52–3, 68 and 74; Belgrave to President of Manama Municipality, n. 1227/8 of 1349, 21 February 1931, R/15/2/1209 IOR.

[7] Political Resident Bushehr to Government of India n. 626-S of 1923, 10 November 1923, R/15/2/127 IOR; minutes by Assistant Political Agent Bahrain, 20 February 1936, R/15/2/1923 IOR.

[8] R/15/2/1227 IOR: I'lan Hukumah al-Bahrayn, n. 753/17 of 1347; Political Agent Bahrain to Collector of Malabar, 10 January 1929, n. 31 of 1929. I'lan Hukumah al-Bahrayn, n. 29 of 1350, R/15/2/1228 IOR; Secretary of Manama Municipality to Belgrave, 13 Jumada al-Ula 1347/27 October 1928, R/15/2/1218 IOR; 'Annual Report for the Year 1365' in *The Bahrain Government Annual Reports, 1924–1970*, vol. III, p. 74.

[9] 'Abd al-'Aziz M. Yusif Bu Hajji, *Lamahat min tarikh al-murur fi al-Bahrayn khilal al-sanawat 1914–1969* (Manama: al Mu'assasah al-'Arabiyyah li al-Tiba'ah wa al-Nashr, 1998), 23–72; Belgrave, *Personal Column*, pp. 174–5.

15 Traffic warden in central Manama with the typical Indian-style police uniform, early 1940s

Attentive to any innovation which might benefit their business, merchants competed to sponsor modern roads soon after the end of World War I, and continued to press for their extension and maintenance after the establishment of the municipality. Automobiles became a much sought-after status symbol for members of the ruling family and for entrepreneurs. By the 1950s the marketing of cars had reached large audiences, as suggested by the ubiquity of car advertising in the local press. In 1926 only ten cars circulated in Bahrain; by 1957 there were 5,595 registered vehicles including cars, taxis and trucks. Between 1960 and 1967 the number of private cars increased by 82 per cent, causing regular rush-hour traffic jams in Manama (see Figure 15).[10]

Thoroughfares were the window onto Manama for the outside world, a vantage point from which the growing number of overseas travellers who reached the city by air and sea en route to India and Europe could observe Bahrain's path towards modernity. The municipality attempted, not always successfully, to enforce a uniform appearance to the frontage of thoroughfares which were visible to car passengers. In 1947 Belgrave

[10] Bu Hajji, *Lamahat min tarikh al-murur*, pp. 31, 296; 'The Bahrain Economy', memorandum by the Ministry of Overseas Development, 15 October 1968, CAB 148/90 PRO; 'Bahrain Annual Review for 1971', Diplomatic report n. 65/72, 31 December 1971, FCO 8/1823 PRO.

lamented the bad publicity which Manama received in the British press following complaints by air passengers in transit.[11] While the network of motor roads which connected Manama to the rest of the islands was established at the beginning of the 1930s and was heavily subsidised by the oil company, the road system in the inner city improved steadily after the establishment of the municipality.[12] During a brief visit in 1923, the British political resident noted that car circulation had improved dramatically and that the new network of motor roads joined the agency and the Customs House and connected Manama to Shaykh Hamad's residence in al-Sakhir. Before the completion of his palace in the new district of al-Qudaybiyyah in 1927, the roads of the inner city were used to stage official parades, and allowed the police to patrol markets and neighbourhoods more efficiently.[13]

In other important respects the control of roads was central to the new engineering of urban space on the part of the government. As roads became the modern services and facilities par excellence, they became antithetical to the unruly layout and messy appearance of *barasti* compounds. The resilience of the *barasti*s in the inner city symbolised the growing political threat posed by Bahrain's lumpenproletariat which was developing around the oil industry. The first official ban on the construction of huts was enforced in 1937 along the main arteries which embraced and intersected the quarters of the old town. Ten years later the area affected was extended to the modern residential area of al-Qudaybiyyah but excluded the popular quarters of northeastern Manama where many informal communities still lived.[14] While modern thoroughfares fixed the geographical boundaries of the old neighbourhoods, they became the showcase of the state administration as they were named after Belgrave, political agents who had served in the 1920s and early 1930s and members of the ruling family.

Bahrain's embryonic bureaucracy also started to categorise the inner city in an orderly and systematic fashion. Since 1939, the publication of *Jaridah al-Bahrayn* (The Bahrain Gazette) contributed to the standardisation of the names of localities as it included the announcement of the sale and purchase of properties issued by the Department of Land Registration. The official nomenclature of roads, neighbourhoods and

---

[11] MMBM, 4 Dhu al-Hijjah 1367/7 October 1948, R/15/2/1932 IOR; 'Annual Report for the Year 1368' in *The Bahrain Government Annual Reports, 1924–1970*, vol. IV, p. 34.

[12] Maps, 'Bahrain Islands', 1938 (BR 477) and 1944 (BH 477), BA.

[13] Political Resident Bushehr to Government of India, 10 November 1923, n. 626-S, R/15/2/127 IOR.

[14] MMBM, 21 Jumada al-Ula 1356/30 July 1937, R/15/2/1924 IOR; I'lan Baladiyyah al-Manamah, 6 Dhu al-Hijjah 1367/9 October 1948, n. 6, R/15/2/1932 IOR.

public buildings entered popular usage only in the late 1950s. As traditional landmarks continued to foster the sense of place and hierarchy of urban residents, the municipality and the government continued to use mosques, *ma'tam*s and upper class mansions in their proclamations to indicate particular districts.[15] Although land registration played a crucial role in fixing the boundaries of both properties and neighbourhoods, it also subverted traditional perceptions of space. The production of detailed title deeds, with measurements and maps, established a new visual language of property ownership which replaced the formulas of the property certificates issued by Shaykh 'Isa (*hibah*s) and by the qadis (*sanad milkiyyah*) in the early twentieth century. Although the plans drawn by *Tabu* officials were often not consistent with the old documentation, land and property disputes were less confrontational than in the villages. In fact, merchants and members of the Al Khalifah family, who were the largest claimants of real estate, were often in a position to produce proof of ownership.[16]

Domestic space continued to be dominated by traditional notions of intimacy. While most of the modern houses were rented to foreigners, old properties built around courtyards were enlarged and repaired, and new rooms added to accommodate family members. The *Hay'ah al-Kashf* (Inspection Committee) of the municipality became the 'privacy' committee par excellence as it was in charge of vetting the extension and repair of buildings. The disputes arbitrated by the municipality reveal the durability of the 'introverted' character of Manama's urbanism which protected traditional notions of morality and family life.[17] In areas of public utility, residents also challenged the authority of the *baladiyyah*. They often claimed portions of roads by opening new entrances to their houses and shops, by building balconies and putting up sun shades and benches. When the municipality started to cover the main thoroughfares of the markets, wealthy merchants started to build their own roofs across shops.[18]

---

[15] Bu Hajji, *Lamahat min tarikh al-murur*, pp. 59–65; MMBM, 3 Jumada al-Ula 1354/3 August 1935 and 3 Dhu al-Qa'dah 1369/17 August 1950, R/15/2/1922 and 1932 IOR; 'I'lanat Idarah al-Tabu' in *Jaridah al-Bahrayn*, Dhu al-Qa'dah 1359–Dhu al-Hijjah 1360 (December 1940–January 1942), MWT; 'Tasjil mabi'at wa ghayr fi al-Tabu' in *al-Jaridah al-Rasmiyyah*, n.1 to n. 39, 15 Rajab 1357–15 Rajab 1370 (23 May 1948–21 April 1951), DSQ.

[16] Manaf Yusif Hamza, *Manar al-Bahrayn fi tarikh al-tabu wa al-misahah*, (Manama: under the auspices of the Council of Ministers, 2000), p. 142; interview with Muhammad Ishaq 'Abd al-Rahman al-Khan, Manama, 8 April 2004.

[17] The word *al-kashf* was also used for privacy in popular parlance.

[18] In 1940 a famous dispute involved 'Abd al-'Aziz al-Qusaybi who had roofed two of his properties on either side of a municipal road. When he informed the municipality, the secretary ordered the structure to be demolished. Although it was eventually taken down, al-Qusaybi got monetary compensation by claiming that he had simply repaired a roof

Inside and outside private residences, the oil era shadowed the emergence of distinctively modern spaces and lifestyles. Although the upper
classes did not abandon traditional housing, furniture and utensils in the
residences of entrepreneurs, merchants, civil servants and professionals
displayed a marked European taste. Tables and chairs replaced mats,
carpets and cushions. Curtains were used for windows, and the *majlis*es of
merchants and entrepreneurs often had a gramophone and a radio set which
with the car became the modernist icon of the 1950s. With electricity,
wealthier households were equipped with refrigerators and fans. Coffee
shops, a traditional institution of Manama's public life, were gradually
transformed with modern furniture and catering facilities. By 1937 the
largest coffee shops started to be referred to by their customers as *al-utils*
(hotels). In the 1940s, the growing popularity of cinemas which showed
Indian, European and American films also contributed a shift in the public
awareness of what constituted modern entertainment and defined the new
style of leisure of Manama's young middle classes (see Figures 16 and 17).[19]

Urban expansion and the land regime

The government supervised and guided urban expansion outside the inner
city through the Department of Land Registration. In encouraging the
fixation of rights of private property, land policies endeavoured to create a
class of smallholders among the *barasti* population who lived on the edge of
town. As early as 1930 most of the non-agricultural land around Manama
not privately owned was classified as property of the state (*miri*). After
1925, the municipality took over on behalf of the Land Department land
occupied by *barasti* compounds in areas such as al-Hurah and Garandor,
which after 1937 became Manama's red-light district. Residents started to
be charged a nominal rent and by the early 1930s tenants who could prove
that they had occupied the area for at least ten years were in a position to
acquire title deeds.[20] In the early 1950s, while the government continued to
encourage the ownership of land and houses on the part of the less affluent
segments of urban society, it started to offer several building loan schemes
with BAPCO in order to encourage oil workers to build modern houses

built before municipal regulations were issued. Belgrave to Political Agent Bahrain, 15
Rajab 1365/15 June 1946, R/15/2/1309 IOR; MMBM, 6 Shawwal and 18 Dhu al-Hijjah
1359/6 November 1940 and 16 January 1941, R/15/2/1924 IOR. Several examples of
disputes over privacy brought in front of the municipal council are included in files R/15/
2/1923, 1924, 1925, 1932 IOR.
[19] 'Administrative Report for the Years 1926–1937' in *The Bahrain Government Annual
Reports, 1924–1970*, vol. II, pp. 54–5.
[20] Files n. 54, 62, 67, 73, 84, 87, 94, 96, IT; MMBM, 9 Dhu al-Qa'dah 1358/20 December
1939, R/15/2/1925 IOR; interview with anonymous informant, Manama, 5 April 2004.

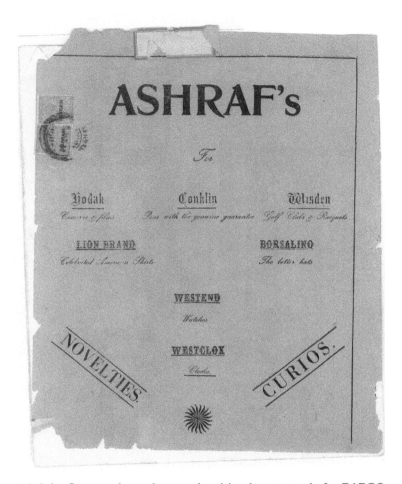

16 Ashraf's general merchants: advertising luxury goods for BAPCO
European and American employees and for Bahrain's emerging middle
class, 1937

with sanitation and electricity. These schemes encountered mixed success.
If on the one hand most of the grants were used for that purpose, on the
other the new dwellings were often rented out at very high prices following
the boom of the rental market.[21]

---

[21] *The Bahrain Government Annual Reports, 1924–1970*: 'Annual Report for the Year 1371',
vol. IV, p. 35; 'Annual Report for the Year 1372', vol. V, p. 35; Belgrave, *Personal Column*,
p. 181.

17 Advertising for Quaker Corn Flakes, 1961. The last line reads: This is the food of the modern age, enjoy it!

In granting security of tenure to large segments of the population, land provisions were instrumental in integrating Manama's shanty towns into the emerging modern city in the 1940s and 1950s, particularly al-Hurah and al-Dawawdah in the east and al-Zarari'a in the west, including Garandor. In the agricultural belt in the south and southwest, the Land Department had to come to terms with the claims of the peasantry who continued to contest rights of ownership against the claims of the Al

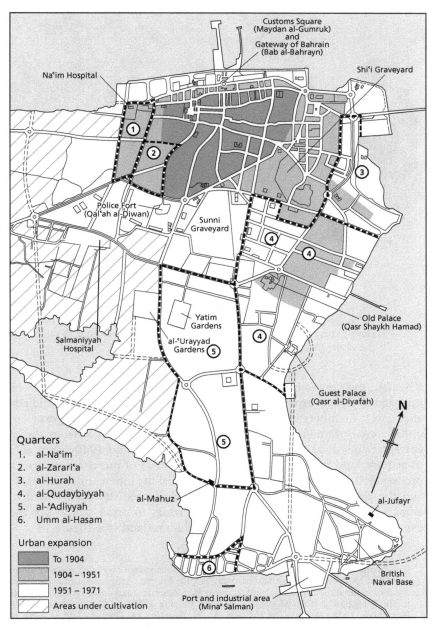

Customs Square
(Maydan al-Gumruk)
and
Gateway of Bahrain
(Bab al-Bahrayn)

Na'im Hospital

Shi'i Graveyard

Police Fort
(Qal'ah al-Diwan)

Sunni
Graveyard

Old Palace
(Qasr Shaykh Hamad)

Salmaniyyah
Hospital

Yatim
Gardens

al-'Urayyad
Gardens

Guest Palace
(Qasr al-Diyafah)

N

al-Mahuz

al-Jufayr

Quarters
1. al-Na'im
2. al-Zarari'a
3. al-Hurah
4. al-Qudaybiyyah
5. al-'Adliyyah
6. Umm al-Hasam

Urban expansion

To 1904

1904 – 1951

1951 – 1971

Areas under cultivation

British
Naval Base

Port and industrial area
(Mina' Salman)

5 Manama urban expansion, 1904–71

18 The wealthy Persian merchants and landowners of al-'Awadiyyah, 1951. Second from the right Ahmad 'Arshi, a relative of the owner of Bayt Faruq. First from the left Muhammad Tahir Khunji, a relative of the philanthropist Abd al-'Aziz Lutf 'Ali

Khalifah, their customary overlords. Further, in spite of the restrictions imposed by the government on the alienation of the Al Khalifah holdings after 1927, members of the ruling family continued to sell properties to old merchant families such as the Kanus and the rich Persian Sunni entrepreneurs of al-'Awadiyyah who in the 1930s and 1940s were able to acquire land fairly cheaply.[22] The penetration of merchant capital, a process well under way since the last quarter of the nineteenth century, [23] and the absence of a master plan effectively forced the government to enter a partnership with private entrepreneurs in order to oversee the expansion of Manama into its agricultural hinterland (see Figure 18).

[22] The claims of the peasantry were not successful with the exception of the case of eviction started in 1928 by Shaykh Muhammad ibn 'Isa, the brother of the ruler, against some of the former inhabitants of Zulmabad. It seems that Belgrave intervened, refusing to expel them. R/15/2/1923 IOR; MMBM, 9 and 23 Jumada al-Ula 1347/23 October and 6 November 1928; Belgrave to Political Agent Bahrain, 26 Dhu al-Qa'dah 1354/20 February 1936 n. 1299-1 of 1354; minutes by Political Agent Bahrain, 27 February 1936. Belgrave to Political Agent Bahrain, 28 March 1938, R/15/2/807 IOR.
[23] See pp. 89–90, 102–4.

The first of such partnerships was the new neighbourhood of al-Qudaybiyyah, developed on land which was partly owned by the government (*miri*) and partly by Mustafa 'Abd al-Latif, the wealthy entrepreneur from Lingah and one of Manama's largest property owners. The area started to develop in the late 1930s around the palace of Shaykh Hamad, which was completed in 1927, and around the new quarters of the Al Khalifah family. Besides being the new stronghold of the ruling family in Manama, by the end of World War II al-Qudaybiyyah had become important to the expanding British political and military establishments: the Royal Air Force owned an airfield in the vicinity of the palace compound, and plans were put forward by the political agency in 1946 to erect the headquarters of its Indian clerical staff.[24] Mixing old and new styles of patronage, al-Qudaybiyyah became the first of Manama's planned residential districts. The Land Department took on the role of planning office in order to keep away the evils which beset the inner city, particularly random building patterns. The government built roads, sponsored two cinemas, and by the early 1950s initiated the construction of Buyut al-'Ummal, a housing project for junior civil servants and oil workers. In parallel, Mustafa 'Abd al-Latif who was the largest private landowner in the area, instructed the Department of Land Registration to sell his land at a nominal price in small allotments to poor immigrants from Iran.[25] *'Ard Mustafa* (the land of Mustafa), as the area owned by the rich Persian became known, stood alongside the modern al-Qudaybiyyah and continued to grow under the wing of its benefactor, displaying some of the architectural features of the inner city (see Figure 19).

The 1960s ushered in a new phase of urban development inspired by Western concepts of urban planning. Awali, the headquarters of BAPCO, and 'Isa Town, the first modern housing project sponsored by the government outside Manama, provided the model for al-'Adliyyah, a new residential district built in the 1960s with modern housing compounds and residential villas surrounded by private grounds.[26] Old merchant families

[24] Political Agent Bahrain to British Resident Bushehr, 8 January 1946, n. 91–18/8, R/15/2/1309 IOR; interview with Muhammad Ishaq 'Abd al-Rahman al-Khan, Manama, 8 April 2004.
[25] Belgrave, *Personal Column*, p. 181; *The Bahrain Government Annual Reports, 1924–1970*: 'Annual Report for the Year 1365', vol. III, p. 55; 'Annual Report for the Year 1369', vol. IV, p. 38.
[26] Awali was also used as a model for the construction of other purpose-built oil towns, Dhahran in Saudi Arabia and Ahmadi in Kuwait. 'Annual Report for the Year 1365' in *The Bahrain Government Annual Reports, 1924–1970*, vol. III, pp. 78–80; Belgrave, *Personal Column*, pp. 139–41; J. Gornall, 'Some Memories of BAPCO', typescript, May 1965, BA; *Madinah 'Isa/'Isa Town* (Ministry of Housing, Municipalities and Environment, State of Bahrain, c. 1996), p. 2.

19 Mustafa 'Abd al-Latif, the Persian entrepreneur and landowner, early 1960s

such as the Kanus and al-'Urayyads built their mansions in their garden properties, which they had bought some decades earlier from members of the ruling family. Further west, the al-Salmaniyyah Hospital and the residences of its medical staff formed the first nucleus of al-Salmaniyyah, a quarter which developed after 1968. In the same period the new port of Mina Salman and the British Naval Base at al-Jufayr on the southern coast became the new poles of urban expansion which gathered momentum after independence with the creation of the new residential area of Umm al-Hasam.

By 1971 the landscape of the outskirts of Manama and the geography of its coastline had started to change irreversibly. The green agricultural belt which once surrounded the town shrunk visibly as date gardens disappeared and old agricultural settlements became part of developing commercial and residential areas. Land speculation also altered patterns of land use along the coast. While until the 1950s the Land Department had utilised reclaimed land in order to settle Manama's informal communities, in the following decades land reclamation became a lucrative source of income, particularly for members of the ruling family, a process which continues today (see Figure 20).

Immigrants, nationality and land

Policies on immigration, nationality and land were instrumental in the 'nationalisation' and 'Arabisation' of Manama, processes which in the

20 Aerial view of northeast Manama with modern districts being developed on reclaimed land, 1970

1940s and 1950s unfolded in parallel with the consolidation of the nationalist movement. As after 1937 the right to own land became conditional on the acquisition of Bahraini nationality, the historic communities of Manama viewed Bahraini passports as the new prize of modernity. Immigrants from neighbouring Arab countries and from Iran had similar aspirations, attracted to the town by the almost mythological lure of oil wealth. Throughout the Gulf, Bahrain acquired the reputation of the place where 'all streets are paved with gold'.[27]

With the advent of the reforms and of oil, Manama was no longer the open town of the pearl boom. Soon after the reorganisation of the customs administration in 1923, immigration started to be regulated by a system of visas and passports which were under the control of the port and the municipal authorities. Following the expansion of oil production on the eve of World War II, the government started to encourage the migration

---

[27] Quote from Belgrave, *Personal Column*, p. 103.

of particular communities.[28] In the second half of the 1930s, for instance, the British agency started to favour the entry of labourers from the Indian subcontinent. After 1947, the violence and dislocation which followed the partition of India played into the hands of the agency as some 2,000 impoverished refugees arrived in Manama from India and Pakistan in 1949 alone.[29] The increasing demand for labour in the modern sectors of the economy brought to Manama a new type of immigrant whose arrival in Bahrain was no longer determined by family or personal connections. Economic migrants continued to represent a large proportion of the urban population. In 1941, for instance, more than one-third of urban residents were classed as non-nationals. At least until the mid 1950s, immigration from overseas supported the city's demographic expansion.[30]

With the enforcement of immigration quotas and work permits, the profile of 'illegal' immigrant became firmly established. The failure to control immigration from Iran was a thorn in the side of the government as Persian Shi'is became the largest foreign community with no passports or recognised travel papers. Renewed Iranian claims to Bahrain and the increasing popularity of the Iranian Communist party (*Tudeh*) in the early 1950s reinforced the belief that the Persian immigrants constituted either a fifth column of the Pahlavi government or the vanguard of a leftist revolution. Large numbers were routinely rounded up by the police between 1939 and 1956, and then either imprisoned or expelled from Bahrain.[31] Many immigrants used the nationality papers and travel documents issued by the various British political agencies around the Gulf to enter Bahrain. Between 1945 and 1947 some 3,000 Persians arrived in

---

[28] *The Bahrain Government Annual Reports, 1924–1970*: 'Annual Report for the Year 1365', vol. III, p. 74; 'Annual Report for the Year 1369', vol. IV, p. 7; 'Annual Report for the Year 1956', vol. V, p. 94. Secretary of Manama Municipality to Belgrave, 13 Jumada al-Ula 1347/27 October 1928, R/15/2/1218 IOR.

[29] Lawson, *Bahrain: The Modernization of Autocracy*, p. 50; 'Annual Report for the Year 1955' in *The Bahrain Government Annual Reports, 1924–1970*, vol. V, p. 94.

[30] The urban population increased from 25,000 in 1904 to 41,000 in 1941, and in 1959 it reached approximately 61,000. *The Fourth Population Census of Bahrain: A Brief Analytical and Comparative Study* (Finance Department, Statistical Bureau, State of Bahrain, August 1969), p. 5; 'Papers Concerning the Population Census of 1941', R/15/2/1289 IOR. *The Bahrain Government Annual Reports, 1924–1970*: 'Annual Report for the Year 1365', vol. III, p. 74; 'Annual Report for the Year 1369', vol. IV, p. 7; 'Annual Report for the Year 1956', vol. V, p. 94.

[31] R/15/2/494 IOR, particularly 'Deportations of Persians from Bahrain, 1938–1944'; Belgrave to Political Agent Bahrain, 17 February 1948, D.O. n. 782, R/15/2/485 IOR; Belgrave to Political Agent Bahrain, 17 Rabi' al-Awwal 1367/27 January 1948, n. 666 and minutes by Political Agent Bahrain, 17 February 1948, R/15/2/490 IOR. *The Bahrain Government Annual Reports, 1924–1970*: 'Annual Report for the Year 1369', vol. IV, p. 7; 'Annual Report for the Year 1955, vol. V, p. 44; 'Annual Report for the Year 1956', vol. V, p. 94.

Manama after a brief stay in Dubai or Sharjah, where they were given local travel papers as British-protected subjects, despite the restriction enforced by the agency in Bahrain.[32] By the late 1940s, however, the government and the agency were forced to encourage migrations from Arab Gulf countries as the non-Arab labour force came increasingly under attack from the nationalist movement. After the enforcement of a new Order-in-Council in 1952, visas and work permits were no longer required for Arab nationals as jurisdiction over them was transferred from the British agency to the Bahrain Government. By 1957–8 they represented the largest group of immigrants in the registries of both the port and aviation authorities.[33]

Alongside the profile of immigrant, government intervention reshaped the legal meaning of 'foreigner' as non-national. The transfer of British extraterritorial jurisdiction to the Bahrain Government gathered momentum in 1937 with the issue of the Bahrain Nationality and Property Law, a milestone in the history of Manama.[34] The transfer of jurisdiction had already started before the discovery of oil as also suggested by the consolidation of municipal authority in the late 1920s over large segments of the urban population.[35] Moreover, after 1929 children of immigrants became subjects of the Shaykh of Bahrain by default unless their parents had registered them in the political agency at birth.[36] As part and parcel of the process of state centralisation, the 1937 legislation promoted a new policy of 'land for Bahrainis'. As the right to own real estate became conditional to the acquisition of Bahraini nationality, the government targeted the foreign propertied classes of Manama, particularly rich Persian entrepreneurs who were forced to acquire Bahraini passports in order to retain ownership of their assets. This legislation also responded to concerns with national security; it was widely feared that the Pahlavi government could use the disproportionate economic influence of the Persian community of Manama in order to gain a foothold in Bahrain.

Yet by World War II only a fraction of local Persians born before 1929 had opted for Bahraini nationality. These were usually the richest Sunni

---

[32] It seems that this continued until 1971. Minutes by Political Agent Bahrain, 17 February 1948, R/15/2/490 IOR; Belgrave to Political Agent Bahrain, 17 February 1948, R/15/2/485 IOR.

[33] 'Annual Report for the Year 1372' in *The Bahrain Government Annual Reports, 1924–1970*, vol. V, p. 38. Political Resident Bahrain to Foreign Office, 6 March 1959, FO 371/140273 PRO; Al-Baharna, *British Extra-Territorial Jurisdiction*, p. 38.

[34] I'lan Hukumah al-Bahrayn, 27 Safar 1356/8 May 1937, R/15/2/1976 IOR.

[35] See pp. 123–4.

[36] I'lan Hukumah al-Bahrayn, n.1101/17/1347, 17 Ramadan 1347/27 February 1929 and n. 50/1351, 4 Dhu al- Hijjah 1351/31 March 1933, R/15/2/150 IOR; Belgrave to Political Agent Bahrain, 9 September 1933, n. 541–9A, R/15/2/150 IOR; I'lan Hukumah al-Bahrayn n. 53/1356, 27 Sha'ban 1356/1 November 1937, R/15/2/151 IOR.

merchants who were traditionally hostile to the Iranian government.[37] Many Shi'i entrepreneurs, who were either members of the municipal council or had connections to the Al Khalifah, became the proud possessors of dual citizenship. When they visited Iran, they obtained travel documents and were treated as Iranian subjects, a status which they often expressed openly in Manama. Some of those who had acquired Bahraini passports in 1937 also attempted to register their properties in the name of their children born after 1929.[38] In contrast with the reluctance of rich Persian residents to sever links with their motherland, immigrants relentlessly pursued their quest for property and nationality. As applications for passports became conditional on the ownership of property, many Persians and coastal Arabs used land acquisition to attempt to legalise their position in Bahrain. A large number of Persians and labourers from al-Ahsa', for instance, requested a passport after they had acquired small plots of government land in the outskirts of Manama. Inundated with applications by the early 1940s, the passport office started to turn down requests, particularly from Persians. Between 1948 and 1950 all applications for nationality lodged by Persians were refused while Arab nationals continued to be treated favourably in order to assuage the sensibilities of nationalist protesters and leaders.[39]

The stirrings of Arab nationalism also forced the administration to uphold its policy of 'land and country' for public consumption. In 1949, a ban was enforced on the sale of 'Arab' land owned by Bahrainis to foreigners. Three years later, in the tense climate which preceded *Fitnah al-Muharram* and the establishment of *al-Ha'yah*, legislation was issued to the effect that the sale of real estate owned by Iranians, Saudis and citizens of other Arab Gulf countries was restricted to Bahrainis in an attempt to limit the property drain.[40] As suggested by this legislation, the avowed policy of 'land for Bahrainis' was clearly incongruent with developments on the ground. Since the late 1930s the position of Manama as the commercial centre of the Gulf's nascent oil industry had boosted foreign investment in real estate. During the war the property market thrived.

---

[37] In 1948 only 233 local Persians had Bahraini nationality. Belgrave to Political Agent Bahrain, 21 March 1948, R/15/2/490 IOR.

[38] R/15/2/152 IOR: I'lan Hukumah al-Bahrayn n. 53 of 1356, 27 Sha'ban 1356/1 November 1937; 'Abd al-Rahim ibn Shaykh Muhammad Khoeij to Political Agent, 22 February 1938.

[39] *The Bahrain Government Annual Reports, 1924–1970*: 'Annual Report for the Year 1365', vol. III, p. 56; 'Annual Report for the Year 1369', vol. IV, p. 7; 'Annual Report for the Year 1370', vol. IV, p. 39; 'Annual Report for the Year 1371', vol. IV, p. 38.

[40] *The Bahrain Government Annual Reports, 1924–1970*: 'Annual Report for the Year 1368', vol. IV, p. 33; 'Annual Report for the Year 1372', vol. V, p. 35. Political Agent Bahrain to Political Resident Bahrain, 8 February 1958, FO 371/132893 PRO.

Between 1942 and 1945 prices increased six-fold and in 1954, Belgrave noted, the prices of building sites per square foot were comparable to those in London. While land and houses became popular investments for any resident who was able to capitalise on the black market, many properties were acquired by rich non-nationals who were willing to pay very high prices to establish their business in the city. By the mid 1950s Persian and Saudi entrepreneurs owned extensive properties along the seafront and in the inner city, and had also made inroads into the agricultural belt.[41]

Provisions concerning immigration, nationality and land transformed Manama into a new national and trans-national space. The open port town of the pearl boom became the exclusive domain of passport- and property-holding nationals. Immigrants, who had been the building blocks of pre-oil Manama, turned into possessors of visas and travel documents, a disciplined labour force subservient to the new economy. Inevitably, with the imposition of new legal and political identities on the urban population, the historical 'town of foreigners' became the theatre of novel trans-national conflicts, most notably involving the Persian community. Moreover, urban real estate (and land in particular) acted as a new source of political identity in tune with processes of urban modernisation and state centralisation. Before oil, the control of land defined the material and symbolic relationship between Bahrain's rulers and the merchant classes of Manama. By the 1950s, the control of urban real estate had become the centrepiece of a new nationalist rhetoric promoted by a government which was becoming increasingly intertwined with the national and Arab character of the oil state.

'Rationalising' the rural world: the politics of land

The new legislation on immigration and nationality did not have major repercussions on the agricultural districts of Bahrain, as no foreigners resided there. In contrast, land policies represented the main instrument of government intervention in the countryside until the administrative reorganisation of village communities under the newly established Department of Rural Affairs (*Idarah al-Shu'un al-Qaryawiyyah*) in 1957. After 1925, the Land Department essentially upheld the status quo ante by granting the Al Khalifah family permanent rights of ownership over large portions of their agricultural estates. In some areas, the confusion of

---

[41] Political Agent Bahrain to Political Resident Bahrain, 8 February 1958, FO 371/132893 PRO; Belgrave, *Personal Column*, p. 204. *The Bahrain Government Annual Reports, 1924–1970*: 'Annual Report for the Year 1362', vol. III, p. 25; 'Annual Report for the Year 1365', vol. III, pp. 56–7; 'Annual Report for the Year 1372', vol. V, p. 35.

property rights obstructed a comprehensive legal settlement of disputes. A useful parallel can be drawn with Transjordan, where a modern land department was established by the British mandatory administration in 1927. Here, the British authorities were able to solve disputes over tribal land after they completed a land survey in the mid 1930s. In the villages of Bahrain, land settlement was still a top priority in 1957 before the Department of Rural Affairs set out to enforce health provisions and to establish modern educational facilities. Soon after independence, approximately 99 per cent of cases brought before the Bahraini courts dealt with disputes over real estate.[42] Moreover, the Department of Rural Affairs acquired complete jurisdiction over those areas which were not under municipal administration, that is major urban centres, only in 1967, four years before independence.[43]

The protection of the rights of Shi'i agriculturalists played a considerable part in British thinking about reform before World War I. By the 1890s the land regime in force in Bahrain's agricultural estates was placing an increasing burden on the peasantry, as suggested by their frequent complaints to the British agency in Manama. The condition of servitude of the cultivators was worsened by the demographic growth which affected the ruling family and by the increasing number of matrimonial alliances with other tribes which had enlarged the rank and file of the inner circle of Shaykh 'Isa. As more individuals entered the entourage of the ruler, they demanded their own share in the Al Khalifah family estate.[44] Yet political considerations prevented the new Land Department from undertaking registration outside Manama until Belgrave arrived in Bahrain in 1926. Major Daly, the first political agent in charge of land matters, often refused to recognise title deeds, and became renowned for his inclination to tear up certificates in front of applicants, including members of the ruling family. At the same time he showed little or no sympathy for the plight of the cultivators. The Political Resident A. P. Trevor summarised in 1923 the considerations which underscored this course of policy: 'We should not involve ourselves in this matter [land registration, survey and revenue in the villages] because most of the land belongs to the al-Khalifa

---

[42] For land policies in Transjordan see M. R. Fischbach, *State, Society and Land in Jordan* (Leiden: Brill, 2000). 'Annual Report for the Year 1958' in *The Bahrain Government Annual Reports, 1924–1970*, vol. VI, p. 113; interview with Majid Asghrar, Manama, 20 April 2000.

[43] 'The Bahrain Government Rural Affairs Department (Powers and Duties) Ordinance 1967', annex to 'The Bahrain Government Rural Affairs Department (Powers and Duties) (Amendment) Regulation 1968', 8 August 1968, FCO 8/123 PRO.

[44] See file R/15/1/336 IOR for peasants' complaints; Political Agent Bahrain to Political Resident Bushehr, 31 December 1904, n. 204, R/15/2/10 IOR.

family and the other to the Baharna. If we collected the revenue from the Baharna only, we would provoke their anger against us.'[45]

The ethos of the *Tabu* Department vis-à-vis Bahrain's rural world changed after it was taken over by Belgrave. The new line of policy conformed to the advisor's developmental vision: the burden of rural folk was to be eased by involving rulers and cultivators in the process of establishing legal rights over land ownership.[46] Besides land, the department started to supervise water and fishing rights, which were crucial to supporting the ailing village economy. The new system offered a degree of protection to the rural population, giving villagers an opportunity to challenge their landlords in front of *Tabu* officials. They could also apply for the registration of their houses, small agricultural plots and fish traps. During the pearl crisis, *Tabu* officials played a role in protecting cultivators and pearl divers from the claims of boat captains, tribal entrepreneurs and urban-based merchants as they became involved in the supervision of properties which were mortgaged against the repayment of debt.[47]

In the late 1920s the *Tabu* personnel in charge of surveying Manama (Indian technicians recruited from the Bombay Government) started to turn their attention to the rural districts. As was the case in Manama, the drawing of property boundaries on maps, and the record of details of tenancies and water rights was an important step in the bureaucratisation of government. Moreover, as these surveys were conducted with innovative techniques employed in British India, they became one of the manifestations of the rationality and the rigour of the reforms.[48] On the ground, however, both surveyors and *Tabu* officials were faced with a far more ambitious undertaking than in Manama. Apart from the reticence of villagers who feared the imposition of further taxation, their daily routine was hampered by the absence of land legislation before the reforms and by an arbitrary customary system.[49] It soon became clear that the confused layout of property rights and the increasing number of disputes over title deeds represented a dangerous battleground which pitted agriculturalists against tribesmen and villages against the Al Khalifah. Fearing rural unrest and political turmoil, the administration encouraged the

---

[45] Belgrave to Political Agent Bahrain, 19 November 1931, R/15/2/708 IOR. Quote from Rumaihi, *Bahrain*, p. 51.

[46] Evidence is included in files n. 1–37, and n. 45–76, IT.

[47] 'Administrative Report for the Years 1926–1937' in *The Bahrain Government Annual Reports, 1924–1970*, vol. II, p. 26.

[48] Political Agent Bahrain to Surveyor General of India, 28 April 1925, n. 37/9/03, R/15/2/130 IOR.

[49] A useful comparison can be made with the Land Department established by the British in Iraq in 1921 which made extensive use of Ottoman legislation. See P. Sluglett, *Britain in Iraq: Contriving King and Country* (London: I. B. Tauris, 2007), pp. 167–8, 178–80.

registration of existing rights but did not make it compulsory. After 1929 only properties for sale, or gifted by the ruler, had to be vetted by land officials who issued title deeds after having verified claims of ownership, and solved disputes with the support of the courts.[50] Further, in order to assuage the sensibilities of large landowners (members of the Al Khalifah family, tribal leaders and urban entrepreneurs) no land tax was imposed with the exception of a stamp duty on sales, which was replaced by a fixed percentage on the value of the transactions after 1948.[51]

In common with urban Manama, government policies tended to protect the interests of rural landowners while rationalising customary practice. In theory, the institution of private property and the fixation of categories of land tenure entailed the separation of individual rights form collective ownership and the detachment of properties of the Al Khalifah from those of the state.[52] In practice, the new land regime recognised collective ownership but encouraged the parcelling up of agricultural land in order to create a class of small landholders and increase agricultural production.[53] In the case of the estates under the control of the Al Khalifah, they were classed as private property and could be registered in the name of individual holders but ultimately were considered family assets and could not be alienated outside the group. Land Registration faced considerable difficulties in enforcing the new provisions as suggested by the several proclamations issued between 1927 and 1932 which banned the purchase of land from members of the family.[54] Land sales by the Al Khalifah resumed during World War II, when the

---

[50] I'lan Hukumah al-Bahrayn, n.1 of 1349, R/15/2/1923 IOR; 'Memo on Land Registration in Bahrain' by Belgrave, c. 1934, R/15/2/1715 IOR.

[51] In the early years the stamp duty was of one rupee. In 1930 new fee brackets were introduced according to the value of the properties, and in 1948 the stamp duty was fixed at 3 per cent. I'lan Hukumah al-Bahrayn n. 1 of 1349, and n. 1 of 1367, Hamza Archive (hereafter HA).

[52] The cadastral survey recognised *awqaf al-sunnah, ja'fariyyah and dhurriyah* (family endowments), *amlak al-waratah* (properties shared by partners in inheritance), and *miri* and *rahmaniyyah* land, the former controlled by the government and the latter including areas with no agricultural value. *Awqaf dhurriyah* and government land did not undergo systematic registration, while *rahmaniyyah* plots became by default property of the state after 1942. Khuri, *Tribe and State in Bahrain*, pp. 37–49, 101–107; interview with anonymous informant, Manama, 12 September 2004; I'lan Hukumah al-Bahrayn n. 1 of 1361, HA.

[53] Manaf Yusif Hamza, *Mu'jam al-ta'mir wa al-khara'it wa al-watha'iq al-'aqariyyah al-Bahrayniyyah* (Manama: Dar Akhbar al-Khalij, 2001), p. 79–80; files n. 9, 11 and 14, IT.

[54] I'lan Hukumah al-Bahrayn, n. 10 of 1350 and n. 42 of 1351, R/15/2/1228 IOR; I'lan Hukumah al-Bahrayn, 3 Jumad al-Awwal 1347/17 October 1928, R/15/2/1227 IOR. *The Bahrain Government Annual Reports, 1924–1970*: 'Annual Report for the Year 1349', vol. I, p. 27; 'Annual Report for the Year 1362', vol. III, p. 26.

prices of date gardens soared as a result of restrictions on date imports from Iraq and from the mainland.[55]

The economic considerations which underscored land registration undermined the rationale of land settlement on political grounds. After 1929 the land claimed by members of the royal household covered more than three-quarters of the productive area of Bahrain, including large tracts of the agricultural belt surrounding Manama. As noted by Belgrave in 1931, if these claims had been granted, the state treasury would have lost control over much of the countryside. At the same time, the Land Department was not in a position to start land distribution anew as Shaykh 'Isa, the deposed ruler, was alive and in theory he was still the 'land controller'. In other words, if the government interfered with customary practice it would have denied political legitimacy to the household as a whole.[56] After the death of Shaykh 'Isa in 1932, Shaykh Hamad did not recover family properties as the new ruler. Land grants started to be redistributed on an *ad hoc* base under the supervision of the family council, a body which pre-dated the reforms.[57] Regrettably, it is impossible to draw a detailed picture of land rights after the reforms. What is clear is that the Al Khalifah family remained in control of the most productive land in the northern region of the main island. For instance, Shaykh Muhammad ibn 'Isa, the brother of Shaykh Hamad, became the largest owner of rural property in the 1930s.[58]

One notable outcome of the conservative nature of the new land regime was that it did not enforce new hierarchies of authority in the countryside, essentially preserving the profile of landlord, tenant and agriculturalist. It upheld the position of *wazirs*, members of village communities who had supervised tenancies and tax collection on behalf of landlords before the reforms. Under the supervision of the *Tabu*, cultivators enjoyed rights of usufruct (*tasarruf*) by written agreement which replaced oral contracts of lease. Arrangements between tenant and landlord/shaykh continued to be negotiated on a sharecropping basis or, in the case of palm groves, bound

[55] 'Annual Report for the Year 1365' in *The Bahrain Government Annual Reports, 1924–1970*, vol. III, p. 56.
[56] Belgrave to Political Agent Bahrain, 19 November 1931, R/15/2/807 IOR. *The Bahrain Government Annual Reports, 1924–1970*: 'Annual Report for the Year 1348', vol. I, p. 160; 'Annual Report for the Year 1351', vol. I, pp. 369–71.
[57] 'Annual Report for the Year 1351' in *The Bahrain Government Annual Reports, 1924–1970*, vol. I, pp. 369–71. R/15/2/804 IOR, in particular minutes of Al Khalifah family council, 4–11 October 1934, and Belgrave to Political Agent Bahrain, 18 March 1935, n. DO 36; Khuri, *Tribe and State in Bahrain*, pp. 101–7.
[58] 'A Note on Land Tenure by the Ruling Family in Bahrain' by Belgrave, 23 December 1931, R/15/2/807 IOR.

the cultivators to pay a fixed rent in kind.[59] Yet the emphasis on agricultural development and the increasingly lucrative prospects offered by
artesian wells played a part in the adjudication of land rights in the
1930s. The *Tabu* issued title deeds for small plots on the basis of ten
years of occupancy to reward cultivators for having maintained produc-
tivity. To a certain extent it endorsed the Islamic principle of *ihya'* (regeneration) invoked in the nineteenth century by Shi'i clerics in order to
bolster the claims of villagers over uncultivated land whose ownership
(according to Shi'i jurisprudence) had reverted to God. In many cases this
practice, popularly known as *wada'a al-yad* (literally, to lay one's hand;
i.e., to claim usufruct), allowed villagers to appropriate open grounds
located at the margins of cultivated areas.[60] Moreover, the *Tabu* protected
the interests of Shi'i rural communities by allowing village committees to
participate in the redrawing of the boundaries of plots.

The decline of agriculture and the ideology of rural resistance

In contrast with Manama, the landscape of Bahrain's agricultural hamlets
in the oil era continued to be characterised by poverty and decay, a reflection of the social and economic realities of a vanishing rural world. In
speech and appearance villagers continued to be noticeably different from
townsfolk, easily distinguished in the crowds at the markets of Manama and
in the oil fields where many of them came to be employed. The oil company
provided the only form of modern transport for villagers, although during
World War II they started to organise buses to take agricultural produce to
Manama. The marketing of both foodstuffs and modern commodities
continued to be heavily dependent on peddlers who purchased provisions
in Manama, in some cases until the early 1960s.[61] Isolation from the outside world epitomised the seemingly unchanging and backward nature of
Shi'i rural society in contrast with Manama's 'modern' life blessed by
consumerism, Western influence and technological innovation.

In spite of the efforts of the Land Department, a number of factors dealt
the final blow to Bahrain's traditional village economy. First, the government did not earmark funds for the development of Bahrain's rural infrastructure until the administrative reorganisation of the agricultural regions

---

[59] I'lan Hukumah al-Bahrayn, n. 1112/17 of 1347, R/15/2/1227 IOR; Khuri, *Tribe and State in Bahrain*, pp. 37–49.

[60] Hamza, *Mu'jam*, p. 98; I'lan Hukumah al-Bahrayn n.1 of 1361, HA.

[61] 'Annual Report for the Year 1365' in *The Bahrain Government Annual Reports, 1924–1970*, vol. III, pp. 104–5. H. A. Hansen, *Investigation in a Shi'a Village in Bahrain* (Copenhagen: National Museum of Denmark, 1967), p. 61.

of the islands in 1957. Second, a chronic lack of funds impaired the revival of agriculture which in the late 1930s started to be promoted by the administration to compensate for the uncertain prospects of oil exploitation. Investment failed to revive large-scale cultivation as it was channelled towards experimental projects which sought to introduce new crops and agricultural techniques. Third, after 1940 restrictions on the drilling of artesian wells which were depleting Bahrain's underground water supplies weakened further agricultural output. By 1951 gardens were no longer profitable investments as dates ceased to be an essential item in the local diet while the majority of vegetables started to be imported.[62]

The decline of agriculture combined with the development of the oil industry slowly changed the profile of peasant communities. In the early 1930s the inability of the government to fix fair rents and place them on a monetary basis led to the further impoverishment of the rural population. Agriculturalists took out leases which were higher than they could afford in an attempt to obtain the best plots. Landlords complained that their margin of profit was unacceptable and brought villagers to court to recover their dues. Many were imprisoned as they had no properties to auction to repay their debts.[63] In 1934 landowners started to employ salaried labour, mainly Shi'i cultivators from al-Ahsa'. By the mid 1950s the majority of date groves and gardens were tended by Omani immigrants as villagers opted for the secure wages offered by the oil company and construction firms.[64]

While Shi'i villages ceased to be an integral part of the traditional spatial and social economy of Manama, the decline of agriculture marked the dissolution of the economic bonds between the peasantry and their land. By 1959 only 5 per cent of the labour force of Jidd Hafs and Sitrah, two hamlets which started to grow as satellites of Manama and of the oil refinery, was employed in agriculture.[65] For many peasants turned oil and service workers, however, modernisation did not mean physical dislocation from their homes. Until the late 1950s, the rural workforce did

---

[62] *The Bahrain Government Annual Reports, 1924–1970*: 'Annual Report for the Year 1357', vol. II, pp. 28–9; 'Annual Report for the Year 1358', vol. II, pp. 34–5; 'Annual Report for the Year 1359', vol. II, p. 35; 'Annual Report for the Year 1362', vol. III, p. 37; 'Annual Report for the Year 1371', vol. IV, p. 35; 'Annual Report for the Year 1955', vol. V, p. 41. Rumaihi, *Bahrain*, pp. 53–4.

[63] R/15/2/176 IOR: Political Agent Bahrain to Political Resident Bushehr, 7 November 1934, D.O.N. C/882; Belgrave to Political Resident Bushehr, 12 November 1934. 'Annual Report for the Year 1349' in *The Bahrain Government Annual Reports, 1924–1970*, vol. I, pp. 2–3.

[64] *The Bahrain Government Annual Reports, 1924–1970*: 'Annual Report for the Year 1353', vol. I, pp. 555–6; 'Annual Report for the Year 1955', vol. V, p. 41.

[65] *The Population of Bahrain. Trends and Prospects* (Directorate of Statistics, State of Bahrain, January 1979), pp. 84–5.

not contribute to the demographic growth of Manama, which was fuelled mainly by immigration from overseas. The continuity of settlement maintained a degree of social unity among old village communities, serving to keep alive religious codes and traditions. In the 1940s a young trading elite which had benefited from the oil boom started to establish 'official' houses of mourning in rural communities organised around family factions, which were modelled upon the *ma'tam*s which had mushroomed in Manama at the turn of the century.[66]

Religious ideology did not provide the main impetus for the political mobilisation of the workforce of rural extraction against the government in the 1950s. As we have seen their cause was taken up instead by the nationalist and labour activists based in Manama. The response of the villagers to the nationalist agitations was largely determined by their occupation and by the political inclinations of their traditional leaders, particularly men of religion and families which controlled *ma'tam*s.[67] In 1958 a member of the staff of the British residency commenting on the prospects of the newly formed Department of Rural Affairs envisaged that many villagers might turn into supporters of the Al Khalifah given that Arab nationalism had left the sectarian and traditionalist outlook of Bahrain's rural society 'comparatively untouched'.[68]

The conservatism of rural society reproduced the tensions between the Shi'i population and the Al Khalifah family which had dominated Bahrain's agrarian question before the reforms. With the gradual disappearance of the indigenous agricultural economy, the importance of land as ideological capital increased. Partly encouraged by the failure of land registration to break the monopoly of the Al Khalifah, Shi'i clerics and mullas used the loss of agricultural land as a rallying cry against the 'neo-tribal' regime supported by Belgrave. Revisiting the old popular myth of Bahrain as the 'Islands of Paradise', they voiced their opposition to the new government by condemning the 'alien' tribal culture of the Al Khalifah which continued to wreak havoc amongst Bahrain's native population. The loss of land also featured prominently as a major topic of sorrow and reproach among Shi'is of rural extraction living in Manama who accused a number of prominent families of collaboration with the Al Khalifah in the early nineteenth century.[69] Contrary to the predictions of the British residency, the failure of

---

[66] Lawson, *Bahrain: The Modernization of Autocracy*, p. 58.
[67] See for instance the case of the village of al-Diraz split between the al-Shihab and al-'Asfur families. Khuri, *Tribe and State in Bahrain*, pp. 162–3.
[68] Minutes by W. J. Adams, 18 September 1958, FO 371/132531 PRO.
[69] N. Fuccaro, 'Understanding the Urban History of Bahrain', *Journal for Critical Studies of the Middle East*, 17 (2000), 48–82 (63–5); I. A. Schumacher, 'Ritual Devotion among Shi'i in Bahrain', unpublished PhD dissertation, University of London (1987), p. 70.

Arab nationalism to make inroads into Shiʻi rural society did not turn former villagers into Al Khalifah supporters but sowed the seeds of the renewed sectarian conflict which unfolded in the 1970s. The threat posed to the government by land grievances is also suggested by the relentless public ceremonies staged by the Department of Rural Affairs in the 1960s to mark the distribution of title deeds to villagers.[70]

Conclusion

The outcome of state intervention and oil modernisation in Manama can be measured by the growing economic, political and social distance between Bahrain's new capital city and its historic agricultural hinterland. The contrast between the urban and rural landscapes of modern Bahrain reveals the uneven transformative powers of oil, besides pointing to a degree of continuity with the nineteenth century. In Manama state centralisation had an unprecedented influence on urbanisation and urban life. Immigration and nationality laws, in particular, transformed the position of urban residents vis-à-vis the state. In contrast, the old agricultural villages survived as a mere appendix of the new political and economic order. By the 1960s, this new urban–rural divide started to be expressed through traditional ideals of Shiʻi political and social emancipation, suggesting the continuation of the fractured political culture which had become apparent after the Al Khalifah occupation of Bahrain in 1783. Under modern conditions Shiʻism did not cease to provide an ideology of rural 'resistance' against state power, testimony to the profound inequalities enforced by the modern state.

The land policies enforced by the government demonstrate the ways in which the rhetoric of social and political development championed by Belgrave failed to bridge the gap between urban and rural society. Title deeds were the symbols of social progress and 'civilisation', a corrective to the abuse of authority perpetrated by the ruling family, by tribal landowners and by the urban propertied classes. In Manama, the fixing of rights of private property partially achieved this goal. Title deeds granted security of tenure to large segments of the city's informal communities and integrated the shanty towns of the pearl boom into the modern city. In contrast, the land regime enforced in the villages ultimately protected the interests of the Al Khalifah and hindered the creation of a land market, also contributing to the demise of Bahrain's agricultural economy. Land policies provide an illuminating example of how the practices of the modern state failed to empower of Shiʻi rural society.

[70] 'Bahrain's Newsletter' n. 3, 9 February 1958, FO 371/132756 PRO.

Conclusion

Challenging the received wisdom on the Gulf

Over the two centuries between the Al Khalifah occupation and independence from British control, urban development and urban life in Bahrain continued to mirror the broader social and political transformations of the coastal regions of the Persian Gulf. Before oil the dynamics of these frontier societies were expressed in the visual and cultural language of expanding port towns in a way which resembles – albeit in a different economy of scale – the growth of Gulf cities in the age of oil and globalisation. In approaching the city as a separate theme in Gulf history, this study has revisited the political and social evolution of Manama and Bahrain in the age of tribal expansion, British rule and oil. The analysis of Manama's urban history as the world centre of pearling, the hub of British imperial influence and the capital of the modern state of Bahrain challenges standard portrayals of the politics, society and urbanism of the Gulf littoral.

Manama and its agricultural hinterland constitute an excellent vantage point for observing the multiple facets and composite nature of state and nation building in the Gulf before and after oil. The interface between tribe and state in Bahrain, and more generally along the Gulf coast, has thus to be understood in the context of the complex society of its historic port settlement. The histories narrated in this book question earlier accounts centring on tribal elites and ruling families as 'state makers', shifting the emphasis to notables, merchants, pearl divers, immigrants, peasants, oil workers and national activists. Bahrain's tribal administration did not occupy a hegemonic position in the town of the pearl boom. Although strong tribal and sectarian solidarities supported the rule of the Al Khalifah family, tribal authority was clearly enmeshed in economic interests spatially anchored in the port and in the markets, and in political manoeuvres for the control of revenue and real estate. The evolution of the urban body politic in the modern era presents a contrasting picture. On the one hand, tribes no longer featured as political units unlike the old networks of patronage, quarter solidarities, and professional and religious associations which played so large a part in the popular mobilisation of the 1940s and 1950s. On the other hand, old-style tribal authority survived in the local markets, where the Al Khalifah family continued to own real estate until and after independence. In some important respects, it was overseas immigrants who represented the crucial force in the development of Manama. Before and after the discovery of oil, migrant workers provided a reservoir of subaltern groups which sustained Manama's economic and demographic expansion. The discontinuities in the geopolitics of migration apparent since the late 1930s can be readily explained by the emergence of Bahrain's oil industry and by the centralisation of Manama's port economy, as well as by the new international conjunctures which characterised the interwar period. This book has argued that it was the changing social, legal and political position of Manama's migrant workers which measured the pace of state and nation building in Bahrain.

Turning to the imperial context, the dynamics of British expansion into the Persian Gulf explain the precocious development of Manama in comparison with the capitals of the other Arab Gulf states. The partial integration of Bahrain's leading port into the world economy in the late nineteenth century paved the way for its transformation into the centre of a modernising state in the 1920s and early 1930s. In the following two decades, Manama rose to prominence as the 'central place' of oil modernity in the Gulf, the hub of a modern service economy which satisfied the needs of oil industries and societies in the making across the region. It was only in the 1960s that Saudi Arabia and Kuwait started to import modern goods and services for their populations directly from Europe, Japan and the United States. As oil modernisation came to fruition in other Gulf countries, Bahrain relinquished its role as the beacon of regional development. As early as 1958 the gap between the wealth of Kuwait and the 'relative' poverty of Bahrain was already growing wide as a result of the decreasing oil reserves of the islands.

Alongside the early discovery and exploitation of oil, the influence of the British Empire brings into sharper focus the importance of a historical approach in the study of Gulf urban milieus. In this respect, this history of Manama challenges standard portrayals of urbanisation based upon ideal types of urban development as epitomised by recent studies on the Oil City.[1] As suggested in this book, oil alone cannot explain the emergence of Manama as a modern city. Its spatial and socio-political organisation was also profoundly influenced by the pearl economy, the rise and fall of the

---

[1] See for instance S. Khalaf, 'The Evolution of the Gulf City Type, Oil, and Globalization' in Fox, Mourtada-Sabbah and al-Mutawa (eds.), *Globalization and the Gulf*, pp. 244–65.

British Empire in the Middle East and India, and by the growth of Arab nationalism. A more organic and cross-regional approach to urban development also provides a much needed framework for comparison within the region and across different historical periods. For instance, Kuwait and Trucial Oman (since 1971 the United Arab Emirates) did not occupy as prominent a place as Bahrain in the political geography of the British Empire. It can be argued that their relatively weak imperial connections had a strong impact on the formation of national identities. Neither countries nor their capital cities experienced Arab nationalism as part of independence movements as was the case in Bahrain and Manama. In the United Arab Emirates, for instance, only after independence has a self-conscious effort at emphasising the Arab character of the state and of urban centres become apparent.

Notwithstanding these differences, the case of Manama calls for a re-evaluation of the assumption that the oil era constituted a rupture with the urban past of the region. The distinction between the 'traditional' and the 'modern' Gulf city which has gained considerable currency in recent years is clearly rooted in the disproportionate academic attention devoted to the Oil City as an ideal type of urban development. Moreover, the reconstruction of idealised 'traditional' settings in the heart of the hypermodern contemporary Gulf capitals – old neighbourhoods, pearl diving villages and market areas – has undoubtedly reinforced this trend in the minds of both academics and urban planners. At least until independence, modern Manama retained the socio-economic life and spatial features of the port settlement of the pearl boom, characterised by an intimate relationship between the waterfront, the markets and residential neighbourhoods. Revenue from the port economy also supported the city's infrastructural development until the 1960s. Evidence from Manama also frees the historical experience of Gulf urban societies from the aura of 'exceptionalism' which surrounds them. Petro-urbanism – a definition first used at the height of the oil boom of the early 1980s – is often analysed as a revolutionary way of life which entailed the sudden entry of 'backward' indigenous populations into the hectic world dominated by the forces of global capitalism. Before independence, and in spite of oil, the residents of Manama experienced modernity as a gradual process of change; their experience was not that dissimilar to that of other peoples outside Europe in the age of colonisation and decolonisation. The modern world became manifest in the transformation of the lifestyle of the new middle classes and old merchant elites, in the emergence of new notions of private and public spaces, in improved communications with the outside world and, last but not least, in the growth of a new nationalist awareness which reshaped the boundaries of ethnic groups and of communal life.

The state and changing hierarchies of space, place and sect

The transformation of the social, political and spatial topography of Manama after World War I reflected the integration of Bahrain and of the Gulf coast into a world of nation states in the making. The organisation of urban neighbourhoods and the ways in which their residents experienced state authority are a case in point. In the pre-modern era, patron–client relations, immigration flows and merchant capital defined the spatial identity and social texture of al-firjan of the town. By the 1950s, the organisation and social hierarchies of the quarters of the inner city had become increasingly dependent on, and identified with, new practices of state control. The government redrew the lines of privilege among their residents through the enforcement of land registration, censuses, municipal taxation and immigration and nationality laws which created new legal and political divisions between nationals and non-nationals, and between Arabs and non-Arabs.

The episodes of unrest discussed in Chapter 5 illustrate the ways in which places, spaces and urban institutions became the sites of new forms of popular and elite mobilisation against the state. Before the emergence of modern politics in the late 1930s, civic conflict erupted most often at the market place, the core of Manama's pre-modern economy, as with the incidents of factional violence involving Persians and Arabs in 1904 and 1923. The mobilisation of class and intersectarian interests against the modern administration in the era of nationalist upheaval gradually shifted the focus of popular activism to the residential areas. Here by the 1950s protesters and their leaders commandeered houses of mourning and mosques. The government buildings, the municipality and the foreign enterprises on the seafront became the target of widespread resentment, pitting Manama's old quarters against the new political centres of the modern city.

In this respect, it is evident how not only the state but also modern politics appropriated the residential areas of the inner city, in contrast with the situation in Damascus in the interwar period. In the Syrian capital, the elite Arab nationalists of the mandate period who led the movement against the French administration transferred their operational base from the old city to the modern residential districts which had developed as a result of colonial urbanism.[2] In Manama, the new nationalist leadership operated from the old neighbourhoods, contributing to maintaining their spatial and political unity. Perhaps for this reason, the inner-city

---

[2] P. Khoury, 'Syrian Urban Politics in Transition: The Quarters of Damascus during the French Mandate', International Journal of Middle East Studies, 16 (1984), 507–40.

areas have continued to act as a source of historical memory and political identity even after the relocation of their residents to modern residential districts after the 1970s. Today for Bahraini nationals to claim to be a *Mukharaqi*, a *Fadhili* or a *'Awadi* – either by birth or because their parents and extended family resided there – is still a prestigious symbol of urbanity which transcends the grim realities of the decaying landscape of the old quarters now inhabited largely by poor Asian migrant labourers.

State intervention and modernisation had equally momentous implications for the tribal towns established after 1783 whose economic and political importance decreased in parallel with that of former agricultural districts. Muharraq remained the second largest settlement of Bahrain but the transfer of the residence of the ruler to al-Sakhir in 1927 and the lack of public and private investment over the following decades undermined its demographic and economic development. al-Hidd and al-Budayya' never recovered from the collapse of the pearling industry; by 1959 the population of the former had halved while the latter suffered considerably from the migration of its al-Dawasir settlers to the mainland in the 1920s. In contrast, in the 1960s al-Rifa', which had become the residence of the members of the ruling family, emerged as Bahrain's third largest settlement, absorbing the historic towns of Rifa' al-Sharqi and Rifa' al-Qibli.[3]

Turning to Bahrain's village communities, their situation after independence continued to deteriorate. By the 1980s, the accelerated expansion of Manama into its rural hinterland created a new 'dialectics of suburbanism'. As neatly planned, orderly and relatively affluent housing projects mushroomed around Manama to accommodate the new Shi'i middle classes of urban extraction, old villages such as Jidd Hafs and Bilad al-Qadim turned into satellites of Manama without modern housing and adequate public services. The latter, a form of suburbanism that Fuad Khuri has termed 'dormitory' communities,[4] did not represent a transitional stage in the process of integration of the Shi'i underclass into the social and economic fabric of modern Bahrain. It fostered a culture of 'marginality', underdevelopment and political militancy which drew on the ethos and historical memory of the old agricultural communities. This process started to become manifest in the 1960s and gathered momentum in the political mobilisation of religiously inspired Shi'i groups after the Iranian Revolution of 1979.

---

[3] Lorimer, *Gazetteer*, vol. II, pp. 237–8; Belgrave, *Welcome to Bahrain*, p. 16; *Bahrain Census of Population and Housing – 1981: Trends and Prospects* (Directorate of Statistics, State of Bahrain, *c.* 1981), p. 74.
[4] Khuri, *Tribe and State in Bahrain*, pp. 253–4.

It is striking how categories of 'urban' and 'rural' have continued to demarcate the sectarian divide long after the disappearance of agricultural and tribal landscapes. In the mid 1970s Fuad Khuri noted that: 'Rural, urban, city, town, and village are not clear-cut social categories when applied to Bahrain society today – these are historical traditions and must be understood in this context.'[5] A decade later the new suburban Shi'i dormitory communities were still identified with the 'backward' and militant rural milieus of the pre-oil era. As Ilse Schumacher noted during her fieldwork in Bahrain, 'Shi'i is defined as a villager, farmer or labourer, illiterate, emotional and revolutionary' in stark contrast with the stereo-typed image of the Sunni as 'peace-loving, urban, wealthy and educated'.[6] By the 1980s, the urban arena was construed as the symbol of the pro-gressive agenda of the Sunni-dominated state against the perceived reli-gious and social conservatism of the Shi'i rural population. The persistence of this domain of sectarian contestation is the most poignant testimony of the legacies of the past and of the contemporary relevance of Bahrain's urban and rural histories.

The city as the evolving frontier of modern Gulf politics

The British Empire and Arab nationalism acted as the key forces of 'global' development in the making of the modern city. They also fostered the emergence of Manama as a space of modern political contestation against the state in the first half of the twentieth century. The analysis of imperial reform and of the emergence of proto-nationalist sentiments in the 1920s frees the early modern history of the town from the teleological vision of oil wealth as the agent of change. That said, the prominence accorded to labour issues in the nationalist struggle of the 1950s certainly reflected the paramount influence of the oil industry in promoting new class solidarities among the urban population. As in Iraq, the combined effect of imperial rule, the onset of oil production and integration into the world economy produced a powerful nationalist movement. Yet the symbols, rhetoric and channels of popular and elite mobilisation did not differ substantially from those which characterised nationalist and anti-British movements in those cities which did not experience oil modernisation. New nationalist slogans, class divisions and ideas of social progress were closely intertwined with old patronage politics, quarter solidarities, manifestations of religious devotion and religious organisations.

[5] Khuri, *Tribe and State in Bahrain*, p. 249.   [6] Schumacher, 'Ritual Devotion', p. 53.

Many of these similarities with other cities of the Middle East and India can be explained by the incorporation of Bahrain into the 'global' networks of nationalist awakening which shaped the colonial and postcolonial worlds. For instance, urban residents drew inspiration from India to stage strikes as a form of modern political protest. The award of the British mandates in the Arab Middle East in 1920 created another momentous imperial connection. Over the following decades this would become central to the popularisation of Arab nationalism as the Arab residents of Manama increasingly identified with the anti-British and anti-Zionist struggles unfolding in Palestine, Egypt and Iraq. After World War II, the threat posed by grass-roots mobilisation in Bahrain's capital city forced the government to adopt Arabism as an instrument of statecraft. This served to consolidate the position of the Al Khalifah family as the elites of the new state, particularly to counter Iranian claims on the islands. Ironically, while Belgrave and the ruling family started to promote the Arab character of Manama in public policy and discourse in the early 1950s, Arab nationalism posed the most formidable challenge to the survival of the regime.

State-led Arabisation gathered momentum after the suppression of the nationalist movement in 1957 and embraced many aspects of urban life: from the strict supervision of the curricula of educational institutions, particularly the Iranian school, to the establishment of a censorship board which vetted films from India and Iran.[7] During the 1960s the Arabisation of Manama paralleled the expansion and centralisation of the state bureaucracy and the consolidation of the Al Khalifah family in the apparatus of government. While key posts in technical departments such as Customs and Public Works continued to be held by British expatriates, the influence of the imperial order decreased, reflecting the progressive devolution of authority to the indigenous administration. After 1957 the position of Charles Belgrave was taken over by a British secretary to the government who was far less influential than the advisor. Although still in charge of coordinating administrative affairs, he exercised authority as a member of the Administrative Council, a body established in 1956 which included several Al Khalifah shaykhs and a handful of merchants. The announcement of the British withdrawal from the Persian Gulf in 1968 and the declaration of Bahrain's independence three years later left the Al Khalifah family in charge of the state administration.[8]

---

[7] Political Resident Bahrain to Political Agent Bahrain, 19 March 1958, FO 371/132911 PRO.
[8] Lawson, *Bahrain: The Modernization of Autocracy*, pp. 68–71, 73–8. On the circumstances surrounding the British withdrawal from the Gulf and Bahrain see Balfour-Paul, *The End of Empire*, pp. 118–36.

It was in 1971 that Manama officially became the capital of an Arab state. In the lengthy negotiations which preceded the declaration of independence, the future of the city aroused strong emotions throughout the Arab world, partly as a result of renewed claims to the islands on the part of Iran. This strong emotional appeal is echoed in a report of the Gulf correspondent of the Egyptian Gazette published in April 1970:

An Arab arriving in Manama is soon overwhelmed by feelings which prompt him to seek to discover their motives. Such tumultuous feelings would remain with him all through his stay in the Arab emirate [Bahrain]. They might have their apparent justification, for an Arab would react to Bahraini Arab society with surprising speed, and would appear to have turned into part and parcel of that society without any sense of being a stranger.[9]

As in the 1950s, Egypt continued to provide impetus to Arab nationalist fervour. From the late 1960s, the Egyptian national anthem was played in the cinemas of Manama before film screenings. Schools were closed in 1971 to mourn the death of President Nasser, while the state radio broadcast tributes to the Arab leader.

In the 1960s, the locus of political mobilisation against the government shifted from the old quarters, ma'tams and mosques to the modern milieu of the classroom. In March 1965, the students of the secondary and technical schools of Manama ignited a new wave of protests following demonstrations in Muharraq. In the words of the Political Agent Anthony Parsons, writing a few months after his arrival in Bahrain, these youths were no longer self-declared Arab nationalists but longed for 'the paraphernalia of independence and progress: a national assembly, trade unions, elections and political newspapers'.[10] These demands continued to trigger widespread student protests until 1972, supported by intellectuals and poets such as Qasim al-Haddad who became the new conscience of the movement.

By the mid 1960s, the political landscape of Manama mirrored the explosive economic and demographic situation of Bahrain. Between 1941 and 1965 the islands' population had doubled. The great advance in the provision of state education also produced increasing numbers of secondary-school leavers who were ready to enter the job market. Moreover, three decades of oil development and decreasing oil reserves had worsened labour conflict. While the oil industry stabilised employment in the early 1960s, in 1965 foreign labourers still represented

---

[9] 'Bahrain on the Road to Independence', *The Egyptian Gazette*, 8 April 1970, FCO 8/1369 PRO.
[10] 'Annual Review of Bahrain Affairs, 1965' in Political Agent Bahrain to Political Resident Bahrain, 2 January 1966, FO 371/185327 PRO.

between 40 and 50 per cent of the workforce.[11] Following the footsteps of *al-Ha'yah*, a host of underground organisations inspired by Nasserism, Ba'thism and Communism supported the student movement in 1965 and coordinated strikes among civil servants and oil workers, paralysing oil production and public services.[12] Radio Baghdad became one of the voices of the movement championing Ba'thist propaganda from Iraq, which rehearsed themes familiar to the old Nasserist rhetoric: the condemnation of the vicious imperialist apparatus of rule supported by Great Britain and of the 'anachronistic' regime of the Al Khalifah.[13]

The pluralistic and autonomous tradition of the town of the pearl boom survived in the guise of a thriving and subversive public life and modern political culture. The Suez crisis of 1956 highlighted the strikingly different reaction of the urban population of neighbouring Kuwait, the other hotbed of Arab nationalist sentiment in the region. In April 1957 the representative of the British Council in the Persian Gulf duly noted that 'Kuwait reacted with a cold and disciplined hostility; Bahrain rioted.'[14] Despite the constraints on political activism posed by the government after 1957 and 1965, grass-roots organisation continued to proliferate in the city. By 1970 professional associations gathering together lawyers, writers, pharmacists and intellectuals, cultural clubs, sports teams and even musical bands presented a striking cross section of Manama's population as they attracted individuals of different age groups, status and wealth.[15] At the time of writing similar associations are still in place, providing continuity to the corporate identity of Manama and a challenge to the government still under the control of the Al Khalifah family.

Manama since 1971

Since independence, Manama's inner city has changed beyond recognition. Gone are the days of cosmopolitan Manama and of the city of

[11] 'The Bahrain Economy', memorandum by the Ministry of Overseas Development, 15 October 1968, CAB 148/90 PRO; 'Report by the UN Good Offices Mission Bahrain to Secretary-General of the United Nations', 24 April 1970 in 'Note by the Secretary-General of the United Nations to the Security Council', 30 April 1970, p. 6 and annex 1, FCO 8/1370 PRO.

[12] These disturbances have not yet been studied. Details are included in FO 371, files 179788 to 90 PRO.

[13] Political Agent Bahrain to Political Resident Bahrain, 1 May 1965, FO 371/179746 PRO; interviews with 'Ali Rabia', London, 10 September 2006 and with 'Ali Akbar Bushehri, Manama, 16 and 23 April 2004.

[14] 'Annual Report for 1956–57' by British Council Persian Gulf Representative, 29 April 1957, BW 114/6 PRO. I am indebted to James Onley for this reference.

[15] 'Report by the UN Good Offices Mission Bahrain to Secretary-General of the United Nations', 24 April 1970, in 'Note by the Secretary-General of the United Nations to the Security Council', 30 April 1970, pp. 8–9 and annex 1, FCO 8/1370 PRO.

al-Ha'yah, the grass-roots organisation which started the process of Arabisation of Bahrain's national politics and culture. No longer is the inner city 'Arab', or at least Bahraini. Strolling on a Friday afternoon along the winding roads of the old suq, while immigrant workers enjoy their day off, one could easily be in Mumbai or in Thiruvananthapuram, the capital of the Indian state of Kerala. Today, the landscape of the inner city is the exclusive domain of young bachelors from the Indian subcontinent seeking to earn a living in Bahrain. Even the few remaining Bahraini shop owners shout in Urdu to advertise their products.

October 1973 was the turning point in this remarkable demographic change as the fourth Arab–Israeli war triggered a dramatic increase in the price of crude oil. The economic boom which ensued increased cash flows and allowed the new middle classes and the most affluent residents of Manama to obtain easy loans and to invest in properties outside the inner city. Many of the historical communities such as the Baharna, Persians and Indians left. By the mid 1970s, the exclusive marriage patterns which characterised urban social life in the days of pearling had also started to change. In the markets, even artisans and shopkeepers could now afford to employ Asian labourers. Housemaids from the Indian subcontinent also became a status symbol for the middle classes, a privilege which in the previous decades was the preserve of the rich.

The construction boom of the mid 1970s was the most important development which drew very large numbers of labourers from the Indian subcontinent. By 1981 the number of non-nationals living in the city surpassed that of Bahrainis. Ten years later the ratio was two to one. This figure does not entirely show the extent of the 'Indianisation' of the inner city. Population censuses for Manama, in fact, include also new neighbourhoods such as al-'Adliyyah and al-Salmaniyyah where some of the former residents of the old town relocated from the late 1960s. In the early twenty-first century only very approximate population estimates are available, based on the electoral registers of 2002. Taking into consideration the municipal boundaries of Manama in the late 1950s, only 15,000 residents were Bahrainis (and thus eligible to vote). This is a small proportion of the population of the old city, which in 2001 reached approximately 50,000.

Since independence the historical 'town of foreigners' has undergone yet another transformation. It is ironic that the Indian subcontinent has once again played so large a role in defining its character. In the first half of the twentieth century the British Raj had transformed Manama into the western frontier of British India and the outpost of modernisation in the Gulf. By the end of the century, the new Indian 'connection', the result of the new geopolitics of the Gulf region, has somewhat reversed the process of urban modernisation initiated by the municipality in the 1920s. In an era of relentless globalisation, government neglect and the absence of a consistent policy of urban regeneration and of heritage revival have left the inner city in decay. Its landscape now appears almost as disorderly as it did before the establishment of the *baladiyyah* in 1919.

Politically, the Iranian Revolution of 1979 shifted the platform of contestation against the state from historical Manama to its new Shiʻi suburban communities. The attempted *coup d'état* of 1981 which sought the establishment of an Islamic Republic in Bahrain and the unrest of 1994–7 marked a turning point in the more recent history of political activism. Both events placed suburban districts such as Bani Jamrah, al-Diraz and Bilad al-Qadim on the new map of Shiʻi radical politics stretching from Lebanon to Pakistan. In 1994–7, leading clerics and a disaffected generation of angry young men spoke a new language of welfare for the Shiʻi community that rehearsed the demands for democracy, parliamentary rights and political participation which had inspired the turmoil of the mid 1950s and 1960s. Mass demonstrations and strikes, the trademark of the nationalist politics of *al-Haʼyah*, were replaced by guerrilla tactics and arson in Manama's suburban areas, which were routinely besieged by the security forces. The graffiti which covered their walls became part and parcel of this language of political communication with the government. Essentially, they demanded the reinstatement of the Parliament which was formed in 1973 and dissolved in 1975. In the immediate post-independence years, parliamentary politics was a crucial feature of Bahrain's political life. After 1975, it became the rallying cry of the opposition to the government, which continued to be dominated by the Al Khalifah.

Manama has regained its position as the centre of political militancy in the new age of political liberalisation which followed the accession of Shaykh Hamad ibn ʻIsa Al Khalifah in 1999. Elections for the municipal council were held in 2002, the first since 1965, and again in 2006. That the reinstatement of the council as an elected body could be used as a platform for the enlargement of political participation in Bahrain was an idea ventilated by the British residency on the eve of independence. In 2002 and 2006, new municipal councils were formed in connection with the first parliamentary elections held in the country since 1972. The composition of the new councils mirrored the new political realities of Bahrain rather than reflecting the demographic and social make-up of the inner city and of its metropolitan areas. Out of the ten members successful at the ballot box, seven belonged to *Jamʻiyah al-Wifaq al-Watani al-Islamiyyah* (popularly known as *al-Wifaq*), a Shiʻi political organisation which emerged out of the unrest of the 1990s. Although several municipal councils were elected throughout Bahrain, Manama municipal politics was central to the rise to power of *al-Wifaq*. The organisation boycotted the 2002 parliamentary elections and transformed the municipal council into the launch pad for its entry into national politics in 2006.

The municipal by-laws issued before the 2002 elections have curtailed considerably the administrative powers of the council dominated by *al-Wifaq*. To a certain extent, however, the municipality has been successful in proposing a new vision for the development of the city. In 2005 the residents of the last shanty town of modern Manama were resettled outside the municipal boundaries in purpose-built housing. Under *al-Wifaq*, central Manama has also become the target of a new wave of public morality which reflects the Islamisation of national politics. In the first speech delivered after the municipal elections of 2002, the president of the council emphasised the need to keep prostitution and alcohol consumption away from residential areas in order to restore public decency. This was a clear reference to Manama's growing weekend sex industry serving many Saudis and Gulf nationals in hotels and furnished apartments. This 'morality zoning' is still a subject of debate at the time of writing, involving residents, the *baladiyyah*, the government and members of the Parliament.

Significantly, this 'morality zoning' is reminiscent of that enforced by Belgrave in 1937, when he relocated Manama's prostitutes to the red-light district of Garandor. In fact, the sex industry of the contemporary city stands as a legacy of the cosmopolitan port town of the nineteenth and twentieth centuries. No longer are Manama's sex workers African, Omani, Iranian or Indian, as they had been in the pearl and early oil eras, but come from Russia, Eastern Europe and the Far East. As part of the present wave of public morality the municipality was also successful in renaming a road in the inner city connecting several of its old *ma'tam*s after Imam Husayn in 2006. This was indeed a highly symbolic achievement which draws attention to the enduring relationship between Manama, national politics and the vexed issue of sectarian contestation.

The novel cosmopolitanism of the early twenty-first century and the new groups of migrants who now populate the inner city prompt a reflection upon the broad contours of Manama's history. Although rooted in different political, economic and social realities, this cosmopolitanism evokes the multicultural world of the 'town of foreigners' during the pearl boom. Significantly, old and new cosmopolitan traditions are in contrast with the Arabism which transformed Manama into the centre of Bahrain's national culture in the mid twentieth century. Contrary to the nationalist narratives now promoted by the state, it is this transformation which represents the evident discontinuity in the history of the city.

Bibliography

ARCHIVAL SOURCES

GREAT BRITAIN

India Office, London

R/15/1	Bushehr Political Residency, 1763–1947
R/15/2	Bahrain Political Agency, 1900–47
R/15/3	Bahrain Political Agency: Political Agent's Court, 1913–48
L/P&S/7	Political and Secret Letters from India, 1875–1911
L/P&S/9	Political and Secret Correspondence outside India, 1781–1911
L/P&S/10	Political and Secret Subject Files, 1902–31
L/P&S/11	Political and Secret Annual Files, 1912–30
V 23	Selections from the Records of the Government of India, 1849–1937

Public Record Office, London

FO 371	Political Departments: General Correspondence, 1906–66
FO 1016	Political Residencies and Agencies, Persian Gulf: Correspondence and Papers, 1917–72
FCO 8	Foreign Office and Foreign and Commonwealth Office: Arabian Department and Middle East Department, 1967–76
CAB 148	Cabinet Office: Defence and Overseas Policy, Minutes and Papers, 1964–77
BW 144	British Council: Registered Files, Persian Gulf, 1947–80

Arab World Documentation Unit, University of Exeter

Charles D. Belgrave, Personal Diaries, 1926–57

BAHRAIN

Private collections
Bushehri Archive, Manama
  British Native Agency Records, 1833–1900
  Minutes of General Merchants' Association (since 1945 Bahrain Chamber of Commerce), 1939–47

Firdawsi Club, 1946–60
Ma'tam al-'Ajam al-Kabir and Persian School, 1913–57
Photographs and Miscellaneous, 1907–68
Typescripts, 1990–2006
Hamza Archive, Manama
Miscellaneous, 1913–65

Government collections
Bahrain National Museum, Manama
Miscellaneous, Archives of the Municipality of Manama, 1938–63
Directorate of Legal Affairs (Da'irah al Shu'un al-Qanuniyyah), Manama
al-Jaridah al-Rasmiyyah (The Government Gazette), n.s. 1–38, 1948–51
Historical Documentation Centre (Markaz al-Watha'iq al-Tarikhiyyah), Rifa'
American Board of Foreign Missions Correspondence, 1893–1912
Miscellaneous
Land Registration Department (Idarah al-Tabu), Ministry of Justice and
Islamic Affairs, Manama
Real Estate Registration Files, n. 1 to n. 230 (my numbering), 1925–40
Ministry of Housing and Municipalities (Wizarah al-Iskan wa al-Baladiyyat),
Manama
Aerial Photos of Bahrain, 1951

COLLECTIONS OF DOCUMENTS AND OFFICIAL PUBLICATIONS

BRITISH GOVERNMENT

The Affairs of Arabia, 1905–1906, ed. by Robin Bidwell, 2 vols. (London: Cass, 1971)
Arab Gulf Cities, ed. by Richard Trench, 4 vols. (Slough: Archive Editions, 1996)
Arabian Gulf Intelligence: Selections from the Records of the Bombay Government, new series, no. XXIV, 1856, ed. by R. Hughes Thomas (Cambridge: Oleander Press, 1985)
The Arabian Mission: Field Reports, Quarterly Letters, Neglected Arabia, Arabia Calling, 8 vols. (Gerrards Cross: Archive Editions, 1993)
The Bahrain Government Annual Reports, 1924–1970, 8 vols. (Gerrards Cross: Archive Editions, 1986)
The Gazetteer of the Persian Gulf, Oman and Central Arabia, by John George Lorimer, 2 vols. (Calcutta: Office of the Superintendent Government Printing, 1908; repub. by Gregg International, Farnborough, 1970)
The Gulf Pilot by C. G. Constable and A. W. Stiff (London: Hydrographic Office, 1864)
Historic Maps of Bahrain, 1817–1970, ed. by Robert L. Jarman, 3 vols. (Gerrards Cross: Archive Editions, 1996)
The Persian Gulf Administration Reports 1873–1949, 10 vols. (Gerrards Cross: Archive Editions, 1986)

The Persian Gulf Précis, 1903–1908, by Jerome Anthony Saldanha, 8 vols. (Gerrards Cross: Archive Editions, 1986)
Persian Gulf and Red Sea Naval Reports, 1820–1960, ed. by Anita Burdett, 15 vols. (Slough: Archive Editions, 1993)
Political Diaries of the Persian Gulf, 1904–1958, 20 vols. (Farnham Common: Archive Editions, 1990)
Records of Bahrain: Primary Documents, 1820–1960, 8 vols. (Slough: Archive Editions, 1993)

BAHRAINI GOVERNMENT

Bahrain Census of Population and Housing – 1981: Trends and Prospects (Directorate of Statistics, State of Bahrain, *c.* 1981)
al-Bahrayn bayna al-madhi wa al-hadhir/Bahrain Past and Present (Ministry of Housing, Municipalities and Environment, State of Bahrain, *c.* 1996)
Development of Bahrain Villages, 1958–1969 (Rural Affairs Department, State of Bahrain, [n.d])
The Fourth Population Census of Bahrain: A Brief Analytical and Comparative Study (Finance Department, Statistical Bureau, State of Bahrain, August 1969)
al-Ihya' al-iskaniyyah/Housing Neighbourhoods (Ministry of Housing, Municipalities and Environment, State of Bahrain, *c.* 1990)
Ihya' madinah al-Manamah al-qadimah/Manama Urban Renewal Project (Ministry of Housing, Physical Planning Directorate, State of Bahrain, 1987)
al-Iskan wa al-tanmiyah al-'umraniyyah/ Housing and Urban Development (Ministry of Housing, Municipalities and Environment, State of Bahrain, 1996)
Jaridah al-Bahrayn, 1939–44
al-Jaridah al-Rasmiyyah (Government Gazette), 1948–51
al-Khifaz 'ala khasa'is al-madinah al-'Arabiyyah wa 'ala turathiha al-'Arabi al-Islami, by Ibrahim 'Uthman (Central Municipal Committee, State of Bahrain, [n.d])
Madinah 'Isa/'Isa Town (Ministry of Housing, Municipalities and Environment, State of Bahrain, *c.* 1996)
al-Malamih al-'umraniyyah li al-mudun al-taqlidiyyah fi al-Bahrayn (Ministry of Housing, Physical Planning Directorate, State of Bahrain, [n.d])
Ma'rad khara'it al-Bahrayn: tarikh wa suwar (Ministry of Housing, State of Bahrain, 1992)
The Population of Bahrain: Trends and Prospects (Directorate of Statistics, State of Bahrain, January 1979)
Sawt al-Bahrayn: Majallah Adabiyyah wa Ijtima'iyyah, 4 vols. (Beirut: al-Mu'assasah al-'Arabiyyah li al-Dirasat wa al-Nashr, 2003)
Thamanun 'am min 'umr al-baladiyyah fi al-Baharyn, by 'Abd al-Razzaq Yusuf al-'Awadi (State of Bahrain, Ministry of Housing, [n.d.])

DISSERTATIONS

Gleave, Robert, 'Akhbari Jurisprudence in the Writings of Yusuf b. Ahmad al-Bahrani (1186/1772)', unpublished PhD dissertation, University of Manchester (1996)
Kanna, Ahmed, 'Not Their Fathers' Days: Idioms of Space and Time in the Arabian Gulf', unpublished PhD dissertation, Harvard (2006)

Khalifa, Aisha Bilkhair, 'Slaves and Musical Performances in Dubai: Socio-Cultural Relevance of African Traditions', unpublished PhD dissertation, University of Exeter (2003)
Mandeel, Fa'eq Juma, 'Planning Regulations for the Traditional Arab-Islamic Built Environment in Bahrain', unpublished MA dissertation, University of Newcastle upon Tyne (1992)
Razavian, Muhammad Taghi, 'Iranian Communities in the Persian Gulf: A Geographical Analysis', unpublished PhD dissertation, University of London (1975)
Schumacher, Ilsa Amelia, 'Ritual Devotion among Shi'i in Bahrain', unpublished PhD dissertation, University of London (1987)

UNPUBLISHED MATERIALS AND PAMPHLETS

Ashrafs: 75 Years (Manama: Commemorative pamphlet, *c.* 1988)
Bushehri, 'Ali Akbar, 'Archeological evidence on the graves of the *shuyukh al-ra'is* of Bahrein', typescript, 12 pages, 1996
  'The Jews of Bahrain', typescript, 5 pages, December 2003
  'National Union School', typescript, 17 pages, [n.d.]
  'The Struggle of a Family', typescript, 225 pages, [n.d.]
  'Struggle of (sic) National Identity', typescript, 47 pages, 1995
Facts about Bahrain – Historical Highlights (London: Bahrain Freedom Movement, [n.d.])
Fahbji, N., *Taqrir 'an al-madinatayn al-qadimatayn al-Muharraq wa al-Manamah fi al-Bahrayn* (Tunis, Arab League, Educational, Cultural and Scientific Section, 1980)
Gornall, John, 'Some Memories of BAPCO', typescript, May 1965
Hamza, Manaf Yusif, *Manar al-Bahrayn fi tarikh al-tabu wa al-misahah*, (Manama: under the auspices of the Council of Ministers, 2000)
  'Min al-turath al-'aqari al-Bahrayni', typescript, 44 pages, [n.d.]
Nadi al-Muharraq: ra'id al-nahdah al-riyadiyyah (Manama: Commemorative pamphlet, *c.* 1981)
Nadi Ras Rumman: thalathun 'am 'ala ta'sis (Manama: Commemorative pamphlet, *c.* 1986).
Serjeant, Robert B., 'Customary Irrigation Law among the Shi'ah Baharinah of al-Bahrayn', typescript, 33 pages, 1960
al-Shuja'i, M. 'al-Idtihad al-'irqi fi al-Bahrayn "al-'Ajam" ', typescript, 74 pages, [n.d.]

BOOKS AND ARTICLES IN ARABIC AND PERSIAN

'Abdallah, Sulayman Da'wud, *Samahij fi al-tarikh* (Manama: [n.pub.], 1996)
Ayyam zaman /Old Days (Manama: Matbu'at Banurama al-Khalij, 1986)
al-Baharna, Taqi Muhammad, *Nadi al-'Urubah wa khamsun 'am, 1939–1989* (Manama: Matba'ah Wizarah al-'Ilam, 1991)
al-Bahrani, 'Ali ibn Hasan, *Anwar al-badrayn fi tarajim 'ulama' al-Qatif wa al-Ahsa' wa al-Bahrayn* (Najaf: Matba'ah al-Nu'man, 1960)
al-Bahrani, Yusuf ibn Ahmad, *Lu'luat al-Bahrayn fi al-ijazat wa tarajim rijal al-hadith* (Najaf: Matba'ah al-Nu'man, 1966)

al-Bakir, 'Abd al-Rahman, *Min al-Bahrayn ila al-manfa*, 2nd edn (Beirut: Dar al-Kunuz al-'Arabiyyah, 2002)

'al-Baladiyyah insha'at bi amr shafahi' lakinnha kanat tushabbih bi hukumah', *Akhbar al-Khalij*, 23 July 1980

Bashmi, Ibrahim, *Ahdath wa waqa'i wa mashaykh Bastak wa Khunj wa Lingah wa Lar* (Manama: Mu'assah al-Ayyam, 1993)

al-Bassam, Khalid, *al-Najdi al-tayyib: Sirah al-tajir wa al-muthaqqaf Sulayman al-Hamad al-Bassam, 1888–1949* (Beirut: al-Mu'assasah al-'Arabiyyah li al-Dirasat wa al-Nashr, 2008)

   Rijal fi jaza'ir al-lu'lu (Manama: al-Mu'assasah al-'Arabiyyah li al-Tiba'ah wa al-Nashr, 1991)

   Tilka al-ayyam: hikayat wa suwar min bidayyah al-Bahrayn (Manama: Matbu'at Banurama al-Khalij, 1986)

   Yawmiyyat al-manfa: 'Abd al-'Aziz Shamlan fi Sant Hilana, 1956–1961 (Manama: [n.pub.], 2006)

Bu Hajji, 'Abd al-'Aziz M. Yusif, *Lamahat min tarikh al-murur fi al-Bahrayn khilal al-sanawat 1914–1969* (Manama: al Mu'assasah al-'Arabiyyah li al-Tiba'ah wa al-Nashr, 1998)

Bushehri, 'Ali Akbar, 'Bilad al-jadid – mawlid madinah al-Manamah' and 'Mashad 'asimah al-Bahrayn' in *al-Wasat*, July 2003

   'al-Manamah al-qadimah: dhakaraha al-Burtughaliyyun wa al-'Uthmaniyyun', *Banurama al-Khalij*, July 1991

al-Ghanim, 'Abdallah Khalifah, *Jawanib min tarikh al-shurtah fi al-Bahrayn* (Manama: Matba'ah Wizarah Shu'un Majlis al-Wuzara' wa al-'Ilam, 2000)

Ghulum, Ibrahim 'Abdallah, *'Abdallah al-Za'id wa ta'sis al-khitab al-adabi al-hadith: Jaridah al-Bahrayn, 1939–1944* (Muharraq: Dar al-Tiba'ah wa al-Nashr, 1996)

Hamza, Manaf Yusif, *Mu'jam al-ta'mir wa al-khara'it wa al-watha'iq al-'aqariyyah al-Bahrayniyyah* (Manama: Dar Akhbar al-Khalij, 2001)

al-Jasim, Muhammad 'Abd al-Qadir and Sawsan 'Ali al-Sha'ir, *al-Bahrayn: qissah al-sira' al-siyasi, 1904–1956* (Manama: [n.pub.], 2000)

al-Jawdar, Salih ibn Yusif, *Ibn Jawdar qadhi al-Muharraq* (Manama: al-Khalij al-'Arabi, 1999)

al-Jur, Salah ibn Yusuf, *Masajid al-Muharraq: tarikh wa athar* (Manama: Ministry of Islamic Affairs, 2003)

Kanu, 'Abd al-Latif Jasim, *'Abr al-tarikh* (Manama: al-Matba 'ah al-Hukumiyyah li Wizarah al-'Ilam, 1985)

Kazeruni, Muhammad Ibrahim, *Athar shahr-ha-ye-bastani savahil va jaza'ir-i Khalij-i Fars va darya-ye 'Umani*, annotated by Ahmad Iqtidari (Teheran: [n.pub.], 1996)

   Tarikh banadir va jaza'ir Khalij-i Fars (Teheran: Mu'assasah-i Farhangi-i Jahangiri, 1367 [1988–9])

Al Khalifah, Mayy Muhammad, *Mi'ah 'am min al-ta'lim al-nizami fi al-Bahrayn: al-Sanawat al-ula li al-ta'sis* (Beirut: al-Mu'assasah al-'Arabiyyah li al-Dirasat wa al-Nashr, 1999)

   Muhammad ibn Khalifah 1813–1890: al-Usturah wa al-tarikh al-muwazi (Beirut: al-Mu'assasah al-'Arabiyyah li al-Dirasat wa al-Nashr, 1999)

Khatam, Muhammad Gharib, *Tarikh 'Arab al-Huwilah* (Beirut: al-Mu'assasah al-'Arabiyyah li al-Dirasat wa al-Nashr, 2003)

al-Khatir, Mubarak, *al-Muntada al-Islami: Hayyatihi wa atharihi, 1928–1932*, 2nd edn (Manama: al-Matba'ah al-Hukumiyyah li Wizarah al-'Ilam, 1993)

Nabighat al-Bahrayn: 'Abdallah al-Za'id (Manama: Matbu'at Banurama al-Khalij, 1996)

al-Qadhi al-ra'is Qasim ibn Mahza, 2nd edn (Manama: Matba'ah Wizarah al-'Ilam, 1986)

al-Khayri, 'Abd al-Rahman ibn 'Abdallah, *Qala'id al-nahrayn fi tarikh al-Bahrayn* (Manama: al-Ayyam, 2003)

al-Madani, Hasan, *Hikayat al-nawadi: tajribah shakhsiyyah fi Nadi al-'Urubah* (Manama: al-Ayyam, 1996)

al-Madani, Salah 'Ali and Karim 'Ali al-'Urayyad, *Min turath al-Bahrayn al-sha'abi* (Beirut: Matba'ah Samia, n.d.)

al-Muraykhi, Khalil ibn Muhammad, *Ahdath al-zaman: watha'iq 'an tarikh al-Bahrayn* (Manama: [n.pub.], 1995)

Lamahat min madhi al-Bahrayn (Manama: Banurama al-Khalij, 1987)

Musameh, 'Abd al-Rahman, *Muqaddimah fi tarikh al-Bahrayn al-qadim* (Manama: [n.pub.], 1998)

al-Nabhani, Muhammad, *al-Tuhfah al-Nabhaniyyah fi tarikh al-Jazirah al-'Arabiyyah* (Beirut: Dar Ihya' al-'Ulum, 1976)

al-Nuwaydri, Salim, *'Alam al-thaqafah al-Islamiyyah fi al-Bahrayn khilal arba'at 'asharah qarn*, 3 vols. (Beirut: al-'Arif, 1992)

'al-Usar al-'ilmiyyah fi al-Bahrayn', *al-Mawsim*, 11.3 (1990), 847–911

al-Qasimi, Nurah Muhammad, *al-Wujud al-Hindi fi al-Khalij al-'Arabi, 1860–1947* (Sharjah: Da'irah al-Thaqafah wa al-'Ilam, 2000)

al-Rihani, Amin, *al-Muluk al-'Arab*, 2 vols. (Beirut: al-Mu'assasah al-'Arabiyyah li al-Dirasat wa al-Nashr, 1970)

Sayf, 'Abdallah, *al-Ma'tam fi al-Bahrayn*, 2 vols. (Manama: al-Matba'ah al-Sharqiyyah, 1995; Maktabah Fakrawi, 2004)

al-Shayji, Hilal, *al-Sihafah fi al-Kuwayt wa al-Bahrayn mundhu nash'atiha hatta ahd al-istiqlal* (Manama: Matbu'at Banurama al-Khalij, 1989)

Sulaybikh, Khalifah, *Hikayat min al-Hurah* (Manama: [n.pub.], 2004)

Tajir, Muhammad 'Ali, *'Aqd al-lal fi tarikh al-Awal* (Manama: al-Maktabah al-'Ammah, 1994)

al-'Urayfi, Rashid, *al-'Imarah al-Bahrayniyyah* (Manama: al-Matba'ah al-Sharqiyyah, 1978)

al-'Urayyad, 'Abd al-Karim, *Nafidhah 'ala al-tarikh: Bayt al-'Urayyad* (Manama: al-Mu'assasah al-'Arabiyyah li al-Tiba'ah wa al-Nashr, [n.d.])

Wali, Tariq, *al-Bayan wa al-tibyan fi al-'imarah wa al-'umran* (Manama: [n.pub.], 1993)

al-Muharraq: 'umran madinah khalijiyyah 1783–1971 (Manama: Matbu'at Banurama al-Khalij, 1990)

'al-Yahud bayna al-Bahrayn', *al-Mar'at al-Yawm*, 9 July 2002

al-Zayyani, Amal Ibrahim, *al-Bahrayn bayna al-istiqlal al-siyasi wa al-intilaq al-duali* (Cairo: Dar al-Kutub, 1977)

al-Zayyani, Rashid, *al-Ghaws wa al-tawwashah* (Manama: al-Ayyam, 1998)

BOOKS AND ARTICLES IN ENGLISH AND OTHER
EUROPEAN LANGUAGES

BAHRAIN, THE PERSIAN GULF AND THE MIDDLE EAST

Abdullah, Thabit A. J., *Merchants, Mamluks and Murder: The Political Economy of Trade in Eighteenth-Century Basra* (Albany: State University of New York Press, 2001)

Abu-Hakimah, Ahmad Mustafa, *Eastern Arabia: Historic Photographs*, 3 vols. (London: Hurtwood, 1984–95)

History of Eastern Arabia, 1750–1800: The Rise and Development of Bahrain, Kuwait and Wahhabi Saudi Arabia (Beirut: Khayats, 1965)

Aghaie, Kamran Scott, *The Martyrs of Karbala: Shiʻi Symbols and Rituals in Modern Iran* (Seattle: University of Washington Press, 2004)

Algar, Hamid, 'The Oppositional Role of the Ulama in Twentieth-Century Iran' in N. Keddie (ed.), *Scholars, Saints and Sufis: Muslim Religious Institutions in the Middle East since 1500* (Berkeley: University of California Press, 1972), pp. 231–56

Alghanim, Salwa, *The Reign of Mubarak al-Sabah: Shaikh of Kuwait, 1896–1915* (London: I. B. Tauris, 1998)

Allen, Calvin H., 'The State of Masqat in the Gulf and East Africa, 1785–1829', *International Journal of Middle East Studies*, 14 (1982), 117–27

Alster, Robert, 'Dilmun, Bahrain and the Alleged Paradise in Sumerian Myth and Literature' in D. T. Potts (ed.), *Dilmun: New Studies in the Archaeology and Early History of Bahrain* (Berlin: Reimer, 1983), pp. 39–74

Altorki, Soraya and Donald P. Cole, *Arabian Oasis City: The Transformation of ʻUnayzah* (Austin: University of Texas Press, 1989)

Anscombe, Fredrick, *The Ottoman Gulf: The Creation of Kuwait, Saudi Arabia and Qatar* (New York: Columbia University Press, 1997)

Al-Arayyed, Salim A., *Islamic Law as Administered in British India and in Joint British Courts in the Arabian Gulf, 1857–1947* (Manama: Al Ayam Press, 2001)

Aubin, Jean, 'Le royaume d'Ormuz au début du XVIe siècle' in *Mare Luso-Indicum* (Geneva: Droz, 1973), vol. II, pp. 77–179

Ayubi, Nazih N., *Over-Stating the Arab State* (London: I. B. Tauris, 1995)

Baer, Gabriel, 'The Beginnings of Municipal Government in Egypt', *Middle Eastern Studies*, 4.2 (1968), 118–40

Egyptian Guilds in Modern Times (Jerusalem: Israel Oriental Society, 1964)

Al-Baharna, Husain M., *The Arabian Gulf States: Their Legal and Political Status and International Problems* (Beirut: Librairie du Liban, 1978)

British Extra-Territorial Jurisdiction in the Gulf, 1913–1971 (Slough: Archive Editions, 1998)

Balfour-Paul, Glen, *The End of Empire in the Middle East: Britain's Relinquishment of Power in Her Last Three Arab Dependencies* (Cambridge University Press, 1991)

Bayly, Christopher A. and Leila Tarazi Fawaz, 'Introduction: The Connected World of Empires' in L. T. Fawaz and C. A. Bayly (eds.), *Modernity and Culture: From the Mediterranean to the Indian Ocean* (New York: Columbia University Press, 2002), pp. 1–27

Beblawi, Hazem and Giacomo Luciani (eds.), *The Rentier State* (London: Croom Helm, 1987)

Beiling, Willard A., 'Recent Developments in Labor Relations in Bahrayn', *The Middle East Journal*, 13.2 (1959), 156–69

Belgrave, Charles, *Personal Column* (London: Hutchinson, 1960)

The Pirate Coast (Beirut: Librairie du Liban, 1972)

Belgrave, James, *Welcome to Bahrain*, 8th edn (Manama: The Augustan Press, 1973)

Bent, Theodore, *Southern Arabia* (London: Smith and Elder, 1900)

Bianca, Stefano, *Urban Form in the Arab World: Past and Present* (London: Thames and Hudson, 2000)

Bibby, Geoffrey, *Looking for Dilmun*, 2nd edn (London: Stacey International, 1996)

Billecocq, Xavier Beguin, *Un vaisseau français à Bahreïn 1842: une première diplomatique/A French Ship's Journey to Bahrain 1842: A Diplomatic First* (Paris: [n. pub.], 2001)

Bonine, Michael E., 'Oil and Urban Development: The Transformation of the Small Arab Town in the United Arab Emirates' in *Petites villes et villes moyennes dans le monde arabe* (Tours: URBAMA, 1986), pp. 621–36

Braude, Benjamin and Bernard Lewis (eds.), *Christians and Jews in the Ottoman Empire: The Functioning of a Plural Society*, 2 vols. (New York: Holmes and Meier, 1982)

Brown, L. Carl (ed.), *Imperial Legacy: The Ottoman Imprint on the Balkans and the Middle East* (New York: Columbia University Press, 1996)

Brown, Nathan J., *The Rule of Law in the Arab World: Courts in Egypt and in the Gulf* (Cambridge University Press, 1997)

Bushehri, 'Ali Akbar, 'The Master Builder of Bahrain', *The Gulf Mirror*, February 1987, issue n. 8

'The War of No Battle – Bahrain in 1559', *Dilmun*, 18 (1999–2000), 20–27

Celik, Zeynep, *Urban Forms and Colonial Confrontations: Algiers under French rule* (Berkeley: University of California Press, 1997)

Chalcraft, John T., *The Striking Cabbies of Cairo and Other Stories: Crafts and Guilds in Egypt, 1863–1914* (Albany: State University of New York Press, 2004)

Clarke, Angela, *Bahrain: Oil and Development, 1929–1989* (London: Immel, 1990)

Through the Changing Scenes of Life: The American Mission Hospital Bahrain, 1893–1993 (Hong Kong: Wing King Tong, 1993)

Cleveland, William L., 'The Municipal Council of Tunis, 1858–1870: A Study in Urban Institutional Change', *International Journal of Middle East Studies*, 9.1 (1978), 33–61

Cole, Juan R., 'Rival Empires of Trade and Imami Shi'ism in Eastern Arabia, 1300–1800', *International Journal of Middle East Studies*, 19.3 (1987), 177–204

Roots of North India Shi'ism in Iran and Iraq: Religion and State in Awadh, 1722–1859 (Berkeley: University of California Press, 1988)

Cottrell, Alvin J. et al., *The Persian Gulf States: A General Survey* (Baltimore: John Hopkins University Press, 1980)

Crystal, Jill, 'Civil Society in the Arabian Gulf' in Augustus Richard Norton (ed.), *Civil Society in the Middle East*, 2 vols. (Leiden: Brill, 1995), vol. II, pp. 259–86

Oil and Politics in the Gulf: Rulers and Merchants in Kuwait and Qatar (Cambridge University Press, 1990)

Cursetjee, Manockjee, *The Land of the Date* (Reading: Garnet, 1994)

Curzon, George Nathaniel, *Persia and the Persian Question* (London: Longmans, 1892)

Davie, May, 'Être Beyrouthin en 1800' in *La Citadinité en questions* (Tours: URBAMA, 1996), pp. 59–68

Davis, Eric, 'Theorizing Statecraft and Social Change in Arab Oil-Producing Countries' in E. Davis and N. Gavrielides (eds.), *Statecraft in the Middle East: Oil, Historical Memory and Popular Culture* (Miami: Florida International University Press, 1991), pp. 1–35

Dessouki, Assem, 'Social and Political Dimension of the Historiography of the Arab Gulf', in E. Davis and N. Gavrielides (eds.), *Statecraft in the Middle East: Oil, Historical Memory and Popular Culture* (Miami: Florida International University Press, 1991), pp. 96–115

Dieulafoy, Jane, *A Suse: journal des fouilles, 1884–1886* (Paris: Hachette, 1888)

Denoeux, Guilain, *Urban Unrest in the Middle East: A Comparative Study of Informal Networks in Egypt, Iran and Lebanon* (Albany: State University of New York Press, 1993)

Dresch, Paul, *Tribes, Government and History in Yemen* (Oxford: Clarendon Press, 1989)

Eldem, Edhem, Daniel Goffman and Bruce Masters (eds.), *The Ottoman City Between East and West: Aleppo, Izmir and Istanbul* (Cambridge University Press, 1999)

Farah, Talal Toufic, *Protection and Politics in Bahrain, 1869–1915* (Beirut: American University, 1985)

Fattah, Hala, *The Politics of Regional Trade in Iraq, Arabia and the Gulf, 1745–1900* (Albany: State University of New York Press, 1997)

Fawaz, Leila Tarazi and Christopher A. Bayly (eds.), *Modernity and Culture: From the Mediterranean to the Indian Ocean* (New York: Columbia University Press, 2002)

Field, Michael, *The Merchants: The Big Business Families of Saudi Arabia and the Gulf States* (New York: Overlook Press, 1985)

Finnie, David, 'Recruitment and Training of Labor: The Middle East Oil Industry', *Middle East Journal*, 12.2 (1958), 127–43

Fischbach, Michael Richard, *State, Society and Land in Jordan* (Leiden: Brill, 2000)

Floor, Willem, 'Dutch Trade with Mascat during the Eighteenth Century', *Journal of Asian and African Studies*, 16 (1982), 197–213

The Persian Gulf: A Political and Economic History of Five Port Cities, 1500–1730 (Washington: Mage, 2006)

Fox, John W., Nada Mourtada-Sabbah and Mohammed al-Mutawa (eds.), *Globalization and the Gulf* (London: Routledge, 2006)

Fox, John W., Nada Mourtada-Sabbah and Mohammed al-Mutawa, 'Heritage Revivalism in Sharjah' in J. W. Fox, N. Mourtada-Sabbah and M. al-Mutawa (eds.), *Globalization and the Gulf* (London: Routledge, 2006), pp. 266–87

Fuccaro, Nelida, 'Ethnicity and the City: The Kurdish Quarter of Damascus between Ottoman and French Rule, c. 1724–1946', *Urban History*, 30.2 (2003), 206–24

'Mapping the Transnational Community: Persians and the Space of the City in Bahrain, c.1869–1937' in M. al-Rasheed (ed.), *Transnational Connections in the Arab Gulf* (London: Routledge, 2005), pp. 39–58

'Understanding the Urban History of Bahrain', *Journal for Critical Studies of the Middle East*, 17 (2000), 48–82

'Visions of the City: Urban Studies on the Gulf', *Middle East Studies Association Bulletin* 35.2 (2001), 175–87

Gelvin, James L., *Divided Loyalties: Nationalism and Mass Politics in Syria at the Close of Empire* (Berkeley: University of California Press, 1998)

'The Social Origins of Popular Nationalism in Syria: Evidence for a New Framework', *International Journal of Middle East Studies*, 26.4 (1994), 645–61

Ghoul, Bernard, 'Les Transformations d'une cité-marchande: Doubaï, 1971–2001: impact global et dynamique interne', *Monde Arabe Maghreb-Machrek*, 174 (2001), 70–4

Hannoyer, Jean and Seteney Shami (eds.), *Amman: ville et societe/The City and its Society/al-Madinah wa al-mujtam'i* (Beirut: CERMOC, 1996)

Hansen, Henny Arald, *Investigation in a Shi'a Village in Bahrain* (Copenhagen: National Museum of Denmark, 1967)

Hanssen, Jens, *Fin de siècle Beirut: The Making of an Ottoman Provincial Capital* (Oxford: Clarendon Press, 2005)

Hardy-Guilbert, Claire and Christian Lalande, *La Maison de Shaikh 'Isa a Bahrayn* (Paris: ADPF, 1981)

Harrison, Paul W., *The Arab at Home* (London: Hutchinson, 1925)

Heard-Bey, Frauke, *From Trucial States to United Arab Emirates* (London and New York: Longman, 1999)

Holes, Clive, *Language Variation and Change in a Modernising Arab State: The Case of Bahrain* (London and New York: Kegan Paul, 1987)

Hourani, Albert, 'Ottoman Reform and the Politics of Notables' in A. Hourani, P. S. Khoury and M. Wilson (eds.), *The Modern Middle East: A Reader* (London: I. B. Tauris, 1993), pp. 83–109

Ibn Khaldun, *al-Muqaddimah: An Introduction to History*, trans. by Franz Rosenthal, 3 vols. (London: Routledge and Kegan Paul, 1958)

Ilbert, Robert, 'De Beyrouth à Alger: La fin d'un ordre urbain', *Vingtième Siècle*, 32 (1991), 15–24

Ismael, Jacqueline S., *Kuwait: Dependency and Class in a Rentier State* (Gainesville: University of Florida Press, 1993)

Ismail, Salwa, *Political Life in Cairo's New Quarters: Encountering the Everyday State* (Minneapolis: University of Minnesota Press, 2006)

Issawi, Charles, 'British Trade and the Rise of Beirut, 1830–1860', *International Journal of Middle East Studies*, 7 (1977), 91–101

Kanoo, Khalid M., *The House of Kanoo: A Century of an Arabian Family Business* (London: Centre of Arab Studies, 1997)

Keating, Aileen, *Mirage: Power, Politics and the Hidden History of Arabian Oil* (Amherst, NY: Prometheus, 2005)

Keddie, Nikkie, 'The Roots of 'Ulama Power in Modern Iran' in N. Keddie (ed.), *Scholars, Saints and Sufis: Muslim Religious Institutions in the Middle East since 1500* (Berkeley: University of California Press, 1972), pp. 211–30

Keddie, Nikkie (ed.), *Scholars, Saints and Sufis: Muslim Religious Institutions in the Middle East since 1500* (Berkeley: University of California Press, 1972)

Kelly, John B., *Britain and the Persian Gulf, 1795–1880* (Oxford: Clarendon Press, 1968)

Kent, Marian, *Moguls and Mandarins: Oil, Imperialism and the Middle East in British Foreign Policy* (London: Cass, 1993)

   Oil and Empire: British Policy and Mesopotamian Oil, 1900–1920 (London: Macmillan, 1976)

Kervran, Monik, *Bahrain in the 16th Century: An Impregnable Island* (Manama: Ministry of Information, 1988)

Khalaf, Sulayman, 'The Evolution of the Gulf City Type, Oil, and Globalization' in J. W. Fox, N. Mourtada-Sabbah and M. al-Mutawa (eds.), *Globalization and the Gulf* (London: Routledge, 2006), pp. 244–65

   'Globalization and Heritage Revival in the Gulf: An Anthropological Look at Dubai Heritage Village', *Journal of Social Affairs* 19.75 (2002), 13–41

al-Khalifah, Abdullah ibn Khalid and Michael Rice (eds.), *Bahrain through the Ages: The History* (London: Kegan Paul International, 1993)

Al Khalifah, Khalid, 'Hawalla Arabs and the English East India Company in the 18th Century: Trade and Rivalry', *Dilmun*, 16 (1993–4), 57–64

Khoury, Dina Rizk, 'Merchants and Trade in Early Modern Iraq', *New Perspectives on Turkey*, 5–6 (1991), 53–86

Khoury, Philip, *Syria and the French Mandate: The Politics of Arab Nationalism, 1920–1946* (London: I. B. Tauris, 1987)

   'Syrian Urban Politics in Transition: the Quarters of Damascus during the French Mandate', *International Journal of Middle East Studies*, 16 (1984), 507–40

   Urban Notables and Arab Nationalism: The Politics of Damascus, 1860–1920 (Cambridge University Press, 1983)

Khoury, Philip and Joseph Kostiner (eds.), *Tribes and State Formation in the Middle East* (Berkeley: University of California Press, 1990)

Khuri, Fuad I., *From Village to Suburb: Order and Change in Greater Beirut* (University of Chicago Press, 1975)

   Tribe and State in Bahrain: The Transformation of Social and Political Authority in an Arab State (University of Chicago Press, 1980)

King, Jeoffrey, *Traditional Architecture of Saudi Arabia* (London: I. B. Tauris, 1998)

Kostiner, Joseph, *The Making of Saudi Arabia: From Chieftaincy to Monarchical State* (Oxford University Press, 1993)

Kubicek, Robert, 'The Proliferation and Diffusion of Steamship Technology and the Beginnings of "New Imperialism"' in D. Killingray, M. Lincoln and N. Rigby (eds.), *Maritime Empires: British Maritime Trade in the Nineteenth Century* (Woodbridge: Boydell Press, 2004), pp. 100–10

Larsen, Curtis E., *Life and Land Use on the Bahraini Islands: The Geoarchaeology of an Ancient Society* (University of Chicago Press, 1983)

Lawson, Fred H., *Bahrain: The Modernization of Autocracy* (Boulder: Westview, 1989)

Lewcock, Ronald, *Traditional Architecture in Kuwait and Northern Gulf* (London: Archaeology Research Papers, 1978)

Liebesny, Herbert J., 'Administration and Legal Development in Arabia: The Persian Gulf Principalities', *Middle East Journal*, 1 (1956), 37–42

Lienhardt, Peter, *Shaikhdoms of Eastern Arabia*, ed. by Ahmad al-Shahi (Basingstoke: Palgrave MacMillan, 2001)

McLachlan, Keith S., 'Kuwait City: A Study of Discrete Social Zones in an Oil Economy' in *Eléments sur les centres-villes dans le monde arabe/Materials on City Centres in the Arab World* (Tours: URBAMA, 1988), pp. 17–35

McPherson, Kenneth, 'Port Cities as Nodal Points of Change: The Indian Ocean, 1890s–1920s' in L. T. Fawaz and C. A. Bayly (eds.), *Modernity and Culture: From the Mediterranean to the Indian Ocean* (New York: Columbia University Press, 2002), pp. 75–95

Majed, Ebrahim Issa, *The Traditional Construction of Early Twentieth Century Houses in Bahrain* (Doha: Arab States Folklore Centre, 1987)

Marchal, Roland, 'Dubai: Global City and Transnational Hub' in M. al-Rasheed (ed.), *Transnational Connections in the Arab Gulf* (London: Routledge, 2005), pp. 93–110

Munif, Abdelrahman, *Cities of Salt*, trans. by Peter Theroux (New York: Random House, 1987)

Nakash, Yitzak, *The Shi'is of Iraq* (Princeton University Press, 1994)

Nakhleh, Emile A., *Bahrain: Political Development in a Modernising Society* (Toronto and Massachusetts: Lexington Books, 1976)

Al-Naqeeb, Khaldun, *Society and State in the Arabian Peninsula: A Different Perspective* (London: Routledge, 1990)

Niebuhr, Carsten, *Travels through Arabia, and other Countries in the East*, trans. by Robert Heron, 2 vols. (Edinburgh: R. Morison & Son, 1792)

Okruhlik, Gwenn, 'Struggle over History and Identity: "Opening the Gates" of the Kingdom to Tourism' in M. al-Rasheed and R. Vitalis (eds.), *Counter-Narratives: History, Contemporary Society and Politics in Saudi Arabia and Yemen* (New York: Palgrave Macmillan, 2004), pp. 201–28

Onley, James, *The Arabian Frontier of the British Raj: Merchants, Rulers, and the British in the Nineteenth-Century Gulf* (Oxford University Press, 2007)

'Britain's Informal Empire in the Gulf, 1820–1971', *Journal of Social Affairs*, 22.87 (2005), 29–48

'The Politics of Protection in the Gulf: The Arabian Rulers and the British Resident in the Nineteenth Century', *New Arabian Studies* 6 (2004), 30–92

'Transnational Merchants in the Nineteenth-Century Gulf: The Case of the Safar Family' in M. al-Rasheed (ed.), *Transnational Connections in the Arab Gulf* (London: Routledge, 2005), pp. 59–89

Onley, James and Sulayman Khalaf, 'Shaikhly Authority in the Pre-Oil Gulf: An Historical-Anthropological Study', *History and Anthropology*, 3 (2006), 189–208

Palgrave, William Gifford, *Narrative of a Year's Journey through Central and Eastern Arabia (1862–63)*, 2 vols. (London and Cambridge: Macmillan, 1865)

Potts, Daniel T. (ed.), *Dilmun: New Studies in the Archaeology and Early History of Bahrain* (Berlin: Reimer, 1983)

al-Qasimi, Sultan ibn Muhammad, *Power Struggles and Trade in the Gulf, 1620–1820* (University of Exeter Press, 1999)

Qubain, Fahim I., 'Social Classes and Tensions in Bahrain', *The Middle East Journal*, 9.3 (1955), 269–80

al-Rasheed, Madawi, *A History of Saudi Arabia* (Cambridge University Press, 2002)
    Politics in an Arabian Oasis: The Rashidis of Saudi Arabia (London: I. B. Tauris,
    1991)
al-Rasheed, Madawi (ed.), *Transnational Connections in the Arab Gulf* (London:
    Routledge, 2005)
al-Rasheed, Madawi and Robert Vitalis (eds.), *Counter-Narratives: History,
    Contemporary Society and Politics in Saudi Arabia and Yemen* (New York:
    Palgrave Macmillan, 2004)
Raymond, André, *Artisans et commerçants au Caire au XVIIIe siècle* (Damascus:
    Institut Français, 1973–4)
Risso, Patricia, 'Muslim Identity and Maritime Trade: General Observations and
    some Evidence from the 18th-century Persian Gulf/Indian Ocean Region',
    International Journal of Middle Eastern Studies, 21 (1989), 381–92
Rosenthal, Steven, 'Minorities and Municipal Reform in Istanbul, 1850–1870' in
    B. Braude and B. Lewis (eds.), *Christians and Jews in the Ottoman Empire: The
    Functioning of a Plural Society*, 2 vols. (New York: Holmes and Meier, 1982),
    vol. 1, pp. 369–85
Rumaihi, Muhammad G., *Bahrain: Social and Political Change since the First World
    War* (London and New York: Bowker, 1976)
Salati, Marco, 'La Lu'lua al-Bahrayn fi l-ijâza li qurratay al-'ayn di Šayh Yûsuf b.
    Ahmad al-Bahrânî (1107–1186/1695–1772): per lo Studio della Šî'a di
    Bahrayn', *Annali di Ca' Foscari*, 28.3 (1989), 111–45
Savory, Roger M., 'A.D. 600–1800' in A. J. Cottrell et al., *The Persian Gulf States: A
    General Survey* (Baltimore: John Hopkins University Press, 1980), pp. 14–40
al-Sayegh, Fatima, 'Merchants' Role in a Changing Society: The Case of Dubai,
    1900–90', *Middle Eastern Studies*, 34 (1998), 87–102
Seikaly, May, 'Haifa at the Crossroads: An Outpost of the New World Order' in
    L. T. Fawaz and C. A. Bayly (eds.), *Modernity and Culture: From the Mediterranean
    to the Indian Ocean* (New York: Columbia University Press, 2002), pp. 96–111
Serjeant, Robert B., 'Customary Irrigation Law among the Baharna of Bahrain' in
    A. Ibn K. al-Khalifah and M. Rice (eds.), *Bahrain through the Ages: A History*
    (London: Kegan Paul International,, 1993), pp. 471–96
    'The Interplay between Tribal Affinities and Religious (Zaydī) Authority in the
    Yemen', *al-Abhath*, 30 (1982), 11–50
al-Shayeb, *Al-Jubayl: Saudi Village* (Doha: Arab States Folklore Centre, 1985)
Shibar, Saba Jurj, *The Kuwait Urbanisation: Documentation, Analysis, Critique*
    (Kuwait: Kuwait Government Printing Press, 1964)
Slot, B. J., *The Arabs of the Gulf, 1602–1784*, 2nd edn (Leidschendam: the author,
    1995)
Sluglett, Peter, *Britain in Iraq: Contriving King and Country* (London: I. B. Tauris,
    2007)
al-Tajir, Mahdi Abdallah, *Bahrain 1920–1945: Britain, The Shaikh and the
    Administration* (London: Croom Helm, 1987)
Teixeira, Pedro, *The Travels of Pedro Teixeira*, trans. by William F. Sinclair
    (London: Hakluyt Society, 1902)
Waly, Tarek, *Private Skies: The Courtyard Pattern in the Architecture of the House in
    Bahrain* (Manama: Al-Handasah, 1992)

Yapp, Malcolm, 'British Policy in the Persian Gulf' in A. J. Cottrell et al., *The Persian Gulf States: A General Survey* (Baltimore: John Hopkins University Press, 1980), pp. 70–100

'The Nineteenth and Twentieth Centuries' in A. J. Cottrell et al., *The Persian Gulf States: A General Survey* (Baltimore: John Hopkins University Press, 1980), pp. 41–69

Zahlan, Rosemarie Said, *The Making of the Modern Gulf States*, 2nd edn (Reading: Ithaca Press, 1998)

al-Zayyani, Rashid, *Memories and History* (Manama: Al-Ayyam, 1999)

Zubaida, Sami, *Islam, the People and the State: Political Ideas and Movements in the Middle East* (London: I. B. Tauris, 1993)

CITIES AND EMPIRE

Abu Lughod, Janet, 'The Islamic City – Historic Myth, Islamic Essence and Contemporary Relevance', *International Journal of Middle East Studies*, 19 (1987), 155–86

Anderson, David M. and Richard Rathbone (eds.), *Africa's Urban Past* (Oxford: Currey, 2000)

Banga, Indu, *Ports and their Hinterlands in India* (New Delhi: Manohar, 1992)

Basu, Dilip K., *The Rise and Growth of the Colonial Port Cities in Asia* (Berkeley: University of California Press, 1985)

Bayly, Christopher A., *Imperial Meridian: The British Empire and the World, 1780–1830* (Harlow: Pearson Education, 1989)

Rulers, Townsmen and Bazaars: North Indian Society in the Age of British Expansion, 1770–1870 (New Delhi: Oxford University Press, 1992)

Braudel, Fernand, *The Mediterranean and the Mediterranean World in the Age of Philip II*, trans. by Sian Reynolds, 2 vols. (London: Collins, 1972–3)

Broeze, Frank (ed.), *Brides of the Sea: Port Cities of Asia from the 16th-20th Centuries* (Kensington: New South Wales University Press, 1989)

(ed.), *Gateways of Asia: Port Cities of Asia in the 13th-20th Centuries* (London and New York: Kegan Paul, 1997)

Brooke, John L., 'Reason and Passion in the Public Sphere: Habermas and the Cultural Historians', *Journal of Interdisciplinary History*, 29.1 (1998), 43–67

Chaudhuri, Kirti N., *Asia before Europe: Economy and Civilisation of the Indian Ocean from the Rise of Islam to 1750* (Cambridge University Press, 1990)

Chutintaranond, Sunait and Chris Baker (eds.), *Recalling Local Pasts: Autonomous History in Southeast Asia* (Chiang Mai: Silkworm Books, 2002)

Cole, Juan R., *Roots of North Indian Shi'ism in Iran and Iraq: Religion and State in Awadh, 1722–1859* (Berkeley: University of California Press, 1988)

Cooper, Frederick and Ann Laura Stoler, *Tensions of Empire: Colonial Cultures in a Bourgeois World* (Berkeley: University of California Press, 1997)

Crinson, Mark, *Modern Architecture and the End of Empire* (Aldershot: Ashgate, 2003)

Cunningham Bissel, W., 'Conservation and the Colonial Past: Urban Space, Planning and Power in Zanzibar' in D. Anderson and R. Rathbone (eds.), *Africa's Urban Past* (Oxford: Currey, 2000), pp. 246–61

Davies, Philip H., *Splendours of the Raj: British Architecture in India, 1660–1947* (London: Murray, 1985)

De Certeau, Michel, *The Practice of Everyday Life*, trans. by Steven Rendall (Berkeley: University of California Press, 1984)

Dharmasena, K., 'Colombo: Gateway and Oceanic Hub of Shipping' in F. Broeze (ed.), *Brides of the Sea: Port Cities of Asia from the 16th–20th Centuries* (Kensington: New South Wales University Press, 1989), pp. 156–69

Dossal, Mariam, *Imperial Designs and Indian Realities: The Planning of Bombay City, 1845–1875* (Bombay: Oxford University Press, 1991)

Freitag, Sandria, *Collective Action and Community: Public Arenas and the Emergence of Communalism in North India* (Berkeley: California University Press, 1989)

Freitag, Ulrike and William Clarence-Smith (eds.), *Hadrami Traders, Scholars and Statesmen in the Indian Ocean, 1750s-1960s* (Leiden: Brill, 1997)

Furet, François, *Interpreting the French Revolution*, trans. by Elborg Forster (Cambridge University Press, 1981)

Gaubatz, Piper Rae, *Beyond the Great Wall: Urban Form and Transformation on the Chinese Frontiers* (Stanford University Press, 1996)

Grossman, Patricia A., *Riots and Victims: Violence and the Construction of Communal Identity among Bengali Muslims, 1905–1947* (Boulder: Westview Press, 1999)

Hosagrahar, Jyoti, *Indigenous Modernities: Negotiating Architecture and Urbanism* (London and New York: Routledge, 2005)

Jalal, Ayesha, *Self and Sovereignty: Individual and Community in South Asian Islam since 1850* (London and New York: Routledge, 2000)

Kaur, Raminder, *Performative Politics and the Cultures of Hinduism: Public Uses of Religion in Western India* (New Delhi: Permanent Black, 2003)

Killingray, David, Margaret Lincoln and Nigel Rigby (eds.), *Maritime Empires: British Maritime Trade in the Nineteenth Century* (Woodbridge: Boydell Press, 2004)

King, Anthony D., *Colonial Urban Development: Culture, Social Power and Environment* (London: Routledge and Kegan Paul, 1976)

    Global Cities: Post-Imperialism and the Internationalization of London (London and New York: Routledge, 1990)

    Urbanism, Colonialism and the World Economy: Cultural and Spatial Foundations of the World Urban System (London: Routledge, 1990)

Lapidus, Ira M., 'The Muslim Cities as Plural Societies: The Politics of Intermediary Bodies' in *The Proceedings of the International Conference on Urbanism and Islam (ICUIT)*, 4 vols (Tokyo: The Middle East Culture Centre, 1989), vol. I, pp. 134–63

Lefebvre, Henri, *The Production of Space*, trans. by Donald Nicholson-Smith, 24th edn (Oxford: Blackwell, 2007)

Lombard, Denys and Jean Aubin (eds.), *Asian Merchants and Businessmen in the Indian Ocean and in the China Sea* (Delhi: Oxford University Press, 2000)

Low, Setha. M. and Denise Lawrence-Zúñiga (eds.), *The Anthropology of Space and Place: Locating Culture* (Oxford: Blackwell, 2003)

McNeill, William H., *Europe's Steppe Frontier, 1500–1800* (Chicago University Press, 1964)

The Great Frontier: Freedom and Hierarchy in Modern Times (Princeton University Press, 1983)

Markovits, Claude, *The Global World of Indian Merchants, 1750–1947: Traders of Sind from Bukhara to Panama* (Cambridge University Press, 2000)

Metcalf, Thomas R., *An Imperial Vison: Indian Architecture and Britain's Raj* (New Delhi, Oxford University Press, 1989)

Murphey, Rhoads, 'Colombo and the Re-Making of Ceylon' in F. Broeze (ed.), *Gateways of Asia: Port Cities of Asia in the 13th–20th Centuries* (London and New York: Kegan Paul, 1997), pp. 195–209

'On the Evolution of the Port City' in F. Broeze (ed.), *Brides of the Sea: Port Cities of Asia from the 16th–20th Centuries* (Kensington: New South Wales University Press, 1989), pp. 223–46

Myers, Garth Andrew, *Verandahs of Power: Colonialism and Space in Urban Africa* (New York: Syracuse University Press, 2003)

O'Connor, Richard A., 'A Regional Explanation of the Tai *Müang* as a City-State' in Moregns Herman Hansen (ed.), *A Comparative Study of Thirty City-State Cultures* (Copenhagen: Kongelige Danske Videnskabernes Selskab, 2000), pp. 431–44

Pandey, Gyanendra, *The Construction of Communalism in North India* (Delhi: Oxford University Press, 1990)

Reid, Anthony, 'The Organisation of Production in the Pre-Colonial South Eastern Asian Port City' in F. Broeze (ed.), *Brides of the Sea: Port Cities of Asia from the 16th–20th Centuries* (Kensington: New South Wales University Press, 1989), pp. 54–74

Sato, Tsugitaka (ed.), *Islamic Urbanism in Human History: Political Power and Social Networks* (London and New York: Kegan Paul International, 1997)

Singerman, Diane, 'Informal Networks: The Construction of Politics in Urban Egypt' in T. Sato (ed.), *Islamic Urbanism in Human History: Political Power and Social Networks* (London and New York: Kegan Paul International, 1997), pp. 77–106

Sutherland, Heather, 'Eastern Emporium and Company Town: Trade and Society in Eighteenth-Century Makassar' in F. Broeze (ed.), *Brides of the Sea: Port Cities of Asia from the 16th–20th Centuries* (Kensington: New South Wales University Press, 1989), pp. 97–128

Tilly, Charles, 'Revolutions and Collective Violence' in F. I. Greenstein and N. W. Ponsby (eds.), *Handbook of Political Science*, 8 vols. (Reading, MA, 1975), vol. III, *Macropolitical Theory*, pp. 503–25

Warner, Michael, 'The Mass Public and the Mass Subject' in C. Calhoun (ed.), *Habermas and the Public Sphere* (Cambridge, MA: Massachusetts Institute of Technology Press, 1999), pp. 377–401

Index of persons, tribes and families

Index of subjects

agriculture
  debate on 120
  decline of 21, 217–18
  and land regime before the reforms 212
'Arab 29, 154
Arab Nationalism 120, *see also al-Ha'yah
  and* Pan-Arabism
  and land policies 210–11
  mobilisation in Manama 147–8
  and rural society 218
al-'arish
  al-bahrani 35
  al-manami 35
al-'asabiyyah see tribalism
'ashura', 23, 91, 101, 106, 107, 164, *see also
  ma'tam and* Muharram rituals
  divisions between Arabs and Persians 165
  and *ma'tams* 38, 97, 107
  parades 165, 166
awqaf ja'fariyyah
  control by the clergy 23–4
awqaf al-sunnah 90
a'yan see merchants in Manama: notables

Bahrain 5, 6, 119
  administration 3
  as a frontier society 9, 16
  Islands of 2, 8–9
  as the 'Islands of Paradise' 22, 29, 218
Bahrain National Congress 158
Bahrain Order-in-Council
  of 1913 113–14, 115, 116
  of 1952 209
Bahrain Petroleum Company *see* BAPCO
al-baladiyyah see Municipality (Manama)
BAPCO (Bahrain Petroleum Company)
  132, 169, 172, 179, 191, 200–1
barastis 36, 72, 90, 92, 103, 192, 193,
  198, 200
  dwellers 130–1, 155
al-barriyyah 93, 94

Bayt al-Dawlah (British Political Agency)
  64–5, 123
bidun 4
British India Steam Navigation Company
  100, 106, 169
British informal empire 1, 8, 10
  in Bahrain 113–14
  and British Indian law 28, 125
  in the Gulf 5, 50
  rhetoric of 120
British Overseas Airways Corporation
  (BOAC) 50, 132, 196
British Political Agency *see* Bayt al-
  Dawlah
British Political Residency (Bushehr) *see*
  Residency, British (Bushehr)

Civil List 114
clubs 177–8
  the Arab Club (*Nadi al-'Urubah*)
  177–8, 179
  the Bahrain Club (*Nadi al-Bahrayn*)
  177–8, 179
  Firdawsi 187
  and football 178

Dar al-Hukumah 28, 33, 38, 39, 70,
  77, 153

East India Companies 45
  Dutch 45
  English 44, 49–57
Egyptian Gazette 227
Egyptian Revolution (1952) 120, 174, 182
extraterritorial jurisdiction 28, 72,
  156, 159
  and 1861 Treaty 122–3
  application of 121–3
  and establishment of native agency
  court 80
  transfer of 209

Index of places

Abu Dhabi 8, 45, 52
Aden 47
al-Ahsa' 16, 17, 18, 28, 40, 48, 92, 99, 130, 155, 210, 217
al-'Ajman 52
Aleppo 5
Alexandria 47, 124
al-'Ali 82
Arabian Peninsula 1, 7, 8, 85, 86
Awal 18
Awali 170, 191, 205
'Ayn al-'Adhari 23
'Ayn Sujur 22

Bab al-Bahrayn 193–4
Bani Jamrah 230
Basra 43, 44, 45–6, 50, 58
Bayt Faruq 37
Bayt Khadim 36
Bayt Shaykh 'Isa 38, *see-also* al-Nabhani
Bayt al-Shuyukh 96
Beirut 5, 47
Bilad al-Qadim 18, 23, 25, 40, 62, 91, 104, 224, 230
Bombay (Mumbai) 46, 54, 83, 229
Brazajan 101
al-Budayya' 24, 27, 29, 163, 224
  neighbourhood organisation 31
Bushehr 20, 43, 46, 50, 53, 101, 166
Buyut al-'Ummal 205

Cairo 5, 152
Central Arabia 2, 8, 29, 97
Colombo 46

Damascus 5, 103
  colonial urbanism 223
  notables and Arab nationalism 189
al-Damistan 20
al-Dammam 27, 99, 105
Dasht 101
Delhi 5

al-Diraz 20, 22, 27, 91, 230
Doha 8
Dubai 2, 3, 45, 52, 56, 209
  heritage village 3
  rise of 54
  as a 'world' city 7

Eastern Arabia 26, 99
  battle for 16–17

al-farij (firjan) 30, 223
Farij al-'Adliyyah 205–6, 229
Farij al-'Awadiyyah 37, 93, 100, 103, 147, 204
Farij al-Bastakiyyah 36
Farij Bu Sirrah (al-Na'im) 92, 95, 99
Farij al-Dawawdah 94, 138, 202
Farij al-Fadhil 93, 95, 100, 138, 147
Farij al-Hammam 91, 92, 95, 108
Farij al-Hurah 182, 200, 202
Farij Kanu 93–4, 95, 147
Farij al-Mukharaqah 92–3, 95, 99, 101, 107, 109, 146
Farij al-Qudaybiyyah 198, 205
Farij al-Salmaniyyah 206, 229
Farij Umm al-Hasam 206
Farij al-Zarari'a 202
Fars 101
forts 52–3
  and Portuguese mercantilism 53
funeral house *see ma'tam*

Garandor 200, 202, 231
Garash 86

Haifa 47
al-Ha'il 8, 29
halat 94
  Halah Ibn Anas 94
  Halah Ibn Iswar 94
Harran 4

CAMBRIDGE MIDDLE EAST STUDIES 30